Pastors and Pluralism
in Württemberg,
1918–1933

DAVID J. DIEPHOUSE

Pastors and Pluralism

in Württemberg

1918–1933

PRINCETON
UNIVERSITY
PRESS

Copyright © 1987 by Princeton University Press

Published by Princeton University Press, 41 William Street,
Princeton, New Jersey 08540
In the United Kingdom: Princeton University Press, Guildford, Surrey

Library of Congress Cataloging in Publication Data will be
found on the last printed page of this book

ISBN 0-691-05501-7

Publication of this book has been aided by the
Whitney Darrow Fund of Princeton University Press

This book has been composed in Linotron Aldus

Clothbound editions of Princeton University Press books
are printed on acid-free paper, and binding materials are
chosen for strength and durability. Paperbacks, although satisfactory
for personal collections, are not usually suitable for library rebinding

Printed in the United States of America by Princeton University Press,
Princeton, New Jersey

For my Parents

CONTENTS

CONTENTS

PREFACE

𝕿HIS STUDY grew out of an interest in the social and political
dynamics of Weimar Germany as well as a concern to understand the contours of German religious history, particularly
the development of the Protestant territorial churches. Although often overshadowed in historical analyses by the Church
Struggle of the 1930s, the Weimar era can legitimately be
viewed as a watershed in the history of the German churches.
The collapse of the monarchy in 1918—and with it the symbiotic
alliances of throne and altar that for centuries had shaped Protestant institutional consciousness—not only triggered a temporary crisis in church-state relations; more importantly, it forced
churchmen out of the deceptive security of an apparently stable
public order, confronting them with their increasingly marginal
position in a society where the currents of modernization threatened to make "church religion" practically irrelevant. The present book is a case study in this crisis of ecclesiastical purpose. It
deals primarily with churchmen's responses to a changing institutional environment, their struggles to reconcile traditional
values and loyalties with the pluralism of an emerging mass society. In so doing, it seeks to make a modest contribution to what
has lately become a sizable body of scholarship on the role of the
Protestant churches during the years between the November
Revolution and the consolidation of the Hitler regime. By con-
centrating on the territorial church in Württemberg, it also seeks
to broaden the focus of inquiry found in previous works on this
topic, which have dealt largely if not exclusively with Prussia.

Although it deals with churchmen, this study is not conceived
as church history in any narrow sense. It treats theological developments only tangentially and only to the extent that they
bear upon the central theme of the church's position in society.
Nor is it primarily an exercise in theory-building, although I
have made casual use of certain social science categories and

ix

would hope that my notions about the church's institutional character might be of some broader conceptual interest. My chief intent has been to provide an analytical narrative that illuminates both general patterns and specific textures of historical experience. This is, in short, the work of a historian, not a theologian or social scientist, and as such no doubt reflects all the limitations (though I hope also a few of the strengths) of its chosen scholarly genre. To claim total objectivity for such an enterprise would be more than a little foolhardy, not to say presumptuous; I will be satisfied if I have managed to achieve a fair measure of both empathy and critical distance, at least to the degree possible for someone who is neither German nor Lutheran.

This book has been uncommonly long in the making, and space will not permit a complete listing of the many persons and institutions who have helped me along the way. My first debt is certainly to Arno Mayer, who has been prodigal with counsel and encouragement since I first broached the topic as a graduate research project; that any resemblance between the resulting doctoral thesis and the present work is largely coincidental represents a tribute to his forbearance, as it does to the trenchant critiques of Carl Schorske and James Obelkevich. I also owe much to Hartmut Lehmann, who shared with me his intimate knowledge of Württemberg church affairs. Daniel Borg generously read successive drafts of the manuscript, and his suggestions improved the final product more than either of us would probably care to admit. Beate Ruhm von Oppen and Richard Gutteridge provided helpful advice at an early stage. So too did Hans Mommsen, who saved me from several elementary blunders, and also, somewhat later, my friend and former colleague Joseph Held. At Princeton University Press, appreciation is due to R. Miriam Brokaw, who first advised on the manuscript, and to Joanna Hitchcock, who saw it through the publication process. To my fellow historians at Calvin College, among whom much of the work took shape, I owe thanks for support and charity quite beyond the bounds of collegial duty; among those who read, discussed, or otherwise helped foster development of the project, special mention should be made of Bert De Vries, who prepared the map, and also Frank Roberts, Dale Van Kley, and Edwin Van Kley. To all of the above, and to others not mentioned by name, belongs much of the credit for whatever virtues the book may possess. The flaws that surely remain must of course be laid to my account alone.

Financial support in the form of a National Defense Education Act fellowship and travel grant from Princeton University made possible an extended initial research stay in Germany; of subsequent shorter visits, one was underwritten in part by a summer award from the Deutscher Akademischer Austauschdienst. Completion of the project was aided materially by a stipend from the National Endowment for the Humanities as well as sabbatical support from Calvin College. In Stuttgart I received unstinting assistance from staff members at the Landeskirchliches Archiv. I should like to thank especially the director, Gerhard Schäfer, who placed the archive's facilities so generously at my disposal, as well as Hermann Ott, who was the soul of hospitality both personal and professional. I am also grateful to the Evangelischer Oberkirchenrat for permission to explore at will among its files. The staffs of various libraries, especially the Württembergische Landesbibliothek, Princeton University's Firestone Library, the Speer Library of Princeton Theological Seminary, and the Calvin College and Seminary Library, were invariably accommodating. Virginia Bullock, Marie Westveer, and Heidi Vanden Akker shared the task of wordprocessing with what often seemed quite unwarranted enthusiasm; Cindy Boender performed heroics in coordinating the work and preparing the final copy for publication.

For myriad kindnesses on my several visits to Stuttgart, I owe a special debt of appreciation to Brünhilde and Epifanio Proietto; their friendship and generosity will never be fully repaid. My daughters Rachel, Amy, and Miriam have done everything in their very considerable power to alter their father's priorities, and if their own projects have substantially delayed completion of this one, they have also helped keep it in proper perspective. My greatest debt, as in everything, is to my wife, Evelyn. She has shared in the work from its inception, somehow finding time in her own busy schedule as parent and professional to dispense advice, encouragement, and needed doses of healthy Frisian common sense. That she has not lost her good humor in the process seems little short of miraculous. I trust that she appreciates the true scope of her contribution.

LIST OF ABBREVIATIONS

ARCHIVES

DA	Dekanatsarchiv
LKA	Landeskirchliches Archiv (Stuttgart)
LKA/SS	Landeskirchliches Archiv, Sammelstelle für evangelisches Schrifttum
OKR/AR	Evangelischer Oberkirchenrat (Stuttgart), Altregistratur
Gen.	Generalia
OA	Ortsakten
Pers.	Personalia
PfB	Pfarrberichte

ORGANIZATIONS

CSVD	Christlich-Sozialer Volksdienst
DDP	Deutsche Demokratische Partei
DEKA	Deutscher Evangelischer Kirchenausschuss
DkA	Dekanatsamt
DNVP	Deutschnationale Volkspartei
DVP	Deutsche Volkspartei
EPW	Evangelischer Pfarrverein in Württemberg
EVB	Evangelischer Volksbund für Württemberg
KM	Kultusministerium
LKT	Landeskirchentag
LKV	Landeskirchenversammlung
NSDAP	Nationalsozialistische Deutsche Arbeiterpartei
PfA	Pfarramt
SPD	Sozialdemokratische Partei Deutschlands
USPD	Unabhängige Sozialdemokratische Partei Deutschlands
WEK	Württemberg Evangelisches Konsistorium

ABBREVIATIONS

PERIODICALS

BWKG	*Blätter für württembergische Kirchengeschichte*
CW	*Die Christliche Welt*
EGBfS	*Evangelisches Gemeindeblatt für Stuttgart*
EKBfW	*Evangelisches Kirchenblatt für Württemberg*
EVB, *Mit-teilungen*	*Mitteilungen des Ev. Volksbundes an seine Mit-glieder*
KAfW	*Kirchlicher Anzeiger für Württemberg*
KJ	*Kirchliches Jahrbuch*
MfPT	*Monatsschrift für Pastoraltheologie*
RGG	*Religion in Geschichte und Gegenwart*
SAfW	*Staatsanzeiger für Württemberg*
SDZ	*Süddeutsche Zeitung* (Stuttgart)
SES	*Stuttgarter Evangelisches Sonntagsblatt*
SHW	*Statistisches Handbuch für Württemberg*
SM	*Schwäbischer Merkur*
SNT	*Stuttgarter Neues Tagblatt*
ST	*Schwäbische Tagwacht*
ZfWLG	*Zeitschrift für württembergische Landesgeschichte*

Pastors and Pluralism
in Württemberg,
1918–1933

INTRODUCTION

𝕵ɴ Nᴏᴠᴇᴍʙᴇʀ 1918, imperial Germany collapsed in the trenches of the Western Front. Even before hostilities ceased, the streets of most major cities belonged to the revolution; by November 9, with the Wittelsbachs already forcibly deposed in Bavaria, Philipp Scheidemann had impulsively declared a republic in Berlin, and the kaiser was seeking refuge across the border in Holland. In Stuttgart, King Wilhelm II of Württemberg, who had often declared that his person should never become an obstacle to his subjects' welfare, abdicated the throne and motored off into exile at a royal hunting lodge near the old university town of Tübingen. In Tübingen itself, Paul Wurster, professor of pastoral theology in the university's Protestant theological faculty, was registering the shock waves of defeat and upheaval in an essay whose title—"What Now for Our Church?"—expressed what for many Evangelical churchmen seemed to be the burning question of the day.[1] Wurster's was no isolated voice. To Friedrich Naumann, one-time pastor and the spiritus rector of German liberalism, the chorus of ecclesiastical crisis sounded all but deafening. Shortly before his death in 1919, Naumann would remark that his erstwhile brethren of the cloth seemed "more worried about the [potential] collapse of the church than about the downfall of the state."[2]

What now, indeed? Scarcely a year earlier German Protestants had celebrated the four hundredth anniversary of Martin Luther's revolt in Wittenberg. Over these four centuries an intricate web of legal, theological, and emotional associations had

---

[1] Paul Wurster, "Was nun mit unsrer Kirche?" *MfPT* 15 (1918–19): 66. This study uses the terms *Protestant* and (less often) *Evangelical* synonymously for the generic German designation *evangelisch*; cf. Daniel R. Borg, *The Old-Prussian Church and the Weimar Republic: A Study in Political Adjustments, 1917–1927* (Hannover and London, 1984), p. xiii.

[2] Friedrich Naumann, *Werke* (Cologne and Opladen, 1964), 1:942.

grown up, binding the territorial churches to the monarchical order. Alliances of throne and altar, while strained at times, were still reasonably secure when the war began; the German princes still commanded allegiance as both sovereign and *summus episcopus*. Now, at war's end, with the "Holy Protestant Empire of the German Nation" in shambles, the old symbiotic relationships had suddenly become inconceivable. In sweeping away the dynastic order, the November Revolution struck at the historic cornerstone of established German Protestantism. Moreover, the prominence of socialists in the new regime portended the triumph of an ideology that proclaimed religion to be a purely private affair and demanded the abolition of established churches, the restriction of their influence in such historic ecclesiastical preserves as education, and their transformation from privileged public agencies into simple voluntary associations. In sharp contrast to their Catholic counterparts, who could fall back on an authority structure unshaken by revolution and who could mobilize powerful mass support through the Center party, Protestant churchmen entered the new era constrained by the legacy of the old particularist formula *cujus regio ejus religio*, their institutional position problematic and their mass support cast into doubt by the fragmentation of the bourgeois political front. Scanning the new republic for reassuring signs of a Christian order, they saw instead an apparently secular polity in which their own status, both legal and moral, threatened to be at best ambiguous.[3]

In retrospect this sense of vulnerability appears considerably exaggerated, particularly when measured against the more spectacular challenges of the Hitler era. The specter of disestablishment that preyed upon Wurster and a host of fellow churchmen proved insubstantial indeed. To cite the classic verdict of Arthur Rosenberg, the November Revolution "destroyed the German

[3] For a general comparison of Protestant and Catholic conditions, see Klaus Scholder, *Die Kirchen und das Dritte Reich*, vol. 1: *Vorgeschichte und Zeit der Illusionen, 1918–1934* (Frankfurt am Main, 1977), pp. 3–25, and Ernst C. Helmreich, *The German Churches under Hitler: Background, Struggle, and Epilogue* (Detroit, Mich., 1979), pp. 17–117.

dynasties [but] failed to effect any other important change in the character of the German state."[4] Heirs to power they were ill-prepared to exploit, Social Democratic moderates of Friedrich Ebert's stamp preferred to shore up existing structures, even at the cost of promoting counterrevolutionary interests, rather than risk the uncertainties of a root-and-branch transformation. Reform owed a prior debt to stability. Social change must wait upon the establishment, in Ebert's words, of an "orderly government supported by the army and the National Assembly."[5] Hoping to consolidate its modest improvised democracy against militants on both flanks, but especially on the left, the Ebert regime made quick peace with the army and the bureaucracy, both powerful and intrinsically antirepublican mainstays of the old empire. This pivotal rapprochement, reinforced by the stalemate between the cultural policies of Weimar's major mass parties, the Social Democrats and the Catholic Center, yielded major dividends for the churches. Fears of a new Kulturkampf proved largely groundless. The feckless efforts of a few isolated radicals aside, Weimar's reluctant revolutionaries mounted no challenge to ecclesiastical privileges. While the Weimar constitution provided for the separation of church and state, this disestablishment proved extremely limited in practice. Indeed, the terms of the settlement were far more generous than any clerical Cassandra could have anticipated.[6]

It is hardly surprising, therefore, that interpretive perspec-

[4] Arthur Rosenberg, *A History of the German Republic* (London, 1936), pp. 52–53.

[5] Quoted in Franz Neumann, *Behemoth* (1942; reprint, New York, 1966), p. 11.

[6] The churches retained their privileged status as "public corporations" (*Körperschaften des öffentlichen Rechts*), the same legal designation employed for local units of government. On the constitutional settlement, see Henri Cazelles, *Église et état en Allemagne de Weimar aux premières années du IIIe Reich* (Paris, 1936); Helmreich, *German Churches under Hitler*, pp. 61–73; Borg, *Old-Prussian Church*, pp. 83–97; and Johannes Schneider, ed., *Kirchliches Jahrbuch für die evangelischen Landeskirchen Deutschlands, 1921* (Gütersloh, [1921]), pp. 372–415, *1925* (Gütersloh, [1925]), pp. 516–47 (hereafter cited as *KJ 1921*, etc.).

INTRODUCTION

tives on Weimar Protestantism have been colored less by the issues of 1918 than by those of 1933. Charting the churches' course through the shoals of Weimar politics, most observers have stressed the baleful effects of Protestant thought and practice on German politics. There is general agreement that, like other surviving pillars of the empire, the churches fostered a strong antipathy to the values of a democratic and liberal polity, that despite their favored status in the new order they persisted in their allegiance to the fallen powers of monarchism and privilege. Hierarchical traditions and the prevailing social conservatism of Protestant theology, it is argued, had long worked to isolate the established territorial churches from those forces of movement that in 1918 merged, however briefly and ineffectively, to launch the Weimar experiment. With a few notable exceptions, Protestant pastors and church officials had preserved from the previous century an ethic, derived from Luther's famous doctrine of the "two kingdoms" (spiritual and worldly), that stressed subservience to temporal authority and found the source of social ills not in the structure of society but in the moral shortcomings of individuals. Few Protestant leaders displayed any official understanding, let alone enthusiasm, for the values of a pluralistic democracy. Constitutionalism, at least in the liberal individualistic sense, remained as alien a frame of reference for most churchmen in 1918 as in 1848.[7]

---

[7] The classic statement of this thesis is Fritz Fischer, "Der deutsche Protestantismus und die Politik im 19. Jahrhundert," *Historische Zeitschrift* 171 (1951): 473–518; an insightful reformulation can be found in Borg, *Old-Prussian Church*, pp. 1–28. See also Karl Kupisch, *Das Jahrhundert des Sozialismus und die Kirche* (Berlin, 1958); Kupisch, *Zwischen Idealismus und Massendemokratie: Eine Geschichte der evangelischen Kirche in Deutschland von 1815–1945* (Berlin, 1955); William O. Shanahan, *German Protestants Face the Social Question*, vol. 1: *The Conservative Phase, 1815–1871* (Notre Dame, Ind., 1954); Klaus Pollmann, *Landesherrliches Kirchenregiment und soziale Frage: Der evangelische Oberkirchenrat der Altpreussischen Landeskirche und die sozialpolitische Bewegung der Geistlichen nach 1890* (Berlin, 1973); Robert M. Bigler, *The Politics of German Protestantism: The Rise of the Protestant Church Elite in Prussia, 1815–1848* (Berkeley and Los Angeles, 1972); Gottfried Mehnert, *Evangelische Kirche und Politik, 1917–1919: Die politischen Strömungen im*

6

INTRODUCTION

From this it follows quite naturally that, in the shock and confusion of the postwar period, church leaders should for the most part regroup under the banner of an unreconstructed conservatism. Instinctively suspicious of change and haunted by a self-perceived loss of function in an increasingly secular society, the clergy manifested a peculiar crisis mentality whose salient impulse was the glorification of a bygone golden age, a world in which the authority of throne and altar still prevailed. This ecclesiastical resort to mythology in turn linked the church, wittingly or not, to authoritarians and counterrevolutionaries of every stripe who both preached and practiced the destruction of democracy. By lending to the motley antirepublican coalition its authority and influence over public opinion, the church helped to nurture the distrust of democracy in key segments of the German population, not least among those masses of the aggrieved who, battered by successive psychic and economic shocks, flocked for redress to National Socialism. In sum, Protestant ideology and the weight of institutional tradition cast the churches fully in the mold of what Fritz Stern has called German "illiberalism." At best, church officials rallied to the republic only when collapse was imminent; at worst, they acted as willing heralds of that collapse.[8]

---

deutschen Protestantismus von der Julikrise 1917 bis zum Herbst 1919 (Düsseldorf, 1959); William R. Ward, *Theology, Sociology, and Politics: The German Protestant Social Conscience, 1890–1933* (Bern, 1979); and E. I. Kouri, *Der deutsche Protestantismus und die soziale Frage, 1870–1919: Zur Sozialpolitik im Bildungsbürgertum* (Berlin and New York, 1984).

[8] Fritz Stern, *The Failure of Illiberalism* (New York, 1971; reprint, Chicago, 1971), pp. 3–25. For a political model based on the German Nationalists, see Annelies Thimme, *Flucht in den Mythos: Die Deutschnationale Volkpartei und die Niederlage von 1918* (Göttingen, 1969). The general issue of the churches is posed succinctly in Karl Dietrich Erdmann, "Die Geschichte der Weimarer Republik als Problem der Wissenschaft," *Vierteljahreshefte für Zeitgeschichte* 3 (1955): 18–19, and in different terms in Kurt Nowak, " 'Entartete Gegenwart': Antimodernismus als Interpretament für die Begegnung von Protestantismus und Nationalsozialismus in der Weimarer Zeit," *Theologische Zeitschrift* 35 (1979): 102–19, and Manfred Jacobs, "Kirche, Weltanschauung, Politik: Die evangelischen Kirchen und die Option zwischen dem zweiten und dritten Reich," *Vierteljahreshefte für Zeitgeschichte* 31 (1983): 108–35; cf. also Harry

INTRODUCTION

Such, in broad outline, is the prevailing interpretation. In its own terms it is a compelling one, qualifications and occasional demurrals notwithstanding.[9] At the same time, however, it reflects a subtle tendency to see modern Germany primarily as a case study in political pathology—a perspective that, by treating Weimar as a republic under seige, tends to narrow the interpretive frame of reference to an accounting for the strength of authoritarianism and the failure of democratic alternatives. Recent

Eckstein, *A Theory of Stable Democracy*, Center of International Studies Research Monograph no. 10 (Princeton, 1961). Specific analyses of the churches include Borg, *Old-Prussian Church*; Karl-Wilhelm Dahm, *Pfarrer und Politik: Soziale Position und politische Mentalität des deutschen evangelischen Pfarrerstandes zwischen 1918 und 1933* (Cologne and Opladen, 1965); Jochen Jacke, *Kirche zwischen Monarchie und Republik: Der preussische Protestantismus nach dem Zusammenbruch von 1918* (Hamburg, 1976); Karl Werner Bühler, *Presse und Protestantismus in der Weimarer Republik: Kräfte und Krisen evangelischer Publizistik* (Witten, 1970); J. R. C. Wright, *"Above Parties": The Political Attitudes of the German Protestant Church Leadership, 1918–1933* (London, 1974) (expanded German version: *"Über den Parteien." Die politische Haltung der evangelischen Kirchenführer, 1918–1933* [Göttingen, 1977]); Herbert Christ, *Der politische Protestantismus in der Weimarer Republik: Eine Studie über die politische Meinungsbildung durch die evangelischen Kirchen im Spiegel der Literatur und der Presse* (Ph.D. diss., Bonn University, 1967); Guenther van Norden, *Kirche in der Krise: Die Stellung der evangelischen Kirche zum nationalsozialistischen Staat im Jahre 1933* (Düsseldorf, 1963); Rita Thalmann, *Protestantisme et nationalisme en Allemagne (de 1900 à 1945)* (Paris, 1976); Walter Bredendiek, *Zwischen Revolution und Restauration: Zur Entwicklung im deutschen Protestantismus während der Novemberrevolution und in der Weimarer Republik* (Berlin, 1969); and Kurt Nowak, *Evangelische Kirche und Weimarer Republik: Zum politischen Weg des deutschen Protestantismus zwischen 1918 und 1932* (Göttingen, 1981).

[9] Notably Claus Motschmann, *Evangelische Kirche und preussischer Staat in den Anfängen der Weimarer Republik: Möglichkeiten und Grenzen ihrer Zusammenarbeit* (Hamburg and Lübeck, 1969); see also Frank J. Gordon, "The Evangelical Churches and the Weimar Republic, 1918–1933" (Ph.D. diss., University of Colorado, 1977), and Helmreich, *German Churches under Hitler*, pp. 75–94, 121–52. Jacke, *Kirche zwischen Monarchie und Republik*, also suggests a different emphasis, albeit within the general framework of interpretation outlined above; similarly, Walter Bredendiek, "Zur Rezeption des 'progressiven Erbes' im deutschen Protestantismus des 19. und 20. Jahrhunderts—Thesen," in Bredendiek et al., *Zwischen Aufbruch und Beharrung: Der deutsche Protestantismus in politischen Entscheidungsprozessen* (Berlin, 1978).

scholarship, in contrast, suggests that the problems of the Weimar era must be seen in a different light, that political questions must be related more systematically to the development of social and economic structures. Because the November Revolution in fact failed to alter the basic coordinates of German society, it resolved few of the intramural rivalries—between capital and labor, between shop and factory, between the civilian and the military—that had already strained the fabric of the Wilhelmian empire. Authoritarian structures may have given way in some cases to more pluralistic arrangements, and cooptation may have begun to replace coercion as a preferred means of social control, but the underlying nexus of power remained surprisingly constant. This being so, the stability of the republic depended less upon ideological commitments or mass democratic instincts than upon shifting power balances within a far from uniform network of organized social, economic, and cultural interest groups. While the collapse of the Weimar system certainly involved specifically political factors, it was no less a function of the capacity of republican institutions to channel and mediate interest group conflicts. The crisis of the early 1930s testified in part to the inability of the dominant groups and institutions in Weimar's highly pluralistic society and polity either to forge stable coalitions around common interests or to mobilize the mass support necessary to develop an effective system of parliamentary blocs.[10]

[10] The range of recent scholarship is suggested by the essays in Hans Mommsen, ed., *Industrielles System und politische Entwicklung in der Weimarer Republik* (Düsseldorf, 1974); Charles S. Maier, *Recasting Bourgeois Europe: Stabilization in France, Germany, and Italy in the Decade after World War I* (Princeton, 1975), provides a stimulating comparative perspective. See also Gerald D. Feldman, *Iron and Steel in the German Inflation, 1916–1923* (Princeton, 1977); F. L. Carsten, *The Reichswehr and Politics, 1918–1933* (London, 1966); Wolfgang Runge, *Politik und Beamtentum im Parteienstaat: Die Demokratisierung der politischen Beamten in Preussen zwischen 1918 und 1933* (Stuttgart, 1965); Heinrich and Elisabeth Hannover, *Politische Justiz, 1918–1933* (Frankfurt am Main, 1966); Henry A. Turner, Jr., *German Big Business and the Rise of Hitler* (New York, 1984); and David Abraham, *The Collapse of the Weimar Republic: Political Economy and Crisis*, rev. ed. (New York, 1986).

This perspective suggests new and useful points of departure for examining the role of the churches in the Weimar system. Piety requires a different calculus than politics; one ought not simply equate religious institutions, let alone religious beliefs, with economic interests and interest groups.[11] Yet after allowing for the uniqueness of the church's concerns, the institutional affinities between the churches and other forms of social organization remain numerous enough, at least in Germany, to invite further exploration. Without ignoring any illiberal influence that churchmen may have exerted over their coreligionists, it is important to ask how they went about mobilizing a constituency in support of their particular cultural agenda and the extent to which these mobilization efforts in fact succeeded.[12] As powerful and prominent fixtures in German life, with a nominal membership comprising some two-thirds of the population, the Protestant territorial churches provide a microcosm of the political, economic, and cultural tensions endemic to Weimar society. The major purpose of the present study is to trace the various ways in which the church sought, within its own precincts and in terms of its own priorities, to deal with the problems of pluralism and consensus faced by this larger society. To give focus to the inquiry I propose to concentrate on developments in a single territorial church, the Evangelical-Lutheran church in Württemberg, during the fifteen years separating the fall of the Second Reich and the establishment of the Third.

Some preliminary remarks may be in order regarding the institutional character of the German churches, the general nature of the problems they confronted after 1918, and especially the idea of a Volkskirche, a concept central to the Protestant outlook during the Weimar era and beyond. Despite their typically hierarchical structures and strongly conservative ethos, the churches cannot be classified simply as authoritarian survivals.

[11] For a useful introduction to the vast literature on this question, see Joachim Matthes, *Kirche und Gesellschaft* (Reinbek bei Hamburg, 1969).

[12] Jacke, *Kirche zwischen Monarchie und Republik*, puts forward some suggestive links between this perspective and the earlier literature; cf. Borg, *Old-Prussian Church*.

In the context of interwar Germany they are in fact particularly interesting because of their status at the intersection of "state" and "society," between the sphere of public authority and coercive power and the sphere of private attitudes and voluntary action. In one sense the church was preeminently a bureaucratic agency, the preserve of an officialdom whose concern for rank and whose claims to public status differed only superficially from the outlooks of, for example, army officers, or judges, or the upper echelons of the civil service. At the same time, however, the church was an incipient mass organization, a semivoluntary association whose efforts to establish and maintain a vital center for its heterogeneous nominal membership perforce resembled those of other private interest groups and voluntary associations.

This dual identity—as both a pillar of public order and a voluntaristic spiritual community, a *corpus Christianorum*—had already become problematic long before the Great War. It became a vital concern once the November Revolution, by sweeping away the territorial dynasties, destroyed its key integrative element. The problem, in essence, was how the church could hope to exert either spiritual or temporal influence in a society for which ecclesiastical institutions—high levels of nominal membership notwithstanding—appeared to provide an increasingly marginal basis for personal and corporate values. Paul Wurster's rhetorical "What Now?" of 1918 suggested as much. The salient issue, Wurster argued, was not what could still be salvaged from the wreckage of the old order—that is, whether the church could manage to preserve some functional equivalent of the historic alliance between throne and altar. Rather, freed from its previous dependence upon the crown, the church must turn to the larger task of renewing what Wurster called the "historic ties linking *Staatsvolk* and *Kirchenvolk*," civil community and religious community. Wurster thereby anticipated a theme elaborated some years later by Otto Dibelius, general superintendent of Prussia, in his controversial and surprisingly triumphalist book *Das Jahrhundert der Kirche* (1927), which advanced the thesis that only through emancipation from the state could

11

an authentic church community develop in Germany. As both Wurster and Dibelius perceived it, the Weimar crisis proved quite literally opportune. A turning point rather than a disaster, it did not necessitate an embittered retreat into some nostalgic authoritarian utopia. On the contrary, it demanded a renewed commitment to society as actually constituted, and this in the name of the church's own self-defined pastoral tasks.[13]

Hence it is not altogether surprising to find in Weimar Protestantism something of the same renascent spirit found in German Catholicism during the prewar heyday of *Rerum novarum*. Stimulated by a revival of Luther scholarship after 1917 and above all by the fresh impulses of Karl Barth's dialectical theology, theologians subjected optimistic liberal Protestant commonplaces to searching reexamination. The Weimar years also saw a notable upsurge in Protestant social action recalling and at the same time superceding that of J. H. Wichern and Gustav Werner three generations earlier. No longer able to rely on the powers of a cooperative prince, churchmen took upon themselves the burden of preserving in Germany the marks of a Christian society. Despite their national-conservative loyalties, most church leaders soon joined the company of Weimar's *Vernunftrepublikaner*; old alliances of conviction between throne and altar resurfaced in alliances of convenience between the church and the civil bureaucracy. Symptomatically, a small but vocal minority of clergymen broke with their bourgeois heritage to identify the cause of the gospel with the precepts of latter-day socialism.[14]

---

[13] Wurster, "Was nun mit unsrer Kirche?" pp. 66–67; Otto Dibelius, *Das Jahrhundert der Kirche: The Autobiography of Otto Dibelius* (Berlin, 1927). In his memoirs, written after World War II, Dibelius remarked that while he still agreed with the thrust of his earlier work, he would no longer "write such a book in so sanguine a manner" (Dibelius, *In the Service of the Lord*, trans. Mary Ilford [New York, 1964], pp. 111–12). On the more sober diagnosis of the liberal Protestant Ernst Troeltsch, see, e.g., the essays by Hermann Fischer, Rudolf von Thadden, Hartmut Ruddies, and Friedrich Wilhelm Graf, in Horst Renz and Graf, eds., *Troeltsch-Studien*, vol. 3: *Protestantismus und Neuzeit* (Gütersloh, 1984).

[14] Scholder, *Die Kirchen und das Dritte Reich*, 1:26–64; Borg, *Old-Prussian*

Whether pragmatic or principial, these openings to a complex modern world were vital to the church's position. In an age of the masses, strength lay in numbers. Purely spiritual authority aside, churches had long derived much of their influence from a quasi-official status. While by no means inclined to abjure those prerogatives that survived the revolution, churches nevertheless moved increasingly to seek new strength in a mobilized constituency. "If everything we have boasted about the church is more than mere words," Wurster prophesied in 1918, "then there must be a large body of parishioners who would rise up to defend their church. The crisis is still a serious one, but . . . once the acute phase is past a turn for the better may come."[15] The alarms and confusion of 1918 gradually gave way to a general if often ambivalent acceptance of the new order. Regardless of political prejudices, perceptive churchmen could not fail to recognize that the republic granted them an unprecedented freedom of movement and that this freedom in turn challenged them to a reappraisal of traditional goals and methods.

How could spiritual authority be enhanced in a world of cities and factories, the wireless and the cinema? The heart of this challenge lay in the long-implicit religious pluralism that the new German order legitimized. If it did not wholly eliminate ties between church and state, the republic did recognize religion as, in effect, a private affair. The monarchy had at least acknowledged the ideal, even if it often denied the substance, of Luther's Christian state; the republic reflected little of either ideal or substance. The cultural ferment and self-conscious modernism that have fascinated so many subsequent observers of the Weimar era aroused scant admiration among contemporary clerics. They could find little to applaud in a nation whose capital seemed even to so broad-minded a visitor as Stefan Zweig to deserve the epi-

---

Church; Wright, *"Above Parties."* On the rise of Religious Socialism, see Renate Breipohl, *Religiöser Sozialismus und bürgerliches Geschichtsbewusstsein zur Zeit der Weimarer Republik* (Zurich, 1971), and Friedrich-Martin Balzer, *Klassengegensätze in der Kirche: Erwin Eckert und der Bund der Religiösen Sozialisten* (Cologne, 1973).

[15] Wurster, "Was nun mit unsrer Kirche?" p. 67.

thet Babylon of the World.[16] Berlin only confirmed conservative Protestants in the conviction that, left to their own designs by a morally neutral state, individuals would inevitably turn away from a godly walk of life. Traditional piety was by no means dead, to be sure, even in decadent Berlin. Often, though, it had the appearance of an insubstantial residue, a facade of customary practices whose confessional basis had more or less disintegrated. The faith of the fathers seemed in grave danger of becoming simply one alternative among many in the marketplace of values, subject to the verdict of an autonomous private conscience and to the competition of new outlooks and forms of sociability.

In this, of course, Germany was far from unique. If German churchmen found the problem peculiarly acute, the reason may have been, ironically enough, that the general process of secularization was arguably less advanced in Germany than in other parts of industrialized Europe. In any event, the causes of the church's decline as a self-evident moral arbiter for society could not be found in the fact of revolution or the strength of any organized anticlerical tradition; this the ecclesiastical settlement of 1919 would clearly demonstrate. At issue, rather, was the church's capacity to counter alternative value systems and shape the attitudes and practices of its nominal members. Pluralism, not disestablishment, was the vital challenge of the postwar years.[17]

[16] Stefan Zweig, *The World of Yesterday* (New York, 1953), p. 313.

[17] This formulation follows generally from those developed in Thomas Luckmann, *The Invisible Religion: The Problem of Religion in Modern Society* (New York, 1967), and Justus Freytag and Kenji Ozaki, *Nominal Christianity: Studies of Church and People in Hamburg*, trans. Marjorie Sandle (London, 1970), pp. 49–123. It is manifestly impossible to discuss here in detail the problem of secularization, which has spawned a veritable cottage industry among sociologists of religion. David Martin has argued cogently that the very term has become too vague and internally contradictory to serve any useful conceptual purpose (Martin, *The Religious and the Secular: Studies in Secularization* [New York, 1969], pp. 9–22). With this in mind, I have chosen to employ the term *pluralism*, as loosely defined in the text, to refer to that aspect of the phenomenon most acutely relevant to Weimar churchmen. For a bibliographical introduction to the

The peculiar significance of Weimar for the church therefore lay less in any sharp break with a nurturing past than in the recapitulation and politicization of trends extending well back into the previous century. With its overt cultural modernism, the new order posed the problems of pluralism with particular urgency. If churchmen felt this urgency as something novel, it was because the older "defensive alliance"[18] between church and state throughout much of Germany had helped to buffer deeper currents of secularization. Germany's physical and social landscape had changed dramatically in the generation before the Great War, with far-reaching effects on religious practice. That workers and intelligentsia were seldom to be found in the churches was a nineteenth-century truism, but the structural changes went farther and affected more than just understaffed and overpopulated urban parishes. By the late nineteenth century, the institutional church was everywhere facing eclipse as a primary matrix of religiosity. Contrary to some appearances, people had not ceased to be religious, even by fairly conventional standards, but religiosity often came to be merged with, and expressed in terms of, a new constellation of values, among which individualism was paramount. By elevating private belief over public participation, religious individualism almost imperceptibly redefined the church as a voluntary community of believers rather than as the fixed superstructure of personal and communal life. In consequence, the church's central task shifted from one of maintaining external structures of belief—public worship, the sacraments, religious holidays, Sunday observance—to one of nurturing the individual's private religious commitment.[19]

---

subject with special reference to Germany, see Ursula Boos-Nunning and Egon Golomb, *Religiöses Verhalten im Wandel: Untersuchungen in einer Industriegesellschaft* (Essen, 1974).

[18] Thus Jacke, *Kirche zwischen Monarchie und Republik*, pp. 15–20.

[19] Freytag and Ozaki, *Nominal Christianity*, pp. 56–58; see also Hermann Fischer, "Die Ambivalenz der Moderne: Zu Troeltschs Verhältnisbestimmung von Reformation und Neuzeit," in Renz and Graf, eds., *Troeltsch-Studien* 3:54–77.

On this and other points, Protestants faced a more complex challenge than did their Catholic counterparts. Catholic teaching, most would agree, shared little of the individualistic emphasis so often characteristic of Protestantism, and in Germany the Catholic church flourished chiefly in rural areas, where a communal spirit was more likely to persist than in the anonymity of the cities. Moreover, the experience of the Kulturkampf had stimulated the formation of a fairly coherent Catholic subculture, reinforced by a wide range of church-related occupational and age-group organizations, in which civil and religious communities remained largely fused. By contrast, as its crazy-quilt institutional structure suggested, Protestantism had to contend constantly with a tendency towards fragmentation, a tendency that manifested itself most vigorously in the area of personal attitudes, beliefs, and cultic practices. By the nineteenth century, most educated Protestants were deriving their values less from the pulpit than from the library and the laboratory. In working-class districts, where vast blocks of tenements often shut out even a glimpse of the occasional church steeple, the masses found their doctrines and liturgies in socialism and in the growing spectacle of sports. This mass society emerging behind the quasi-feudal facade of the Wilhelmine empire challenged the comfortable verities of ecclesiastical tradition. A church that equated authority, hierarchy, and established social structures with a divine order found itself proclaiming not self-evident truth but increasingly controversial partisan slogans.[20]

On several levels, both institutional and intellectual, the November Revolution posed these long-term problems of status and function in a clearer and more pressing form. The broad challenges facing churchmen were how, in an increasingly pri-

[20] John E. Groh, *Nineteenth-Century German Protestantism: The Church as Social Model* (Washington, D.C., 1982), pp. 531–91. The classic comparison of confessions is Martin Offenbacher, *Konfession und soziale Schichtung* (Tübingen and Leipzig, 1901); cf. Max Weber, *Gesammelte Aufsätze zur Religionssoziologie* (Tübingen, 1922), 1:17–30. See also O. Hackler, *Soziale Eigentümlichkeiten der Konfessionen in Deutschland* (Bückeburg, 1936), and the references in notes 3 and 7, above.

vate society, to reconcile an inherited institutional status with the continuing decline in participation by nominal members, and how, in an increasingly politicized society, to defend an inherited vision of community without mortgaging the church to a narrowly partisan cause. As many saw it after 1918, the specific task was twofold. On the one hand churchmen had to defend the primacy of historic Protestant values in the public forum. On the other hand they had to find ways of instilling in parishioners both a renewed awareness of these values and a commitment to the church as an indispensable spiritual community—in short, to translate nominal membership into integral membership.[21]

By what criterion was this daunting project to be attempted? An assumption most churchmen shared was the notion of the church as properly a *Volkskirche* ("people's church"), the ultimately untranslatable term that became a Protestant rallying cry in the early days of the republic. Since it meant different things in different contexts and to different elements of the Protestant community, the term requires some explanation. On one level it served to distinguish the roughly two dozen territorial churches (*Landeskirchen*), supported by public funds and claiming most of the population as nominal members, from the various smaller Protestant sects and "free churches," in which membership and financial support was individual and voluntary.[22] On another level, *Volkskirche* connoted an integrative role that combined social and religious impulses. As in the free churches, pastors in the territorial churches ministered most directly to a core group of active parishioners, a mere fraction of the entire nominal membership, who came together either for sociability or out of loyalty to the gospel and the church's historic creeds. But even

[21] Freytag and Ozaki, *Nominal Christianity*, pp. 56–62; the typology of "private" and "politicized" societies derives loosely from Jürgen Habermas, *Strukturwandel der Öffentlichkeit: Untersuchungen zu einer Kategorie der bürgerlichen Gesellschaft* (Neuwied, 1962).

[22] "The hallmark of the 'free church' is that it involves an act of personal volition to belong, and the hallmark of the Volkskirche is that it involves an act of personal volition not . . . to belong" (Johannes Schneider, "Kirchliche Zeitlage," *KJ 1921*, p. 372).

17

for nominal members who did not avail themselves of this more intimate cultic fellowship, the church still presented itself as an agent of social integration, standing in an otherwise fragmented community as a source of common moral and civic values.[23]

The Volkskirche, in short, sought at the same time to be a creedal institution and a voluntaristic fellowship that transcended individual differences in social status and theological outlook. This assumption can be seen in the semiofficial Protestant yearbook, the *Kirchliches Jahrbuch*, whose editor, Prussian pastor Johannes Schneider, was an influential spokesman for the mainstream of nationalist-conservative churchmen. The territorial church, Schneider insisted in 1921, must not be allowed to become a "conventicle." It must serve as "the conscience of the people, independent of all . . . political influence, even independent of the favor of the masses." In this paternalistic fashion the Volkskirche would symbolize "that there is still a German-Protestant nation within the boundaries of the German state."[24]

Ideally, pastoral and paternalistic roles should complement one another, just as church and state should fulfill separate but compatible functions. In a society charged with overlapping religious and civic values, the institutional church held a special commission as the moral counterpart of the state: the latter guaranteed civil order, the former spiritual community. The church spoke to the individual heart, encouraging the citizen in obedience to established authority. The state, for its part, would enforce standards of conduct appropriate to an ordered Christian society. Linking the two, in the historic Lutheran vision, should

---

[23] Groh aptly terms this the church's "modeling function" in society: "The life and work of the churches should demonstrate for society how persons and institutions could and should live 'freely' within an authoritarian structure" (*Nineteenth-Century German Protestantism*, p. xii). The most recent analysis of Volkskirche ideology is Kurt Meier, *Volkskirche, 1918–1945: Ekklesiologie und Zeitgeschichte* (Munich, 1982). For classic sociological perspectives, see Reinhard Köster, *Die Kirchentreuen: Erfahrungen und Ergebnisse einer soziologischen Untersuchung in einer grosstädtischen evangelischen Gemeinde* (Stuttgart, 1959), and Dieter Goldschmidt, F. Greiner, and Helmut Schelsky, eds., *Soziologie der Kirchengemeinde* (Stuttgart, 1960).

[24] *KJ 1921*, pp. 372–73.

be the Christian prince, concerned with both civic and religious well-being. To be sure, flaws in this conception had become apparent long before the modern era. Luther's famous doctrine of the two kingdoms, which effectively if not intentionally accorded the state absolute authority in secular affairs, ultimately subordinated the church's precepts to the coercive powers of the territorial sovereign. While the devout Christian prince might serve the dictates of the faith, there was little to prevent him from manipulating the church for his own purposes. Religion might be rendered compatible with *raison d'état*, but often at the expense of its own vitality. A classic case in point was the Prussian church union of 1817, which amalgamated Lutheran and Calvinist churches into a single hierarchy in the name of administrative efficiency and with apparent disregard for the theological sensibilities of the affected churchmen.[25]

The nineteenth-century church thus served as a major prop to monarchical and conservative interests, and it was in part the problems attendant on this status that brought the idea of a Volkskirche into general circulation. The strongest proponents of the Volkskirche ideal were initially Protestant liberals, including activists concerned with the much-debated "social question" and academics determined to reconcile Protestant theological traditions with the new perspectives of scientific positivism or philosophical Idealism. These joint heirs of Wichern and Friedrich Schleiermacher—Naumann, Adolf von Harnack, and their fellows—sought to avoid defining the church according to a narrow confessional position while at the same time seeking to translate the old ideal of the Christian state into terms appropriate to an emergent industrial society. From this perspective, a "people's church" based upon active lay participation better em-

[25] Other states, including Hesse, the Palatinate, and Baden, also established Union churches. See Karl Kupisch, *Die deutschen Landeskirchen im 19. und 20. Jahrhundert* (Göttingen, 1966), and Walter Elliger, ed., *Die Evangelische Kirche der Union* (Witten, 1967). For a still reliable introduction and recent perspectives on the Lutheran heritage—here considerably simplified—see Hajo Holborn, *A History of Modern Germany: The Reformation* (New York, 1967), pp. 183–200, and Günther Wolf, ed., *Luther und die Obrigkeit* (Darmstadt, 1972).

bodied basic Evangelical principles than did a clerical-conservative "pastors' church" based upon royal patronage. Rather than merely serving the crown, the church must embody the nation. The parish should not function as a unit of civil administration but must become the core of a revitalized cultural community. Understood in this way, as a kind of ethical common denominator for society, the church must remain flexible enough to accommodate divergent theological viewpoints in the name of Protestant freedom, just as the political community should accommodate divergent social and economic interests in the name of civic freedom. Such a task was only conceivable in a church open to new intellectual currents. Without openings to the worlds of science and social reform, the church could not hope to improve communications with nominal parishioners for whom it otherwise meant little more than black-frocked officials, arcane dogmas, and the traditional rituals of passage between birth and death.[26]

Liberals were not, however, the only Protestants to raise the call for a genuine Volkskirche. Understood as a summons to lay involvement, the slogan also found considerable resonance among pietists, many of whom had long criticized territorial hierarchies for subordinating edification to administration, personal devotion to the parson's authority. Pietists rarely shared liberals' political enthusiasms. However, it was theological differences far more than political instincts that separated the two camps. Their biblical literalism and devotion to a religion of the heart made pietists instinctively suspicious of the liberal mind, which they saw as dangerously worldly and latitudinarian. The liberal model of a Protestant community, they feared, could only be effected by sacrificing the doctrinal rigor and traditions of the "faith of the fathers."[27]

---

[26] Shanahan, *German Protestants Face the Social Question*, 1:302–416; Johannes Rathje, *Die Welt des freien Protestantismus: Ein Beitrag zur deutsch-evangelischen Geistesgeschichte, dargestellt an Leben und Werk von Martin Rade* (Stuttgart, 1952); Theodor Heuss, *Friedrich Naumann: Der Mann, das Werk, die Zeit* (Stuttgart, 1937); Pollmann, *Kirchenregiment und soziale Frage*; Kouri, *Protestantismus und soziale Frage*.

[27] Useful interpretations of the pietist tradition include Hartmut Lehmann,

Despite obvious differences in orientation, both liberals and pietists shared certain reservations about the nineteenth-century Protestant establishment. Yet church officials themselves also came increasingly to speak the language of the Volkskirche. In the official vocabulary, the church's role as a "people's church" reflected and thereby justified its claim to act as ultimate arbiter of society's values. In the absence of a truly Christian state, church leaders saw all the more reason for their own commanding presence in the home, the marketplace, and the halls of power. Without questioning either the value of lay participation or the ideal of social integration, they insisted first on the preservation of institutional status independent of the favor of the masses that the Volkskirche claimed to embrace. Only from this high ground of institutional security, argued Johannes Schneider and those of like mind, could the church speak authoritatively to a divided and changing society.[28]

If, then, the Volkskirche ideal meant different things to different churchmen, it was an ideal most if not all segments of German Protestantism had come to embrace by 1918.[29] The sundering of throne and altar made this ideal particularly compelling, as common terminology and a shared crisis briefly encouraged cooperation between and among competing ecclesiastical factions.[30] Some have suggested that the well-nigh universal invocation of Volkskirche assumptions after 1918 was little more than an exercise in self-delusion or, worse, a cynical calculation, a "vital lie" propagated to justify the favored status of a church

Pietismus und weltliche Ordnung in Württemberg von 17. bis zum 20. Jahrhundert (Stuttgart, 1969); Carl Hinrichs, *Preussentum und Pietismus: Der pietismus in Brandenburg-Preussen als religiös-soziale Reformbewegung* (Göttingen, 1971); and Gerhard Kaiser, *Pietismus und Patriotismus im literarischen Deutschland: Ein Beitrag zum Problem der Säkularisation* (Wiesbaden, 1961).

[28] See Ernest Bramsted, "The Position of the Protestant Church in Germany, 1871–1933," *Journal of Religious History* 2 (1963): 314–34, 3 (1964): 61–79; Daniel R. Borg, "Volkskirche, 'Christian State,' and the Weimar Republic," *Church History* 35 (1966): 186–206.

[29] For the possible permutations of meaning during the Weimar era, see Meier, *Volkskirche, 1918–1945*, pp. 14–46.

[30] See Martin Greschat, ed., *Der deutsche Protestantismus im Revolutionsjahr 1918/19* (Witten, 1974), pp. 143–85, for representative documents.

largely bereft of significant functions and popular support.[31] Certainly such considerations played a part, especially in the early months of the republic. Equally important, however, is the fact that church leaders' rhetoric reflected a new awareness of the problems of ecclesiastical reform. Once invoked, the term Volks-kirche produced as much argument as concord. While the ideal might imply different things to different people, it was not immediately clear that the institution to which it referred could in fact be all things to all people. Did the mobilization of lay support require the introduction of ecclesiastical democracy and the dismantling of hierarchical structures? Did conditions demand a holy war against pluralism, or did prudence dictate some sort of compromise with the modern order? In its self-ascribed role as moral preceptor, could the church take official stands on controversial public issues without alienating parishioners who might hold differing views? What arenas were in fact proper for public action? Moved equally by fears of social superannuation and by hopes for religious revival, clergy and church leaders struggled with such questions as the nation struggled from crisis to crisis during the Weimar decade.

One immediate product of these reflections was a drive to achieve greater unity between and among the various territorial churches. With its welter of confessions and administrative hierarchies, German Protestantism had seldom spoken with a single voice; no Protestant equivalent existed for the Catholic bishops' conference. To be sure, most of the territorial churches participated in a loose consultative forum, the Eisenach Conference, established in 1852. Since 1903, moreover, a central committee, the Deutscher Evangelischer Kirchenausschuss (DEKA), had functioned as an informal mouthpiece for Protestant interests in Berlin. After the November Revolution, when the status of the churches became a constitutional issue, these consultative agencies took on new importance. At national church congresses in 1919 and 1921—the latter convened in Stuttgart—representatives of the territorial bodies moved to establish a formal Prot-

---

[31] Thus Jacke, *Kirche zwischen Monarchie und Republik*, p. 332 and passim.

estant church federation (*Kirchenbund*), complete with representative assembly and senate, for which the existing DEKA was to function as a standing executive committee. The Kirchenbund came into being in 1922 at a mass assembly in Wittenberg, the symbolic citadel of German Protestantism. Its founders hailed the event as a sign that the churches were at last forging a common identity and transcending historic constraints of particularism. Inevitably, perhaps, the new Kirchenbund bore a distinctly Prussian stamp. The head of the sprawling Prussian Union church, whose several provinces together embraced half or more of all nominal German Protestants, served as permanent chairman of the DEKA and hence as a de facto national spokesman for the Protestant cause.[32]

In view of this, it is hardly surprising that most studies of Weimar Protestantism have concentrated on Prussia or on national church leadership. Yet one should not exaggerate the effects of the unity movement or the influence of the Prussian church. Like the Eisenach Conference that preceded it, the Kirchenbund of 1922 had no power to establish binding policies. Although it served an often significant function as a vehicle of communication between member churches and as a collective mouthpiece in dealings with the national government, it did not and could not produce confessional or administrative uniformity. After 1918 as before, German Protestantism remained an aggregation of autonomous territorial bodies—some twenty-eight in number, not including the various "free churches" such as Methodists and Baptists or those in former German areas lost under the Treaty of Versailles—each with its own peculiar church polity and tradition of relationships to secular authority. Religious customs, liturgical practices, and popular attitudes were equally diverse. For this reason, despite the broad similarities in situation and outlook between and among the various churches, a full analysis of Weimar Protestantism requires attention to its local context. In church affairs as in politics and cul-

[32] Wright, "*Above Parties*," pp. 28–31; Helmreich, *German Churches under Hitler*, pp. 30–36, 69–73; Scholder, *Die Kirchen und das Dritte Reich*, 1:26–45.

23

ture, one must avoid the temptation to equate Prussia and Germany, to limit the horizons of inquiry to the boundaries of Berlin. To trace pastors' struggles with Weimar pluralism, it is often useful to strike a balance between the high ground of academic theology or national church politics and the hedgerow world of the local parish, the village schoolroom, and the humbler outposts of ecclesiastical endeavor.

For this purpose the study of one of the smaller territorial churches has much to commend it. Here it may be possible to mark most clearly the church's transformation from self-confident Wilhelmian bureaucracy to the divided and embattled community of the Nazi era. The church in Württemberg provides an instructive case study of this sort. Not only did it have close historic ties to the state both institutional and emotional, but it also remained to some extent a genuinely popular institution, a recognized force in the life and customs of the people. Württemberg's social structure and political traditions, moreover, afford at least a modest counterbalance to the Prussian paradigm, which, as noted, has typically dominated studies of this topic. Once the salient features of this Swabian social and ecclesiastical landscape have been sketched, our aim will be to identify specific influences on churchmen's self-understanding after 1918, tracing the ways in which they sought to adapt Volkskirche traditions to the changed circumstances created by the November Revolution. The first concern will be to examine the practical impact of revolution, both on the church's relationship to the state and on its internal polity. Attention can then shift to the search for ecclesiastical identity and purpose reflected in churchmen's efforts both to maintain a commanding presence in the schools and to expand the Protestant social presence. This will lead in turn to a reassessment of the church's place in the Weimar political constellation and its role in the passage from democracy to dictatorship after 1930.

What emerges from the inquiry is a picture of the Weimar years as a watershed in the church's development, a period in which one can detect at least the preliminary signs of a shift in the center of its institutional gravity. If the church had historically defined itself in terms of the state, after 1918 it grappled increasingly with the problems of a definition in terms of society. If churchmen had earlier concerned themselves with modelling established order and authority, they now felt compelled to concentrate increasingly on firming their tenuous base among nominal members. The dimensions of this shift were not yet fully evident when Hitler sealed the collapse of the Weimar experiment. As developments after 1933 and particularly after 1945 would confirm, however, the November Revolution helped create a church that, despite its traditionalism and for better or worse, was becoming more pluralistic in social and political outlook and certainly more conscious of the ambiguities involved in any project for accommodating the Volkskirche heritage to the complexities of a changing modern world.

ONE

Church, State, and Society
in Württemberg before 1918

𝕿HE EVANGELICAL-LUTHERAN CHURCH in Württemberg ranked fourth in size among German churches after World War I; besides the vast Prussian church, only those in Saxony and Hannover were larger. According to the census of 1925, it numbered some 1,722,189 nominal members, or two-thirds of the total Württemberg population, a proportion of Protestants nearly identical to that in Germany as a whole.[1] This demographic coincidence does not mean, of course, that generalizations about German Protestantism can be applied without qualification to Württemberg. Like many of the territorial churches, and perhaps more than most, the Württemberg church reflected peculiar local social and economic conditions, folkways, and political values, the characteristic features of a culture in which it was itself a prominent fixture. The history of Württemberg religious life is a history of mutual interpenetration between church, state, and society. To understand churchmen's aims and actions after 1918, it is helpful to see them in terms of the church's historical environment, the particular configurations of society in which it was embedded, and the institutional arrangements that it had inherited from nearly four centuries of monar-

---

[1] *KJ 1926*, pp. 652, 611–81 passim. Institutionally speaking, the large Evangelical church by no means exhausted the possibilities of Württemberg Protestantism, which abounded in small sects and free churches, among them Methodists and Baptists, Huguenots, Darbyists, and a variety of holiness groups. While of considerable local significance in some areas, such groups nevertheless attracted only a tiny fraction of the Protestant population; for our purposes they played a marginal if sometimes highly visible role in the religious life of the region.

chical order. It is equally important to have some sense of the church's place in popular culture. We begin, therefore, with a brief survey of civic traditions, ecclesiastical structures, and religious practices in Württemberg on the eve of the November Revolution.

In 1918 the kingdom of Württemberg was the largest state in the German southwest. Its heartland lay in the upper Neckar basin, where the old Swabian duchy of Württemberg, with its capital at Stuttgart, had stood as a bastion of Lutheranism since 1534. Württemberg attained the status of a kingdom in the early nineteenth century when, under Napoleonic aegis, its frontiers expanded to absorb parts of Protestant Franconia, the largely Catholic Habsburg holdings in Upper Swabia, and a number of former imperial free cities such as Heilbronn and Ulm. Together with Bavaria and Baden, its neighbors to the east and west, Württemberg formed part of the loose triumvirate of southern states that served at least intermittently as a counterweight to Prussian hegemony in intra-German affairs.

The German southwest has sometimes been called, affectionately, the *Musterländle*, that "model land" where the bigger world beyond can be found reduced to an intimate human scale. Just as the gentle hills and quiet stream valleys of old Württemberg reflected in miniature the topography of the larger German landscape, so too the contours of its social, political, and religious landscape tended to mirror national conditions, yet always with distinctive features of their own. As one of its most distinguished historians has observed, interwar Württemberg represented a happy medium among the German states. Neither condemned to political insignificance nor committed, like its larger neighbor Bavaria, to self-assertion at any price, it followed the general course set in Berlin, but at a distance great enough for its own profile to remain visible.[2]

[2] Waldemar Besson, *Württemberg und die deutsche Staatskrise, 1928–1933* (Stuttgart, 1959), p. 18. A standard history is Ernst Marquardt, *Geschichte Württembergs* (Stuttgart, 1961); for the Weimar period, see also Wolfgang Benz, *Süddeutschland in der Weimarer Republik: Ein Beitrag zur deutschen Innenpolitik, 1918–1923* (Berlin, 1970).

This profile has been the subject of considerable popular commentary, much of it fairly fanciful. Recurrent themes, however, include the area's comparative prosperity and its generally harmonious class relations. Above all, observers have emphasized the characteristic Swabian *Lebensdemokratie*, a casual but passionately felt individuality, at once deferential and egalitarian, which militated against rigid or arbitrary distinctions in rank and status. By popular account, Württemberg's rulers before 1918 could expect loyal subjects to address them not as "Your Majesty" but as "Herr König," with "king" connoting the same occupational dignity accorded "butcher," "lawyer," or "farmer."[3]

This complex of traits, to which might be added a proverbial Swabian predilection for hard work, was closely linked to the pace and character of Württemberg's economic development. During the 1920s Württemberg appeared to many to offer a productive blend of tradition and modernity. In some respects it stood at the forefront of progress, sharing in the industrial transformation that by 1900 had made imperial Germany the economic giant of Europe. According to occupational figures in the 1925 census, 40 percent of the Württemberg population earned a livelihood either directly or indirectly from industry, roughly the same as the national average. The half-century before the Great War had seen the capital, Stuttgart, grow from a sleepy royal residence into a prosperous city of more than three hundred thousand people, the hub of an expanding industrial conurbation along the Neckar River between Heilbronn and Esslingen. With its modest skyscrapers and Bauhaus apartment projects, its avant-garde art galleries and well-tended parks, Stuttgart was by no means the least among the cities of Europe.

---

[3] Paul Wurster, *Das kirchliche Leben der ev. Landeskirche in Württemberg* (Tübingen, 1919), pp. 24ff.; Theodor Heuss, *Schwaben: Farben zu einem Portrait* (Tübingen, 1967). While Württemberg was not exclusively Swabian, Swabian values also enjoyed an informal hegemony in the territories annexed after 1800. The *Volkskundler* Wilhelm Heinrich Riehl noted that "in the inns of Weikersheim and Mergentheim one hears Franconian in the public rooms and Swabian in the lounge where the civil servants sit" (Riehl, "Ein Gang durchs Taubertal," *Wanderbuch*, 3d ed. [Stuttgart, 1892], p. 152).

The peripatetic Ilya Ehrenburg, who visited briefly during the Weimar years, found it one of the most attractive and "American" towns of its size on the Continent.[4]

At the same time, however, Württemberg retained many distinctive features of an older way of life. Although industrial development began comparatively early, it proved less overwhelming in pace and scale than it became farther north and east. Württemberg entered the Weimar decade still largely a land of small towns and villages. Besides Stuttgart, the only city with more than fifty thousand inhabitants was Ulm, Württemberg's commercial gateway on the upper Danube; in only four others—Heilbronn, Ludwigsburg, Esslingen, and Reutlingen—did the population exceed twenty-five thousand. Roughly 60 percent of the population lived in towns of under five thousand inhabitants, a full 25 percent in villages of one thousand or less.[5] The vineyards and wooded slopes that extended into the heart of Stuttgart itself and tempered even the harshest industrial precincts of the Neckar valley served as a reminder of the persistent traditional rhythms of the countryside.

The countryside itself was largely a preserve of smallholders. The agricultural census of 1882 showed that less than 2 percent of all rural holdings exceeded 250 acres, scarcely one-tenth the national average. A resident landed gentry existed only in the annexed Franconian district of Hohenlohe, and even there to nothing like the extent found in the Prussian latifundia east of the Elbe. To be sure, the distribution of holdings varied considerably in different parts of the kingdom. Midsized family farms were the rule in the Catholic south, while in the Protestant heartlands, where primogeniture was seldom practiced, the subdivision of the land into successively smaller plots produced

---

[4] Ilya Ehrenburg, *Menschen Jahre Leben: Autobiographie*, trans. Alexander Kaempfe (Munich, 1962), 1:718; cf. Walter Laqueur, *Weimar: A Cultural History* (1974; reprint, New York, 1976), pp. 26–27. Statistics are from *Statistisches Handbuch für Württemberg, 1928* (Stuttgart, 1928), pp. 20–22, 30 (hereafter *SHW 1928*).

[5] *SHW 1928*, pp. 20–24.

widespread misery and often heavy emigration during the several periods of agricultural crisis in the nineteenth century.[6] The proliferation of microfundia also exerted an influence on industrial culture. Württemberg's factories clustered most densely in those areas where uneconomic smallholdings were most common, producing a characteristic interpenetration of urban-industrial values and practices with those of the small towns and the surrounding countryside. Vast tenement suburbs on the model of Berlin or Essen were all but nonexistent. Indeed, while less than 40 percent of the population earned its primary livelihood from farming at the turn of the century, fully 55 percent still lived either directly on the land or in small farming villages. In many districts, particularly along the Neckar and its tributaries, a new commuter population grew up as marginal farmers who maintained households in villages sought work in neighboring cities while, conversely, urban workers in search of better living conditions found homes—and often brides—in the countryside. If urban migrants infected village life with the alien ways of the city, it was equally typical for factory workers to retain a relationship to the soil in the form of a family vineyard, or *Schrebergarten*. As a result, the influence of the land remained stronger than could be measured in gross occupational statistics alone. "With its private homes and small plots of land, the working class wears a largely petty bourgeois face"; this is how the pastor of one Stuttgart suburb summarized local social conditions as late as the 1920s.[7]

Württemberg industry bore little resemblance to the blast-furnace kingdoms on the Ruhr. A lack of basic raw materials militated against the development of heavy primary industries,

[6] Ibid.; Klaus Simon, *Die württembergischen Demokraten, 1890–1920* (Stuttgart, 1969), pp. 4–6.

[7] Plattenhardt, Pfarrbericht 1928, OKR/AR PfB. For studies of worker mentalities in Württemberg, see Peter Borscheid, *Textilarbeiterschaft in der Industrialisierung: Soziale Lage und Mobilität in Württemberg (19. Jahrhundert)* (Stuttgart, 1978); Wolfgang von Hippel, "Industrieller Wandel im ländlichen Raum: Untersuchungen im Gebiet des mittleren Neckars, 1850–1914," *Archiv für Sozialgeschichte* 19 (1979): 43–122.

with the result that the industrial sector rested principally on comparatively small-scale enterprises, first in textiles and housewares, then increasingly in finishing industries such as machine-tool works, electrochemical concerns, and first-generation automotive production. Here, continued reliance on skilled labor identified the factory more with older handicraft methods than with those of the assembly line. Tuttlingen, a small city in southern Württemberg known for its shoe- and implement-making firms, was typical of many. A former resident recalled that at the turn of the century, "the factories were located on residential streets. The smaller enterprises would hardly have been identified as such except for the work noises which they emitted."[8] Even when they applied the most advanced entrepreneurial methods, factory owners bore the stamp of the older merchant and professional classes from which most had come. The result was a stable, sober, and self-sufficient class of small-town burghers and urban notables who admired honesty and hard work more than wealth or social display.

Württemberg, in short, was preeminently a land of free farmers, skilled laborers, and commercially vigorous burgher-entrepreneurs, with neither a large urban underclass nor a Junker-like elite of rural grandees. This social configuration in turn left an imprint on political attitudes. Its clearest legacy was doubtless the broadly democratic and populist traditions that distinguished Württemberg from many parts of the country. In Württemberg, democracy enjoyed the sanctity of tradition. Democratic instincts had their social roots in the burgher classes of former imperial cities and provincial estates, whose persistent struggles on

[8] August Springer, *Der Andere, der bist Du: Lebensgeschichte eines reichen armen Mannes* (Tübingen, 1954), p. 20. See also Theodor Heuss, *Robert Bosch* (Tübingen, 1946), and Paul Gehring, "Das Wirtschaftsleben in Württemberg unter König Wilhelm I," *ZfWLG* 9 (1949–50): 196–257. For a general analysis of Württemberg economic statistics, see Klaus Megerle, "Regionale Differenzierung des Industrialisierungsprozesses: Überlegungen am Beispiel Württembergs," in Rainer Fremdling and Richard N. Tilly, eds., *Industrialisierung und Raum: Studien zur regionalen Differenzierung im Deutschland des 19. Jahrhunderts* (Stuttgart, 1979), pp. 105–31.

behalf of their "good old rights" had moved Charles James Fox, the eighteenth-century English Whig, to declare that, next to Britain, Württemberg was the only European state with a constitution worthy of the name.[9] The estates fought to temper, though they could not totally check, the absolutist designs of the Württemberg ruling family. After years of stormy confrontations involving the crown, burghers, churchmen, and petty imperial nobility, the constitution of 1819 finally laid the foundations for a genuine parliamentary order. By the early twentieth century, in contrast to the sham constitutionalism of Bismarck's Prussia, the Württemberg system had eliminated virtually all its residual absolutist features. Württemberg's last king, Wilhelm II, who took the throne in 1891, was a far cry from his Prussian namesake. A constitutional monarch by both choice and temperament, Wilhelm enjoyed wide popularity as a patron of social and political reform. Under his benevolent aegis a series of constitutional revisions in 1909 removed the remaining barriers to a fully representative state government. In 1916, on the twenty-fifth anniversary of Wilhelm's coronation, Württemberg's Social Democratic chieftain Wilhelm Keil created a local legend by writing that if Württemberg were suddenly to become a republic, little would change, since "if the decision were left to the people, no one would have a better prospect of being elected head of state than the present king."[10]

The political party structure reflected this tradition of democratic conservatism and the mediating effects of Württemberg's economic evolution. By and large state politics retained a strong centrist cast, rooted in stable economic blocs and little affected by extremist influences on either the right or the left. In contrast with much of Germany, political liberalism was able to maintain

[9] Quoted in Francis L. Carsten, *Princes and Parliaments in Germany from the Fifteenth to the Eighteenth Century* (Oxford, 1959), p. 5.

[10] Wilhelm Keil, *Erlebnisse eines Sozialdemokraten*, 2 vols. (Stuttgart, 1947–48), 1:377–378. The king apparently had plans to include Keil on his birthday decorations list for 1917, withdrawing the offer privately only after Keil replied that it would be in the best interest of both if no Social Democrat were so honored.

a genuinely popular base in Württemberg during both the Wilhelmian and Weimar periods. The prewar national-liberal Deutsche Partei drew upon a stable core of academic, professional, and commercial supporters. Most notable, however, was the strength of the anti-Prussian Volkspartei, a branch of the left-liberal German Progressive movement, whose electoral achievements in Württemberg remained unmatched anywhere in Germany during the Second Empire. Drawing heavy support from middling farmers and small entrepreneurs, skilled laborers, and many Catholics of *grossdeutsch* persuasion, the Populists dominated the Württemberg lower chamber during the unification era and again during the decade after 1895, when they controlled nearly half of the seats in the chamber.

By World War I, economic change had begun to erode the Populist hegemony and to create new party alignments along interest-group lines. On the right an agrarian party, the Bauernbund, emerged as a fixture in rural Protestant districts, often working in concert with its urban counterpart, the Bürgerpartei, which represented conservative burghers, academics, and many Protestant state officials. At the same time the two major mass parties on the Wilhelmian spectrum, the Social Democrats and the Catholic Center, began to draw off former supporters of the Volkspartei. A negligible force before 1900, Social Democrats more than tripled their strength in the decade that followed; by 1912 they held 17 of 92 seats in the provincial diet, or Landtag. On the whole the party presented a moderate image in state affairs, a stance to which the comparative traditionalism of many of its supporters may have contributed. Pockets of working-class militancy did emerge, to be sure, in the greater Stuttgart area and in newer industrial centers like Göppingen and Schwenningen, providing a productive training ground for such left socialist leaders as Klara Zetkin and Arthur Crispien. Still, local conditions hardly encouraged the formation of a large and radicalized industrial proletariat. The Württemberg party apparatus remained securely in the hands of technicians like Wilhelm Keil, pragmatists who, as Keil himself admitted, saw no reason for "putting the preservation of party dogmas ahead of practical political tasks."[11]

Like Social Democracy, political Catholicism came into its own as a public force only after 1900. The Kulturkampf of the 1870s had largely bypassed Württemberg, and in part for this reason the Catholic Center did not emerge as a separate organization there until 1894. Before that time, as already noted, many Catholics supported the Volkspartei, a party with which the Center continued a limited collaboration on certain political and procedural issues. Cultural interests, however, and the heavily agrarian character of the Catholic electorate, increasingly drove the Center to make common cause with the conservative Protestant Bauernbund. At the outbreak of World War I, the Catholic Center and the coalition of Bauernbund and Bürgerpartei controlled as many Landtag seats as the liberal and socialist parties combined.

The realignments that occurred after the war altered party labels but otherwise had little effect on the prewar political configuration. A merger of the progressives and the left wing of the former liberal faction produced the German Democratic party (DDP), an amalgam of populists and professors that persisted as a respectable force in Württemberg until 1933, long after its national counterpart had faded into insignificance. The old national-liberal right either affiliated with Gustav Stresemann's new moderate-conservative German People's party (DVP) or

---

[11] Keil, *Erlebnisse*, 1:205. On Social Democrats in Württemberg, see Carl E. Schorske, *German Social Democracy, 1905–1917: The Development of the Great Schism* (Cambridge, Mass., 1955; reprint, New York, 1955), pp. 130–33. Major interpretations of Württemberg political culture include Besson, *Württemberg und die deutsche Staatskrise*; Simon, *Württembergische Demokraten*; Walter Grube, *Der Stuttgarter Landtag, 1457–1957* (Stuttgart, 1957); Rosemarie Menzinger, *Verfassungsrevision und Demokratisierungsprozess im Königreich Württemberg* (Stuttgart, 1969); James C. Hunt, *The People's Party in Württemberg and Southern Germany, 1890–1914* (Stuttgart, 1975); Dieter Langewiesche, *Liberalismus und Demokratie in Württemberg zwischen Revolution und Reichsgründung* (Düsseldorf, 1974); and David Blackbourn, *Class, Religion, and Local Politics in Wilhelmine Germany: The Centre Party in Württemberg before 1914* (New Haven, Conn., 1980).

joined prewar Protestant conservatives in an expanded Bürger-partei, which, together with the surviving Bauernbund, constituted Württemberg's variant of the rightist German National People's party (DNVP).

When the monarchy collapsed in 1918, Social Democrats stepped into the breach in Stuttgart as in Berlin, forming a Weimar-style coalition with the Catholic Center and the DDP. Once a new state constitution had been adopted, however, they withdrew to their accustomed position as a loyal opposition. Thereafter the Center served as the anchor of every government coalition, first with the DDP and then, after 1924, with the Protestant right. While Württemberg thus participated in the general rightward trend of Weimar politics, the cabinet instability that plagued national government was not to be found in Stuttgart. In effect Württemberg experienced only one political shift during the 1920s, from center to center-right in 1924, and the presence of the Center party in every cabinet provided an element of continuity that enhanced Württemberg's image as a "peaceful island" in Weimar's stormy political seas.[12]

Though the Catholic Center was a pivotal parliamentary force throughout the 1920s, Catholics otherwise played only a modest role in public life. While one branch of the ruling family professed the Roman faith, and while nineteenth-century kings pursued a policy of more than benevolent neutrality towards the Catholic church, Württemberg's strong historical identification with Protestantism, reinforced by the state's social and confessional structure, left the bureaucracy in effect a Protestant preserve. In the absence of a Junker class, the bureaucracy functioned both as a recruiting ground and as a preferred field of endeavor for Swabian notables. As a result the Protestant church, and particularly its administrative hierarchy, became solidly identified with the local mandarin class; religious confession reinforced education and family connections as linchpins of social standing.[13]

[12] Thus Marquardt, *Geschichte Württembergs*, pp. 366–67.
[13] The 19th-century background is analyzed effectively in Blackbourn, *Class,*

This interplay of caste and confession found a clear focus in Tübingen, which, as Württemberg's sole university, played an indispensable part in the formation of a local administrative elite. Like the area it served, the university was peacefully biconfessional. Yet the prevailing ethos was unambiguously Protestant, just as it was distinctively Swabian. Of pivotal importance in both respects was the university's famous and venerable Protestant seminary, or Stift. Established by ducal fiat in 1536, the Tübingen Stift and its several preparatory seminaries offered state-subsidized classical educations to those who achieved success in the rigorous qualifying examinations. The original and still primary purpose of the Stift was of course to train candidates for the Protestant clergy; David Friedrich Strauss once described it as a "theological mousetrap with fellowships as the bait."[14] A career in the church was not the only option, however, and many *Stiftler* went on to professional or civil service positions. The system therefore served as a key selection mechanism for future leadership, and because access depended as much upon merit as upon birth, the Stift provided an important and uniquely Swabian vehicle for social mobility. On the eve of World War I, for example, nearly 75 percent of all higher civil servants in Württemberg had the honor of being the first in their families to have earned a university degree.[15]

Through the shared experiences of classroom and dormitory, a complex web of personal relationships bound together pastors, professors, and government officials. The alliance of throne and altar replicated itself socially in the bloodlines of the bureaucracy and the Protestant burgher class. Representative of this mandarin caste was Hermann von Zeller, who in 1918 was president of the Protestant Consistory (Konsistorium), the supreme ad-

---

Religion, and Local Politics, pp. 61–99. For contemporary comments, see "Parität in Württemberg?" *Deutsches Volksblatt*, Oct. 30, 1926, and "Die Parität im württ. Beamtentum," *SDZ*, Nov. 10, 1926.

[14] Quoted in Wurster, *Kirchliches Leben*, p. 186.

[15] Karl Weller, *Die Staatsumwälzung in Württemberg, 1918–1920* (Stuttgart, 1930), p. 5. On the Stift, see Martin Leube, *Das Tübinger Stift 1770–1950* (Stuttgart, 1954).

ministrative body of the Württemberg church. A high official in the state Ministry of Finance for most of his career, Zeller came from a large and influential family of businessmen, clergy, and civil servants. A listing of his family connections, by blood and marriage, constitutes a veritable compendium of Swabian notables.

The church's institutional structure derived from a model first established for Old Württemberg in the General Church Order of 1559. Under this charter Württemberg's rulers exercised their authority as bishops through the Protestant Consistory in Stuttgart. Part state bureau, part ecclesiastical committee, the Consistory comprised about ten officials, both clergy and laymen, appointed by the sovereign and acting in his name to set church policy, to supervise clerical personnel, and in general to oversee the spiritual and material welfare of the church. Spiritual supervision was primarily the concern of prelates, or general superintendents, who served as ex officio members of the Consistory and carried out episcopal functions within the church's several administrative regions. During the period with which we are concerned, the church was divided into four dioceses, centered in Heilbronn, Ludwigsburg, Reutlingen, and Ulm. The diocese of Heilbronn included all of northern Württemberg. That of Ludwigsburg, in the historic Protestant heartland, was smallest in area but largest in population, including as it did Stuttgart and its densely settled environs. The diocese of Reutlingen encompassed both western and south-central Württemberg between the Black Forest and the Swabian Jura and, nearer Stuttgart, the district of Esslingen. To the east and south sprawled the diocese of Ulm, whose seemingly disproportionate size—more than half the state—was explained by the fact that it included virtually all the predominantly Catholic regions in Württemberg (see map, p. 38).

The church's basic administrative unit was of course the local parish, of which there were about one thousand in 1920, served by some twelve hundred pastors. As elsewhere, parishes varied widely in size and social composition, from rural diasporas in

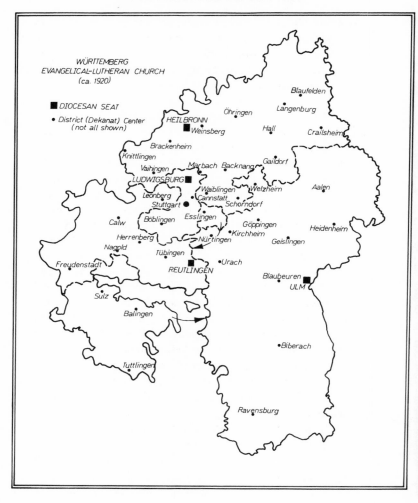

WÜRTTEMBERG
EVANGELICAL-LUTHERAN CHURCH
(ca. 1920)

■ DIOCESAN SEAT

● District (Dekanat) Center
(not all shown)

which a single pastor might serve as many as a dozen scattered
hamlets to the mass congregations of Stuttgart and Heilbronn,
where the roll of nominal parishioners might exceed twenty
thousand and where church affairs required the talents of an entire subhierarchy of clergy and lay officials. For the most part,

however, Württemberg's small-town character reflected itself in the size and distribution of parishes.[16]

Parishes were in turn grouped into forty-nine districts (*Dekanate*), most contiguous with civil administrative districts (*Regierungsbezirke*). Each was administered by a *Dekan*, or dean, accountable to the regional prelate and to the Consistory in Stuttgart. The Dekans were pivotal figures in the Württemberg hierarchy. On the one hand they served as the Consistory's official representatives in dealing with the parish clergy. On the other hand they too had parish responsibilities, since the post of Dekan was invariably tied to a preaching position in the principal town of the district. In this dual capacity the Dekan stood *primus inter pares* among area clergy and was responsible for maintaining collegial relations and for serving as an intermediary between fellow pastors and higher church authorities. The responsibility and esteem that attached to the office of Dekan made appointment to such posts a matter of great interest and no little political maneuvering. Theophil Wurm, head of the church during the Hitler era and himself a former Dekan, would note wryly in his memoirs that there was no other aspect of church administration in which the leadership could count upon such a surfeit of unsolicited advice.[17]

Until 1918, as already noted, ultimate ecclesiastical authority rested with the king as summus episcopus. While the church functioned in most respects as an autonomous institution, it also filled a variety of quasiofficial roles, notably in the supervision of the state school system. Prelates and members of the Consistory, who throughout the nineteenth century sat as members of

---

[16] For a detailed structural analysis, see Günther Bormann and Sigrid Bormann-Heischkeid, *Theorie und Praxis kirchlicher Organisation: Ein Beitrag zum Problem der Rückständigkeit sozialer Gruppen* (Opladen, 1971), particularly pp. 61–90. Basic sourcebooks for the Weimar period include Friedrich Kühnle, *Die ev. Kirchenstellen in Württemberg*, 4th ed. (Esslingen, 1931), and the periodic compilations of clergy and clerical positions in Wilhelm Breuninger, ed., *Magisterbuch*, 38th ed. (Stuttgart, 1920) and following. For a fine brief historical introduction, see Gerhard Schäfer, *Kleine württembergische Kirchengeschichte* (Stuttgart, 1965).

[17] Theophil Wurm, *Erinnerungen aus meinem Leben* (Stuttgart, 1953), p. 67.

the Landtag, were appointed by the king and served at his pleasure. The equation of throne and altar was further reinforced by financial arrangements. In 1806 a royal decree secularized ecclesiastical rents and properties in Württemberg, holdings that at one time had amounted to nearly one-third of all the land in the duchy. As compensation, clerical livings gradually came under the purview of the state Ministry of Education (Kultusministerium), and the old system of parish tithes and payments in kind gave way by midcentury to a uniform salary scale informally assimilated to that for civil servants.

In part this arrangement reflected the crown's determination to centralize and rationalize administration of state finances. It also reflected the complexities involved in administering new territories acquired between 1802 and 1809, in which church finances remained a patchwork of private endowments, rents, and local tithes. The effect, in any case, was to leave the Württemberg church with few financial resources of its own. As a result it was more heavily dependent on the state's largesse than was its Catholic counterpart, not to mention the many other Protestant territorial churches that won the right, in the course of the century, to supplement public support with direct or indirect taxes on their members. At the beginning of World War I, only 570,000 M, less than one-tenth of the Württemberg church's annual budget of about 6 million M, represented specifically ecclesiastical income, largely in the form of interest from commutation payments on properties not subject to secularization in 1806. Of the remainder, only about 3 million M was judged to represent the income value of the pre-1806 *Kirchengut*. Roughly one-third of the total budget therefore came from unsecured state subsidies, the legal status of which were always open to debate. While the Württemberg constitution of 1819 affirmed the church's right to a separately administered endowment, a variety of obstacles prevented implementation of this provision. Despite intensive negotiations on the subject as late as 1914, the entire matter of finances remained unresolved at the time of the November Revolution.[18]

[18] "Die finanzielle Lage der evangelischen Landeskirche Württembergs,"

It is hardly surprising that, in Hegel's native land, Protestants should identify their cause so fervently with the welfare of the state and the royal family. The state church tradition was not without critics, however, even among the clergy. Although financial bonds remained tight, the nineteenth century saw a gradual relaxation of administrative ties between church and state. This was one legacy of the long reign of Württemberg's King Wilhelm I (1816–64), a self-styled enlightened despot of no great religious convictions who, many churchmen believed, judged candidates for ecclesiastical positions less by their theological qualifications than by their political reliability—an understandable concern, perhaps, in view of the fact that the several Protestant prelates, by virtue of their office, sat in the upper chamber of the Landtag. The revolutionary currents of 1848 also had an effect: democratic spokesmen who protested the overweening bureaucratic character of government in Württemberg often extended their criticism to encompass the church as well. Internal dissatisfaction and external criticism led, at least indirectly, to a series of structural reforms between 1851 and 1868, which provided for a greater measure of ecclesiastical autonomy. Lay participation in church government increased through the establishment of elected parish councils (*Kirchengemeinderäte*) and a general church synod with limited legislative powers. Theoretically this synodical system created a new balance in church life, with a modest democratic impulse—rooted in the lay membership, which voted for members of parish councils and, through the latter, for the general synod—counterposed to the bureaucratic authority vested in crown and Consistory. In practice, to be sure, the balance of power still heavily favored the latter. Nevertheless, the resulting synodical-consistorial hybrid would provide a ready model for reorganization after 1918.[19]

---

memorandum [1919], LKA A26/1238; Karl Mayer, "Die finanziellen Beziehungen zwischen der Ev. Kirche und dem Staat in Württemberg, 1806–1919," *BWKG* 36 (1932): 108–38. About 65% of the church budget went to pay clergy salaries, another 20% to fund pension and survivors' benefits; the remainder represented construction and maintenance costs and expenses for the preparatory seminaries.

[19] Gerhard Schäfer, "Das Ringen um neue kirchliche Ordnungen der würt-

Prospects for still greater ecclesiastical autonomy increased at the end of the nineteenth century with passage in 1898 of the so-called *Reversaliengesetz*, or law of succession for the summus episcopus. The Württemberg royal family, we have noted, included both a Protestant and an ancillary Catholic line. Because the reigning sovereign, Wilhelm II, was the only living male in the Protestant line and had no direct heirs, his death seemed likely to result in a Catholic successor. The law of 1898, proposed by the Consistory and supported by the crown, was designed to deal with the anomaly of a Catholic sovereign at the head of a Protestant church. It provided that if, through incapacity or accident of succession, there should be no Protestant to serve as summus episcopus, formal episcopal authority would devolve upon a five-member collegium composed of two Consistory representatives and three Protestant members of the Württemberg cabinet. In the event that the latter were unavailable, unable, or unwilling to serve, church officials would be empowered to name all five members. This law took on unanticipated significance in 1918, since its provision for a statutory transfer of authority effectively insulated Württemberg churchmen from the traumatic and confusing jurisdictional struggles that briefly convulsed the Prussian church and that contributed not a little to the strained relations between Protestant officials and the new republican state.[20]

Despite the church's bureaucratic and hierarchical structure, with its ranks of Dekans, its prelates, and its *Konsistorialräte*, distinctions of rank and authority had less importance than might be expected within the Württemberg clerical caste. The same ties of family and friendship that linked churchmen and

---

tembergischen Landeskirche in der ersten Hälfte des 19. Jahrhunderts," *BWKG* 62 (1962): 282–308.

[20] *Regierungsblatt für das Königreich Württemberg* (1898), p. 75 (hereafter, *Regierungsblatt*); *Amtsblatt des Württ. Ev. Konsistoriums*, 16 (1912): 135 (hereafter, *Amtsblatt*); cf. Max Mayer, "Die Aenderung des Gesetzes, betreffend die evangelische Kirchenregierung," speech to Evangelischer Bund, Stuttgart, Oct. 1911, copy in LKA A26/214. Some other German states, such as Saxony, had similar ordinances.

their civil service counterparts also tempered and attenuated lines of division between pastors and Dekans, higher and lower clergy. One Württemberg pastor in three was himself a pastor's son. In many families the line of occupational succession extended unbroken for generations, with the result that family ties often united the loftiest prelate and the lowliest vicar. Despite the potential for social mobility afforded by the Tübingen Stift—or perhaps, indeed, because of it—the clergy remained a stable and homogeneous element in Württemberg society, enjoying a status somewhere between that of the professional and bureaucratic mandarins and the humbler orders of shopkeepers and village schoolmasters. Clergy and intermediate classes together furnished nearly 90 percent of all candidates for the parish ministry. Occasionally the son of an academic or commercial notable might choose a theological career; workers' sons generally lacked both opportunity and inclination. While the church was proverbially strong in the countryside, farmers' sons were a rarity among pastors, primarily because few enjoyed access to the classically oriented preparatory schooling necessary to compete successfully on the state examinations. These proportions are borne out by a table of Württemberg theologians killed during World War I. Of the 238 men listed, 91 were sons of pastors or missionaries, 42 sons of schoolmasters, and 27 sons of civil servants, while 21 came from the commercial classes and 18 from small business or industry. Farmers and artisans each supplied 9, while 13 were sons of salaried employees, and only 4 each came from working-class and professional families.[21]

In a society that recognized university training as a key to social standing, pastors' academic credentials set them apart from most of their parishioners. Academic experience was also basic to the clergy's occupational esprit. For the fortunate fifty or so

[21] *Gedenktafel für die Kriegsopfer des Württ. Pfarrhauses und Pfarrstandes* (Stuttgart, 1936). For further social statistics, see Joseph Haller, *Das evangelische Pfarrhaus in Württemberg* (Berlin, 1937), and Alfons Neher, *Die katholische und evangelische Geistlichkeit Württembergs (1813–1901)* (Ravensburg, 1904); for an earlier period, Martin Hasselhorn, *Der altwürttembergische Pfarrstand im 18. Jahrhundert* (Stuttgart, 1958).

young men normally admitted each year to theological training, the subsequent regimen of common study and the boarding-school discipline of the lower seminaries and Stift proved a powerful formative influence. This self-encapsulated world produced poets like Eduard Mörike and no less a thinker than Hegel, as well as a phalanx of journalists, bureaucrats, and academicians. To be sure, the cloistered atmosphere also fueled the rebellion of such free spirits as Hermann Hesse, whose novel *Unterm Rad* describes the author's brief and unhappy tenure as a seminarian at Maulbronn. For most, however, theological commitment or a compulsion to succeed overcame adolescent impulses towards independence, and shared experiences did much to temper subsequent distinctions of rank and achievement.[22]

Given all these incentives to cohesion, it is hardly surprising either that the clergy's political and theological orientations should have covered a fairly limited spectrum or that differences of outlook that did exist tended to be muted by caste consciousness. In both politics and theology, churchmen divided themselves loosely into two groups, a broad conservative majority and an active liberal minority. While it is tempting, and not wholly illegitimate, to assume a correlation between political and theological outlook, such correlations were scarcely automatic, for if political liberals almost invariably leaned towards a liberal theology, a commitment to some species of theological liberalism by no means precluded a solidly conservative social or political outlook. By any standard, certainly, Württemberg churchmen were more conservative than the population as a whole. This was particularly true at the upper levels of administration, thanks to the mechanisms of royal appointment and the self-replicating character of the hierarchy. Major political issues after 1848 found church leadership strongly identified with the forces of order. Many high-ranking churchmen, for exam-

[22] Leube, *Tübinger Stift*; Hans Voelter, "Lebensgefühl und Lebensschicksal der alten Generation: Erinnerungen an die Jahrhundertwende," *BWKG* 59 (1959): 171–87; Voelter, "Die Welt der Vikare um die Jahrhundertwende," typescript, LKA/SS R 5/7; Karl Heim, *Ich gedenke der vorigen Zeiten: Erinnerungen aus acht Jahrzehnten* (Hamburg, 1957), pp. 29–56.

ple, sided with Württemberg's *kleindeutsch* minority during the unification debates of the 1860s, not only because of their preference for the Protestant Hohenzollerns over the Catholic Habsburgs but also out of antipathy towards the left-liberal democrats that supported the particularist cause.[23]

This basic conservatism notwithstanding, social-liberal impulses in fact found greater resonance in Württemberg than in many German churches. Populist sympathies shaped the political outlooks of not a few younger clergy during the latter decades of the nineteenth century. They drew reinforcement from the growing prominence of the so-called "social question" in the wake of accelerating industrialization. During the 1880s, the Berlin City Mission, under the direction of the subsequently controversial court preacher Adolf Stoecker, served as a magnet for these interests. According to the Württemberg church's official historian, "there was scarcely a Swabian theology student in those days who did not seek out Stoecker . . . and return home full of enthusiasm."[24]

Not everyone, however, remained content with Stoecker's social-conservative synthesis. In a prophetic gesture of sorts, a young graduate of the Stift, Theodor von Wächter, withdrew his name from the roster of potential pastors in 1893 to devote his energies to work for the Social Democratic party (SPD). A cause célèbre erupted a half-decade later around the younger Christoph Blumhardt, Protestant chaplain in Bad Boll, near Göppingen, and scion of one of Württemberg's best known clerical families. Outraged by the notorious Penitentiary Bill placed before the Reichstag in 1899, Blumhardt made public protest by enrolling in the SPD. Within a year the party had nominated him as a parliamentary candidate, launching him on a brief and frustrating career as a member of the Württemberg Landtag. Violently attacked in the religious and conservative press, Blumhardt had his preaching credentials revoked by the Consistory. "A sincere

[23] Gerhard Schäfer, "Die württembergische Landeskirche und die Deutsche Einigung, 1864–1871," *ZfWLG* 26 (1967): 421–31.
[24] Heinrich Hermelink, *Geschichte der evangelischen Kirche in Württemberg von der Reformation bis zur Gegenwart* (Stuttgart and Tübingen, 1949), p. 444.

Christian cannot be a Social Democrat," thundered one critic, "and a sincere Social Democrat cannot remain a Christian."[25]

To the right of Wächter and Blumhardt, a significant and self-conscious party of movement emerged around the turn of the century among the Evangelical-Social followers of Friedrich Naumann, who held the Reichstag mandate for Heilbronn and whose famous break with Stoecker came at a Stuttgart congress in 1896. Not all Württemberg churchmen in the Protestant social movement sided with Naumann; still, his moderate liberalism tapped a substantial reservoir of support. The immediate Naumann circle included more than one Swabian pastor, and his star was very much in the ascendancy among Stiftler and younger pastors after 1900. Naumann's efforts to rescue the working classes for Wilhelmian respectability attracted warm support, as the efforts of a small but vigorous Evangelical Workers' Association (Evangelischer Arbeiterverein) attested. Undiscriminating conservatives outside Württemberg could find little to distinguish the Swabian Evangelical-Social front from the outcast Social Democrats. In 1913, when the Württemberg Consistory named a prominent Evangelical-Social, Theodor Traub, to the coveted post of Dekan in Stuttgart, shock waves were felt as far away as Berlin, where the reactionary Protestant *Kreuzzeitung* raged about the impunity of offering a high church office to so notorious a "socialist apostle of the working classes." That even conservative churchmen in Württemberg found such a reaction incomprehensible says something about the sense of collegiality and moderation prevailing in the Protestant southwest.[26]

Most Naumannites linked social liberalism with a broad construction of the Volkskirche and sympathy for the liberal currents in nineteenth-century Protestant theology. Württemberg liberals tended away from the sober biblicism that had long been

[25] Quoted in Lehmann, *Pietismus*, pp. 285–86; see also Eugen Jäckh, *Christoph Blumhardt* (Stuttgart, 1950), pp. 209–13.

[26] Hans Voelter, "Die evangelisch-soziale Bewegung in Württemberg und die Bietigheimer Tage," *BWKG* 59 (1959): 3–91; cf. Theodor Heuss, *Erinnerungen, 1905–1933*, 5th ed. (Tübingen, 1964), pp. 28–64; Heuss, *Friedrich Naumann: Der Mann, das Werk, die Zeit*, 3d ed. (Munich, 1968), pp. 111–347.

a hallmark of academic theology at Tübingen, preferring the more optimistic historical-critical perspectives of Adolf von Harnack and Albrecht Ritschl that then reigned supreme in north German theological faculties. In 1912, when a former colleague was suspended without a hearing by the Prussian church for publishing articles critical of the hierarchy, Württemberg liberals banded together in the Association for a Free Volkskirche (Freie volkskirchliche Vereinigung) to plead for ecclesiastical freedom of thought and for a broad definition of Protestant traditions in doctrine and practice. At the time of World War I, this association numbered among its members about two hundred pastors, one-sixth of the Württemberg clergy. One of the group's guiding spirits, Jakob Schoell, emerged after the November Revolution as a dominant force in church affairs. Born in 1866 and appointed to the Consistory in 1918 as prelate for Reutlingen, Schoell was that rarity among churchmen, a farmer's son. He represented an important clerical type in Württemberg, combining as he did erudition and earthy social consciousness, theological sophistication and a Swabian yeoman's sober-minded realism and disregard for personal pretense. Although comparatively little known outside ecclesiastical circles, he brought the force of his outlook and personality to bear on virtually every aspect of church life during the 1920s.[27]

Despite his influence among church leaders, Schoell remained the spokesman for a minority position both within the clergy and among active laity. To some, indeed, his theology—though moderate enough by contemporary academic standards—smacked of rank unbelief. The vital center in church politics remained solidly conservative, a fusion of classic Lutheran ortho-

[27] On the development of the liberal party, see Hermelink, *Geschichte der evangelischen Kirche in Württemberg*, pp. 442–47; Theodor Daur and Paul Weitbrecht, *Weg und Aufgabe eines freien Protestantismus in der Evangelischen Kirche* (Hanau, 1961), pp. 1–13; and press clippings in Julius Gmelin Personalakten, LKA A27/936. For appreciations of Schoell: Gottlob Egelhaaf, *Lebens-Erinnerungen*, ed. Adolf Rapp (Stuttgart, 1960), p. 143; Wilhelm Pressel, *Die Kriegspredigt 1914–1918 in der evangelischen Kirche Deutschlands* (Göttingen, 1967), pp. 228–30; M. Haug to Anna Schoell, Nov. 1966, Schoell Personalakten, OKR/AR Personalia.

doxy and the various deeply ingrained strains of Württemberg pietism. What resulted was an outlook consciously rooted in the Reformation, with a strong emphasis on personal spirituality, uncompromising doctrinal purity, and a personalistic social ethic derived more or less explicitly from the Sermon on the Mount. Consummated in the midnineteenth century by such church officials as the pietist prelate Sixt Carl Kapff, the conservative alliance found organizational expression in the Evangelische-kirchliche Vereinigung (Evangelical Church Association), a group founded in 1895 by Christian Römer, then Dekan in the Black Forest pietist stronghold of Nagold. Born in 1854, Römer rose to become titular prelate and chief preacher in Stuttgart's historic Stiftskirche. Here he followed in a long line of churchmen, including Kapff and Ludwig Hofacker, who worked to marshal the pietist "quiet ones in the land" as a bulwark of confessional purity and political conservatism. Where liberals like Schoell prized toleration and theological flexibility, Römer typified a more defensive mentality that elevated doctrinal orthodoxy as the true hallmark of the church. Although liberal and orthodox groups boasted roughly equal membership in 1914, Römer's association undoubtedly drew upon a broader reservoir of sympathy in the church at large, particularly among active laity.

If pietism provided a healthy impetus to Protestant conservatism in Württemberg, this conservatism bore a distinctively Swabian stamp. Unlike Prussian pietism, for example, with its strong aristocratic features, Württemberg pietism emerged out of the heart of traditional burgher society. Strongest among the small farmers, artisans, and shopkeepers of the Neckar basin and eastern Black Forest, it reflected a self-confident lay mentality whose democratic notions of ecclesiastical authority reflected something of the small-town populist spirit so significant for Württemberg's political culture. Pietism itself was no homogeneous phenomenon. Its manifestations ran the gamut from intellectualism to mysticism, from separatism to a strong Volkskirche orientation. Mainstream "Old Pietists" traced their roots back to such eighteenth-century theologians as Johann Albrecht Bengel or, outside Württemberg, to Zinzendorf's Herrnhut

Brethren. Led for the most part by theologians and schoolmasters, these groups maintained an ambitious range of apologetic and charitable undertakings, some of which—for example, the Württemberg Bible Society and the social-welfare Evangelische Gesellschaft (Evangelical Society)—became fixtures of nineteenth-century Württemberg life. More idiosyncratic, perhaps, were the followers of such charismatic eighteenth-century figures as Michael Hahn and Christoph Gottlob Pregizer, most of them farmers and humble artisans who concentrated in one way or another on the cultivation of an inner piety. Yet another movement, associated primarily with the pietist mission center in Bad Liebenzell, brought to a German context traces of Anglo-Saxon revivalism. While the total number of pietists can only be estimated, it was probably at least fifty thousand at the turn of the century—a far from negligible proportion of Württemberg's active Protestant laity.[28]

Contrasting theological viewpoints naturally made for tensions in church life. To doctrinaire liberals, insistence on the letter of confessional formulations seemed narrow-minded and a denial of Protestant freedom. For their part, conservatives were tempted to regard liberal Protestantism, even in its moderate Württemberg form, as an advance guard of unbelief. In most of the larger territorial churches, such tensions had produced open factionalism and party formation by the turn of the century. While to some extent the same was true of Württemberg, strong mediating factors kept disputes over doctrine and practice within fairly narrow bounds. Significantly, a majority of pastors chose not to affiliate formally with either Schoell's or Römer's association. An unwritten precept, moreover, enjoined every pastor to serve members of his flock without partiality. Whatever his own doctrinal position, nothing in his public behavior should cast doubt on the pastor's trustworthiness as a *Seelsorger*, a provider of spiritual care and guidance.

Hence it is not surprising to find that pivotal figures in church

---

[28] On the history and social character of Württemberg pietism, see Lehmann, *Pietismus*, and Joachim Trautwein, *Religiosität und Sozialstruktur: Untersucht anhand der Entwicklung des württembergischen Pietismus* (Stuttgart, 1972).

politics often proved to be those who, like Tübingen's Paul Wurster, could move more or less freely in both theological camps. While sympathetic to new currents in academic theology and in fact a sometime leader of the liberal pastors' association, Wurster, an adopted son of the pietist-minded Reutlingen philanthropist Gustav Werner, also enjoyed widespread confidence among conservatives. Theophil Wurm, the dominant church figure at the end of the Weimar era, was cast in the same mediating mold. Indeed, Wurm's powerful base of support in Württemberg during the Hitler-era Church Struggle derived precisely from his ability to mobilize understanding and personal support from every segment of the church community. While he could point to impeccable pietist credentials, having served for nearly fifteen years as a pastor with the Evangelische Gesellschaft in Stuttgart, Wurm also kept open cordial lines of communication with liberal colleagues. Wurm's career provides a paradigm of ecclesiastical mobility in Württemberg during the Weimar era. Appointed in 1913 as assistant pastor in Ravensburg, a center of the Protestant diaspora in southern Württemberg, he assumed the influential position of Dekan in Reutlingen in 1920 and rose to the Heilbronn prelature in 1927. Two years later, a deadlock between liberal and conservative factions in the church assembly made him the obvious compromise candidate for election to the presidency of the church.[29]

At the time of the November Revolution, then, the Württemberg church boasted a fair degree of institutional cohesion and a clerical esprit de corps, which, theological controversies notwithstanding, provided a significant base of strength for churchmen in the ensuing struggle to redefine relationships between church and state. No less important, if more difficult to measure, was the image of the institutional church among its nominal membership. From an aggregate statistical standpoint, Württemberg

---

[29] On Wurster see Paul Klemm, "Paul Wurster," in *RGG*, 3d ed. (Tübingen, 1962), 6:1848. On Wurm, in addition to Wurm's *Erinnerungen*, see Reinhold Sautter, *Theophil Wurm: Sein Leben und sein Kampf* (Stuttgart, 1960). For a sociological analysis of clerical relationships in Württemberg, see Bormann and Bormann-Heischkeid, *Theorie und Praxis kirchlicher Organisation*, pp. 91–149.

Protestants deviated little from national norms in their religious practice. Baptismal and communicant figures generally remained well above those for churches to the north, but they fell below those for the minority Protestant churches in neighboring Baden and Bavaria. The broad declines in popular religiosity often associated with nineteenth-century urbanization and industrialization also applied to Württemberg, albeit with local variations. By 1900, certainly, a majority of Württemberg Protestants, like those throughout Germany, retained only nominal ties to the church and played no part in its internal discussions.[30]

Still, statistics alone cannot reflect the full flavor of religious attitudes and behavior. In a major survey of Württemberg church life published in 1918, Paul Wurster noted that some of the most generous contributions to Protestant charities regularly came from parishes and districts where statistical measures suggested a low level of religiosity. Whether deserved or not, Württemberg in fact had a reputation elsewhere in Germany as an unusually God-fearing land. A visitor to Stuttgart in the 1880s wrote that it seemed the only major city in the nation that on Sundays still gave the "appearance of a pious town."[31] This image no doubt benefited from the comparatively tranquil pace of modernization in Württemberg. The stability of small-town burgher society, with its attendant traditionalism, fostered an atmosphere in which respect for the church, the clergy, and the values they represented was common even among groups whose actual participation in church life may have been minimal. Demographic shifts and social dislocation, the frequent concomitants of economic change, were at best tangential in Württemberg. As late as 1907, nearly two-thirds of the population still

---

[30] For comparative statistics, see, e.g., *KJ 1926*, pp. 80–137.

[31] Quoted in Wurster, *Kirchliches Leben*, p. 83; cf. ibid., pp. 285–90. A brief survey of traditional piety can be found in Martin Scharfe, "Bildzeugnisse evangelischer Frömmigkeit," in Scharfe, Rudolf Schenda, and Herbert Schwedt, *Volksfrömmigkeit: Bildzeugnisse aus Vergangenheit und Gegenwart* (Stuttgart, 1967), pp. 43–49; see also the case studies from old-regime Württemberg in David W. Sabean, *Power in the Blood: Popular Culture and Village Discourse in Early Modern Germany* (Cambridge, 1984).

51

resided in their places of birth.[32] When migration did occur, it did not automatically signal destruction of face-to-face relationships or the traditions of the *Heimat*. A parish report from Urach, on the edge of the Swabian Jura near Reutlingen, noted in 1924 that variations in religiosity within the local proletariat often enabled pastors to deduce workers' birthplaces in the Jura hinterland: persons from villages with traditionally strong churchgoing habits tended to retain them even after moving into the larger town. Nor was this an isolated case in Württemberg.[33] On another level, the importance of the Stift in the formation of a Swabian ruling elite guaranteed continued contact between the church and the educated bourgeoisie, a class whose religious indifference had become proverbial in many areas. Furthermore, pietism's strong roots among the middling elements of Württemberg society encouraged a positive orientation towards religion in general, and the church in particular, within this numerically significant segment of the population.

In summary, if the ideal of the Volkskirche was to be more than an empty rhetorical construct, then social and cultural patterns in Württemberg provided a best-case argument in its favor. Noted pastor and theologian Günther Dehn, whose decades of service in the Prussian church gave him ample basis for comparison, concluded as much after spending several years during World War II serving a parish in Ravensburg. Dehn later recalled that "it was quite an experience . . . to be able to work in a church that was still fairly well rooted in the life of the people. The pastor is a respected figure here, and many Dekans seemed to me to enjoy the prestige of a district official."[34] Precisely because the Württemberg church appeared to be thus "rooted in the life of the people," a study of developments there may help to mark out the boundaries of the Protestant presence in Weimar society and beyond.

[32] See Hunt, *People's Party in Württemberg*, p. 21.

[33] Urach, Pfarrbericht 1924, and Böblingen, Pfarrbericht 1928, both in OKR/ AR OA/PfB.

[34] Günther Dehn, *Die alte Zeit, die vorigen Jahre: Lebenserinnerungen*, 2d ed. (Munich, 1964), p. 346.

TWO

Beyond Throne and Altar

By the early 1920s, it was clear even to clerical doomsayers that, as yearbook editor Johannes Schneider put it in 1921, the territorial church system had "weathered the first wild storm of the revolution era." "State props have fallen; the churches still stand," wrote Schneider—proof positive that official Protestantism was "far less a state church than [critics] assumed."[1] The latter statement was arguably more notable for triumphalism than for strict accuracy. If the churches indeed lost a powerful prop in the November Revolution, it was the prop of monarchy rather than the state. Despite formal disestablishment, and although separation of church and state became a common shibboleth of the immediate postwar era, most Protestant churches retained extensive institutional ties with the state, ties rooted in a dense web of both law and custom. In this and in other respects, Schneider's "wild storm" dissipated before it could gather force.

As a result, the disestablishment of the Weimar period was less a matter of separation than of adaptation, the adjustment of a church thoroughly imbued with monarchical tradition to the particular constraints of a republican "party state." While this relationship has often been explored from the standpoint of political and ideological influences, considerably less attention has been paid to its specifically institutional dimensions. The importance of the latter, however, should not be underestimated. A decisive aspect of the republican state-building project in Germany after 1918 was its nearly total subordination of ideology to administrative precedent. This legalism is particularly apparent in policy towards the churches. Where separation of church and

[1] *KJ 1921*, p. 330.

state was concerned, political theory and theologies of the state played only peripheral roles compared to such practical determinants as church finance.

It follows that the substance of disestablishment, with its implications for ecclesiastical identity and action, should be sought not so much in the letter of constitutional law as in the concrete procedure of bureaucratic routine. If the latter provides strong evidence of continuity between monarchy and republic, it also hints at a subtle but important change in the church's institutional status, a change that, though perhaps undramatic in itself, would nevertheless affect churchmen's notions of their position vis-à-vis state and society. The nature of this change in Württemberg can perhaps best be defined by examining the pattern of relationships between church and successive state administrations during the Weimar years. The lineaments of a new stance first manifested themselves during the early months of the republic in the context of preliminary contacts with the socialist-dominated provisional government; they were confirmed in the drafting of a comprehensive state church law, approved in 1924 at the behest of a center-left cabinet; they underwent further elaboration in dealings with the conservative coalitions of the middle and late 1920s.

SEPARATION OF CHURCH AND STATE

"God grant that these new leaders can keep their feet on the ground and . . . recognize that . . . *we* also have a place in a republican state." Thus wrote Württemberg's senior prelate, Heinrich von Planck, in the first uncertain days after the monarchy's collapse.[2] As it happened, the "new leaders" in Stuttgart did little to give Planck or his colleagues cause for concern. Whereas revolutionary regimes in some parts of Germany, notably Prussia and Thuringia, made at least token attempts to diminish church power in the name of socialist or democratic principles, the Württemberg government regularly and with little

---

[2] Planck to Zeemann, Nov. 15, 1918, LKA D1/26,9.

resistance deferred to churchmen's interests. It would be a pardonable exaggeration to say that Württemberg church leaders were left to draw up the terms of their own disestablishment. If these terms derived formally from the Weimar constitutional settlement of 1919, they also reflected informal institutional arrangements, working relationships between and among churchmen, civil servants, and political leaders. The basic shape of these relationships became clear during the first months of the republic. It reflected churchmen's efforts to reconcile conflicting impulses to beat back the specter of revolution while affirming a prominent role in the new state the revolution was creating.

Württemberg's political climate in 1918 helps explain the passivity of the local regime in ecclesiastical matters. The new leadership in Stuttgart inherited the loosely Burkean attitude towards reform that historically characterized virtually the entire ideological spectrum in Württemberg. With the exception of a vocal but politically negligible left, represented by such figures as Klara Zetkin and Arthur Crispien, no party was prepared to claim a mandate for fundamental change, civil or ecclesiastical. Like their fellows in much of Germany, the mainstream Social Democrats who dominated the provisional government became republicans more by force of circumstance than by conviction. The party's parliamentary leader, Wilhelm Keil—the same Keil who in 1916 had hypothetically nominated Württemberg's Wilhelm II for the presidency of a Swabian republic—doubtless spoke for most when he confessed that the idea of abolishing the monarchy had simply never occurred to him; there seemed "neither subjective nor objective reason" for doing so, especially in Württemberg.[3] Thrust into power with little warning and with few clear programmatic principles beyond a scrupulous regard for legality, Keil and his colleagues were only too ready to embrace a caretaker role in the new state. From the beginning they turned to the parties of the bourgeois center for advice and assistance. On November 10, anticipating the short-lived national Weimar Coalition, the cabinet was expanded to include

[3] Keil, *Erlebnisse*, 1:470.

representatives of both the Catholic Center and what became the DDP. Ignoring voices on the left, the regime set about the tasks of maintaining order and of fostering an all-party consensus on future constitutional reforms.[4]

This emphasis on legality and continuity militated against a critical scrutiny of the church's status or its relationship to the state. Under the 1898 law of episcopal succession, invoked by Wilhelm II hours before his abdication, ecclesiastical authority automatically devolved upon a five-member governing committee.[5] Hence the church's legal position was never in doubt, and the regime saw no cause for special measures. Wilhelm Keil, whose own family included devout, active church members, was prepared to believe that with the personal alliance of throne and altar broken, the church would be sufficiently emancipated from the old order for its "moral force" to become progressively engaged with the moral vision of Social Democracy.[6] Others less sanguine were simply reluctant to stray into what for many was alien administrative territory. At the Ministry of Education, the agency with the most extensive jurisdiction in ecclesiastical matters, the new Social Democratic minister, Berthold Heymann, was concerned chiefly to keep from blundering into the pitfalls of a confessional landscape with which he—a Prussian, a Jew, and, in the view of the liberal democrat Theodor Heuss, a "loyal, cautious man"—lacked all native familiarity. Meeting with Consistory president Hermann von Zeller on November 11,

---

[4] In addition to Keil, contemporary accounts include Wilhelm Blos, *Von der Monarchie zum Volksstaat*, 2 vols. (Stuttgart, 1922); Ludwig von Köhler, *Zur Geschichte der Revolution in Württemberg* (Stuttgart, 1930); Theodor von Pistorius, *Die letzten Tage des Königreiches Württemberg* (Stuttgart, 1935); Karl Weller, *Die Staatsumwälzung in Württemberg* (Stuttgart, 1930); and Hermann von Zeller, *Die württembergische evangelische Landeskirche in der Revolution von 1918 und der Deutsche Evangelische Kirchenbund* (Stuttgart, 1933).

[5] Neurath to WEK, Nov. 11, 1918, LKA A26/214. As early as October 31 the king had initialed a contingency decree to this effect, suggesting that the role of summus episcopus might have been terminated even without the impetus of abdication. See Hans Voelter, "Revolution von 1918," *BWKG* 62 (1962): 320, and Zeller, *Landeskirche in der Revolution*, pp. 2–4.

[6] Keil, *Erlebnisse*, 2:532, 688–89.

Heymann assured churchmen that they need fear no interference from him. All he asked from the church was an official pledge of political neutrality. Throughout the crucial early months of the republic, Heymann deferred to others on religious questions, taking counsel with pastors and laymen from the old Naumann circle recommended to him by Heuss.[7] Wilhelm Blos, the veteran party functionary who headed the provisional government, likewise refused to press any claims to influence. Although a nominal Protestant, he declined to accept one of the two seats on the church governing committee allocated to Protestant cabinet ministers under the law of 1898; the Consistory, he was sure, did not want a Social Democrat for an overlord.[8] Finance Minister Theodor Liesching, a prominent former Progressive, followed suit. Though anything but unsympathetic to Protestant interests, coming as he did from a large, prominent family of pastors and civil servants, Liesching likewise deemed it prudent to avoid any appearance of meddling in internal church affairs, hoping thereby to defuse antagonism toward the new state among conservative parishioners.[9]

From the beginning, therefore, in contrast to Prussia, the Württemberg regime regarded ecclesiastical autonomy as self-evident. Indeed, the absence of cabinet ministers on the new Evangelical governing committee, which formally convened on December 5, left the church with greater autonomy than it would have enjoyed had the law of 1898 taken effect without the catalyst of revolution. The Consistory had solid legal and procedural grounds for the oft-repeated claim that the Protestant church was bound to no specific form of government.[10]

[7] Richard Fischer, "Die Geschichte des Kirchenkampfes in Württemberg (1933–1945)," typescript, LKA, 1:6–7; Heuss, *Erinnerungen, 1905–1933*, p. 235. A Consistory decree urging the clergy to refrain from political activity is in *Amtsblatt* 18 (1919): 33.

[8] Blos, *Monarchie zum Volksstaat*, 1:42; Blos adds that he took it for granted that church officials expected him to decline the position.

[9] Zeller, memorandum, Nov. 11, 1918, and Liesching to WEK, Nov. 22, 1918, both in LKA A26/214.

[10] Mehnert, *Kirche und Politik*, p. 93.

Although the November Revolution left churchmen with virtually unrestricted freedom of movement, the Consistory's actions during the early weeks of the republic nevertheless reflected a pervasive sense of uncertainty over the church's institutional standing. Two concerns predominated during late 1918 and early 1919. One was the possibility that militants outside Württemberg might attempt to impose a radical disestablishment policy on all Germany by way of the national constitution. From Prussia and other north German states came alarming rumors of a new Kulturkampf, led by such anticlerical firebrands as the Independent Socialist Adolf Hoffmann, a veteran parson-baiter who briefly shared the portfolio of Prussian education minister and in that capacity became identified with plans aimed at drastically restricting the churches' influence and reducing them to the status of mere private voluntary associations. Even with Hoffmann's specter removed, however, there remained the unresolved question of the Württemberg church's financial basis. For more than a decade, socialists and left liberals had been urging a binding determination of state subsidies based on a narrow construal of the value of ecclesiastical properties secularized in 1806. Only three months before the November Revolution, Social Democrats in the Württemberg assembly had voted against church appropriations to protest the lack of such a settlement.[11] Churchmen therefore had reason to assume that a regime controlled by Social Democrats would insist on writing its views into any new legislation. Since, according to the most exhaustive prewar calculations, little more than half of existing subsidies could be interpreted as legal obligations, the prospect of a crippling disendowment seemed only too likely. A Consistory position paper summarized the leadership's fears on this point:

> In view . . . of the [insufficiency of income from historic church holdings], the fact that, . . . in the absence of definite legal norms, [church appropriations] depend to a great extent on the goodwill of state agencies, that the church's

11 Württemberg Landtag, 2. Kammer, *Verhandlungen* (1918), pp. 6320–21.

right to its historic holdings is not legally guaranteed, and that the protection of the constitution has become undependable since the revolution, the church's financial status for the future must be described as grave.[12]

These overlapping concerns had the immediate effect of driving the Consistory into a defensive alliance with the Protestant career bureaucracy. If civil servants' sense of duty kept them from seeking to subvert the republic—"the result," an Interior Ministry official later wrote, "would have been, not the restoration of the monarchy, but anarchy"—it also reinforced their inclination to see themselves as the true embodiment of the state, as legitimate guardians of public authority in contrast to the merely temporary occupants of ministerial posts.[13] For the ministries directly concerned with church affairs—education and finance—it meant implicit recognition that the regulation of church-state relations properly fell within the purview of the bureaucracy. Officials who had worked long and hard on abstruse problems of finance did not propose to see their achievements preempted by inexperienced politicians caught up in the passions of the moment. The bureaucrat's natural instinct for territoriality found further stimulus in ties of kinship and education, which, as previously noted, linked Protestant officialdom in Württemberg at every level. It was no accident that the de facto head of the church, president of the Consistory Zeller, had spent most of his public career in the Württemberg Finance Ministry. Nor was it surprising that the principal official in the Education Ministry concerned with church finances, Robert Meyding, had

---

[12] "Finanzielle Lage der Landeskirche"; cf. Fritz Lenckner, *Das Recht am altwürttembergischen evangelischen Kirchengut* (Stuttgart, 1919), pp. 52–64. Studies conducted between 1912 and 1914 had concluded that of a total state appropriation (1914) of 6,300,000 M, between 3,370,000 M and 4,270,000 M, depending on the method of calculation, represented binding obligations and income from former church holdings.

[13] Köhler, *Revolution in Württemberg*, pp. 130, 160. Cf. Protokoll ("Vertraulich"), Verband von Vereinen höher geprüfter württ. Staatsbeamten, Verbandssitzung, Stuttgart, Nov. 20, 1918, copy in LKA D/EPW 28.

a father and a brother in the clergy and was himself a former Tübingen Stiftler.

For reasons of both sentiment and self-interest, therefore, the Protestant establishment in Württemberg found a common rallying point in the process of disestablishment. Churchmen and civil servants alike saw their best interests served by a strategy aimed at circumventing party-political decisions and shielding any review of the church's legal status behind a protective barrier of bureaucratic "objectivity." By Christmas of 1918 they had seized the initiative in formulating a constitutional settlement. The key figure in this effort was Meyding, working in close consultation with Zeller and other members of the Consistory.

Early in December the Blos cabinet appointed a committee, chaired by Wilhelm Keil, to draw up a draft constitution for submission to the constituent assembly to be elected in Württemberg the following month. Keil's committee commissioned a preliminary text from one of its three nonsocialist members, Wilhelm von Blume, a Tübingen professor of law. Both the Consistory and sympathetic officials such as Meyding harbored suspicions about committee intentions, not only because of its socialist majority but also because Keil had made no effort to solicit preliminary advice or otherwise involve career officials in the drafting process. With the blessing of the Consistory as well as Education Minister Heymann's designated deputy for church affairs, Meyding approached Blume unofficially with an offer to draw up the paragraphs on religion himself, "in view of the importance that, experience shows, attaches to the first draft of a proposal." While skeptical that political conditions would allow for "doing the right thing," Blume had no objection to this plan. As a result, the draft laid before the Keil committee corresponded less to the conceptions of the Social Democratic platform than to those of the church leadership itself.[14]

Meyding's proposed language generally confirmed existing

[14] Meyding, memorandum, "Zur Entstehung des Par. 63 Abs. 1 Satz 2 der Verfassungsurkunde vom 25. September 1919," Apr. 20, 1920, LKA A100/23,3.

relationships while leaving maximum room for maneuver in the area of finance. The draft recognized the three major religious bodies—Protestant, Catholic, and Jewish—as privileged public corporations with the authority to levy taxes on their members. Church taxes were common practice in other German states, including Prussia and neighboring Baden, and offered an obvious recourse for the Württemberg church in the event of reductions in direct state subsidies. As for subsidies themselves, Meyding and church leaders had agreed to advance a provision reaffirming the church's right to a guaranteed subsidy, the precise amount to be determined by subsequent legislation "according to the churches' existing needs." The postponement of a definitive decision would not only reassert the prior claims of the bureaucracy but would also provide officials and churchmen considerable latitude for negotiation, since Meyding's language did not necessarily bind the state to any particular interpretation of the church's legal claims.

That this formula encountered little opposition within the provisional government shows the extent to which Protestant forces of order misinterpreted the intentions of Württemberg's new leaders, particularly their devotion to legality and their almost naive respect for existing institutional structures. The only substantive challenge came in fact from Blume, who altered Meyding's purposely vague reference to the church's "existing needs" to specify a settlement based on "present needs."[15] Within the Keil committee, the expected socialist front failed to materialize. The two members from the Independent Socialist party (USPD) took little active part in deliberations, deferring to those more versed in the conventions of statecraft. Keil, himself anything but an ideological purist, placed a premium on consensus, and under the circumstances this normally entailed compromising with the wishes of his committee's bourgeois minority. Keil's attitude is indicated by his willingness to assign responsi-

---

[15] Ibid. This emendation involved such factors as pensions and survivors' benefits where increases mandated in earlier legislation had not yet completely taken effect. Meyding's language was intended to leave latitude for including future increases, Blume's to exclude them.

bility for the church paragraphs to the committee member most closely identified with the Protestant establishment: Johannes Hieber, vice-chairman of the new Württemberg DDP. A former National Liberal, Hieber had briefly occupied a parish pastorate in the early 1890s and had thereafter remained prominent in church life as a member of synods, as leader of the hyper-Protestant Evangelical League, and as director of the supervisory committee for Protestant schools (Oberschulrat) in the Württemberg Education Ministry. Equally telling was Keil's willingness to accept a reinstatement of Meyding's original language on finances, which Hieber proposed at the Consistory's behest. "Doing the right thing" thereupon became a foregone conclusion; the committee approved the Meyding-Blume text with only perfunctory debate. Where church-state relations were concerned, the forces of bureaucratic order had launched a preemptive campaign for self-preservation only to find the putative foe willingly marching in their own ranks.

Ironically enough, the same prophylactic impulses that led churchmen to seek institutional immunity from politics drove them simultaneously in the opposite direction, towards a mobilization of the Protestant population as a political force in its own right. For all its claims to stand "above parties," the church quickly became a lightning rod for partisan energies. In the turbulence and uncertainty of the immediate postwar period, when the streets seemed to belong to drifters, demonstrators, and political vigilantes of every stripe, when every wall seemed plastered with election appeals and every hall seemed reserved for party functions, few groups remained immune from pressures to mobilize. Where the institution itself became a major political issue, as in the church's case, some sort of mobilization seemed imperative. To be sure, the shock of revolution initially reinforced the quiescent inclinations of some church folk. The collapse of accustomed authority encouraged pietists in particular to retreat from involvement in a world perceived as hostile to their hopes for the Kingdom of God. Christian Römer, the guiding spirit of pietist orthodoxy in Württemberg, warned against the temptations of political activity in a New Year's meditation for 1919. The affairs of the day, he wrote, were purely temporal; politics, being "of time and for time," could be "no concern of ours."[16] However, this spirit of passivity and indifference to events—what one pastor later called an attitude of "comfortable depression"—only served to heighten the sense of urgency felt by those churchmen and active lay people for whom political action seemed, in the words of the liberal pastor Hans Voelter, a "matter of life and death."[17]

Such activist impulses were perhaps strongest in the Naumannite wing of the Württemberg church, where natural democratic sympathies combined with the residual optimism of a liberal Protestant tradition that identified the church with a progressive realization of the Kingdom of God in history, encouraging hopes that emancipation from the crown would free the church to assume a positive role in bringing stability and moral purpose to the new state. As early as November 13, speaking to a gathering of fellow National Liberals, Stuttgart pastor Eduard Lamparter declared that while he could not greet the end of the monarchy with a "light heart," he had confidence that a truly all-embracing church could serve as the catalyst to a new civil order. Lamparter's Stuttgart colleague Albert Esenwein, for years a tireless laborer in the vineyard of Progressive politics, likewise called upon the church to exert an "educative force" in republican society. The liberal Association for a Free Volkskirche formally endorsed this position at a meeting in Stuttgart on November 30. The theme of cooperation in building a new order found vigorous expression at a major rally of Evangelical-Social forces in Stuttgart on December 9. Those assembled, including Education Minister Heymann, heard Württemberg's last court preacher Richard Lempp insist that the church "offer the same service to the new democratic state as to the old conservative state." In response, Heymann once again emphasized the compatibility of

[16] Christian Römer, "Herr, bleibe bei uns!" *EKBfW* 80 (1919): 1.

[17] Urach, Pfarrbericht 1924, OKR/AR OA/PfB; Voelter, "Bietigheimer Tage," p. 13; Lehmann, *Pietismus*, p. 298. On developments elsewhere in Germany, see Nowak, *Kirche und Republik*, pp. 17–53, 85–108; Mehnert, *Kirche und Politik*; Borg, *Old-Prussian Church*, pp. 56–83.

socialist and republican ideals with the principles of the religious confessions, promising a fraternal and mutually satisfactory settlement of constitutional questions. Speaking at the same meeting, Albert Esenwein projected a hopeful vision of democratization as a mutual process linking church and society. To become a bulwark of the democratic state, the church must shed the vestiges of an old authoritarian "pastors' church" for a new role as a less centralized, more parish-oriented "people's church." The church should hasten social integration and stability by fostering in individual parishioners a greater sense of responsibility for both church and community affairs.[18]

Those churchmen who appealed in this way to Württemberg's populist and democratic traditions remained, however, a minority. The Protestant mainstream, including virtually the entire church leadership, was less concerned to define a common task with the new state than to mobilize across a broad bourgeois front in defense of the inherited order. Separation of church and state might be desirable, but only in a formal sense; the church could not surrender its influence on "state, law, and morality." Practically speaking, this meant pressing for solid guarantees of "the necessary funds and the necessary influence over the youth."[19] To be sure, the Consistory's first pastoral letters after the revolution urged the faithful to cooperate with the provisional regime and to work to restore stability, but they coupled such exhortations with ringing appeals to band together in "faith, steadfastness, and perseverance" to withstand the "storm [that] has broken over us and still rages."[20]

Seeking to exploit an apparent weakness—the lack of a Protestant equivalent to the Catholic Center—church leaders launched an offensive designed to capture the entire spectrum of nonsocialist parties for the church's cause. Their strategy was twofold. On one hand they pressured all parties to take public stands in support of their constitutional agenda, while on the

18 *SM*, Nov. 14, Dec. 2, 11, 1918; also Hans Voelter, notes, LKA D12/1.
19 Thus Oscar F. Mauer, "Trennung von Kirche u. Staat," speech to Schorndorf Bezirkssynode, Dec. 27, 1918, copy in LKA/SS P 5/3.
20 *SM*, Nov. 17, 1918.

other they encouraged politically active church members to press vigorously within their chosen parties for the nomination of candidates committed to defend Protestant interests both at Weimar and in the Württemberg assembly. In Stuttgart, a working group organized by Naumannite Dekan Theodor Traub drew up a manifesto of church demands, which it published with the Consistory's approval on December 12. Asserting that the church required a stronger rather than a weaker position in the new order, the Traub statement demanded that the state commit itself to providing continued financial support. It challenged all political parties to adopt official positions regarding the church's future legal and financial status as well as the place of religious instruction in Württemberg schools. Loyal Protestants were urged to support only those parties whose responses proved favorable. The Traub committee's manifesto provides a pioneering example of tactics employed in most German states as well as by national church leaders.[21]

The manifesto's immediate and predictable effect was to deepen the historic rift between Protestant burgherdom and Social Democracy. Parties in the socialist camp could only respond "favorably" by abandoning long-established platforms, while those of the right and center had everything to gain by catering to an aroused Protestant populace. Predictably enough, the conservative coalition of Bürgerpartei and Bauernbund embraced the church's cause without reservation. Propaganda equated a vote for the right with a vote for the church—hardly surprising for a party whose leadership ranks were studded with prominent church figures. One of the Bürgerpartei's chief parliamentary leaders, Gustav Beisswänger, was a former pastor; its list of candidates for the elections on January 12 included, among others, Tübingen professor Paul Wurster and future Dekan and church president Theophil Wurm, then a pastor in Ravensburg.[22]

[21] *SM*, Dec. 9, 13, 27, 1918. The DEKA in Berlin issued a similar set of demands to national party leaders later in December; cf. *Frankfurter Zeitung*, Jan. 1, 1919; Helmreich, *German Churches under Hitler*, p. 62.

[22] Fischer, "Geschichte des Kirchenkampfes," 1:9; Lewis Hertzman, *DNVP: Right-Wing Opposition in the Weimar Republic* (Lincoln, Neb., 1963), p. 56.

The liberal center in Württemberg was not to be outdone in staking its claim to a Protestant identity. The DDP platform affirmed support for the churches' privileged legal status and for a continuing role for religion in public education, though it took no position on the question of a specific financial settlement. Here too, however, party rolls reflected the strength of a liberal Protestant subculture. Besides former pastor Johannes Hieber, candidates virtually assured of election to the Württemberg assembly in January included pastors Albert Esenwein and Eduard Lamparter as well as Johannes Fischer, a Protestant layman prominent in the Evangelical-Social workers' movement. In Lamparter's case, favorable placement on the party list came as a direct result of church pressures, the militantly Protestant Evangelical League having exploited its ties to the former national-liberal wing of the new party by threatening to boycott the DDP if Lamparter were not granted special consideration. [23]

As the tempo of political agitation accelerated, churchmen cast about for ways to build and sustain a mass base for their cause. Concern for the masses arose out of both political and evangelistic motives. While mass support obviously represented an important bargaining tool in dealings with state and parties, some churchmen also hoped to reinvigorate church life by rallying marginal parishioners to a broad Protestant consensus. From the latter standpoint, suggested Christian Schnaufer, a pastor in Esslingen and the chairman of the Württemberg Pastors' Association (Pfarrverein), the November Revolution ought to be considered "not a bane but a blessing." Schnaufer reminded the Pfarrverein's executive board that churchmen had "tried who knows how often [in the past] to mobilize these parishes," and in this he saw no hope for success "unless the whole [state church] system is changed." [24] Speaking in mid-December to a Stuttgart crowd of more than a thousand people, Richard Lempp urged dedicated Protestants to infiltrate the ranks of every party, in-

[23] Simon, *Württembergische Demokraten,* p. 215.
[24] EPW, Vertrauensmännerversammlung, Jan. 2, 1919, Protokollbuch II, LKA D/EPW 22.

cluding the SPD. If the church had previously alienated working-class members by its close identification with an antisocialist order, a new wave of lay activism might win back the proletariat, not to some vestigial authoritarian state but to the life of the church itself.[25]

Most churchmen, to be sure, had less interest in making gestures towards the new order than in shoring up the defenses of their accustomed constituencies. In Urach, where, as previously noted, there persisted a tradition of marginal working-class piety, the clergy found to their dismay that church rallies initially appeared to draw more attention from local Social Democrats than from conservative parishioners. Mobilization of the latter population required a hastily organized leaflet campaign carried out in concert with the Evangelical Press Association, the propaganda arm of the Inner Mission in Württemberg.[26] Women, newly enfranchised, were a particular target of appeals. Early in December, representatives of the major Protestant women's organizations in Württemberg met in Stuttgart to plot strategy for mobilizing church women as a force at the polls. The result was the establishment of an umbrella committee pledged to the "preservation and cultivation of moral and religious forces in society." Constituent groups recruited popular speakers and exploited such customary channels of sociability as sewing circles and study groups to raise members' consciousness regarding the political issues of the day.[27] Church officials devoted similar attention to the Protestant diaspora in southern Württemberg, seeking to engender heightened loyalties to the larger church community through concentrated propaganda and a network of new parish organizations. One of the principal architects of this effort was Theophil Wurm, pastor in predominantly Catholic Ravensburg. With the Consistory's approval, Wurm took a

[25] SM, Dec. 20, 1918.

[26] Urach, Pfarrbericht 1924, OKR/AR PfB; "Was wir Evangelischen für unsere Kirche von den Parteien fordern müssen," pamphlet (Stuttgart, 1918), copy in LKA/SS P 5/3.

[27] SM, Dec. 9, 19, 24, 1918; Christian Römer, "Frauenwahlrecht und Kirche," EKBfW 80 (1919): 9.

leave of absence from parish duties to devote himself to electoral campaigning and to the church's counteroffensive in conservative circles.[28]

By the end of 1918 crusading impulses had all but submerged calls for rapprochement with the parties of movement. This can be seen, for example, in the minutes of the Pfarrverein's executive committee, which met in Stuttgart on January 2 for a confidential tour of the political horizon. No one present seriously questioned the dictum that blunting socialist power, thus reducing the danger of unfavorable constitutional settlements, should be a chief aim of the Protestant mobilization. Max Mayer-List, a Stuttgart liberal, noted that the church could not survive financially in anything like its present form if forced to become a private voluntary organization. Since in public, at least, the Social Democrats, not to mention the USPD, continued to insist on the Erfurt Program as their official platform, self-interest dictated that churchmen lend aid and comfort to the party's foes. The principal question was simply what strategy would best achieve the desired end. Stuttgart Dekan Theodor Traub warned against a frontal assault, not so much because Consistory president Hermann von Zeller had pledged the church to neutrality but because overt action would only serve to alienate the Social Democratic remnant still active in the Württemberg church. Nor should churchmen become otherwise identified with the interests of a single party; formal neutrality was advisable both on pragmatic grounds and for the sake of a "clear conscience." Eduard Lamparter agreed but suggested that individual Social Democrats might be vulnerable to private pressure from their pastors. Where opportunities arose, Lamparter urged, the clergy should not shy away from "confronting . . . Social Democrats with a *crise de conscience.*" Of the other parties, the Catholic Center must be dismissed as a dubious ally in any "holy war" against revolution, since it lacked a proper understanding of the Volkskirche tradition and remained oriented towards an alien conception of church-state relations. As a prospective assembly

---

[28] Wurm, *Erinnerungen*, p. 65.

delegate on the DDP list, Lamparter understandably insisted that the democratic center should become the basis for a Protestant coalition embracing the entire bourgeois front. He discounted the prospect of any lasting alliance between the DDP and the SPD while emphasizing evidence of his own party's good faith on issues of religion. The Pfarrverein discussion ended in an informal consensus that matters should be allowed to run their course. As an institution the church should hold to the high ground of neutrality. Pastors should keep official duties and regular church functions free of any political taint; in particular they should avoid partisan appeals in sermons or pulpit statements. At the same time, however, they should permit no relaxation of the campaigns underway to propagandize parishioners, nor should they hesitate to speak up in defense of church interests, particularly at political meetings open to the public.[29] What churchmen hoped to achieve was precisely the effect that the sympathetic Stuttgart *Schwäbischer Merkur* noted five days before the January balloting, when it declared: "The movement presently underway among our church-minded folk is so strong that it cannot be ignored by any regime that seriously claims to be considered a popular government."[30]

Mobilization and neutrality were, however, all but incompatible aims. Rather than establishing the church as an independent reference point in the political landscape, churchmen only propelled themselves further down the byways of conservative reaction. Events in one working-class Stuttgart parish reveal the operative mentality of many in the clergy during this period. At a parish assembly convened on January 8, the presiding pastor declared that for his part he could support no party but the conservatives. Social Democrats in attendance requested an opportunity to respond, but the pastor brushed them aside with the remark that since he was not himself a member of any political group and had not called the parish meeting to "benefit or harm

[29] EPW, Vertrauensmännerversammlung, Jan. 2, 1919, Protokollbuch II, LKA D/EPW 22.
[30] *SM*, Jan. 7, 1919.

the cause of any party," it could not be considered a political assembly; nor did he have any obligation to yield the floor to spokesmen for other viewpoints.[31]

Instances of this sort were by no means uncommon. The pastor in a small town near Reutlingen, an area with a heavy concentration of pietists, openly defended political sermons on the grounds that such preaching was necessary to combat the civic lethargy of his flock.[32] Even where pastors kept official silence, volunteers of the Evangelical Press Association stood at church doors distributing explicitly antisocialist literature to departing worshipers. At least one pastor gave the same material to children in his confirmation class with instructions to pass it along to their parents. The same pastor became embroiled in a conflict with local Social Democrats after several of their number, detailed to monitor a prayer meeting in the parish hall, interrupted to protest allegedly partisan statements. When the exchanges grew heated, some members of the audience slipped away and summoned the town constable, who escorted at least one of the protestors home with threats to arrest him for the "Spartacist" disruption of a religious function. The local SPD committee lodged a formal complaint charging intimidation, but the provisional government declined to take action—one of several similar instances that served to confirm the regime's passivity where church interests were involved.[33]

In Württemberg, as throughout Germany, churchmen's behavior during the election period bore witness to a traditional conception of clerical office, rooted in the social image of the pastor as an authority figure with an inherent right—indeed duty—

[31] Ernst Wurzbach to Arbeiter- und Soldatenrat Stuttgart, Jan. 13, 1919 (copy); Alfred John statement, n.d.; and Traub to WEK, Jan. 25, 1919; all in LKA A26/151.

[32] Hermelink to WEK, Mar. 12, 1919; also G. Franck to Arbeiterrat Stuttgart, Jan. 23, 1919 (copy), and Fleck to Dekanatsamt Ludwigsburg, Feb. 13, 1919; all in LKA A26/151.

[33] Sozialdemokratischer Verein Horrheim to Arbeiter- und Soldatenrat Stuttgart, Jan. 22, 1919 (copy); Findeisen to WEK, Feb. 7, 1919; and Welsch to WEK, Feb. 10, 1919; all in LKA A26/151.

to inculcate proper attitudes among his parishioners. There is some evidence that such authority still carried weight in Württemberg, even on the margins of the core Protestant community. One small-town Social Democrat, complaining that the local pastor had remarked in a sermon that he had "already thrown two ballots [Social Democratic and Independent Socialist] into the fire," insisted plaintively that the sermon had cost his party "a number of votes" on January 12.[34] That "Christian" and "Social Democrat" were mutually exclusive categories seemed as axiomatic for churchmen as ever. In this sense the November Revolution served to expose the inherently political character of the old social contract between throne and altar. Moreover, in seeking to capture the political arena for their own institutional advantage, churchmen themselves became to some extent captives of the political process.

For the moment, however, Protestant leaders could celebrate the achievement of their minimum program in Württemberg. Though no party won a clear victory on January 12 and though the Protestant right managed only 25 of 150 seats in the state constitutional assembly, the forces of republican movement were already beginning to lose whatever momentum they had enjoyed since November. The SPD, with 52 seats, formed the largest single bloc in the assembly, confirming Wilhelm Blos as chief cabinet minister and *Staatspräsident*. Even with the addition of four members of the USPD, however, the socialist front fell far short of an absolute majority. Parliamentary and administrative initiative consequently rested with the center, where the Catholic Center (31 seats) and the DDP (38 seats) held the balance. Results of the elections to the National Assembly held a week later duplicated this pattern on a national scale. While threats of violence would force the National Assembly to forsake Berlin for the more placid setting of Weimar, political calm had returned to Stuttgart by the time the Württemberg assembly convened on January 23. From the beginning, its proceedings

[34] Klumpp to Arbeiter- und Soldatenrat Stuttgart, Jan. 15, 1919 (copy), and Dipper to WEK, Feb. 6, 1919, both in LKA A26/151.

71

were marked by an unspoken agreement to subordinate ideology to the practical task of expediting approval of the new state constitution. Theophil Wurm, a successful candidate on the Bürgerpartei list, later recalled the deliberations as marked by an unusual degree of cordiality, permitting him to enjoy friendly relations even with such ideological antagonists as the militant Independent Socialist Klara Zetkin.[35]

While delegates labored in committee and plenum to refine other parts of the draft constitution, they showed little inclination to tinker with the compromises on religious matters struck by the Keil committee.[36] To the left's principal objections came the invariable rejoinder that the regulation of church-state relations was not a question of "philosophy" but simply a practical matter of ratifying the express wishes of the "state."[37] At the final reading, in late April, the draft won overwhelming support. Nor did anyone challenge the Ministry of Education budget for 1919 when it included an indefinite extension of existing subsidy arrangements with the churches pending future legislation on commutation.[38]

Besides running true to established form for Württemberg, this willingness to defer to bureaucrats on church-state questions also reflected the fact that the crucial struggles over future church-state relations were those taking place more or less simultaneously in Weimar. The ultimate shape of any local settlement naturally depended on the framework provisions of the national constitution. Hence although work on the state constitution absorbed their immediate energies, church leaders were not disposed to remain merely passive observers of events at Weimar. Through the DEKA, through communications with

---

[35] Wurm, *Erinnerungen*, p. 66.

[36] Württemberg, Verfassungsgebende Landesversammlung, Verfassungsausschuss, Sitzungsbericht, Feb. 25, 1919, typescript copy in LKA A26/226; Wurster to Merz, Feb. 25, 1919, LKA A26/226. A review of committee decisions is included in its report of Apr. 15, 1919; Landesversammlung, *Verhandlungen* (1919), Beilageband, pp. 217–300.

[37] Landesversammlung, *Verhandlungen* (1919), pp. 368–76, 415.

[38] Ibid., pp. 988, 1543–60; Beilageband, pp. 441, 454, 510, 780–83, 871.

other churches, and through churchmen's own contacts with principal figures in the National Assembly, the Württemberg church labored to make its mark on the Weimar settlement. This was by no means an unambiguous task. Indeed, churchmen constantly found themselves in the position of having to balance their desire to protect a favorable position at home with pressures to defend the collective interests of all the Protestant churches, including those less favored by local circumstance.

Despite the best efforts of the DEKA to address the National Assembly with a common voice, tension between local and national interests repeatedly created rifts in the Protestant front. To be sure, churchmen without exception decried the preliminary draft constitution prepared by Hugo Preuss; its brief references to religion implied elimination of the churches' privileged legal status and promised to make membership obligations wholly voluntary by freeing individuals of any legal necessity to reveal their religious affiliation—not even, by implication, for purposes of establishing church tax rolls. Although the various churches united in opposing these provisions (they were eliminated in all subsequent drafts) and in demanding a favorable regulation of financial matters, disagreement arose over the preferred course to follow. The progress of local church-state negotiations encouraged Württemberg churchmen to support an essentially particularist formula. The Consistory therefore joined with church leaders from other south German states, where comparable circumstances obtained, in pressuring the National Assembly to leave regulation of church questions to individual states. While it couched its position in quasi-constitutional language, the Consistory admitted candidly that self-interest dictated opposition to a unitary approach, since the terms of any such settlement were likely to be less advantageous than those being contemplated by the Württemberg regime.[39]

For this reason, too, they were reluctant to take up the cause

[39] WEK to DEKA, Dec. 29, 1918, and Traub to WEK, Jan. 31, 1919, both in LKA A26/226. The draft circulated by the DEKA was the preliminary draft of Hugo Preuss, later withdrawn.

of churches in central Germany, where the hostility of local socialist governments made the prospect of a federalist solution appear nothing short of disastrous. Ignoring pleas from embattled colleagues in such states as Thuringia, Württemberg churchmen lobbied vigorously against any common-denominator solution that might impinge on local arrangements. While no Württemberg pastor was an elected member of the National Assembly and although church leaders took a somewhat reserved approach to most DEKA-orchestrated lobbying strategies,[40] their position was well represented behind the scenes at Weimar. In particular they profited from the extensive network of associations between members of the Württemberg social-liberal movement and the influential circle of churchmen and politicians around Friedrich Naumann, who in his capacity as a leader of the DDP played a pivotal role in crafting constitutional agreements favorable to Protestant interests. Reinforcing the Naumann connection was the prominent presence of a Swabian churchman, August Hinderer, at the head of the Evangelical Press Association, a position that afforded access to key assembly figures as well as to the nerve centers of the Protestant establishment in Berlin.[41] For its part, the Württemberg government under Wilhelm Blos also loyally pressed the case for a federalist approach. Blos himself would later write that Social Democratic leaders in Stuttgart had always considered it vital "to guarantee the Württemberg people their own unique way of life as dictated by the historical development of the land."[42] Hence the Blos cabinet agreed on February 11 to appeal "emphatically" that individual states be left free to set their own terms for a separation of church and state.[43] In the Reichsrat, a stronghold of south German particu-

[40] It does not appear, for example, that the Württemberg leadership made any effort to promote the massive signature campaign orchestrated by the Prussian church in support of religious instruction. EVB, *Mitteilungen* 6 (Jan. 1920): 81ff.; DEKA to WEK, Mar. 17, Apr. 26, 1919, LKA A26/1097.

[41] Heuss, *Friedrich Naumann*, p. 624. Cf. Ströle to WEK, Feb. 12, 21, 1919, and Ströle to Rade, Feb. 25, 1919 (copy), all in LKA A26/151.

[42] Blos, *Monarchie zum Volksstaat*, 1:78.

[43] Heymann to Provisorische Regierung, Feb. 11, 1919 (copy), and Heymann to WEK, Feb. 14, 1919, both in LKA A26/226.

larism, Württemberg's representative, the revisionist Social Democrat Karl Hildenbrand, warned of his government's determination to oppose any regulation that would negate or substantially alter elements of the provisional state constitution.[44]

The impact of these efforts, and indeed of church lobbying in general, is difficult to assess. Advocates of particularism failed in the end to carry their point; the Weimar constitution (ARTICLE 10) reserved to the national government the right to establish basic principles regarding the "rights and duties of religious associations." At the same time, however, the specific provisions on religion (ARTICLES 135–141) presented little threat to prior arrangements in Württemberg. The crucial paragraphs of ARTICLE 137 reaffirmed the churches' status as public corporations entitled to impose taxes on members. ARTICLE 138 made a token bow towards particularism by leaving the actual commutation of financial subsidies to the states, albeit within the general framework of Reich legislation. Moreover, ARTICLE 173 obligated states to honor existing financial arrangements until such a national commutation law could be adopted. Other paragraphs (ARTICLES 139–141) reaffirmed the constitutional basis for some historic marks of the Christian state such as the provision of religious services in the military and the designation of Sunday as a day of rest and "spiritual uplift." That these provisions were so generally favorable owed much to the tactical skill of Friedrich Naumann and the far from negligible power-brokering of the Catholic Center, which exploited the growing estrangement between radicals and revisionists in the socialist camp to bring majority Social Democrats into a flexible consensus. It may be that the clamor of the churches encouraged members of the National Assembly's Constitution Committee, beset as they were by a host of other problems, to opt for a settlement that would require a minimum of deviation from existing practices. In any event, the final compromise came quickly; by April, separation of church and state had been eclipsed as an issue by more intract-

[44] Blos to Hildenbrand, Feb. 20, 1919 (copy), LKA A26/226. On the role of south German particularism, see Willibalt Apelt, *Geschichte der Weimarer Verfassung* (Munich, 1946), pp. 71–82.

able problems involving school types and the place of religion in the curriculum, problems whose ramifications for Württemberg will be explored in a later chapter.[45]

Reviewing the constitutional settlement in 1921, Stuttgart's conservative Protestant *Süddeutsche Zeitung* concluded that "in November 1918 no one would have allowed himself to dream that such a strong thread of . . . continuity . . . would remain intact."[46] This statement sums up the attitude not only of churchmen relieved at the passing of a threatened Kulturkampf but also of those who had sincerely expected the November Revolution to bring about genuine disestablishment. One of the lonely voices of protest in the Württemberg assembly was that of Social Democrat Paul Sakmann, professor in a Stuttgart gymnasium and a Stiftler who upon completion of his studies at Tübingen in the 1880s had abandoned the church, later to emerge as one of the leaders of Württemberg's militant conventicle of freethinkers. In a speech given in Stuttgart towards the end of 1919, Sakmann vented his frustration over the passivity of his own party in the face of the Protestant mobilization. The church, he grudgingly admitted, had demonstrated its strength as a pressure group. Its "diplomacy and tactics" within the Württemberg bureaucracy were enhanced by "extraordinary resources of communication—mass organizations, placard missions, press organizations—which hold the press of almost every party firmly in their grasp." Even where the church had once seemed most vulnerable, in the area of finance, it had come away with a favorable interim settlement. "Before the revolution, if worse came to worst, the state could at least reject the education budget; today it is constitutionally obligated to appropriate funds far in excess of the [strict value of secularized] church lands." Token disestablishment had not brought Württemberg, or Germany, closer to the old liberal ideal of a free church in a

[45] Jacke, *Kirche zwischen Monarchie und Republik*, pp. 119–27, 131–45; Borg, *Old-Prussian Church*, pp. 83–97. A standard contemporary analysis of the constitution is Fritz Stier-Somlo, *Die Verfassung des Deutschen Reichs vom 11. August 1919*, 3d ed. (Bonn, 1925).

[46] *SDZ*, July 23, 1921.

free state. If anything, that ideal seemed even more remote than before. "We have," Sakmann concluded, "a free church and an unfree state."[47]

In reality the church was neither so free nor the state so fettered as Sakmann would have it. The status of a "free church," as that term was then understood, was of course precisely what advocates of the Volkskirche tradition had fought to avoid. Though bound by no formal constraints of law, the church therefore remained bound as a matter of choice by its dependence on state subsidies. In the absence of a constitutionally mandated law on commutation (a law, as it happened, that the Reichstag never produced during the Weimar years), the state may have been bound to honor existing subsidy commitments, but the precise definition of these obligations remained open to debate. The constitution thus allowed for considerable continuity while affording church leaders and state officials alike a measure of freedom to maneuver. If churchmen still felt entitled to claim a privileged public position, they had also found themselves impelled to abandon the high ground of Volkskirche preeminence for the power stuggles of the political arena. Constitutional guarantees aside, churchmen's future status and influence would depend in practice upon both the favor of the state and the support of the masses. In this sense, at least, the incomplete separation of church and state accurately reflected an ambiguity inherent in the Volkskirche orientation.

THE CHURCH LAW OF 1924

The Weimar constitution established the general framework for a new church-state order; the Württemberg constitution provided the specific local framework. Many details of implementation, however, remained unresolved. With this in mind, the Ministry of Education began consultations with major church bodies on comprehensive legislation to regulate church matters.

---

[47] "Was fordert die neue Zeit von dem freidenkenden Menschen?" speech, Stuttgart, Nov. 29, 1919, typescript report in LKA D4/24x.

Nearly five years would pass before the task was complete, and this extended interim, marked by frequent and often tedious negotiations, served to underscore the incompleteness of the initial disestablishment process. Although the king's abdication left the church formally autonomous, the Consistory continued to exercise primary control of day-to-day affairs, and in the absence of formal devolution it remained legally an agency of the state, albeit one with only the loosest ties of accountability. The process of negotiation during the early 1920s likewise underscored the already-noted tension between the desire of churchmen to set themselves securely "above parties" and the pressure to brave political struggles in defense of their institutional interests. As Paul Sakmann rightly implied, the church now dealt with the state less as a semiofficial bureau than as a semiprivate pressure group, seeking to gain or preserve benefits that, within limits set by the constitution, only the state could dispense. Despite advantages of organization and communication, the church's freedom of maneuver was limited on one side by bureaucratic punctilio and on the other by political power-brokering, as ostensible allies maneuvered for parliamentary advantage.

Final reordering of church-state relations revolved around a host of specific juridical and administrative details, many highly technical in nature. Since church membership historically involved both ecclesiastical and civil dimensions, new procedures were necessary to regulate resignations and transfers between confessions. Similarly, new legislation was needed to confirm the status of certain ecclesiastical properties and endowments, to regulate the imposition of fees for clerical services, and to confirm rights of jurisdiction in cases of discipline or disputes between clergy and public officials. Overshadowing all such issues, however, was the paramount question of finances. Both sides agreed that the Württemberg church, like most of the larger territorial churches in Germany, should henceforth realize a portion of its revenues through a tax on parishioners, with the state continuing to provide a certain level of support as compensation for the secularization of 1806. The sticking point lay in the specific determination of these continuing subsidies. In Württemberg, where high public officials historically prided themselves on frugality of administration, even where their own salaries were concerned,[48] the church's financial claims were bound to provoke dispute, all the more so in the often desperate economic climate of the early 1920s.

Like any service bureaucracy, the church was a labor-intensive organization. Excluding building and other capital expenses, many of which were funded separately, well over 90 percent of the general church budget went to cover pastors' salaries and pensions. Salaries and salary scales therefore loomed large in any determination of church finances. As noted earlier, one long-term effect of the 1806 secularization decree had been to divorce pastors' compensation from parish tithes, prebends, and livings and to substitute a uniform salary schedule analogous to that for civil servants. While the royal government had never formally recognized the clergy as part of the civil service, comparisons between the two groups were all but inevitable, and it was a common complaint of pastors, especially in outlying areas, that their incomes left them at an unfair disadvantage against public officials of similar rank and training. Clergy salaries in Württemberg, as elsewhere, fell into three basic categories. The ecclesiastical elite—members of the Consistory and a few other high officials, such as the Stuttgart Dekan—enjoyed salaries comparable to those of university professors and ministerial department heads. Most of the parish clergy, by contrast, were assigned to a sliding scale comparable to that for rectors and senior schoolmasters, with supplementary living and dependency allowances that varied according to locale. An intermediate salary group included Dekans and a small number of pastors in particularly demanding parishes, who received "enhanced" salaries of about 10 percent above the normal range. This last group had grown in size from about 50 persons at the turn of the century to perhaps 140 in 1919. The increase in enhancements, however, was too gradual to satisfy rank-and-file clergy, who objected that

---

[48] Besson, *Württemberg und die deutsche Staatskrise*, p. 52.

the existing structure only gave them informal parity with elementary schoolteachers, most of whom were their educational inferiors and who, until shortly before the Great War, had been subordinate to pastors in the latter's capacity as local school inspectors. Only those pastors with "enhanced" salaries, it was argued, received compensation equivalent to that of other university-trained civil servants. Moreover, the limited availability of such positions meant that a significantly smaller proportion of pastors could hope for promotion during their careers than was true for those in the state bureaucracy proper.[49]

The sense of comparative deprivation to which these observations contributed provided one focus for the Württemberg clergy's growing sense of a separate professional identity. Since the late nineteenth century, parity of scale with the civil service had become a fixed objective of the pastors' professional association, the Pfarrverein, and thus a ready litmus test of governmental intentions. If anything, the November Revolution heightened pastors' preoccupation with material concerns. It drove the Pfarrverein into an alliance of convenience with upper-echelon bureaucrats in the Württemberg branch of the Verband höher geprüfter Beamten, an association of university-trained officials organized in 1918 for the explicit purpose of "championing improvements in the incomes of higher officials and seeing to it that . . . an appropriate differential is maintained with respect to the lower salary grades." In exchange for the clergy's support in its general lobbying efforts, the association, claiming about four thousand members in Württemberg, agreed to adopt pastors' call for parity as its own.[50] For its part, the Con-

[49] EPW to WEK, May 12, 1911, and Zeller to KM, Dec. 30, 1913, both in LKA A26/1100.

[50] EPW, Jahresversammlung, Stuttgart, Apr. 30, 1919, Protokollbuch II, LKA D/EPVW 22. See also "Rundschreiben an die Herren Vorsitzenden und Vertreter," Feb. 9, 1925, and Merkbuch für die Mitglieder der der Landesgruppe angeschlossenen Verbände (Cannstatt, 1926), copies of both in LKA D/EPW 28. Concern to maintain distinctions from lesser civil servants led the group to split from the larger public servants' union (Deutscher Beamtenbund) in 1920; see Zeitschrift des Bundes höherer Beamten 2 (June 15, 1920): 1–2, copy in LKA D/EPW 28.

sistory recognized pastors' growing self-consciousness as an interest group by agreeing to the establishment in late 1920 of a formal advisory council (Pfarrerbeirat) through which it would consult with spokesmen for the clergy on matters of salary, benefits, or appointments.[51]

Some months earlier, the Blos government had proposed a revision of the civil service salary code that partially accommodated churchmen's demands. These concessions were largely the work of Johannes Hieber, the DDP parliamentary chief who had replaced Berthold Heymann as education minister after a cabinet shuffle in the fall of 1919. Hieber's party had underscored its commitment to a "positive" relationship between church and state in a revised party platform of July 1919.[52] As a former pastor, Hieber was not insensitive to the clergy's status concerns. Although the new code fell short of granting pastors parity with academic civil servants, it did confirm a modest differential between clergy and schoolmasters.

Since the Württemberg constitution, in harmony with the transitional provisions in ARTICLE 173 of the Weimar constitution, required the state to underwrite the church budget pending agreement on a final commutation formula, these salary adjustments quickly became a test case for conflicting conceptions of a permanent subsidy formula. In proposing the new code, Hieber took the position that salary increases as such could have no bearing on the question of permanent subsidy arrangements. The Finance Ministry, faced with the pressures of a deteriorating economy, took an even stronger position. Objecting to even a temporary increase in outlays, the ministry demanded that the Consistory and the Education Ministry conclude a binding long-term agreement before the submission of the next annual budget—an agreement, moreover, that would not entitle churchmen to automatic subsidy adjustments by virtue of possible future increases in civil service salaries. For its part, the

[51] Draft agreement of Nov. 22–23, 1920, LKA A26/564; Protokoll, LKA D/EPW 21.
[52] *SNT*, July 24, 1919.

Consistory roundly objected to conclusion of such a "premature" agreement, arguing that an equitable resolution could be achieved only after economic conditions had stabilized. The Pfarrverein, eager to consolidate any advantage, however minor, endorsed the Consistory's stand by a resounding majority.[53]

Tactical considerations favored the Consistory's delaying strategy. With state elections scheduled for June 1920, Hieber had good reason to avoid embroiling the Protestant electorate in a controversy about the church policy of either his party or the government coalition. On May 2 Robert Meyding, Hieber's liaison with church officials, met with members of the Consistory to assure them that despite the Finance Ministry's ultimatum Hieber would not hold recent salary adjustments hostage to a quick agreement. Rather, he was prepared for the moment to accept the Consistory's argument that a comprehensive agreement should not be concluded until settled times returned.[54] While Hieber publicly took pains to emphasize that the government was not welcoming the clergy into the civil service by the back door and that salary reforms did not constitute a commitment to escalating state subsidies, the salary law approved by the assembly in late May formally linked the clergy's pay schedule to that of the civil service, the first such action by any German state since the November Revolution.[55]

The June elections in Württemberg continued the general rightward movement in German politics since 1919. Protestant conservatives emerged as the largest single faction in the reconstituted assembly, though with 27 of 101 seats they fell far short of a majority. The SPD, which had suffered the most serious

[53] WEK and LKV-Ausschuss, memorandum, Apr. 20, 1920, LKA A26/226; see also EPVW, Jahresversammlung, Stuttgart, Apr. 28, 1920, Protokollbuch II, LKA D/EPW 22.

[54] "Aufzeichnungen über eine Besprechung im Sitzungssaal des Konsistoriums am 2. Mai 1920," and Meyding to Zeller, May 3, 1920, both in LKA A26/226. Cf. Synodalausschuss meeting, June 15, 1920, Protokoll, LKA A100/24.

[55] "Jahresbericht 1920," KAfW 30 (1921): 70; Regierungsblatt (1920), pp. 367–68; Amtsblatt 19 (1920): 253–63, 423–42; Landtag, Verhandlungen (1920), pp. 2249–50, Beilageband, pp. 1261–64.

losses, withdrew from the governing coalition, leaving the DDP and Catholic Center to form a new cabinet. As leader of the DDP, Johannes Hieber became Württemberg's new president and retained his portfolio as minister of education. The results promised an era of good feeling between church and state, any remaining differences over finance notwithstanding. "Dr. Hieber . . . possesses the confidence of broad segments of the Evangelical population," declared the *Stuttgarter Evangelisches Sonntagsblatt*, a powerful mouthpiece of conservative Protestant opinion; "If he can succeed in extricating questions of school and church from political controversy, this would be a fine and noble act of domestic peacemaking."[56]

Faced with a strong Catholic Center and a resurgent Protestant right, Hieber was in no position to shake such confidence. Early in 1921 he declared in the state assembly that it was "a matter of honor" for the state to continue interim support of the churches "so that the clergy will not have to suffer because of this [period of] transition."[57] During the dizzying inflationary spiral of the next two years, the Württemberg government did everything possible to protect clergy from economic catastrophe. Beginning in 1921, budgets included mechanisms for automatic salary increases pegged to inflation.[58] Other measures waived restrictions on the collection of local parish taxes and approved applications for extraordinary assistance in cases of special need.[59] Real incomes, to be sure, declined dramatically during this period, leaving pastors' salaries in many cases lower than the wages of a typical skilled laborer; nor could legislative

[56] *SES* 54 (1920): 212.

[57] Landtag, *Verhandlungen* (1921), pp. 1581–82.

[58] EPW to WEK, Mar. 4, 1921, and Zeller to Schnaufer, Mar. 4, 1921, both in LKA D/EPW 31; Landtag, *Verhandlungen* (1921), Beilageband, pp. 611–19; typescript salary data for 1922, n.d., LKA A26/229. Bälz to WEK, July 13, 1923; Reichsinnenministerium to KM, n.d. (copy); DEKA to WEK, Aug. 4, 1923; DEKA to WEK, Aug. 31, 1923; and Bälz to WEK, Sept. 4, 1923; all in LKA A26/230. *Amtsblatt* 20 (1922–23): 63–66, 262–66, 279–82, 282–90, 301–2, 21 (1923–24): 33–39; *Reichsgesetzblatt* (1923), 1:494.

[59] Protokoll, Sept. 3, 1923; Bälz to WEK, Sept. 24, 1923; and Bracher to WEK, Nov. 8, 1923; all in LKA A26/1505.

relief shield clergy from the evaporation of savings and investments that became the lot of the entire German middle class. Even so, few if any Württemberg churchmen were reduced to the utter impoverishment that befell colleagues in areas such as Saxony or Thuringia, where unsympathetic state officials paid fixed subsidies in worthless paper currency, forcing some pastors to seek menial jobs in order to fend off starvation.[60]

With the Reich currency reform of November 15, 1923, the era of uncontrolled inflation came to an end. Less than four months later, in early 1924, the Württemberg assembly finally passed a comprehensive church law. The two events were not wholly unrelated. Economic conditions undoubtedly delayed both the drafting process and subsequent parliamentary consideration. Whether they also colored the content of the legislation is less clear. It is reasonable to assume, however, that inflation— and, of course, the absence of a national law on commutation— had something to do with the fact that the 1924 law proved almost as vague as the constitution of 1919 on the specific scope of state subsidies. Former Education Minister Heymann was not far from the truth when he predicted in 1923 that the salary code of 1920 represented not simply an interim expedient but the Hieber government's model for more permanent arrangements.[61]

The Württemberg church law constituted a monument to departmental particularism and bureaucratic consensus-building. The first working draft, a document of ten densely printed, double-columned pages drawn up principally by Robert Meyding, was circulated to officials of the three major confessions late in

[60] Traub to WEK, Oct. 6, 1923, LKA A26/1505; Merz to DEKA, Mar. 18, 1929, OKR/AR Gen. 124/I. Cf. Wurm to Hieber, June 23, 1923: "In Württemberg the clergy did not face the great distress that occurred in other churches . . . during the period of inflation" (OKR/AR Gen. 5a). Most state governments in fact followed a policy similar to that in Württemberg, providing temporary subsidies to a greater or lesser extent; cf. *KJ 1921*, pp. 334–38; *KJ 1924*, pp. 429–30, 476–79; and Borg, *Old-Prussian Church*, pp. 116–19. On comparative wages, see Gerhard Bry, *Wages in Germany, 1871–1945* (Princeton, 1960), esp. pp. 229–30, 438–39.

[61] *ST*, July 27, 1923.

1921. A preliminary chapter elaborated constitutional guarantees of the churches' rights as public corporations. The second chapter established provisions for membership, resignation, and transfer, while the third and longest dealt with procedures for church taxation. Other chapters were devoted to disciplinary matters, ecclesiastical fees and collections, the status of religious endowments, and a variety of administrative details. In accordance with the national and state constitutions, the draft authorized those religious bodies recognized as public entities (that is, Evangelical, Catholic, and Jewish) to levy a tax on their members for the purpose of raising revenues not provided by the state or other sources. This tax was to be collected for the churches by the state tax office in the form of a surcharge on individual income taxes and certain property taxes; specific rates were to be established by church officials in consultation with the Finance Ministry but were not to exceed 10 percent of the civil tax. Although a novelty for Württemberg, these procedures were familiar enough from the practice of states such as Prussia and Baden, where general church taxes had been the norm for a generation or more. The mixture of taxes and subsidies implied a degree of flexibility in budgetary planning. Where subsidies themselves were concerned, the proposed legislation would not obligate the state to a set formula, as some churchmen and state officials insisted, but it also set no ceiling on potential state support.[62]

This Solomonic formula reflected the Hieber ministry's concern to keep open as many administrative options as possible. Specifically, it struck a mediating position between the Finance Ministry's insistence on budgetary restraint and the Consistory's demands for the broadest possible construction of state obligations. It also provided some latitude within which to respond

[62] Synodalausschuss meetings, June 8, 20, Nov. 17, 1921, Protokolle, LKA A100/24. Hieber to WEK, Nov. 30–Dec. 6, 1921, and WEK to KM, Jan. 14, 1922, both in LKA A26/228. Hieber to WEK, Jan. 5, 1921, and Zeller to KM, Mar. 22, 1921, both in LKA A26/409. See also "Das staatliche Gesetz über die Kirchen," SES 55 (1922): 349, and for earlier provisions, Amtsblatt 10 (1892): 4444, 5044–47.

to any future guidelines on commutation laid down by the Reichstag, although this would not seem to have been a primary consideration (and the promulgation of such guidelines hardly appeared imminent). Much depended upon the impact of church taxes. Prudence dictated that surcharges be kept modest; above a certain rate they were almost certain to become counterproductive, since they could be expected to precipitate a rash of withdrawals from church membership, which would in turn cut anticipated revenue. Even at the maximum rate allowed, however, church taxes would make up only part of the difference between the total church budget and a subsidy determined strictly on the basis of the 1806 secularization—a shortfall in fact amounting to half or more of the entire budget. Inasmuch as the Hieber proposal would have the state continue to cover this shortfall, continuing negotiations involved not the question of subsidies as such but rather their legal status. Hieber insisted on a nonbinding arrangement; the Consistory, however, held stubbornly to the position that the church had a legal right to public funds for any budgetary needs not otherwise satisfied, and it demanded a clear statement to this effect in the draft law. With other states looking to the Württemberg draft as a model for legislation of their own, the Consistory no doubt hoped in this way to establish favorable precedents for their fellow churchmen elsewhere.[63]

Whatever its legal merits—and on this point observers on both sides were dubious—the Consistory's position had little immediate prospect of success in the Landtag. The Conservative opposition, while sympathetic, lacked the necessary votes; socialist support was inconceivable. Appeals to the Catholic Center's parliamentary spokesman on church-state questions, Ludwig Bauer, failed to dissuade Hieber's coalition partner from supporting the government formula.[64] Hieber himself sent

---

[63] See, e.g., Kühn (Dresden) to WEK, Jan. 10, 1921, and Hoffmann (Anhalt) to WEK, Jan. 10, 1921, both in LKA A26/227; Landeskirchenrat Eisenach to WEK, Sept. 25, 1922, LKA A26/229; *Frankfurter Zeitung*, June 3, 1922; *SM*, Aug. 4, 7, 14, 1922.

[64] Bauer to Schauffler, July 19, 1922, LKA A26/221.

church officials a veiled warning that if they insisted too strongly on their position, his government would see fit simply to "go its own way."[65] Under the circumstances the Consistory had little choice but to accept Hieber's personal assurances that the government would not impose any unreasonable formula and that in any case the church would not forfeit its right to a future judicial determination if questions remained unresolved.[66] By the spring of 1923, when a committee of the Landtag finally began considering the legislation, further negotiations had produced agreement on a general formula for implementation. The proposed arrangement underscored anew church dependence on state support; even after the introduction of church taxes, fully 80 percent of church revenue would represent appropriations through the Education Ministry.[67] In a May circular to the clergy, the Consistory declared this state of affairs to be satisfactory for the present, concluding that while some demands necessarily remained unmet, the church would continue to enjoy a "not unfavorable" position in comparison with many of its German counterparts.[68]

Although the Hieber government anticipated quick assembly action,[69] work on the draft dragged on for more than a year. Not only did the immediate pressures of inflation repeatedly relegate church affairs to secondary rank but the committee assigned to review the legislation found its progress delayed by wrangles over a host of amendments, more than two hundred in all. The committee comprised eighteen members: six conservatives, led by Gustav Beisswänger, a former pastor; one moderate liberal, Gottlob Egelhaaf, a local historian and stalwart Protestant lay

[65] "Staat und Kirche in der Rede des Staatspräsidenten Dr. Hieber am 4. Juli 1922," Jakob Schoell, notes, LKA A26/229; cf. SAfW, July 5, 1922.

[66] Hieber to WEK, Dec. 21, 1922; WEK to KM, Jan. 2, 1923; and WEK to KM, Jan. 30, 1923; all in LKA A26/229.

[67] Memoranda, Feb. 15, 27, 28, 1923, LKA A26/229; Amtsblatt 20 (1922–23): 282–90.

[68] "Erlass an alle Dekanatsämter," May 19, 1923, LKA A26/229.

[69] Landtag, Verhandlungen (1922), Beilageband, pp. 561–80. The draft of July 1922 assumed an effective date of Apr. 1, 1923.

leader; four representatives of the Catholic Center; two Democrats; and five Social Democrats, led by Berthold Heymann.
Each faction sought to press changes of its own, and the committee's composition denied any group a natural majority. Social Democrats fought to alter what they regarded as overly
cumbersome procedures for renouncing church membership, efforts stoutly resisted by the right and the Catholic Center. Protestant conservatives demanded limitations on the state's right to
review church financial records in determining subsidies, a right
defended no less vigorously by Democrats and Social Democrats. For its part, the Catholic Center sought to expand church
taxes to include a surcharge on corporate real estate, in part as a
means of offsetting the effects of limited income in rural districts, where Württemberg's Catholic population was concentrated. Again Democrats and Social Democrats objected
strongly, while conservatives were unable to reach a unified position. Twice, in March and June of 1923, the committee was
forced to suspend its deliberations. Not until the end of the year
did it finally arrive at a compromise. The left abandoned efforts
to modify church membership provisions; the right accepted
some state review of church budgets; the Catholic Center agreed
to defer its tax proposal pending further study.[70]

Once committee hurdles had been cleared, speedy approval by
the full assembly seemed certain. Only a nettlesome USPD minority flatly opposed the draft, and their opposition took the
form of a simple refusal to take part in deliberations in protest of
the lack of any genuine separation of church and state.[71] With

---

[70] The legislative history is included in "Anträge des Kirchenausschusses zu
dem Entwurf eines Gesetzes über die Kirchen," Landtag, *Verhandlungen* (1924),
Beilageband, pp. 579–605, 641–46. WEK to KM, Jan. 14, 1922, LKA A26/220.
Schauffler to Egelhaaf, Nov. 2, 1922, LKA A26/221. "Abänderungsanträge zum
Kirchengesetz," typescript, Dec. 12, 1922 (marginal notation: "Schauffler
11.12.22 mit Bl. 6 an Bazille"), LKA A26/221. Hieber to WEK, Mar. 26, 1923;
KM to Arbeitsministerium, Mar. 26, 1923 (copy); Verband Württembergischer
Industrieller, statement of Apr. 19, 1923; Kübler to WEK, Apr. 19, 1923; and Faut
to WEK, Apr. 28, 1923; all in LKA A26/1505. *SAfW*, Mar. 13, 16, June 28, 1923;
SM, Mar. 23, June 28, 1923; *SDZ*, Mar. 23, June 28, 1923; *SNT*, Mar. 15, 1923.
[71] Landtag, *Verhandlungen* (1922), p. 3926.

varying degrees of enthusiasm, all other factions had already identified themselves with the administrative status quo. The DDP constitutional specialist Wilhelm von Blume spoke for a majority when he asserted that the government had a legitimate interest in supporting religion; any disagreements involved details, not basic principles. Even in opposition, the SPD leadership held loyally to the course set in 1918. If the party had once attacked the churches as instruments of the state, Berthold Heymann stated, such a policy ceased to be necessary "once the state . . . assumes a totally neutral position in questions of religion and the church." This, he insisted, the proposed law would guarantee.[72]

After the previous year's wrangling, the irenic tone of assembly debate was particularly welcome to church leaders. Adoption of the church law by near acclamation would provide symbolic reinforcement of their claims to stand above partisan interests and to represent an institution whose public role was endorsed by every sector of the society it claimed to embrace. The Consistory's position is clearly expressed in the draft of a speech prepared by the Consistory's legislative liaison, Gerhard Schauffler, in consultation with Gustav Beisswänger. Apparently intended by the Bürgerpartei as a programmatic statement to be delivered during the assembly's concluding plenary debate, the speech emphasized the friendly intentions of all participants and praised the law as a reasonable compromise embodying the considered interests of church and state alike.[73]

Final passage on February 8, 1924, however, saw the Consistory's vision of an all-party consensus unexpectedly evaporate. The negative votes came, surprisingly, from the Bürgerpartei itself, the most vocally Protestant of all Württemberg parties and, as the above-mentioned Schauffler draft testified, the one church leaders regarded as their natural ally in the legislative arena. While the precise motives for this reversal remain murky, the

[72] Ibid., pp. 3914–26.
[73] Typescript draft with revisions in Schauffler's hand, LKA A26/221. The same file includes a similar draft of the statement delivered by the Bürgerpartei faction during the first reading of the church law in 1922.

tactical calculations of party chairman Wilhelm Bazille certainly played a key role. With the 1924 elections only weeks away, Bazille apparently hoped to drive a wedge between the existing coalition partners, the DDP and the Catholic Center, by exploiting intramural disagreements over Catholic tax proposals. Playing to rural conservatives of both confessions, Bazille attacked the church law as a shabby surrender to the left, "unresponsive" to the needs of either church or state. On the final vote the conservative faction joined the extreme left in withholding support—a symbolic gesture that was both calculated and safe, inasmuch as a comfortable majority for passage remained assured.[74]

The Bürgerpartei's action left churchmen in an awkward position. Gottlob Egelhaaf, a member of the DVP, who as his party's representative on the Landtag's church committee had also worked closely with the Consistory throughout the legislative process, angrily denounced Bazille for betraying the church's trust. "We can only assume," Egelhaaf wrote in the *Schwäbischer Merkur*, "that either the right has been playing a secret, shabby, and inconceivably malicious game [from the start] or that at the last moment demagogic calculations overpowered political good sense."[75] The Consistory itself lamely sought to downplay the significance of the rift. In an article prepared for a newly launched national Protestant journal, *Das evangelische Deutschland*, Consistory member Hermann Müller emphasized arguments that the Bürgerpartei's action had had nothing to do with the merits of the legislation and that the party had in fact played a central role in seeing it to completion.[76]

Still, the Bürgerpartei affair cast an ironic light on the Consistory's basic strategy since 1918. It accentuated the dissonance inherent in churchmen's efforts to transcend the political arena while at the same time mobilizing within it for their own purposes. Since the revolution, the Consistory had worked to preserve the church as a structural constant in public life, a fixture

---

[74] Landtag, *Verhandlungen* (1924), pp. 5489–97.

[75] "Der Handstreik der Rechten," *SM*, Feb. 11, 1924.

[76] Hermann Müller, "Das württembergische Staatsgesetz über die Kirchen," *Das evangelische Deutschland* 1 (1924): 15.

on the horizon of society beyond party squabbles or conflicts of ideology. Hence it acted wherever possible within the familiar channels of the state bureaucracy. Simultaneously, however, it pursued a perceived need to shore up the church's position on the party-political front, and this largely defensive impulse led to an identification with the Württemberg right that was at once unnecessarily narrow and potentially precarious—narrow because it all but ignored the benevolent intentions of the parties from the democratic center and even moderate left; precarious because it exposed church interests to the vagaries of partisan party tactics.

From this perspective the actual content of the Württemberg church law might well be regarded as less important than the legislative history outlined at length above. Despite protracted debate over specific details, the range of constitutionally feasible options was fairly narrow; moreover, the apparent hard line espoused by some state officials in the course of financial negotiations was a far cry indeed from the sort of conscious bureaucratic subversion practiced during the same period in militant socialist strongholds of central Germany. Passage of the church law brought to an end half a decade of institutional transition in Württemberg. In the process, it also provided churchmen with repeated reminders of the encumbrances facing a self-proclaimed "people's church" in a politically fragmented society.

THE NEW ORDER IN PRACTICE

The church law took effect in April 1924, permitting septuagenarian Consistory president Hermann von Zeller to declare his long-delayed retirement and clearing the way for election of a new president by the state church assembly. The Consistory officially ceased to be an organ of the state; to emphasize its new status, it assumed the name Oberkirchenrat (Supreme Church Council). Changes of nomenclature aside, however, the new order differed from the old in little besides the introduction of church taxes. The law of 1924 in effect brought church-state relations in Württemberg to a point reached decades earlier in most German territories; it took its point of departure less from the recent revolution than from prewar constitutional reforms.[77] During the course of negotiations Robert Meyding once remarked approvingly that the new arrangements had the virtue of adhering to the letter of constitutional requirements for a separation of church and state without seriously disturbing traditional ties between the two.[78]

In the absence of the crown, however, these ties became not so much intrinsic as instrumental. The old social contract had been broken; the church was no longer a self-evident pillar of established authority. Autonomy of action, however, remained limited by the practical fact that where finances were concerned, churchmen were not fully their own masters. The discretionary element still inherent in state subsidies made for a degree of continued uncertainty on the bureaucratic front. Where political tactics were concerned, moreover, recent actions in the Württemberg assembly showed that even the most vocal advocates of the Protestant cause could not automatically be depended upon to recognize churchmen's claims to an institutional position above parties and party interests.

Hence, far from being a temporary expedient, lobbying activity remained a fact of institutional life for church officials throughout the republican era. This was confirmed when the Bürgerpartei—arguably the principal beneficiary of earlier Protestant mobilization—found itself in a position to set government policy. The spring elections in 1924 continued the swing toward the right in Württemberg politics, leaving conservatives with nearly one-third of the seats in the assembly and a comfortable governing majority in coalition with the Catholic Center.[79] Wilhelm Bazille, leader of the Bürgerpartei, replaced Johannes Hieber as Staatspräsident, and like his predecessor he also took re-

[77] Cf. Albert Esenwein, "Zur Auseinandersetzung zwischen Staat und Kirche," *SNT*, Oct. 23, 1920.

[78] Meyding, memorandum, Feb. 27, 1923, LKA A26/229.

[79] The distribution of assembly seats was as follows: Bürgerpartei-Bauernbund 25, Catholic Center 17, Social Democrat 13, Communist 10, Democrat 9, People's Party 3.

sponsibility for the Ministry of Education. Bazille cut an unusual figure in Württemberg politics. Flamboyant, mercurial, and almost obsessively partisan, he was an ambitious tactician with a reputation for ruthlessness that contrasted markedly with the model of self-effacing statesmanship preferred by most Württemberg political leaders. As Waldemar Besson has suggested, there was something appropriate about Bazille's preference for Corsica, the birthplace of Napoleon, as a vacation site.[80]

The perpetual matter of salaries provided church officials with a first test of the new education minister's methods and intentions. Stabilization of the currency in late 1923 necessitated yet another revision of civil service salary schedules, the code of 1920 having been effectively rendered obsolete by inflation before it could be fully implemented. Mandated to pursue budgetary austerity, the Hieber regime in its last months had undertaken to curb salaries and to cashier nonessential public employees.[81] Whether similar economies could be applied in the case of churchmen, informally assimilated as they were into the civil service code, was a question that provoked controversy both in Württemberg and elsewhere. Church officials naturally protested against any unilateral application of austerity policies to the clergy. Not only would this represent unconstitutional interference in church affairs, complained Hermann von Zeller shortly before his retirement, but the "so-called salary improvements" promised since the war had "really brought . . . a steady decrease in income" for pastors.[82] Nor did churchmen find cause for celebration in Hieber's preliminary budget for 1924, which calculated state subsidies to church tax revenues on a ratio markedly below that assumed by church leaders during previous negotiations. In concert with other territorial church administrations, the Württemberg Consistory petitioned Reich finance

[80] Besson, *Württemberg und die deutsche Staatskrise*, p. 37; Wurm, *Erinnerungen*, p. 34; Keil, *Erlebnisse*, 2:288; Marquardt, *Geschichte Württembergs*, p. 370.

[81] *Regierungsblatt* (1923), pp. 537ff.

[82] WEK, memorandum, Jan. 1924, and Zeller to KM, Mar. 12, 1924, both in OKR/AR Gen. 103/I. Cf. Bry, *Wages in Germany*, pp. 229–30.

minister Hans Luther, through the DEKA in Berlin, for an injunction exempting churches from retrenchment measures. This Luther provided; shortly before leaving office, Hieber amended the budget to restore the earlier and more generous subsidy formula.[83]

Although he had attacked austerity policies skillfully during the campaign, Wilhelm Bazille took office ready and willing to continue them. On June 1 Bazille announced his intention to reinstate the formula for church subsidies just abandoned by Hieber. In communications with the Oberkirchenrat and in private conversation with newly elected church president Johannes Merz, Bazille made clear his determination to keep his administrative options open. While assuring Merz that he had no intention of undermining previous agreements, he insisted that economic conditions were still too unsettled to permit any blanket commitments. Churchmen could not expect a hard-pressed state treasury to increase appropriations simply to fund the higher salaries for which clergy continued to clamor. "What is possible now," he remarked in July, "is after all a quite different matter from the days when problems could be solved simply by printing more money."[84]

Bazille's official posturing put heavy pressures on church leadership and especially on the new church president, a mild-mannered man who, unlike his Consistorial predecessor Zeller, had little taste for the tactics of bureaucratic trench warfare. Beyond immediate uncertainties over finances, the Oberkirchenrat also had to contend with the prospect of discontent among the rank-and-file clergy, who since 1920 had been nursing hopes for

[83] *KJ 1924*, pp. 429–30. DEKA to Reichsinnenministerium, Feb. 4, 1924 (copy); Luther to Landesregierung Württemberg, Feb. 9, 1924 (copy); Zwiegert to Landesregierung Württemberg, Feb. 22, 1924 (copy); and Hieber to WEK, Mar. 7, 1924; all in OKR/AR Gen. 103/I. *Regierungsblatt* (1924), p. 183.

[84] Merz to Bazille, June 5, 1924, OKR/AR Gen. 5a. Bazille to OKR, June 26, 1924; Merz to Bazille, June 27, 1924; Bazille to OKR, July 12, 1924; and Bazille to OKR, July 21, 1924; all in OKR/AR Gen. 103/I. Karl Geier, "Die Staatsleistungen an die evangelische Landeskirche," *Württembergische Jahrbücher für Statistik und Landeskunde, 1936–37* (Stuttgart, 1938), p. 115.

improvement in living standards and who, in the words of a formal Pfarrverein protest, had no intention of seeing pastors forced to "bear the burden of austerity."[85] The lack of visible progress during the summer of 1924 now strained the clergy's confidence in the church leadership. Within the Pfarrverein, support grew for a demarche with allied civil service groups independent of the church hierarchy. Militancy was particularly high among rural pastors, who regarded themselves as doubly disadvantaged under existing arrangements. Not only were rural parishes routinely placed in the church's lowest salary category but the limited opportunities for schooling available outside the cities meant that many a pastor, hoping to provide his offspring with an education appropriate to their station, felt obliged to saddle himself with heavy expenses for tutoring or boarding schools.[86] While austerity measures never brought actual reductions in the salary levels established after currency stabilization, this did little to allay critics. Nor did an emergency supplemental grant from the Education Ministry in September; designed to forestall an immediate crisis in church finances, it only appeared to confirm a fear that financial relations with the state were degenerating from a stable contractural arrangement to a patchwork of ad hoc grants for which churchmen would be forced to beg, hat in hand. Meeting with his pastors' advisory council, church president Merz could do little but plead for patience and repeat the claim that compared to other areas of Germany, clergy in Württemberg still enjoyed relatively favorable conditions.[87]

Having failed to advance their case appreciably with Bazille the education minister, church leaders resorted to a flank assault on Bazille the party leader. On November 13 a delegation of

[85] Schnaufer to Bazille, July 10, 1924 (copy), OKR/AR Gen. 426/I; cf. Landeskirchenausschuss, statement, July 7, 1924, OKR/AR Gen. 426/I.

[86] EPW, circular, July 18, 1924, LKA D/EPW 21.

[87] Bazille to Merz, Sept. 24, 1924, and Merz to Bazille, Oct. 25, 1924, both in OKR/AR Gen. 103/I. Bälz to OKR, Oct. 8, 1924, and OKR to KM, Oct. 17, 1924, both in OKR/AR Gen. 426/I. EPW, Beiratssitzung, Nov. 10, 1924, Protokoll, LKA D/EPW 21.

prominent clergy and laymen active in the Bürgerpartei descended upon Bazille in force. The group included former Consistory president Hermann von Zeller; Theophil Wurm, now Dekan in Reutlingen and briefly a member of Bazille's faction in the 1919 assembly; and Heinrich Mosthaf, a retired senior civil servant prominent in a variety of Protestant lay organizations. Others included the chief justice of the Württemberg high court and even Bazille's own parliamentary deputy, the former pastor Gustav Beisswänger. In an intense exchange of views, the group warned that discontent among the clergy might well have damaging repercussions for the party. This veiled challenge to Bazille's leadership apparently accomplished its purpose; after lengthy discussion he eventually consented to return to the formulas agreed upon by Hieber. Additional consultations with the Ministry of Finance and the finance committee of the state assembly produced a definitive revision of policy in early December. The question of subsidies thereafter ceased to be a major source of contention in church-state relations.[88]

More than half a decade of negotiations thus served, ironically, to ratify a settlement based not on adjudicated claims but on "custom and goodwill."[89] Although the state assembly passed a resolution in 1925 calling anew for a definitive judicial review, the initiative proved stillborn. After further discussions with church leaders, the Education Ministry first deferred action and then in 1927 laid the prospect officially to rest with a ruling that since the government had in effect committed itself not to alter existing arrangements to the detriment of the church, no practical reason for litigation existed.[90] This was the context in which the final readjustment in postwar church-state relations

[88] "Aufschrieb über eine Besprechung zwischen Angehörigen der Bürgerpartei und dem Herrn Staatspräsidenten Bazille am 13. November 1924," OKR/AR Gen. 103/I; *SAfW*, Dec. 2, 1924.

[89] Thus Bälz to Finanzministerium Thüringen, Apr. 9, 1925 (copy), OKR/AR Gen. 103/I.

[90] Landtag, *Verhandlungen* (1925), p. 1577. Bälz to OKR, Oct. 9, 1925, and Bazille to OKR, Feb. 16, 1927, both in OKR/AR Gen. 103/II. Geier, "Staatsleistungen," pp. 114–50.

took place. In 1928, nearly a decade after the November Revolution, formal administrative control of the Tübingen Stift and preparatory seminaries passed from the state to the church; Tübingen's theological faculty, however, remained a part of the university and hence subject to the directives of the Education Ministry.[91]

Prospects for a new era of good feeling in church-state relations increased considerably during the economic Indian summer of the mid-1920s. Stable and growing revenues from church taxes helped keep the actual level of state subsidies below 70 percent of the total church budget, rather than the 80 percent churchmen had earlier considered essential. Between 1924 and 1930, a period in which gross tax revenues grew 75 percent, subsidies actually declined slightly as a proportion of the budget.[92] This, combined with the prospect of an expansionary economy, encouraged even the perennially cautious Finance Ministry to accede to more generous outlays for clergy salaries and benefits. Total appropriations for pensions more than doubled during the same period. In 1928, moreover, the state authorized a modest increase in the number of positions carrying "enhanced" salaries, thereby making a further token gesture towards churchmen's conception of parity between clergy and civil servants.

As a symbolic issue, parity was never far from the surface in any discussion of finances. The Oberkirchenrat's own figures showed that whereas roughly 85 percent of all pastors remained in the lowest salary classification throughout their careers, 48 percent of teachers and perhaps 40 percent of district administrators could expect promotion into a higher category.[93] Significant

[91] *SAfW*, Mar. 5, 6, 1928; *SM*, Mar. 5, 6, 1928.

[92] The distribution of revenue in 1924 was: church taxes 2,225,000 M (26.0%), subsidies 5,927,060 M (69.5%), other 385,740 M (4.5%); for 1931 the corresponding figures were: taxes 3,900,000 M (28.9%), subsidies 8,972,100 M (66.4%), other 641,200 M (4.7%). LKV, *Verhandlungen* (1924), Beilageband p. 8; Landtag, *Verhandlungen* (1932), Beilageband p. 36. In 1927 subsidies unexpectedly fell short of costs, forcing the church to draw from its working capital to balance the budget; cf. 1. LKT, *Verhandlungen* (1927), p. 302.

[93] "Gruppeneinteilung der höheren Beamten nach dem Staatshaushaltsplan," tables and notes, Sept. 14, 1925, OKR/AR Gen. 426/I.

relief on this point did not appear possible. Meeting with the Pfarrverein advisory committee in 1925, church president Johannes Merz declared that where demands on the public treasury were concerned the Oberkirchenrat found itself at the "end of the road."[94] When the 1926 revision of civil service salaries contained no improvement for pastors, the Pfarrverein revived its earlier plans for a lobbying effort outside ecclesiastical channels. With the aid of sympathetic civil servants, pastors launched a campaign aimed initially at more than doubling the number of higher-salaried positions, from the existing 140 to 300.[95] By the spring of 1928, these efforts began to show promise of bearing fruit. With still further civil service revisions in prospect, the Education Ministry signaled an intent to provide modest increases in church subsidies, on the basis of which the Oberkirchenrat would be able to expand to slightly over 250 the roster of favored positions. Coupled with a more flexible approach to allocation, these improvements went far towards defusing resentments among rank-and-file clergy. Indeed, in purely statistical terms pastors enjoyed marginally more favorable professional status a decade after the November Revolution than they had in the decade before the monarchy's collapse.[96]

[94] EPW, Ausserordentliche Vertrauensmännerversammlung, Dec. 9, 1925, Protokollbuch II, LKA D/EPW 22; Pfarrerbeiratssitzung, May 8, Sept. 21, 1925, Protokolle, LKA D/EPW 21.

[95] *Amtsblatt* 22 (1926): 1–8. Reichsverband höherer Beamten to Finanzministerium Stuttgart, Oct. 1927 (copy); Kübel to Schnaufer, Oct. 24, 1927; Dekanat Langenburg to EPW Vorstand, Nov. 18, 1927; Umfrid to Schnaufer, Nov. 7, 1927; Schnaufer to Umfrid, Nov. 21, 1927; Wagner to Schnaufer, Nov. 21, 1927; Weller to Schnaufer, Nov. 22, 1927; and Schnitzer to Schnaufer, Apr. 21, 1928; all in LKA D/EPW 31.

[96] Hermann Müller, memorandum, Apr. 4, 1928, OKR/AR Gen. 426/II; EPW, Vertrauensmännerversammlung, Apr. 10, 1928, Protokollbuch II, LKA D/EPW 22; *Regierungsblatt* (1928), pp. 53–91; "Pfarrbesoldungsordnung von 1928," notes of Dec. 21, 1928, OKR/AR Gen. 427/I; *Amtsblatt* 23 (1928), Beiblatt, pp. 1–8. Besides positions that automatically carried higher salaries, the new policy designated a special category of positions, largely in rural areas, that would qualify pastors for promotion after a specified period of service. The Oberkirchenrat also reserved a number of "enhanced" salaries for discretionary allocation. Cf. 1. LKT, *Verhandlungen* (1928), p. 422.

During assembly debate on the 1928 budget, SPD leader Wilhelm Keil found occasion to reflect upon his party's church policies, and in so doing he appealed to principles that, with local variations, served to describe the pattern of church-state relations throughout Germany after the war. Social Democrats, Keil declared, had always advocated the separation of church and state. Separation, however, could not be understood "in the sense that the state denies any obligation to the church whatsoever"; historic commitments must be recognized and honored.[97] This approach found expression both in the Weimar constitution and in subsequent implementing legislation. Despite the initial sound and fury of 1918, the issue of the church's place and prerogatives was a matter of means more than ends, of technical niceties more than basic principles. The changes embodied in the Weimar settlement did little other than confirm long-term trends evident across much of Germany, including Württemberg, all of which pointed toward a clearer institutional demarcation between church and state without prejudice to the church's privileged semiofficial status. One significant if predictable consequence for the Weimar era was that many of the traditions of establishment survived formal separation of church and state. The November Revolution threw up no effective structural barriers to churchmen's self-ascribed role as pillars of public order, and however firmly their heartstrings may have bound them to the old monarchy, their purse strings bound them no less firmly to the new republic.

But if formal changes were slight, the church's institutional status nevertheless underwent a significant shift in character after 1918. Though churchmen may still have regarded themselves as exemplars of proper social order, the monarchy's collapse removed both the source and the chief integrative symbol of their putative hegemony. The ramifications of this change remain to be explored in subsequent chapters. Here it is only necessary to suggest again that, as ongoing financial negotiations demonstrated, the November Revolution encouraged the

[97] Landtag, *Verhandlungen* (1928), p. 5267.

church's transformation into a type of privileged cultural interest group, exploiting bureaucratic alliances and political connections to press its claims on the state and buttress its position in an increasingly pluralistic public arena. Like the formal separation of church and state, this transformation was a gradual process, and at least in Württemberg it was one little affected by ideology. As we have seen, it was precisely the most committed republicans who acted as loyal guarantors of continuity in local church-state relations after 1918, and it was precisely the most vocally Protestant conservatives who by their policies under Wilhelm Bazille confirmed the church's client status where financial arrangements were concerned. These arrangements bespoke the church's more general institutional situation, which benefited from but also was contingent upon the force of custom and goodwill. If disestablishment was a monument to continuity, it also confirmed the peculiar ambiguity of the church's position. Like other Protestant territorial churches, the church in Württemberg emerged from the November Revolution neither truly public nor truly private, consigned by choice and circumstance to an institutional twilight zone between state and society—a state with which it could only partially identify and a society it could only partially control.

THREE

Democracy and the Limits of Church Reform

ELATIONS WITH THE STATE after 1918 bore witness to an inherent duality in churchmen's institutional orientation, a duality that distinguished them from most other vocational and interest groups as well as from the civil and military officialdom to which they have often been compared. To a significant extent the church remained both *Anstalt* and *Verein*, both "pastors' church" and "people's church," both public bureaucracy and voluntary association. Before the November Revolution, precedent and practice had strongly favored the bureaucratic orientation. Yet the church was also held to be in some sense a lay enterprise, grounded in the authentic Lutheran principle of a priesthood of all believers. This latent democratic impulse found ample secular encouragement during the revolutions of 1848, and in the years that followed, many territorial churches, including that in Württemberg, moved to establish church synods, a species of indirectly elected representative assembly open to laity as well as clergy, which provided at least a symbolic counterbalance to consistorial authority. Seventy years later, revolution again created pressures for ecclesiastical reform. Just as separation of throne and altar cast doubt on the church's institutional role as pillar of monarchical order, the upsurge of republicanism brought new calls for a more lay-oriented church polity. The collapse of the monarchy therefore revived a fundamental question of ecclesiastical order: did the church's authority as an institution inhere in its bureaucratic structure, via some Lutheran species of apostolic succession, or was it properly and ultimately vested in its membership, both individual and collective?[1]

In the aftermath of the November Revolution, nearly every territorial church made some provision for greater lay involvement and an expanded role for representative institutions. The nature and extent of this internal democratization is a matter of debate. While some commentators point to a genuine shift in favor of lay representation and synodical power, contemporary critics as well as many subsequent scholars have charged that church leaders failed to grapple seriously enough with the challenge of democracy. Despite initial enthusiasm for reform, a common argument goes, the churches remained preserves of authoritarianism, providing little scope or incentive for genuine lay initiative. Not only did individual churchmen espouse antirepublican sentiments but the structure of church life provided few opportunities for members to assimilate those virtues of citizenship—active participation, sense of personal responsibility, tolerance for diversity—held conducive to a healthy democratic polity. Nor did Protestants have any ready vehicle for mediating hierarchicalism and parliamentarism such as the Catholic church possessed in the Center party. Hence, it has been contended, both clerical attitudes and the shape of the prevailing ecclesiastical order militated against democratic political values and, by extension, Weimar's fragile republican consensus.[2]

While this argument has much to commend it, it nevertheless requires certain qualifications. Specifically, it is important to

---

[1] For a conservative statement of the issue, see Johannes Schneider, "Verfassungsfragen: Allgemeines und Grundsätzliches," *KJ 1921*, pp. 372–91; cf. the compilation of documents in Greschat, ed., *Deutsche Protestantismus im Revolutionsjahr 1918/19*, pp. 146–85.

[2] Helmreich, *German Churches under Hitler*, pp. 68–69, stresses increased lay power. For the general view, see Mehnert, *Kirche und Politik*; Nowak, *Kirche und Republik*, pp. 17–71; Bredendiek, *Zwischen Revolution und Restauration*; Jacobs, "Kirche, Weltanschauung, Politik"; Jacke, *Kirche zwischen Monarchie und Republik*; Karl-Wilhelm Dahm, "German Protestantism and Politics, 1918–1939," *Journal of Contemporary History* 3 (1968): 29–49; and, more generally, Fischer, "Protestantismus und Politik im 19. Jahrhundert," and Eckstein, *Theory of Stable Democracy*.

consider the extent to which it is possible to identify ecclesiastical structures with political behavior and to draw consequences for the fate of the republic from the fate of ecclesiastical democracy. In a pluralistic society, democracy typically connotes not only equal access to participation but also some institutionalization of conflict, through elections, parliamentary debates, and the like.[3] But while ecclesiastical democracy obviously implies some lay exercise of authority, the ideal of the Volkskirche aimed not at the institutionalization of conflict but at its mitigation, not at majority rule but at harmony and fellowship. Furthermore, the nominal attachment of most Protestants to the church meant that in practice the vitality of any church polity depended not simply on its formal structures and procedures but also on the readiness of the laity to exploit them. Without mass participation, formal provisions for democracy would be of little avail.

A further complication arose out of the elective affinity between structural and confessional issues in the church. For at least some liberals, structural democracy should naturally go hand in hand with a democracy of doctrine; toleration of diversity was to be regarded as the hallmark of a healthy Volkskirche and a necessary precondition for expanded lay participation. To theological conservatives, however, such a notion betokened craven surrender to the relativism of the age and, worse, the abandonment of that firm dogmatic basis that alone could give the church identity and purpose. If a liberal party of movement was prepared to relax confessional discipline in the name of Protestant freedom, an orthodox party of order was equally determined to reassert it in the name of ecclesiastical integrity.

Where the church was concerned, therefore, the question of democracy carried both political and pastoral overtones. If the immediate issue was one of power and authority, the relationship between Pfarrkirche and Volkskirche, this could not easily be separated from such pastoral concerns as the relationship be-

[3] The locus classicus on this point remains Ralf Dahrendorf, *Society and Democracy in Germany* (1967; reprint, Garden City, N.Y., 1969), pp. 129–41.

tween active and nominal church membership or the relationship between freedom of conscience and faithfulness of confession. These issues in turn bore directly on the problem of
churchmen's status and vocation. Should pastors regard themselves as servants of the new order or witnesses to the old? Were
they agents of an active laity or shepherds of a passive and dependent flock? Conditions in Württemberg provided ample
scope for all of these options to come into play. The church possessed not only a strong tradition of consistorial government but
also a healthy potential for lay activism, both liberal-populist
and pietist, while the grass-roots strength of the latter movement
ensured that theological considerations would loom large in any
discussion of church reform. Hence, the search for a new church
polity in Württemberg provides insight into both the possibilities and the limits of ecclesiastical reform after 1918. In charting
these developments our concern will be essentially twofold: to
determine the extent to which the experience of political upheaval influenced efforts to reconstruct the church, and to determine whether the resulting church polity served in practice to
foster achievement of such pastoral ideals as active participation
and doctrinal harmony.

The Impact of Revolution

There can be little doubt that in the immediate aftermath of the
November Revolution, secular developments provided the chief
impetus to ecclesiastical reform. With republicanism in the ascendancy, it was hardly difficult to draw appropriate conclusions
for church life. Indeed, even before the end of November 1918,
the Consistory had drawn up and circulated to all Dekans a set of
"Theses on Ecclesiastical Reorganization," which assumed an
expanded role for the laity in church government. The most significant of the proposed changes involved the church synod,
which was recast as a full-fledged legislative body elected directly
by the entire adult church membership, both male and female.
At least by implication, such an assembly would shift the basic

locus of ecclesiastical authority from the administrative heirarchy to the Protestant populace as a whole.[4]

It is noteworthy that this proposal originated with the church leadership. Unlike Prussia, for example, where questions of church organization became the object of complex political and ecclesiastical power struggles,[5] virtually all leaders of the Württemberg church shared some appreciation for parliamentary models. The impact of the revolution was evident in a Pfarrverein resolution of November 22, 1918, which endorsed the expansion of lay influence in church life as appropriate to the spirit of the republican order.[6] In "The Church and the New Age," a programmatic essay written in early 1919, Jakob Schoell, recently appointed prelate for Reutlingen and the Consistory's most influential liberal member, tied the cause of democratization firmly to the church's historic concern for a Christian state. The new age of republicanism, Schoell argued, called for a broadly based church that could afford everyone a "sense of belonging" that transcended class and political interests. In a nation shaken by defeat and domestic turmoil, fragmented into warring economic and ideological camps, the church had a unique responsibility to "preserve and manifest as much as possible the [underlying] spiritual unity of [a] divided people." A democratic church, in short, should serve to mitigate the divisive tendencies of a democratic state.[7]

Forming a dissonant counterpoint to the theme sounded by Schoell, one finds statements of the sort contained in a parish report from the tiny Jura village of Hausen. Ernst Schreiber, the town's pastor since 1908, returned from military service and internment in a French prison camp to find subtle changes in parish life. "The great upheavals of recent years have left their

[4] *Leitsätze zur kirchlichen Neugestaltung* (Stuttgart, 1918); cf. Voelter, "Revolution von 1918," p. 311.

[5] For conflicting interpretations, see Jacke, *Kirche zwischen Monarchie und Republik*, pp. 246–303; Gordon, "Evangelical Churches and Weimar Republic," pp. 91–154; and Borg, *Old-Prussian Church*, pp. 97–110.

[6] *SM*, Nov. 22, 1918.

[7] "Die Kirche und die neue Zeit," *MfPT* 15 (1918–19): 295.

traces in even the smallest and remotest village," he reported. If parishioners still made an outward show of deference to their pastor, this traditional behavior masked a "much freer attitude than formerly" about church matters. Not a few in the village equated the church so closely with the monarchy that they seemed to have written off one with the other. Declared Schreiber: "The nimbus of the church is gone."[8]

On what basis could the church serve as a force for social integration if in even the smallest and remotest village its nimbus had so seriously faded? While not always directly addressed, this question underlay virtually every discussion of ecclesiastical reform. Such discussions were frequent during the early months of the republic, especially between late 1918 and mid-1920, when the Württemberg synod, now called the Church Assembly (Landeskirchenversammlung), was engaged in the task of drawing up a new church constitution. On January 20, 1919, in what one account described as the "last act of the old . . . order,"[9] the former synod ratified a consistorial decree setting June 1 as the date for elections to a constitutional assembly. By this time a rough consensus already existed on the outlines of a future church order, a consensus extending from the Consistory itself to those liberal factions among the clergy and laity pressing for what one manifesto of the period called the "elimination of all bureaucratic fetters" from Protestant church life.[10] Basic to this consensus was the affirmation of a greater role for laity in church government and the assumption that a popularly elected assembly would fulfill such a role.

From the perspective of the hierarchy, reform implied primarily the reconsolidation of existing structures on a more explicit mass basis. To some extent, no doubt, this was a tactical commitment, part of the larger mobilization of friendly forces in defense of Evangelical interests at a time when the church's future legal and financial status remained obscure. Consistory presi-

---

[8] Hausen ob Lontal, Pfarrbericht 1920, LKA A29/1842; cf. *Magisterbuch* (1932), p. 143.

[9] *SM*, Feb. 2, 1919.

[10] *CW* 32 (1918): 487.

dent Hermann von Zeller confidentially assured his counterpart in the Baden church that despite plans for a more active church assembly, the Consistory fully expected to retain ultimate authority, particularly in the absence of a definitive settlement with the state. Pending such a settlement, an elected assembly, acting on behalf of the mass of loyal church members, might help to dissuade the provisional government from attempting to tread heavily on ecclesiastical prerogatives.[11]

However defensive its motives, the Consistory was prepared to take comparatively bold steps to implement them. The existing synod, like those in most of the German churches, had been indirectly elected, with representatives chosen at the district level by members of local parish councils. While as a rule the latter were directly elected, candidates tended to be self-selected, and the franchise was restricted to adult males. The result was typically an assembly of Protestant notables, dominated by the upper ranks of the clergy, the academic bourgeoisie, the large commercial interests, and the landed gentry. For the new assembly, however, the Consistory proposed that election be both direct and based on universal suffrage. All church members over the age of twenty-five, including women, would be eligible to vote; anyone over thirty could stand as a candidate. To guarantee lay influence, less than one-third of the seats would be reserved for clergy, with each voter choosing one lay and one clerical candidate. For this purpose the state was divided into separate local electoral districts, the boundaries of which corresponded for the most part to those of the forty-nine church districts. Except for the larger urban districts, each electoral district was to be represented by one assembly delegate. Parishioners in Stuttgart would elect four representatives, those in Cannstatt, Heilbronn, and Ludwigsburg, two each.[12]

Publication of this electoral decree provoked surprise outside Württemberg. Conservative-minded churchmen objected that since the great majority of the left's supporters, with their pre-

[11] Zeller to Vibel, Feb. 12, 1919, LKA A26/322.
[12] *SM*, Jan. 21, 22, 23, 1919.

sumed anticlerical prejudices, still maintained nominal church membership, an open franchise of the sort proposed in Württemberg might become a constitutional Trojan horse. In the era of Spartacism it was easy enough for nervous conservatives, especially in politically turbulent regions, to conjure up the specter of hostile socialists and communists exploiting their ecclesiastical franchise by the thousands, dispatching to the assembly a corps of delegates pledged to the disruption if not the outright destruction of church structures. Few other territorial churches in fact chose to follow Stuttgart's lead where election procedures were concerned. As late as 1921, when all threat of a cultural revolution had evaporated, Prussian church leaders still felt constrained by pressure from conservatives to employ a system of indirect election designed to thwart participation by the unchurched masses.[13] In Württemberg, where anticlerical agitation had never been particularly effective even in socialist strongholds, church leaders had no such fears. The Consistory correctly calculated that those willing to make use of their franchise rights would be those actively loyal to the church. Moderation seemed further guaranteed by the democratic gesture of extending the franchise to women. "In church life, women are often more knowledgeable and actively committed than the men," wrote Zeller in mid-February, adding frankly that he expected female voters to exercise the same conservative influence in church politics that had already manifested itself in the secular political arena.[14]

From this it might easily be concluded, as some critics at the time charged, that the proposed changes in church order were largely cosmetic, the self-protective maneuvers of a church leadership little interested in promoting genuine ecclesiastical democracy.[15] During the early months of 1919, however, this program provided many points of departure for the broader aims of the church's social-liberal wing, which, with its spokesman Ja-

[13] On the Prussian electoral system, see Borg, *Old-Prussian Church*, pp. 11–12, 99–111. See also Jacke, *Kirche zwischen Monarchie und Republik*, pp. 246–47, and Gordon, "Evangelical Churches and Weimar Republic," pp. 250–54.

[14] See note 11, above.

[15] *SM*, Feb. 12, 1919.

kob Schoell, was prepared to hail an expanded synodical assembly as the centerpiece of a more participatory structure of church government.

For Schoell and his allies, both pragmatism and principle dictated an opening to the people. Expanded lay responsibility, it was hoped, would lead to greater ecclesiastical vitality, while a vigorous and healthy parish life would in turn strengthen the church's claim to social significance. To lay the groundwork for democracy, liberals looked hopefully to a new lay organization, the Evangelischer Volksbund (Evangelical People's League), founded in early 1919. The Württemberg Volksbund was one of many such groups that sprang up throughout Germany during this period to form a short-lived national federation under the aegis of August Hinderer's Evangelical Press Association.[16] Patrons of the Württemberg effort included Schoell; the former Württemberg court preacher Konrad Hoffman; a number of liberal diocesan officials, including Stuttgart Dekan Theodor Traub and Weikersheim Dekan Adolf Dörrfuss; and Hermann Ströle, director of the Evangelical Press Association in Stuttgart. The board of directors included a fair sampling of local Protestant notables, including a prominent member of the petty nobility, Prince Ernst zu Hohenlohe-Langenberg, long a stalwart liberal in church politics.[17] Professedly nonpartisan both in politics and theology, the Volksbund sought to implement the twin ideals of unity and reform in parish life. It would also, not incidentally, function as a permanent pressure group for "religious principles" and the church's interests over against the state. "Of course we want the masses," wrote Schoell in defense of the new league. "The Evangelical church will carry exactly as much weight in public life as it has people behind it."[18]

[16] On the Volkskirche movement generally, see Borg, *Old-Prussian Church*, pp. 72–73, and Gordon, "Evangelical Churches and Weimar Republic," pp. 91ff.

[17] EVB, *Mitteilungen* 1 (June 1919): 2–3; Weitbrecht and Daur, *Weg und Aufgabe eines Freien Protestantismus*, p. 9; Christian Sigel, comp., "Das evangelische Württemberg," 14 vols. in 22, typescript, copies in LKA and Württembergische Landesbibliothek, Stuttgart, 9:381–82.

[18] *Satzungen des Evang. Volksbundes für Württemberg* (copy), LKA D1/59,1; "Was will der Ev. Volksbund?" EVB, *Mitteilungen* 1 (June 1919); *SM*, Mar. 31,

At the same time, however, the architects of the Volksbund hoped that a new ecclesiastical *Sammelpartei* would accomplish what prior Evangelical-Social programs had failed to do, namely extend the boundaries of active church membership to workers and to alienated segments of the middle class. Speaking at an organizational rally for the Volksbund in Stuttgart, the veteran Protestant labor organizer August Springer challenged church authorities to take a strong official stand against social inequities and to defend the concerns of the laboring man. Jakob Schoell, who shared the platform with Springer, picked up this rhetorical gauntlet. Lay responsibility, he declared, was the necessary link between church life and the new political order. Just as the individual was now to exercise a greater voice in affairs of state, so too must he be given a greater voice in the church. The church must take cognizance of its members' needs, particularly those of workers, which had been too often ignored. Individual participation, however, was central; democracy consisted in the first instance of opportunities for participation. By encouraging such participation, the Volksbund proposed to play a vital role in church renewal, mediating between traditional church structures and marginal parishioners while providing opportunities for all social groups to meet on a common ground of ethical and religious concern. An effective mass movement for the laity, in short, would not only underscore the church's claims to power but would also work as a solvent to economic, social, and ideological barriers.[19] In its first months of existence, the Volksbund gave genuine promise of becoming a force of movement in church life, offering a rallying point for lay energies and a well-oiled propaganda machine useful both to reformers and to the church leadership. By the end of 1919, two-thirds of all Württemberg parishes had local chapters; total Volksbund membership already far outstripped that of any other church organization.[20]

1919; Jakob Schoell, "Die Bedenken gegen den evang. Volksbund," *KAfW* 28 (1919): 140.

[19] *SM*, May 2, 1919.

[20] Richard Lempp, "Kirchenaustritt zur Religionslosigkeit in Württemberg 1920," typescript, LKA A26/409.

Unfortunately for liberal aspirations, increased lay participation did not necessarily promote a common sense of purpose. On the contrary, it emphasized traditional divisions, notably that between theological liberals and those on the church's orthodox-pietist wing. Theological tensions ran high in the weeks before church elections on June 1, 1919. "As soon as the future of the church was at issue, passions exploded," recalled one candidate, Hans Voelter.[21] If liberals like Voelter took the offensive in hopes of achieving a more pluralistic church polity, one allowing for greater lay initiative and responsibility, not a few conservatives saw this as a blueprint for weakening the church's confessional identity. Both liberals and conservatives established rudimentary campaign organizations, with a coalition of pietist groups arrayed against an Electoral Committee for a Free Volkskirche. Secular issues likewise encouraged the spirit of factionalism. Given the church's continuing prominence in the constitutional debates of the period, it is not surprising that competing Protestant-oriented parties, especially the DDP and the Bürgerpartei, should seek to turn church elections to their own tactical advantage. While party tactics hardly overshadowed the more basic theological and church-order debates, they nevertheless threatened an unprecedented politicization of church affairs in which an informal amalgam of political and ecclesiastical democrats became pitted against the combined forces of the political and theological right.

The prospect of party strife within the church evoked varied responses. Sometimes churchmen and political functionaries sought to forestall open confrontation by reaching a prior consensus on assembly nominees. This occurred, for example, in the electoral district of Blaufelden, where all factions were able to agree upon the candidacy of Gottlob Egelhaaf, the DVP delegate in the Württemberg Landtag, who had served in several previous church synods to the general satisfaction of theological liberals and conservatives alike. The aging Egelhaaf consented to stand again on condition that the several political parties pledge in ad-

---

[21] Voelter, "Revolution von 1918," p. 313.

111

vance that they would not seek to "adulterate" the election process in any way.[22]

Once political interests became involved, however, "adulteration" proved harder to avoid. In the district of Aalen, the executive committee of the DDP voted in April to nominate a candidate who would stand for "appropriate" liberal reforms in church life and for greater cooperation between the church and the republic. The committee circularized every party member in the diocese urging active support for its nominee.[23] Conservatives seized upon the Aalen initiative to launch a strong counterprotest against "open meddling of political parties in the election," and while church liberals indignantly dismissed any implication that they were mere puppets of outside forces,[24] the conservative propaganda offensive nevertheless left them on the defensive in areas where they might have been expected to fare best. Such was the case in Stuttgart, the largest electoral district, where early efforts to reach a Blaufelden-style consensus collapsed and competing liberal and conservative slates appeared. Most of the liberal nominees could be identified in some way with the DDP, though their supporters would later feel obliged to contend that "the party as such neither drew up the list nor put its organization at the disposal of the candidates."[25] In both Stuttgart and Aalen, the June election brought a crushing defeat for the liberals. Their candidate in Aalen received less than 15 percent of the votes cast, while to the surprise of most observers the pietist-conservative slate swept all four lay seats contested in Stuttgart. The outcome was no different in Maulbronn, to the north of Stuttgart, where local Democrats campaigned openly but to no avail for their preferred candidate.[26]

Indeed, where political and ecclesiastical interests became entangled, it was invariably the "tacit alliance of ecclesiastical and

[22] Egelhaaf, *Lebens-Erinnerungen*, p. 141.

[23] Copy of statement in LKA D1/13,1.

[24] "Die Kirchenwahl und ihre etwaigen Folgen," *SM*, June 17, 1919.

[25] "Ein Wort zu den Wahlen zur Landeskirchenversammlung," *SM*, June 6, 1919.

[26] Knittlingen, Pfarrbericht 1919, LKA A29/2369.

political rightists," in Voelter's words, that carried the day.[27] If open collaboration seldom occurred, this may have been because the social boundaries of the active parish so often corresponded with those of the Bürgerpartei or Bauernbund. While liberal and populist sympathies no doubt remained stronger in Württemberg than in German Protestantism as a whole, they were scarcely strong enough to overcome the historic equation of theological orthodoxy and political conservatism represented by the Bürgerpartei. Nor did this alliance seem out of order to those who benefited from it. The same writer who declared that "the constitution . . . of the Evangelical church is no concern of the Democratic party as such" could justify the widespread involvement of Bürgerpartei notables in many electoral districts with the bland claim that "individual members [of the Bürgerpartei], including those in positions of leadership, [have] a perfect right . . . to stand up for their convictions."[28] Whether tacit or open, the conservative coalition generally proved both better drilled and more effective than liberals in exploiting campaign opportunities. Shrewd tactics proved decisive, for example, in the conservative sweep in Stuttgart. There the conservative election committee published a list of its nominees in the form of a sample ballot, copies of which were circulated to all eligible Protestant voters in the city. Many parishioners reportedly appeared at polling places on June 1 carrying these "ballots," mistakenly assuming them to be the official forms. Surprised and outflanked, Stuttgart liberals found themselves defeated by an almost two-to-one margin in what should have been one of their strongholds.[29]

If orthodoxy militant borrowed its strategy and tactics from the political right, it found both mass support and ideological appeals in a resurgent pietism. After a generation of comparative quiescence as the "quiet ones in the land," Württemberg pietists responded to the shocks of 1918 by pressing vigorously for their

[27] Voelter, "Revolution von 1918," p. 313.
[28] SM, June 17, 1919.
[29] SM, June 6, 1919.

cherished vision of the church, and it was this revived activism, more than any other single factor, that determined the subsequent balance of power in church politics. The principal commander of the orthodox forces was Christian Römer, a former Dekan in the pietist stronghold of Nagold, who by 1919 had risen to become titular prelate and senior pastor at Stuttgart's historic Stiftskirche. If Jakob Schoell's name became synonymous with the liberal vision of a socially and theologically inclusive Protestant community, Römer was his counterpart on the conservative wing, an eloquent and tireless apologist for biblicism, creedal orthodoxy, and a personalistic evangelistic ethic. While deeply committed to Württemberg's consistorial traditions of church government, Römer was far from unsympathetic to the idea of an expanded role for the laity. German pietism as a whole always had a distinctly lay character, and in this Württemberg was no exception. Nevertheless, Römer's conviction that doctrinal integrity constituted the essence of a vital church made him profoundly suspicious of the wider implications of liberal reform. A policy of ecclesiastical *Sammlung*, he argued, would exaggerate rather than repair "inner flaws" of indifference and stagnation in church life, flaws he blamed squarely on past compromises with modernism over biblical interpretation and the status of received Lutheran doctrine.[30]

For those who shared these convictions, the church elections naturally became a crusade in defense of orthodoxy. Römer and other pietist leaders, notably Ludwigsburg Dekan Samuel Gauger, Stuttgart pastor and publicist Christian Kohler, and Friedrich Lutz, a director of Inner Mission programs in Württemberg, launched a coordinated campaign to rouse followers and organize them into an effective voting bloc. Open letters and articles in the pietist press urged support for candidates who took a stand "on the basis of the biblical gospel," while warning the rank and file to "distrust all the fine words and promises made by the other side."[31] Not all pietists, to be sure, automatically

[30] *EKBfW* 80 (1919): 31–32; Lehmann, *Pietismus*, pp. 298–300.

[31] Thus Friedrich Lutz in a circular to individual chapters of the Württemberg Old Pietist Federation, copy in LKA D1/14.

heeded such injunctions, at least where they ran counter to local deference patterns. In Bietigheim, two local pietist societies took out advertisements declaring their support for the candidacy of the local pastor, Hans Voelter, one of the most outspoken democrats among the Württemberg clergy and an uncompromising advocate of liberal positions. Voelter probably owed his narrow victory to this gesture, since elsewhere in the district his conservative opponent won a clear if modest majority.[32] In Reutlingen, a district with a strong pietist presence, Jakob Schoell was able to run unopposed, theological scruples apparently taking second place to Schoell's personal popularity and to the understandable reluctance of potential opponents to challenge a prelate in his home territory.[33] In most areas, however, pietist involvement worked heavily to the benefit of the orthodox-conservative front. Of some eighty-two delegates elected on June 1, a clear majority of forty-three affiliated with Römer's conservative faction, which by common consent identified itself thereafter as Group I. The liberals around Schoell, designated as Group II, elected thirty-seven of their number; two delegates—including Stuttgart Dekan Theodor Traub, otherwise an Evangelical-Social stalwart—remained officially independent of both camps.[34] That pietism was a decisive factor in the outcome few disputed. As one liberal commented, the election showed that pietism was "no longer the modest little plant in the church's garden which it has usually been considered, but rather the tree which overshadows the whole."[35]

For some months the significance of the June election for church life remained a matter of debate. Critics pointed to a number of weaknesses in organization and procedure, which, it was argued, distorted the voting process and rendered its results

[32] Voelter won by a mere 33 votes out of some 13,500 cast; cf. clippings and handwritten compilation of votes in LKA D1/14–15; also Lehmann, *Pietismus*, p. 301.

[33] Wurm to Merz, Jan. 11, 1925, LKA D1/8,1.

[34] "Ergebnisse der Wahlen zur Landeskirchenversammlung vom 1. Juni 1919," lkv, *Verhandlungen* (1919), Beilageband pp. 95–99, copy in LKA A26/ 356, with penciled notations of group affiliations.

[35] *SM*, June 6, 1919.

suspect. Many in both theological camps agreed that too many parishioners had cast ballots without an adequate understanding of the issues or personalities involved. Confusion over procedures, as in Stuttgart, compounded the problem. In two districts, Ravensburg and Weikersheim, irregularities forced a repetition of balloting.[36] Some critics objected that conservative preferences were indiscriminate, sweeping into office a number of wholly inexperienced delegates at the expense of others whose expertise the assembly would require, most notably Arthur Schmidt, a Tübingen professor of church law who, together with his colleague Paul Wurster, had been commissioned by the Consistory to draft a new church constitution.[37] Liberals were inclined to question whether the theological balance in the new assembly adequately reflected attitudes in the church at large. Except perhaps for Stuttgart, however, results followed a fairly predictable pattern. Most of those identified with Group II came from such traditional strongholds of Protestant liberalism as Heilbronn and Ulm or from districts dominated by newer industrial towns like Göppingen and Tuttlingen. Areas with heavy pietist concentrations, on the other hand, generally returned conservatives, often with large electoral majorities.

In both numbers and enthusiasm, the election represented the high-watermark of lay mobilization in Württemberg after the war and hence a fair index of the potential for active participation in church life. A self-described liberal layman writing in the *Schwäbischer Merkur* correctly noted that the results confirmed two basic hypotheses about the Protestant community: "First, that . . . the indifferent and those alienated from the church would not participate in the election; second, that within the circle of interested voters the pietist societies were the only organizations sufficiently broad-based and reliable [to stimulate heavy participation]."[38] Throughout Württemberg, slightly less than

[36] LKV, *Verhandlungen* (1919), Beilageband pp. 98–99. In both cases the second ballot confirmed the results of the first.

[37] "Die Landeskirchenversammlung," *SM*, June 11, 1919; cf. Voelter, "Revolution von 1918," p. 315.

[38] "Noch ein Wort zu den Kirchenwahlen," *SM*, June 20, 1919.

42 percent of those eligible to take part actually cast ballots. While sometimes dismissed as disappointingly low,[39] this figure seems in fact remarkably healthy when compared both to earlier Württemberg church elections and to those in other German churches after 1918. In the city of Stuttgart, to take one example, 32.5 percent of eligible voters participated in 1919. To be sure, this was substantially below the statewide average and doubtless a major reason why the city's well-disciplined pietist minority was able to influence the outcome there so dramatically.[40] In Stuttgart's last prewar parish council elections, by contrast, a mere 12 percent of those eligible had voted, and while the comparable figure for parish elections held later in 1919 was 26.7 percent, a clear decline in participation from June, this was still more than double the prewar level.[41] If such figures show that "the indifferent and those alienated from the church" indeed shunned participation, they also suggest that the multiple crises of 1918–19 stimulated most Protestants with at least a modicum of interest in church life to take part.

A principal explanation for the contrast with prewar figures was certainly the extension of franchise rights to women, whose high level of interest in religious life was proverbial if not always easily quantified. On the whole, as might be expected, participation was lowest in urban areas, sinking to 29.6 percent in heavily working-class Cannstatt. At the other end of the spectrum, nearly one-third of all electoral districts—sixteen of forty-nine—recorded participation above 50 percent, with highs of 65 percent in Crailsheim and 64.5 percent in Münsingen. Few raw figures survive, but those that do indicate that in a number of rural and small-town parishes more than 80 percent of those eligible took part.[42] The figures for Württemberg as a whole are particularly striking when compared with those in other

---

[39] Hermelink, *Geschichte der evangelischen Kirche in Württemberg*, p. 462; cf. *SM*, June 11, 1919.

[40] Lehmann, *Pietismus*, p. 301n.

[41] Theodor Traub, *Jahresbericht 1919* (Stuttgart, 1920).

[42] Wörner to Voelter, June 18, 1919, LKA D1/14,1; Werner to Voelter, n.d., LKA D1/13,1; LKV, *Verhandlungen* (1919), Beilageband, pp. 95–99.

churches. When the Prussian church, for example, held preliminary local elections for a constitutional assembly in 1921,
scarcely one eligible voter in ten took part. Under the "sieve" or
"filter" system employed in Prussia, prospective voters were required to register in advance with parish officials. Less than 25
percent of those eligible troubled to do so, and of those who registered less than half actually cast ballots.[43] Both in its procedures and in its results, the Württemberg experiment more
nearly approximated the Volkskirche ideal than did northern
Protestant strongholds—a reflection, perhaps, of the continuing
vitality of mediating institutions such as parish societies and
mission organizations, the integration of many pietist groups
into the mainstream of Württemberg church life, and the perdurance of small-town traditions of religiosity in many parts of
the land.

Moreover, despite liberal claims that the absence of a proportional voting system skewed results in favor of conservatives,[44]
it may well have been the liberals who benefited most from the
system of single-member districts. Allowing for a considerable
margin of error, it seems likely that a strictly proportional system would have left liberals with, if anything, one or two fewer
seats than they in fact won.[45] Single-member districts also
worked to the liberals' benefit in other ways. Of the ten smallest
electoral districts, all with fewer than ten thousand eligible voters, candidates from Group II won in no less than seven. Similarly, ten of the fourteen candidates who ran unopposed were
liberals, and of these ten, four were clergymen who won in areas
that returned lay delegates from Group I. These facts suggest
that where traditions of deference operated, they tended to favor

[43] Jacke, *Kirche zwischen Monarchie und Republik*, p. 247.

[44] *SM*, June 11, 1919.

[45] Precise calculations are difficult, in part because the group affiliations of
some unsuccessful candidates cannot be determined with certainty. As nearly as
can be determined, however, Group II won some 42.7% of votes for lay candidates, 46.1% of those for clergy. Figured proportionally, this would mean 23 lay
seats rather than the 22 actually won but only 12 clergy seats instead of the 15
actually won, for a total of 35 rather than 37 seats.

liberal candidates, many of whom were either lay notables—such as Prince Ernst zu Hohenlohe-Langenburg, who in effect stood for election on his own estates—or prominent church officials, who enjoyed advantages of status and what a later generation would call name recognition. Liberals, in sum, did not fare badly in Württemberg. In Prussia, by contrast, church elections held the following year yielded an assembly overwhelmingly weighted in favor of orthodox-conservative forces.[46]

In Württemberg, no less than in Prussia, democratic procedures served not so much to expand as to confirm the boundaries of active membership. Given the prevailing conservatism of the core community, at least in matters of doctrine, the results were all but inevitable. Significantly, however, loyalty to the Volkskirche tradition kept Württemberg conservatives from exploiting their numerical advantage to run roughshod over the liberal minority. Parliaments might function according to a "politics of force," based on the power of momentary majorities, but the church's affairs must be settled through a "politics of love," based on mutual respect and understanding.[47] Conservative field marshal Christian Römer lost little time in offering an olive branch to his erstwhile adversaries. In a statement shortly after the election he expressed regret over the defeat of certain "deserving" candidates from Group II as well as the hard feelings engendered by some conservative campaign tactics, and he pledged his group to work for an assembly marked by an absence of animosity and a maximum of tolerance and respect.[48] When the assembly convened in October, one of its first official acts was to choose a prominent lay member of Group II—President Haffner of the state bureau of statistics—to serve as presiding officer. Although the two factions met regularly in separate caucuses, party discipline in the parliamentary sense was lax if not nonexistent. Gottlob Egelhaaf would later write affectionately of

---

[46] Jacke, *Kirche zwischen Monarchie und Republik*, p. 250; Borg, *Old-Prussian Church*, pp. 110–11. Of 190 seats in the Prussian church assembly, 127 went to representatives of the orthodox-conservative front.

[47] See, e.g., *Zum Neubau der Kirche* [Stuttgart, 1918].

[48] "Die evang. Kirchenwahl in Stuttgart," *SM*, June 7, 1919.

one venerable old pietist who dozed peacefully through most of the proceedings, rousing himself only to answer roll calls, when he would turn to Egelhaaf—a member of Group II—and ask, in perfect innocence, how he should vote.[49]

In part, this emphasis on fraternity arose naturally out of the assembly's social composition and methods of procedure. Despite deep theological differences, members were bound by the mediating constraints of family, school, and occupational ties. Christian Römer, for example, was a Tübingen fraternity brother of several prominent figures in Group II,[50] and as in the past, local notables of the academy and bureaucracy dominated both theological groups. The delegates' average age was slightly over fifty; only seven were younger than forty. Of clerical seats, less than half were held by ordinary parish pastors, the rest by prelates and Dekans. Civil servants and educators were heavily represented, accounting for half of all lay seats. By contrast, only three members described themselves as farmers, and factory workers were completely absent. The precise occupational composition of each theological group differed slightly, to be sure, and in ways that reflected the traditional social bases of Protestant liberalism and conservatism in Württemberg. Group II drew its members overwhelmingly from among higher academics and civil servants, together with a few entrepreneurs and free professionals. Group I, on the other hand, was made up largely of artisans, schoolmasters, and shopkeepers, as well as the odd farmer. If anything, Group I could claim to be marginally more representative of the populace at large than Group II, despite the latter's advocacy of a socially diverse church community. The differences, however, were scarcely significant. While the assembly's theological balance may have corresponded fairly accurately to that of the active churchgoing population, its social boundaries barely extended to the farmers and craftsmen likely to be found in most parish pews of a Sunday.

[49] Egelhaaf, *Lebens-Erinnerungen*, p. 143.
[50] Ibid.; cf. *BfWKG* 52 (1962): 346.

By the same token, the church's nominal members, many of them workers, went totally unrepresented.[51]

In short, church government remained largely an affair of notables, an elite of *Bildung* and *Besitz* whose shared social and cultural attitudes did more to bind them than theological convictions did to divide. More than half of the delegates had served as members of previous synods. Of the newcomers, many were pietist laymen with good intentions but little experience in church government. Most, like Gottlob Egelhaaf's somnolent neighbor, adopted a largely passive role, preferring to leave decisions to the leadership cadre in each faction. The assembly itself met infrequently; after an initial week of plenary meetings in October 1919, the full assembly recessed and did not reconvene until the following May. As a result, church officials and Stuttgart-based laymen exerted a disproportionate influence, since involvement in interim committee work posed fewer difficulties for them than for most lay delegates, who could not afford the repeated interruptions of work routines or hours of travel to the capital that committee assignments would have entailed.

Under the circumstances it is not surprising that the assembly would invest much of its collective energy in symbolic issues or that deliberations would revolve more around ramifications of doctrine than of democracy. The thorniest challenge of constitution-making, in fact, proved to be drafting a statement of the church's confessional standpoint orthodox enough to satisfy conservatives while flexible enough to accommodate liberals. In

---

[51] Occupational data compiled from election certificates in LKA A100/23; on patterns of church attendance, see Wurster, *Kirchliches Leben*, pp. 88–89. According to the occupational census of 1925 (cf. *SHW 1928*, p. 63), a full 73% of Württembergers earned their livelihoods in agriculture, industry, or crafts, while the corresponding figure for the church assembly was only 20%. Trade and commerce were somewhat overrepresented (nearly 25% of the assembly, compared to 11.6% of the general population), but the most dramatic discrepancy came in the category of "administration," which included less than 5% of the general population but over 50% of lay assembly delegates. (Since clergy would also have been included in this category, the actual discrepancy was of course much greater still.)

their working draft, Arthur Schmidt and Paul Wurster proposed a preamble stating that the Württemberg church, "thankfully mindful of its origins, stands on the foundation of the gospel as attested to in the Holy Scriptures and opened up anew . . . through the Reformation. The gospel is the inviolable basis of its labor and fellowship." Invoking by implication his own dual citizenship in the realms of pietism and liberal Protestantism, Paul Wurster was prepared to defend this formulation as one all factions could embrace without sacrifice of integrity. The church, he argued during opening plenary debate, would remain what it had always claimed to be: a Lutheran church rooted in the heritage of the Reformation. Membership implied a morally binding commitment to this heritage but not a legally binding commitment to one interpretation of that heritage. From the conservative side, Christian Römer conceded that confessional matters should not be subjected to any form of legal compulsion. At the same time, however, he warned that too great an emphasis on Protestant diversity would effectively rob the tradition of any meaningful content. He therefore appealed for a more precise delineation of Reformation heritage. Specifically, he proposed a revision that declared Luther's catechism and the summary of doctrine in the church's confirmation book to be normative for teaching and preaching. Römer's amendment, however, created unease among the members of Group II, who saw in it a veiled attempt to impose a binding theological position too narrow for liberals to accept. When Heilbronn pastor Paul Hinderer implied ulterior motives on the part of the orthodox faction, Römer responded by charging liberal theologians with systematically subverting the doctrinal standards of the younger clergy. The tone of the debate grew progressively sharper, with moderates forced to intervene repeatedly—most dramatically in a prayer for humility by Heinrich von Planck, prelate of Ulm and a member of Group II—to prevent the assembly from dissolving into uproar.[52]

[52] LKV, *Verhandlungen* (1919), pp. 30–78; Voelter, "Revolution von 1918," pp. 316–17.

In hopes of cooling passions, leaders of both groups eventually agreed to suspend debate on the preamble and refer it to a committee for further consideration. The immediate difficulty, it would appear, arose less out of the conflicting theological assumptions of the two groups than out of an unaddressed ambiguity in the conservatives' own position. Römer and his fellow conservatives held an unwavering, not to say passionate, commitment to doctrinal orthodoxy as essential to the church's health and integrity. At the same time they hoped to uphold the Volkskirche vision, with its inherent tolerance for diversity within the bounds of order. The result was a delicate problem of balance: how to advance the cause of orthodoxy without denying a basic institutional postulate of the Volkskirche. Römer himself was unable to reach a satisfactory resolution of this problem. In committee deliberations he showed himself as desirous as anyone to find a compromise formulation.[53] Publicly, however, he held fast to the defense of unbending orthodoxy. His essay *Gospel, Confession, and Church*, published in early 1920,[54] added fuel to the controversy with yet another strongly-worded attack on the liberal stance and appeals for a strict and binding adherence to historic creeds, appeals promptly echoed by many pietists in Römer's following.[55]

This battle cry for orthodoxy proved Römer's last. Only weeks after his pamphlet appeared and before assembly leaders could extricate themselves from the preamble dilemma, Römer died unexpectedly at the age of sixty-six. His mantle fell upon Eugen Reiff, pastor in Mitteltal, a small Black Forest town near Freudenstadt. By preference a pastor rather than a church politician, Reiff came to the continuing discussions with patience, a strong sense of collegiality, and the determination to achieve an edifying compromise. After various alternatives had been considered and discarded, conservatives eventually acceded to the substance of the original proposal, albeit with cosmetic changes

---

[53] Voelter, "Revolution von 1918," p. 318.

[54] *Evangelium, Bekenntnis, und Kirche* (Stuttgart, 1920).

[55] Lehmann, *Pietismus*, pp. 301–2.

in language. Led by Reiff and Stuttgart schoolmaster Friedrich Jehle, the rank and file of Group I joined liberals on May 12 in unanimously adopting this revised preamble, which declared that, "true to the heritage of the fathers," the church stood on the foundation of the "gospel of Jesus Christ, our Lord, given in the Holy Scriptures [and] attested in the confessions of the Reformation."[56] The latitude of interpretation admitted by this formulation was underscored by a further provision, incorporated into Article 22 of the final draft, stipulating that confessional matters were not subject to church legislation; a particular construal of the creeds or catechism could not be invoked to discipline churchmen holding differing views.

The debate over a preamble adumbrated similar struggles in other German churches during the early 1920s. Of these the most spectacular occurred in the Prussian church's constitutional assembly of 1921–22, where orthodox factions combined to force the adoption of a detailed, explicitly conservative formulation, thereby creating bitter divisions within the clergy, laity, and church hierarchy alike. On this point Württemberg and Prussia provide contrapuntal images of Protestant responses to the diversity evident both inside and outside active church ranks. The symbolic victory of orthodoxy in Prussia has been seen as reflecting a broader failure of progressive and democratic impulses to animate the church's dominant bureaucratic-conservative outlook, which, if anything, grew more inflexible and retrograde in reaction to republican conditions.[57] In Württemberg, with its less complex ecclesiastical structures and its deeply ingrained tradition of collegiality, such tendencies never threatened to dominate the church's stance. By reaching compromise on a preamble, the two principal factions in the church assembly were laying joint claim to the local Protestant tradition, which honored both tolerance and orthodoxy. Despite the divisions in their midst, or perhaps because of them, churchmen sought to

[56] LKV, *Verhandlungen* (1920), pp. 851–79; *Amtsblatt* 19 (1920): 199; cf. Voelter, "Revolution von 1918," pp. 317–20.

[57] Jacke, *Kirche zwischen Monarchie und Republik*, pp. 286–98.

settle on those formulations that would divide them least. As the passionate liberal Hans Voelter later stated: "Matters never reached the point where a bare majority triumphed over a strong minority. Rather, everyone transcended their differences for the great common core that all shared."[58]

The same instinct to temper parliamentarism with pastoral concern infused discussions of ecclesiastical organization. Earlier liberal enthusiasm notwithstanding, most members of the assembly showed no inclination to attempt more than superficial modifications to the existing consistorial-synodical framework, contenting themselves with a largely theoretical debate over the nature and exercise of authority in Protestant church polity. What might be called the consistorial party argued for the historic sovereignty of the summus episcopus, locating the source of ecclesiastical authority in the crown's administrative surrogate, the Consistory. In this view, authority and initiative in church affairs flowed downward from the top, through prelates and Dekans, to the local clergy, who performed a dual role as subordinates to the church leadership and paternalistic shepherds to the flock of their parishioners. Counterposed to the consistorial position was a more democratic, lay-oriented conception of church polity. The lay party could likewise appeal to Lutheran tradition, specifically to the doctrine of the priesthood of all believers. From this basis it could be argued that authority ultimately resided not in the hierarchy but in church membership as a whole, to be exercised through popular election of parish councils and the church assembly, which should exercise ultimate oversight in ecclesiastical administration. If the consistorial position held that the terms of royal abdication legitimized continued administrative primacy, the lay interpretation viewed the executive committee established in late 1918 as a symbolic representation of the entire Protestant community. From this standpoint, the end of the monarchy opened the way for the full and final establishment of a church polity achieved only embryonically in the old synodical structure, which had granted an

[58] Voelter, "Revolution von 1918," p. 320.

indirectly elected assembly consultative powers but no effective control over church affairs. Now, argued supporters of this view, the Protestant church could come fully of age. The new church order should be genuinely parliamentary, with a directly elected assembly entrusted with both legislative initiative and administrative review.

The lines separating consistorial and lay parties approximated, though were not identical with, those of the two established theological factions. Consistory president Hermann von Zeller and state attorney general Hermann Roecker of Stuttgart, an influential lay member of Group I, spoke strongly in favor of the argument for administrative continuity. On the other side, about thirty delegates, most of them members of Group II, supported a motion by Ernst Welsch, Dekan in Vaihingen/Enz, to include in the constitution a clause that church officials were ultimately responsible to the church assembly.[59] Debate on this motion, which was eventually defeated, showed widespread ambivalence on all sides as to how ecclesiastical authority ought in practice to be exercised. While most pietists undoubtedly leaned towards a restorationist stance, seeing democratic arguments as a form of surrender to the spirit of the age, the pietist outlook itself was much too lay-oriented and suspicious of overweening officialdom to accept, without qualification, rule by an autocratic hierarchy. For their part, some liberals likewise drew back from the possible consequences of a purely parliamentary church order, especially the divisive prospect of rule by majority in a Protestant community that lacked either theological or social homogeneity and in which liberals themselves were likely a minority. The liberal delegate Heinrich von Mosthaf, a leading spirit in the Volksbund project and anything but unsympathetic to the lay position, spoke for a majority on both sides when he argued that the ideal polity for a self-professed Volkskirche was ''not a parliamentary system but a system in which the powers and duties of the various organs are balanced and equalized, rather than

---

[59] LKV, *Verhandlungen* (1920), pp. 416–68.

having one exercise unconditional authority over the other."[60] Many delegates, indeed, considered it unseemly to include any specific delineation of power relationships in the constitution.[61] These attitudes bore fruit in the final version of the constitution, which the assembly adopted by unanimous vote on May 21, 1920. The new church order envisioned a marginally more prominent role for a church assembly (Landeskirchentag), which, as successor to the old synods, would be elected by direct popular vote and would have power to pass on all major budgetary and policy questions. For its part, the hierarchy would retain primary responsibility for personnel decisions and day-to-day administration. Under the constitution, the Consistory continued as the church's chief administrative agency, although it was given a new name—Oberkirchenrat—to underscore the fact that it would henceforth be a purely ecclesiastical body with no connection to the state. In place of the former Consistory president, the constitution called for a "church president" to be elected for life by two-thirds vote of the church assembly.

The title "president" met with disfavor in some quarters and would come under fire from Nazi elements a decade later because of its alleged republican implications. Nevertheless the Württemberg church assembly overwhelmingly chose to retain it rather than to opt for the alternative of creating an office of bishop. Not only was the idea of a presidency already firmly established in consistorial tradition but it was also argued that creation of a bishop would unnecessarily limit the choice of church leaders to members of the clergy. To militant Protestants, the office of bishop smacked of things Roman Catholic, while to others it raised questions about the status of the prelates, with whom episcopal functions had historically resided in Württemberg. Hence, if the designation *Kirchenpräsident* implied obeisance to republican values, this was a matter of coincidence, not a conscious ideological choice.[62]

[60] Ibid., p. 638.
[61] Voelter, "Revolution von 1918," p. 333.
[62] LKV, *Verhandlungen* (1920), pp. 416–68; Voelter, "Revolution von 1918,"

Linking Oberkirchenrat and church assembly there was to be a supreme executive committee (Landeskirchenausschuss), comprising the church president and presiding officer of the assembly together with one additional assembly delegate. As a kind of symbolic compromise between contending doctrines of authority, this committee typified the prevailing spirit in Württemberg church politics. On one hand, it could be seen as a natural successor to the committee established under the 1918 abdication decree and as such an embodiment of the consistorial argument that ultimate ecclesiastical authority devolved from the crown. On the other hand, the fact that two of the three members were to come from the church assembly—a provision worked out only after considerable negotiation and debate—represented a bow in the direction of ecclesiastical popular sovereignty; for that matter, the third member—the church president—would also be an electee of the assembly. In practice, to be sure, this committee performed little more than a ceremonial function. The permanence of the administrative hierarchy, coupled with the relative infrequency of assembly sessions, meant that the church president and Oberkirchenrat would normally exercise the initiative in setting church policy. As a mouthpiece of parishioners' opinion, the assembly carried on in the supportive and legitimizing role of its synodical predecessor, only rarely seeking to challenge the actions or policies of the hierarchy.[63]

A similar fusion of hierarchical and democratic principles marked provisions dealing with affairs in the local parish. A week after passing the church constitution, the assembly debated an ordinance regulating the appointment of parish clergy. At issue, among other things, was whether the assignment of pastors to parishes should be regarded as a prerogative of church officials or left to the decision of the parishioners immediately concerned. In Württemberg, as in most territorial German

---

pp. 331–32. Contrast the heated debates over titles in Prussia; Jacke, *Kirche zwischen Monarchie und Republik*, pp. 271–77.

[63] LKV, *Verhandlungen* (1919), pp. 30–78, 102–47, 150–83, (1920), pp. 416–68, 472–542, 546–617, 620–83, 686–728, 730–99, 802–32, 836–79, 1076–1153, 1156–87.

churches, clerical appointments had historically been made by the Consistory; in a few districts, largely in the newer territories of the northeast, titular nobility (including Group II delegate Prince Ernst zu Hohenlohe-Langenburg) continued to exercise rights of local patronage. During assembly debate on the appointment ordinance, Consistory president Zeller vigorously defended the continued primacy of the hierarchy. Zeller argued that the power of the leadership to appoint pastors followed reasonably from the fact that it was the church as an institution, not parishioners as individuals, that selected, educated, compensated, and disciplined clergy. Most delegates, however, favored a stronger lay voice in the appointment procedure. By a wide margin the assembly approved an amendment, offered jointly by Group I leader Eugen Reiff and Group II's Hans Voelter, requiring the church leadership to consult with local parish councillors before filling any vacant post. Patronage rights, moreover, would cease upon the death of the incumbent patrons.

To the disappointment of ardent democrats like Voelter, however, the assembly proved reluctant to pursue the logic of these initiatives by empowering parish councils themselves to choose pastors. Several delegates objected that such a procedure would only serve to set one theological faction against another within the parish and to reduce any candidate's potential effectiveness in office by associating him with the interests of the dominant group. Ecclesiastical democracy, from this standpoint, would be better served by the election of delegates to councils and assemblies than by the election of pastors to vacant parishes. A solid majority, cutting across theological boundaries, accepted the view that officials in Stuttgart, having duly consulted local representatives, could be trusted to select the most suitable pastor for a specific parish unswayed by ephemeral considerations of personal popularity or the whims of a particular parish faction. The resulting ordinance did little to challenge a patriarchal model of relationships between pastor and parishioners. Consultation rights aside, supervision of the clergy would remain the business of Dekans and prelates, not the parish laity.[64]

[64] Ibid. (1920), pp. 882–949, 952–1073, 1288–1329; cf. Voelter, "Revolution

Even if this ordinance could be interpreted as a retreat from democratic principles, the basic motives were quite clearly pastoral in nature. Here, as elsewhere, the assembly was not so much concerned to frustrate lay initiative as to prevent parish disharmony. Except for the initial election campaign, the process of church reform bore remarkably few traces of the political turmoil out of which it had arisen. In this respect Württemberg presented a marked contrast to other areas, notably Prussia, where a church constitution provoked bitter struggles, both verbal and tactical, between contending political and theological factions. The comparative lack of acrimony in Württemberg was in part an unacknowledged tribute to churchmen's cautiously friendly relations with local officials, which freed conservatives from the specter of anticlerical meddling in ecclesiastical affairs. Conversely, those Württemberg churchmen who supported the republic were not inclined to regard the existing consistorial church as a bastion of reaction that somehow needed to be neutralized for the sake of the new order. Beyond this, as church elections demonstrated, the adoption of democratic procedures actually worked to the benefit of conservatives, especially pietists, who approached the problem of reform chiefly from the standpoint of preserving confessional orthodoxy. Hence, both the forces of movement and the forces of order within the church generally sought to avoid pitched battles, preferring to reach consensus on the common ground of pastoral concern.

The resulting church order can best be described as an adaptation of inherited structures to a world from which the stabilizing presence of the summus episcopus had been removed. While adoption of universal suffrage may have put Württemberg in the vanguard of German churches where formal assimilation of democratic practice was concerned, lay involvement could hardly be described as structurally essential to church life. The

---

von 1918," pp. 336–39. The normal appointment procedure was for the Consistory (Oberkirchenrat) to declare a vacancy and invite interested pastors to apply for consideration. Candidates would then be ranked informally according to various criteria (e.g., scores on the postseminary service tests), with a final decision made after consulting the parish council in question.

old hierarchy remained intact, and as a result formal democracy brought few practical consequences for churchmen's roles or self-image. By design or default, the clergy retained the initiative in church life. Even when they sought to involve the masses, pastors were more likely to feel a responsibility *for* their parishioners than a responsibility *to* them.

Between Involvement and Indifference

As the reforms of 1919–20 demonstrated, institutional experiments by themselves were unlikely to arouse nominal parishioners to the enthusiasm and sense of personal initiative deemed essential for a strong and healthy Protestant community. Churchmen found themselves perpetually confronted with the question of whether, in a world where strength lay in numbers, a sufficiently broad segment of the membership could be kept mobilized to invigorate church life, or whether the "people's church" would remain, in everything but rhetoric, a "pastor's church." On this score soundings of parish sentiment were less than reassuring. Occasionally, to be sure, churchmen found cause for optimism, as in the working-class Stuttgart suburb of Zuffenhausen, where a Dekan's visitation in 1923 concluded that "despite all the disruption of revolution and the preceding war years, it can still be said that . . . church life has been maintained and even gives welcome signs of prospering."[65] Group II leader Ernst Welsch, Dekan in Vaihingen/Enz, was not alone when he reported that, despite more open criticism of the church, most parishioners in his small city north of Stuttgart remained "deeply concerned that things here be to the pastor's liking, and any comment to the latter effect is received with obvious satisfaction."[66] On the other hand, numerous parish reports of the early 1920s also reflected a sense that democratic initiatives had found little resonance in the population at large. In this regard a report of 1921 from Heilbronn Dekan Hermann Eytel deserves

[65] Zuffenhausen, Visitationsbericht, Mar. 18, 1923, LKA A29/5395.
[66] Vaihingen/Enz, Pfarrbericht 1920, LKA A29/4881.

quotation at some length. While perhaps more pessimistic in tone than most, it nevertheless makes explicit a theme sounded obliquely in scores of similar reports, especially those from larger towns and cities. Declared Eytel:

> As far as the community's private attitudes towards the clergy and clerical office are concerned, it is striking how many people do not even know who their pastor is. The pastor is no longer an authority figure for anyone. In workers' circles, the separation of church and state—which, to be sure, can still hardly be detected—has produced no new appreciation for the pastor; he remains suspect as a reactionary state official, although contacts at baptisms and weddings or house visitations are not unpleasant for the most part. It cannot be denied that many morally stunted "modern" people have little use for him and consider him odious and superfluous. To the sects and free churches he is a paid priest whose faith is automatically suspect and who is hard pressed to convince them that he is a Christian. In polite society he is a desirable ornament at social occasions, whose arrival and timely departure are greeted warmly, but [in other respects] he often has a difficult time representing the church's viewpoint, and the alienation from Christian thought and feeling is starkly apparent.[67]

Churchmen in such circumstances were understandably tempted to devote most of their attention to that more narrowly defined parish in which, as Eytel further noted, they could hope to find an "extensive, serious, understanding, and well-rooted community of those who see in their pastor a preacher of the gospel, a friend and spiritual advisor, and who support him and further his work in a spirit of hearty confidence and loyal devotion."[68] As prospects for structural renewal ebbed and the masses still kept their distance, pastors and church officials

[67] Heilbronn, Pfarrbericht 1921, LKA A29/1909; cf., e.g., Urach, Pfarrbericht 1930, OKR/AR OA/PfB.
[68] Heilbronn, Pfarrbericht 1921, LKA A29/1909.

sought first of all to shore up this perdurable core community against future erosion.

The church constitution of 1920 remained in legal limbo until the spring of 1924, when it finally took effect following the Landtag's passage of the much-delayed state church law. At this time, as noted in the previous chapter, Hermann von Zeller relinquished the office of Consistory president, the Consistory itself was reconstituted as the new Oberkirchenrat, and the church assembly convened to elect the first president of the new era. In his annual report as chairman of the Württemberg Pfarrverein, Esslingen pastor Christian Schnaufer voiced a prevalent attitude, at least among churchmen, when he praised the "clarity of situation" that the church now enjoyed. "What was necessary has occurred," he declared; "We have done what we could."[69]

Whereas Zeller had been a lay civil servant, and while in theory the idea of a lay church president was appealing, as earlier debate over the bishop's title indicated, sentiment in the assembly by 1924 almost unanimously favored election of an ordained person as a means of emphasizing the office's purely ecclesiastical focus.[70] Finding an appropriate candidate, however, proved difficult. Given the symbolic importance of theological considerations, the constitutional requirement of a two-thirds majority for election posed potentially formidable problems. An obvious nominee was Jakob Schoell, arguably the most versatile and gifted member of the old Consistory, who enjoyed a high personal and scholarly reputation throughout Württemberg and beyond. At the same time, he was too prominently identified with liberal theology to pass muster with a majority in Group I. Pietists who admired him as a person could not be brought to award the highest ecclesiastical office to a churchman suspected in hyperorthodox circles of flirting with unbelief. A second possible nominee, Theodor Traub, the titular prelate and Dekan for Stuttgart, presented fewer problems, having refused to affiliate

[69] Christian Schnaufer, "Jahresbericht," *KAfW* 33 (1924): 57; cf. lkv, *Verhandlungen* (1924), pp. 2062–68, 2204–6.
[70] Egelhaaf, *Lebens-Erinnerungen*, p. 145.

formally with either theological faction. Yet he too failed to garner sufficient support, and after eight inconclusive ballots the assembly commissioned a six-member ad hoc committee to find an alternative candidate acceptable to all.

The committee's lot fell upon a relatively little known member of the new Oberkirchenrat, Johannes Merz. Born in 1857, Merz was a pastor's son and a lifelong churchman. After earning doctorates at Tübingen in both theology and philosophy, he spent six years as a pastor in Ludwigsburg before accepting an administrative position in 1894. Nine years later he became a full member of the Consistory and, in 1913, a titular prelate. A student of ancient art and one of the Consistory's specialists on school affairs, he had gained experience in most major areas of church life. Meanwhile, unlike his more controversial colleague Schoell, he had maintained a low theological profile. Associates would later praise him as a patient technician rather than a politician. More open hearted than calculating, both uncharismatic and unabrasive, he embodied an essentially pastoral outlook in which strong leadership took second place to the quiet promotion of harmony and tolerance. Under the circumstances he was an inspired choice, and his nomination won immediate endorsement from the full assembly.[71]

Indeed, Merz's mild-mannered personality and administrative skill ideally suited him for leadership in a period when most churchmen were concerned less with innovation than with the consolidation and defense of established positions. During his comparatively brief tenure as president, which lasted until his death in 1929, the church faced few if any major crises. The prevailing calm, however, mirrored the deeper long-term tendencies towards stagnation, which, after the multiple stimuli of the immediate postwar years, once again began to manifest itself at many levels of church life. Though the church may have lost lit-

[71] Ibid., p. 146; Merz was a close friend of Egelhaaf, who probably suggested his name. See also Max Mayer-List, "Die Wahl des Kirchenpräsidenten," *KAfW* 38 (1929): 109, and *Zur Erinnerung an D. Dr. Johannes Merz, Kirchenpräsident der Evang. Landeskirche in Württemberg, geb. 24.2.1857, gest. 4.5.1929* (Stuttgart, 1929).

tle apparent ground to competitors in the struggle for hearts and minds, churchmen found that frequently the price for stability was passivity. Customs and attitudes changed slowly, for the most part, whether to the benefit or to the detriment of Protestant vitality.

Statistics on church life, while imprecise at best, provide one index of popular attitudes and practice, and by this conventional standard Württemberg Protestants appeared little affected by the changes of the postwar era. Indices for church weddings and funerals, for baptisms, and for attendance at Eucharist all held fairly constant after 1918 at levels little different from those of the prewar decade. The great majority of nominal Protestants, generally 90 percent or more, continued to avail themselves of the church's good offices at marriage and at death. Moreover, fully 97 percent of children born to Protestant parents received the sacrament of baptism, while the annual number of recorded communicants at the Eucharist in the mid-1920s amounted to about 41 percent of the total church membership, very nearly the same proportion (41.6 percent) recorded in 1910. In all of these categories Württemberg ranked slightly above the average for German Protestant churches as a whole. If figures tended to be marginally higher in neighboring south German churches, they were often much lower in the Protestant heartland to the north, where the proportion of communicants, for example, declined to scarcely 25 percent in the Prussian Union churches and Saxony, and to a mere 7 percent in Hamburg.[72]

Another ready statistical measure can be found in gross membership figures. In Württemberg, as throughout Germany, the specter of a mass exodus of nominal parishioners haunted church officials throughout the Weimar era. For Württemberg churchmen, unlike some colleagues to the north, the primary concern was not the anticlerical posture of public officials but rather the very practical fact that, with the approval of the state church law in 1924, membership now carried a direct financial obligation in the form of church taxes. Experience with local church taxes, which were already being levied in nearly three-fourths of all

[72] *KJ 1926*, pp. 82–93, 99, 116, 119.

parishes, suggested potential difficulties. Complaints of inequity plagued many parishes. The most common grievances, especially during the period of hyperinflation, came from persons on salaries and fixed incomes, who argued that the resort to a surcharge on income taxes gave an unfair advantage to those, such as farmers, whose principal assets lay in real goods and whose income, it was alleged, could easily be understated. As in other states, such as Prussia, the practice of assessing taxes by occupation rather than by individual aroused further unhappiness. In novelist Hermann Hesse's boyhood home of Calw, on the edge of the Black Forest, salaried civil servants threatened to leave the church in 1922 if church officials did not adopt procedures deemed more equitable.[73]

The introduction of general church taxes promised to be a boon for anticlerical forces bent on reducing the church's public influence. With the advent of the republic, radical socialists and academic freethinkers in much of Germany had returned with renewed vigor to crusades against church membership interrupted by the war. Nationwide a total of perhaps 150,000 individuals belonged to one or another of the major anticlerical organizations: the League of Freethinkers (Freidenkerbund), the Monists' League, and the communist-oriented League of Proletarian Freethinkers. These groups were most active in the cities of northern Germany, where agitation against church taxes achieved some initial success. Protestant churches in Berlin-Brandenburg, for example, lost 79,000 members in 1919 alone, while withdrawals in Hamburg exceeded 50,000. By middecade the cumulative total of withdrawals had risen to over 1,000,000—a troubling figure for churchmen, though a scant 2.5 percent of Germany's nominal Protestant population.[74]

[73] Compilations on local taxes in LKA A26/1505; also Zeller to Bosler, Oct. 29, Nov. 12, 1921; Bosler to Zeller, Nov. 1, 18, 1921; and Bezirksbeamtenbund Calw to WEK, Feb. 1, 1922; all in LKA A26/1505. Mittelstadt, Pfarrbericht 1923, LKA A29/2869.

[74] *KJ 1921*, pp. 91–94, 339; *KJ 1926*, pp. 135–37. For a general survey, see Jochen-Christoph Kaiser, *Arbeiterbewegung und organisierte Religionspolitik: Proletarische Freidenkerverbände im Kaiserreich und in der Weimarer Republik* (Stuttgart, 1981).

In Württemberg, where freethinking groups remained internally divided and boasted scarcely a thousand members at the beginning of the decade, churchmen heard only faint echoes of this clamor against church membership. Public meetings of freethinkers often drew sparse crowds—less than two dozen people at one widely publicized Stuttgart rally in late 1919—and those in attendance typically included a vocal minority of loyal church members come to heckle or debate. The general conference of the Württemberg League of Freethinkers in 1920 heard complaints that the local populace was "simply too pious" for effective anticlerical propaganda; the worker who cheered at a Communist party rally one day was likely to attend his child's confirmation the next.[75] Despite such obstacles, however, Württemberg freethinkers kept up a steady stream of propaganda against church taxes and clerical influence, led by a renegade trinity of former Protestant theology students: Paul Sakmann, Sakmann's Stuttgart colleague Immanuel Herrmann, and Erich Schairer, an iconoclastic Heilbronn journalist. Their efforts bore at least some fruit: between 1919 and 1921 the annual number of withdrawals in Württemberg more than doubled, from 640 to 1,722, and the following year they reached a historic high of 4,414.[76] Much of the increase for 1922 came in the wake of a coordinated offensive in the left-liberal and socialist press. Exploiting the still unresolved financial negotiations between church and state, advertisements portrayed churchmen as scheming to impose astronomical tax rates on members, particularly the poor and those already straitened by inflation. Included in the ads were detailed instructions on the procedure for opting out of church membership. In Stuttgart alone, nearly two hundred notices of withdrawal arrived at church offices within twenty-four hours after the first such notice appeared.[77]

[75] Notes on meetings, LKA D4/24x; "Kirchenaustritt zur Religionslosigkeit in Württemberg 1920," LKA A26/409.

[76] "Kirchenaustritt im Jahr 1921," LKA A26/409; cf. "Stand der Austritte und Uebertritte bis 1926," OKR/AR Gen. 155.

[77] Traub to WEK, Feb. 17, 1922, LKA A26/409; ST, Feb. 10, 1922; other clippings (undated), LKA A26/409.

The apparently escalating rate of withdrawals led church forces to muster a counteroffensive reminiscent of the early months of the republic. In Stuttgart itself, the district executive committee sought press space to rebut allegations about projected tax rates.[78] Using materials on leading freethinkers accumulated by the Volksbund since the war, pastors and lay volunteers systematically attended their opponents' meetings, exploiting every opportunity to present the church's case.[79] Leaflets by the thousands made their way into potential strongholds of anticlerical sentiment. These evoked lurid pictures of the consequences renunciation of church membership would entail: loss of baptismal rights, the right to a church wedding, the right to stand as godparents, the right to a proper church burial.[80] Pastors were urged to reinforce the threat of social ostracism by refusing to render any service, however innocuous, to those who had left the fold. To do otherwise, the argument went, would encourage the notion that formal membership was superfluous.[81]

Whether measures such as these had their desired effect or whether by middecade the anticlerical movement in Württemberg had simply exhausted its principal constituency, the erosion in church membership soon slowed. In 1923, 1,411 persons declared withdrawals; in 1924, the year church taxes were actually introduced, the figure fell to 941 despite freethinkers' efforts to mount a new propaganda campaign. Thereafter annual figures fluctuated between 1,000 and 2,500, and while as late as 1931 churchmen were still concerned enough to sponsor a four-day workshop on the subject, anticlerical inroads in Württemberg remained negligible. In the 1925 census, less than .5 percent of

[78] *ST*, Feb. 13, 23, 1922. The original notices had presented church tax rates as a flat percentage of income rather than as a surcharge on the existing graduated income tax.

[79] EVB, *Mitteilungen* 3 (Oct. 1919): 10–12, 4 (Nov. 1919): 51, 15 (Apr. 1921): 261–62; cf. Zeller to DEKA, June 1921, LKA A26/409.

[80] Thus *Wie stellen Sie sich zur Austrittsbewegung?* (n.p., n.d.), copy in LKA D12/5.

[81] Christian Schnaufer, "Die Stellung der Kirche zu den Ausgetretenen," *KAfW* 32 (1923): 42.

the Württemberg population acknowledged no confessional affiliation, a figure far below the national average. Moreover, the number of withdrawals was consistently dwarfed by the number of simple transfers between Protestant and Catholic churches.[82]

When collection of church taxes began in 1924, the hierarchy mobilized its propaganda resources not only to counter attacks from without but also to encourage a positive spirit from within. The Volksbund issued a call for prompt and cheerful cooperation, urging that payment be regarded as "a matter of *honor*, of *conscience*, and of the *heart* . . . , a public demonstration that our Evangelical populace still stands by the church."[83] Beginning in 1925, the Oberkirchenrat held annual public news conferences to introduce proposed church budgets, always stressing the strict economies being observed in the allocation of revenues.[84] There were, to be sure, occasional problems of adjustment, and not everyone affected by the new arrangements proved a paragon of cheerfulness or good will. The Dekan in Heidenheim reported in July 1924 that more than fifty people who had given church officials notice of their withdrawal had been assessed taxes because they had failed to carry out the required civil registration within the time specified in Württemberg church law.[85] In not a few households, members who had withdrawn from the church found themselves liable for taxes because spouses or children remained members. Such partial taxation was permissible under the terms of the church law, although it had previously proved a source of contention at the parish level. Among those who left the church there were doubtless others who echoed a disgruntled SPD functionary in Besigheim when he wrote in 1922: "I would

[82] *SHW 1928*, p. 260; *KJ 1927*, p. 223; "Stand der Austritte und Uebertritte bis 1926," OKR/AR Gen. 155; Adolf Schaal, memorandum, June 5, 1925, OKR/AR Gen. 155/2; OKR to DEKA, Feb. 29, 1928, OKR/AR Gen. 151b; notes on Tübingen Ferienkurs, Aug. 24–27, 1931, OKR/AR Gen. 117.

[83] *Evangelischer Volksbund für Württemberg* 6 (May 1924).

[84] *SM*, Nov. 10, 1925; notes on later conferences in OKR/AR Gen. 124/I.

[85] Schönhuth to OKR, July 30,1924; OKR/AR Gen. 155. According to ARTICLE 12(3) of the 1924 church law, a person only became exempt from taxes if civil registration took place within three months after local church authorities issued a certificate acknowledging the intention to withdraw.

have thought the churchwardens might have more sense than to come around and simply charge a half tax on my income for my wife. . . . If I ever hand the business over to my wife and no longer have any say in it, then you can come with a bill like this."[86] As late as 1927, one pastor reported that over half the families in his parish paid only after warning notices had been sent.[87]

In general, however, the system worked smoothly; most church members showed themselves "equal to the test," as Pfarrverein chairman Christian Schnaufer put it in 1926.[88] If parishioners seemed willing to stand by the church on this matter, one reason may have been, ironically, that it required no direct contact with the church, since the state looked after the collection of taxes on the church's behalf. That the tax itself took the form of a surcharge on income taxes may also have served to mask its impact, just as it guaranteed that many among the working poor, for whom a simple head tax would have been a painful exaction, actually contributed only insignificant amounts or nothing at all. By decade's end, at any rate, all evidence suggested that the new tax had become an accustomed if by no means universally popular concomitant of church membership.

Though it might have afforded churchmen cause for satisfaction, this passive token of members' loyalty did not necessarily portend greater personal involvement or lay initiative in church life. To the extent that church taxes served to reinforce the church's image as part of a public establishment, they might well have militated against such involvement. For a host of nominal members, it would seem, the church did provide as it were a horizon of respectability, one of the distant points of reference in a socially ordered life. As such, however, it functioned not as a pri-

[86] Thüringer to Kirchenpflege Besigheim, n.d., and Werner to WEK, Apr. 7, 1922, both in LKA A26/1505. The tax liability of spouses was regulated in ARTICLE 34 of the 1924 church law.

[87] Plattenhardt, Pfarrbericht 1928, OKR/AR OA/PfB.

[88] Christian Schnaufer, "Jahresbericht," *KAfW* 35 (1926): 65; cf. Theodor Traub, *Jahresbericht 1928* (Stuttgart, 1929), p. 7.

mary community of belief, with corresponding claims on individual convictions or commitments, but as one among numerous agencies in modern society whose facilities and services—like those, for example, of a social welfare office—were available when needed but could normally be ignored. If the price for such services was payment of a tax, this too was little different from other public services. Moreover, having thus secured the right of access to the clergy's good offices, the nominal member would likely regard obligations to the institution as fulfilled, unless it be for some general commitment to a moral and honest life.[89]

Hence the challenge of a democratic church order appeared largely unmet, and throughout the period churchmen of every theological persuasion continued to search for ways of expanding the boundaries of lay participation and enthusiasm at all levels of church life. Their most ambitious organizational experiment continued to be the Volksbund, the lay organization founded in the hectic days of early 1919. Although its immediate utility had been as an agency of mass mobilization, the Volksbund's ultimate purpose was to stimulate internal renewal by educating the laity to a new sense of coresponsibility for parish life and worship. For several years the Volksbund grew steadily despite the severe dislocations of the inflation era. It reached a peak in 1923, when membership stood at 225,000 persons in 752 local chapters. By this time it also boasted a small staff of salaried functionaries and a strong cadre of volunteers, especially in the capital. With better than one adult Protestant in four committed at least to the extent of a token membership fee, the Volksbund had become the largest mass organization of any kind in Württemberg.[90]

In moments of self-congratulation, league functionaries could assure themselves that they were indeed establishing a proto-

[89] This construct is necessarily hypothetical, but see the suggestive analysis of postwar attitudes, based on empirical survey research in Württemberg, in Günter Kehrer, *Das religiöse Bewusstsein des Industriearbeiters* (Munich, 1967); cf. Köster, *Kirchentreuen*.

[90] EVB, *Mitteilungen* 27 (Apr. 1923): 470–72; Hermann Ströle, "Vom Evangelischen Volksbund für Württemberg," *MfPT* 17 (1921): 289–97.

type for the vital Volkskirche, an organization embracing all political viewpoints and walks of life. Unlike most church-related bodies, the Volksbund was not wholly an affair of the academic and bureaucratic elite. Though its guiding spirits were the usual churchmen and lay notables—Jakob Schoell; former Heidenheim pastor Hermann Ströle; Heinrich von Mosthaf, retired director of the Württemberg Chamber of Trade and Commerce—one of its most visible functionaries, August Springer, came from solid worker-artisan stock. A decorated war veteran with a long prewar history of involvement in the Evangelical Workers' Association, Springer was a model Evangelical-Social proletarian, an autodidact with the hands of a factory worker and the sensibilities of an artist and philosopher.[91] As of 1925, seven of forty-three persons on the Volksbund governing council were women, and while the familiar occupational triumvirate of clergy, academics, and civil servants still dominated, a substantial minority were tradesmen, shopkeepers, farmers, and professionals; one was a factory worker.[92]

The cornerstone of Volksbund efforts at the parish level, particularly in urban areas, was a network of volunteer "stewards" whose task it was to provide a constant link between clergy and parishioners. One Stuttgart chapter of 1,250 members reported a total of forty-eight such volunteers in 1922, each responsible for between ten and twenty families in the parish.[93] Stewards sought to identify extraordinary needs that might otherwise go unnoticed and, where possible, bring church relief efforts into play. At the same time they served as conduits for information, alerting parishioners to special programs and other activities sponsored by the church. Typically, a local Volksbund group would sponsor one or two major assemblies each year for which the central office in Stuttgart supplied advice, materials, or appropriate speakers. Where feasible, regular social and recrea-

---

[91] See August Springer, *Der Andere, der bist Du: Lebensgeschichte eines reichen armen Mannes* (Tübingen, 1954).

[92] EVB, *Mitteilungen* 36 (June 1925): 4–5.

[93] Stuttgart, Matthäuskirche, Pfarrbericht 1922, LKA A29/4382.

tional activities complemented the neighborhood services coordinated by the stewards.

Grass-roots efforts notwithstanding, the momentum of growth proved impossible to sustain. By middecade membership was already beginning to decline; it fell to 175,000 in 1927 and five years later stood at no more than 130,000, with fewer than six hundred chapters still active. In 1929 members' dues and contributions failed for the first time to cover fixed expenses.[94] The reasons for these disappointing trends were, of course, open to debate. Volksbund leaders themselves speculated that members began to leave after the imposition of church taxes in 1924 because they saw Volksbund dues as a kind of second tax.[95] As a para-ecclesiastical organization, the Volksbund may also have suffered to some extent from an ambiguous relationship to other parish societies. In some areas Volksbund chapters were largely dependent on the initiatives of local clergy, with the result that they stagnated or dissolved when their founders moved on to new positions. In other parishes the reverse was true; chapters atrophied because of indifference or opposition from the local clergy, a minority of whom saw the Volksbund's project to create an umbrella organization of laymen as a potential source of tension with their own parish efforts.[96] Similar tensions existed between the essentially liberal impulses animating the Volksbund—the concern to widen the bounds of church participation irrespective of theological commitment—and the pietist ideals so strongly entrenched in many localities. Where pietist organizations played a prominent part in parish life, supporters of the Volksbund were likely to be frustrated by what they saw as ex-

[94] EVB, *Mitteilungen* 44 (May 1927): 219, 55 (Apr. 1930): 522–38; EVB Vertretertag, Apr. 17–18, 1932, minutes in LKA D1/59,1. The Oberkirchenrat provided a subvention in the form of pension contributions for pastors temporarily in the employ of the Volksbund; see Mosthaf to OKR, June 7, 1924, and Merz to EVB, July 4, Sept. 19, 26, 1924, all in OKR/AR Gen. 117.

[95] EVB, *Mitteilungen* 40 (Mar. 1926): 91.

[96] Stuttgart, Rosenbergkirche, Pfarrbericht 1922, LKA A29/4381; Hausen ob Lontal, Pfarrbericht 1928, OKR/AR OA/PfB; Dopffel to Buck, Mar. 22, 1919, LKA C4/4; *KAfW* 39 (1930): 90, 175.

clusivity and apathy towards broader ecclesiastical "community-building."[97] As late as 1931, Esslingen Dekan Richard Lempp was still urging "many an uncomprehending colleague" to recognize the essential value of a lay organization for promoting parish vitality. The Volksbund, he wrote, should not be dismissed as a "blackamoor who has done his duty and now can be off."[98]

From a purely organizational perspective it was probably true, as delegates to the annual meeting in 1931 were told, that it was "no longer possible to conceive of church life in Württemberg without the Volksbund."[99] The organizers' central purpose, however, remained unfulfilled. After a decade's effort, Heinrich von Mosthaf was forced to admit, many church members showed a "complete lack of understanding for the Volksbund's work, especially in outlying areas."[100] Its appeal had been greatest in the early months of its existence, when the church's future had seemed in jeopardy. With a return to comparative stability came also a return to comfortable old patterns of religious behavior. "The church's situation . . . seems secure," Jakob Schoell commented in 1929, "and [many] therefore believe that the . . . Volksbund is no longer as important as at the time of the revolution."[101]

Impulses similar to those that animated supporters of the Volksbund manifested themselves, especially in certain pietist quarters, in a renewed enthusiasm for popular evangelism of the Anglo-American tent-meeting variety as a tool for reaching the masses outside the core Protestant community. Whereas the Volksbund sought to institutionalize broad-based lay participation, revivalism aimed at personal conversion and deepened spir-

[97] E.g., Denkendorf, Pfarrbericht 1929, OKR/AR OA/PfB.

[98] Richard Lempp, "Ein Wort an manche unbegreifliche Kollegen!" *KAfW* 40 (1931): 27–28; cf. Lempp speech, "Die lebendige Gemeinde im Sturm der Zeit," in minutes of EVB Vertretertag, Apr. 17–18, 1932, LKA D1/59,1.

[99] Heinrich Pfisterer, "Vom Vertretertag des Evang. Volksbundes," *KAfW* 30 (1931): 76.

[100] Mosthaf to OKR, Dec. 24, 1929, OKR/AR Gen. 117.

[101] Ibid., notes of Jan. 9, 1930; cf. the earlier complaint in EVB, *Mitteilungen* 31 (Apr. 1924): 519.

itual intensity. Revivalism itself was hardly new to Württemberg pietism. Since 1900, a society to promote evangelization had existed under the auspices of such church luminaries as Christian Römer, Paul Wurster, and future Ludwigsburg Dekan Samuel Gauger.[102] After the war a new wave of tent meetings and revivals swept the countryside. Sometimes these were sponsored by groups within the church, notably the neopietist Liebenzeller Mission; sometimes they were the work of evangelistic entrepreneurs from throughout Germany and abroad. The revivalist style appears to have found strong if often short-lived resonance in the tense atmosphere of the early 1920s. To judge from numerous pastors' reports, at least, revivalist activity varied with the state of the economy, peaking in intensity during the era of hyperinflation between late 1921 and 1923.[103]

Mass evangelization as a technique of renewal provoked considerable interest within the Württemberg church establishment. For a time the Volksbund leadership itself contemplated the revivalist option, urging the Consistory to promote the training of a cadre of lay evangelists committed to the Volkskirche ideal.[104] In part, no doubt, this reflected a strategic desire to keep the unpredictable currents of revivalism within safe channels. Among the clergy at large, where academic theology and concern for "decency and good order" generally prevailed, the tone and style of tent-meeting evangelism aroused considerable ambivalence. To the extent that local revivals afforded a temporary stimulus to parish life, they earned at least grudging support. Many pastors noted a substantial increase in the number of men attending services and joining parish Bible study groups after an evangelist's visit.[105] At the same time, few pastors found themselves wholly comfortable with the methods and character of revivalism, questioning whether what one pastor, in

[102] Lehmann, *Pietismus*, pp. 280–82.
[103] A collection of reports is filed in LKA A26/564.
[104] Mosthaf to WEK, June 22, 1921, LKA A26/564.
[105] E.g., Lempp to WEK, Feb. 22, 1922; Dieterich to WEK, Feb. 25, 1922; Metzger to WEK, May 1, 1922; Esenwein to WEK, Mar. 31, 1922; and Hahn to WEK, July 26, 1922; all in LKA A26/564.

good academic fashion, labeled an *evangelisatio vulgaris*[106] could be considered compatible with church needs and traditions. "Encouraging such enterprises," Langenburg Dekan Friedrich Pfäfflin wrote at the peak of revivalist activity, would "lead to a heavy Americanization of piety in the church."[107]

Church leaders never adopted an official position on the revivalist enterprise. Their basic stance, however, was defensive and skeptical, not only because the hierarchy doubted the long-term effectiveness of the methods used but also, paradoxically, because they feared that the immediate beneficiary might prove to be not the official church but the sects and free churches that dotted Württemberg's religious landscape, many of whom exploited religious enthusiasm as a matter of course. This probably explains why, for example, an internal memorandum on church membership drafted just after middecade referred to free churches such as the Methodists, who claimed no more than about 12,500 adherents in Württemberg, as "dangerous" to the well-being of the Volkskirche; it seemed they possessed the organizational structure to exploit revivalist instincts at the fringes of the established Protestant community.[108]

Like much else, the main wave of postwar revivalism rather quickly ran its course. Local revivals continued sporadically throughout the decade, while church officials themselves experimented on occasion with less flamboyant forms of lay evangelization. In the final analysis, however, revivalism had little lasting impact on church life. Like the Volksbund program, but for different reasons, it rarely extended the social or ideological boundaries of church life. It exerted its strongest appeal, many reports confirmed, among the already converted; any dividend in the form of increased lay involvement soon spent itself.[109]

[106] Stürner to WEK, June 19, 1922, LKA A26/564.

[107] F. Pfäfflin, note on Weinland, to WEK, Feb. 5, 1923, LKA A26/564; similar views can be found expressed in Leonhardt to WEK, Mar. 27, 1922, LKA A26/564.

[108] "Stand der Austritte und Uebertritte bis 1926" (copy), OKR/AR Gen. 155/2. More informally organized groups, many of them Pentecostals, are dismissed as "harmless."

[109] Typical is Eytel to WEK, Apr. 12, 1922, reporting on events in Heilbronn; LKA A26/564.

A similarly ambiguous catalyst to lay activism was the local Protestant youth movement. Numerically, at least, nominally Protestant groups dominated the youth scene in Württemberg; all told they encompassed nearly two hundred thousand young people, most in their teens, in several branches and over three thousand separate local clubs and chapters. By comparison, Catholic youth groups numbered less than fifty thousand members, socialist-oriented groups perhaps forty thousand, and independent groups of the Wandervogel type at best five thousand. Only sports and recreation clubs, whose membership in any case presumably overlapped that of the other groups, could boast a constituency comparable to that of Evangelical youth work.[110] Although it was customary for pastors to exercise at least honorary leadership of local youth groups, the relationship of such organizations to the parish was often unclear. So too, especially in the case of the young men's associations, was the stance of their members regarding church affairs. Cultural and political currents since 1900 had left a strong mark on Protestant youth, particularly those active in the most important youth group, the Evangelical Young Men's League (Evangelischer Jungmännerbund, commonly referred to as the CVJM although not a part of the international YMCA). The critical idealism of the original Wandervogel movement, with its revolt against the stultifying conformity of an adult bourgeois world, exerted a strong appeal within the organization. It manifested itself, among other things, in a widespread inclination to keep one's distance from the official church, which to many youthful members stood for the world of the fathers over and against which the new generation must forge its own identity. Rather than bringing youth into the mainstream of active parish life, the youth movement tended to become a cause of its own, a source of loy-

---

[110] *SHW 1928*, pp. 280–84. For brief sketches of the major component associations, see Paul Keppler, "Das Gemeinsame und das Unterschiedende der Ev. Jugendverbände," *KAfW* 36 (1927): 154–56, and Dieter von Lersner, *Die Evangelischen Jugendverbände Württembergs und die Hitler-Jugend 1933/1934* (Göttingen, 1958), pp. 11–16.

alty separate from, and often beyond the control of, the institutional church.

In 1924 the Württemberg church assembly unanimously passed a resolution of solidarity with the youth movement. Among other things, it declared churchmen to be "imbued with the conviction that youth and the church belong together, that for the young too the church ought to be able to provide a home."[111] Relations, however, remained strained throughout the period, not only because of youth attitudes but also because churchmen themselves could not agree on how best to achieve the pious hopes expressed in the assembly's resolution. Some took the position of Heidi Denzel, an Evangelical-Social lay activist, who in a 1924 article urged pastors to take seriously the complaints and criticisms of the young, especially those attacking the church for a lack of warmth and spirit of community. Denzel and others, like Inner Mission pastor Daniel Schubert, warned against unrealistic expectations; only through patience and understanding on the part of churchmen could the idealistic energies of the youth movement be harnessed to the broader purposes of the church.[112] Others, however, including Hans Dölker, one of two official youth pastors in Stuttgart, blamed tension between churchmen and youth on the spirit of the youth movement itself.[113] "The young should not be giving advice but taking it," wrote Dölker's Stuttgart colleague Theodor Walther. "They should not criticize but rather immerse themselves for once in the meaning of the church's teachings and become acquainted with its actual contributions."[114] Debates between the advocates of patriarchal and pastoral strategies continued in the church press and at meetings of youth leaders throughout the decade. Individual pastors made efforts to enlist youthful talents

[111] LKV, *Verhandlungen* (1924), pp. 2200–2201.

[112] Heidi Denzel, "Jugendbewegung und Kirche," *EGBfS* 20 (May 25, 1924); Denzel to Voelter, May 15, 1924, LKA D12/2; Daniel Schubert, "Gemeinde und Vereine," *KAfW* 35 (1926): 179–80; Rudolf Daur, "Was steht zwischen Jugend und Kirche?" *Die Volkskirche* 1 (Oct. 15, 1928): 1–3.

[113] Notes on Bietigheimer Tag, May 11, 1924, LKA D12/2.

[114] *EGBfS* 20 (June 1, 1924).

in as many areas of parish life and worship as possible. Brass choirs were a favorite means to this end. "The CVJM and . . . young women's society constitute a gratifying demonstration that there are also Christian young people," a parish report from Balingen declared at the end of the Weimar years.[115] Even strong advocates of accommodation, however, including pastor Paul Keppler, head of the Württemberg CVJM, conceded that any ecclesiastical fruit produced by the Protestant youth movement would probably be both slow to ripen and of uncertain quality.[116]

In different and to some extent contradictory ways, experiences with the youth movement, with revivalism, and with the Volksbund underscored a central dilemma facing churchmen. Formal democratization could not by itself galvanize nominal Protestants to accept personal responsibility for the church's health and well-being. Despite its formal autonomy, the church remained fettered to an inherited statist image. Even those who identified actively with Protestant ideals tended to regard the church more as Anstalt than Verein, as an external structure rather than a voluntary fellowship of coreligionists. Where the latter impulse was present it usually took more private forms such as pietists' devotional groups, and these by their very nature militated against social and especially ideological diversity. Church membership, in the larger sense, meant primarily a passive acceptance of office, a general willingness to leave church affairs in the hands of those officials—that is, the clergy and other hired workers—appointed for the purpose.

The question of lay responsibility once again arose, at least obliquely, when in 1924 the church assembly considered a pair of ordinances regarding parish and diocesan administration. In each case the ostensible purpose was to temper the historic domination of local church government by Dekans and clergy. The means was to be an expanded partnership between churchmen

---

[115] Balingen, Pfarrbericht 1931, OKR/AR OA/PfB.

[116] Paul Keppler, "Wie können wir Pfarrer dem Ev. Jungmännerwerk helfen?" *KAfW* 37 (1928): 172–73; Keppler, "Die Bedeutung der Jungmännerwerk für die Kirchengemeinde," *KAfW* 38 (1929): 94–95. See also *KAfW* 38 (1929): 215, and *EGBfS* 25 (Jan. 20, 1929).

and the lay representatives elected to serve on parish councils and diocesan synods. To be sure, the conception of ecclesiastical office enshrined in the church constitution, which defined the clergy first and foremost as representatives of an institutional hierarchy, precluded any radical alteration in the forms or methods of local church administration. Just as the assembly had voted in 1920 to reserve to the hierarchy the power to appoint pastors, it now narrowly rejected a motion by Hans Voelter to give district synods, composed of pastors and representatives of the lay parish councils, a direct voice in the appointment of Dekans. While the ordinances allowed for lay participation in a variety of routine functions, lay initiative here too remained a largely independent variable in the ecclesiastical equation.[117]

From a sociological standpoint, parish councils were undoubtedly the most representative of all church institutions. Unlike the church assembly, parish councils were not a preserve of academics and bureaucrats, even in the larger towns and cities, but represented at least a rough cross section of the wider Protestant community. If, in 1920, 41 of 180 parish councillors in Stuttgart were civil servants, this proportion was smaller than might have been anticipated in the citadel of Württemberg's Protestant bureaucracy. By the same token, 14 Stuttgart councillors were workers, a like number farmers, 12 were artisans, and some 27 were employed in various forms of commerce. Another 20 were women.[118] Parish councils were also increasingly likely to include Social Democratic members, particularly in towns where the party controlled local government, since law and custom dictated that a nominally Protestant mayor be offered a seat on the local parish council.[119]

---

[117] 1. LKT, *Verhandlungen* (1924), pp. 2231–2307, 2605–2749; Voelter, "Revolution von 1918," p. 335.

[118] Traub, *Jahresbericht 1919*, p. 15.

[119] On parish councils generally, see Friedrich Böhm, "Parochie und Gemeinde im 19. und 20. Jahrhundert" (Ph.D. diss., Marburg University, 1958), pp. 111–13. Because of their presumed administrative experience, mayors were usually welcome members even where they were otherwise cool to the clergy or church life. See Heidenheim, Pfarrbericht 1923, LKA A29/1887; also Alpirs-

Despite their democratic potential, or perhaps because of it, parish councils seldom exercised a salient influence upon local church life. Neither the revolution nor subsequent efforts to stimulate lay involvement had much effect on traditional patterns of deference and passivity. At times pastors or supervising Dekans might note a council's willingness to assume greater responsibilities, but the tone of parish reports suggests that such cases were considered exceptional.[120] More typically a pastor would remark, as in a 1921 report from Birkach, near Stuttgart, that members of the parish council were all "honorable men and well-disposed towards the church" but showed no initiative to confront issues beyond the bounds of the purely routine.[121] Gotthilf Supper, pastor in the Black Forest resort town of Schömberg, voiced a widely shared opinion when he lamented in 1927: "The pastor finds no effective support from members of his parish council. Such is probably almost universally the case in the countryside: that the pastor, in the final analysis, is on his own."[122]

Much the same could be said, mutatis mutandis, of the church assembly, the linchpin of the new democratic church order. The lack of grass-roots activism reflected in the uncertain fortunes of the Volksbund meant in turn that the assembly could not draw upon the energies of an informed lay constituency; as a consequence, its intended role as the democratic counterweight to established administrative authority seldom found more than ceremonial expression. The assembly's failure to capture parishioners' imagination became evident in the church elections of

bach, Pfarrbericht 1927; Ebersbach/Fils, Pfarrbericht 1929; and Göppingen, Pfarrbericht 1931; all in OKR/AR OA/PfB. See also Göppingen Kirchenbezirkstag, Nov. 14, 1932, minutes in DA Göppingen 142.

[120] E.g., Lorch, Pfarrbericht 1920, LKA A29/2637; Ravensburg, Pfarrbericht 1925, OKR/AR OA/PfB.

[121] Birkach, Pfarrbericht 1921, LKA A29/492; almost identical language can be found in Ludwigsburg, Pfarrbericht 1923, LKA A29/2666.

[122] Schömberg, Pfarrbericht 1927, and Hausen ob Lontal, Pfarrbericht 1928, both in OKR/AR OA/PfB. In the former case problems were compounded by theological tensions between the pastor, a liberal inclined towards socialism, and the strong pietist faction in the parish.

February 1925, the first held under the new constitution.[123] Widespread dissatisfaction with the experience of 1919 had led the assembly in 1922 to modify election procedures, although the basic structure of direct popular election in single-member districts remained unaltered.[124] The revised procedures slightly reduced the size of the assembly and streamlined the sometimes confusing system of overlapping lay and clerical districts set up in 1919. A new provision authorized the assembly itself to appoint four additional members of its collective choice, this in an attempt to remedy one perceived defect in the earlier procedure by making it possible for "deserving" candidates and other useful figures to serve even if they failed to win voters' approval. Among those seated by this route in 1925 were Eugen Reiff, the acknowledged leader of Group I, and Reutlingen Dekan Theophil Wurm, neither of whom had chosen to stand for election.

The election of 1925 aroused little public attention. In an essay written at about this time, Jakob Schoell decried the "astonishing public ignorance of church affairs,"[125] and the election provided little evidence to contradict him. An observer in Biberach—where over half the eligible voters cast ballots, one of the best showings of any district—later expressed the conviction that a majority of those who took part could not readily distinguish the theological stances of the two major groups.[126] The Biberach election was actually a formality, since no pastor could be found willing to challenge the liberal candidate, local Dekan Paul Scheurlen. The same was true in Reutlingen, where Jakob Schoell again stood as a consensus candidate despite considerable

[123] Assembly terms ran for six years. That elected in 1925 was officially designated Landeskirchentag in contrast to the constitutional assembly, or Landeskirchenversammlung, of 1919–25.

[124] A substantial number of liberals voted against the 1922 electoral ordinance because it again failed to provide some form of proportional representation. LKV, *Verhandlungen* (1922), p. 1908; cf. Voelter, "Revolution von 1918," pp. 335–36.

[125] Jakob Schoell, "Was bist du an dieser Kirche schuldig?" in Paul Scheuerlen, ed., *Du and Deine Kirche* (Stuttgart, 1925), p. 23.

[126] Rilling to Voelter, Feb. 7, 1925, LKA D1/13,2.

opposition from the district's strong pietist constituency.[127] In all, fully 40 percent of seats were uncontested, more than twice the proportion of six years earlier. In only one district did voting results alter the existing theological balance; in Schwäbisch Hall, where the incumbent conservative chose not to run again, the election went to a liberal, Karl Frasch, well known as director of the church's preparatory seminary in nearby Schöntal. In Stuttgart, the two theological factions this time agreed to coordinate their candidate lists so as to assure liberals at least two of the six seats being contested.

Such arrangements, coupled as they were with the absence of controversial issues, provided little incentive for mass participation. For all of Württemberg, the percentage of those who voted fell from nearly 42 percent in 1919 to 37.4 percent. Participation declined in the great majority of districts, often by a substantial amount; only ten districts recorded increases. Many of the latter were urban areas, such as Cannstatt and Heilbronn, where participation in 1919 had been comparatively low. Here the improvement may well have reflected marginally greater participation among workers. In Heilbronn, for example, the local SPD paper endorsed the candidacy of Hans Voelter, urging party members in good church standing to exercise their franchise. Voelter himself appealed openly for workers' support. For whatever reason, Heilbronn registered one of the few dramatic increases, participation rising from 30.5 percent to 44 percent, well above the churchwide average.[128]

The new assembly virtually replicated its predecessor in outlook and social composition—hardly surprising, since nearly half of those elected were incumbents. If anything the new assembly was more conservative and socially encapsulated than before. The majority for Group I increased slightly, while of the forty laymen elected, twenty-six were academics or civil ser-

---

[127] Wurm to Merz, Jan. 11, 1925, LKA D1/8,1. Wurm, then Dekan for Reutlingen, suggested that Schoell's position as prelate intimidated potential challengers among lower-ranking churchmen (including, by implication, Wurm himself, who had been approached by local pietists).

[128] *Neckar-Echo*, Feb. 1925; clippings in Voelter papers, LKA D1/13,2.

vants; the proportion of those from commerce, industry, and agriculture, by comparison, was reduced below the modest levels of 1919. This shrinkage was most dramatic in Group II, where only three of seventeen lay delegates came from the latter categories—a symptom, perhaps, of an inherent weakness in the liberal Volkskirche position.[129]

During its six-year term the assembly dealt with a variety of theological, liturgical, and organizational matters, including revisions of the service book and administration of the Tübingen Stift, which came under church control in 1928. For the most part, proceedings confirmed that the assembly's primary role was at once prophylactic and integrative. It provided a forum for the church's principal subcommunities to air their differences without turning local parishes into theological battlegrounds and to do so in an atmosphere heavy with the sense and symbolism of a higher unity. The formal designations Group I and Group II did as much over time to promote consensus as to confirm divisions. Eugen Reiff declared in 1927 that it was the informal exchanges within group caucuses, more than the formal plenary debates, that enabled delegates to arrive at positions all could support. Jakob Schoell was quick to agree. Theological differences aside, he asserted, groups were a virtual necessity "for the sake of a practical and expeditious handling of deliberations in the plenum." And Schoell drew lively applause by declaring that, with the church "threatened on all sides, . . . we [in the assembly] cannot . . . permit ourselves the luxury of fighting among ourselves in a manner that could only bring harm to the church."[130]

Far from providing a sounding board for grass-roots opinion, in practice the assembly tended to replicate old patterns of deference, leaving initiative and control securely in the hands of a tightly circumscribed elite. This drift towards self-encapsulation, both social and theological, was the most vivid impression

[129] Election statistics for 1925 in LKA A100/23; 1. LKT, *Verhandlungen*, Beilageband, pp. 1–8.
[130] 1. LKT, *Verhandlungen* (1927), pp. 288–93.

carried away by Gustav Gruner, a pastor elected to the assembly
in 1931 as a member of Group I. "It's the tone that makes the
music," he wrote in a letter to Friedrich Buck, the Waiblingen
Dekan whose diocese he represented. Continued Gruner:

> The groups bickered little among themselves. An official at
> the head table made such a racket that one could only think,
> with all due respect, *si tacuisses*. . . . There is no denying
> it: Group II is and remains the *haute volée*, with not a single
> common person among them. Goodman Tailor, Painter,
> Farmer can be found only in Group I. And eternal optimist
> that I am, I labored under the delusion that one or another
> of the old worthies across the way would favor us raw re-
> cruits with a handshake or a good word, but how wrong I
> was: the princes and dukes, the Privy Councillors and their
> ilk simply ignored us, just like they always have.[131]

One could hardly ask for a more candid commentary on the state
of ecclesiastical democracy at the end of the Weimar decade.

Reflecting on his own experience a generation later, after issues had been cast in a new light by the horrors of Nazism, Hans
Voelter for one had no doubt that the greatest tragedy of the
Weimar period was the church's failure to develop a vital "internal relationship to democracy." The original liberal agenda of
greater lay participation and less authoritarian church government remained unfulfilled. Having failed to educate its members
to democracy as an attitude and way of life, Voelter was convinced, the church must bear partial responsibility for the Third
Reich.[132] Other critics have advanced similar arguments. To
them, the reconstructed Protestant church order of the 1920s,

---

[131] Gruner to Buck, May 4, 1932, DA Waiblingen, LKA C4 4/160. The Latin
allusion is presumably to Plautus, *Poenulus*, 1.2.49: *Si tacuisses, jam istus taceo
non natum foret* ["If you had been quiet, that 'I'm quiet' would never have come
forth"].

[132] Hans Voelter, "Kirche in der Demokratie—Demokratie in der Kirche," address to 1958 Bietigheimer Tag; cf. Voelter, "Bietigheimer Tag"; Hans Gerhard
Fischer, *Evangelische Kirche und Demokratie nach 1945* (Lübeck and Hamburg,
1970), pp. 195–98.

typified perhaps by Prussia, can be considered a monument to the insecurity of the traditional ecclesiastical elite, whose distrust of the unchurched masses and deeply ingrained inclinations towards authoritarian categories militated against any prospect of genuine lay self-government. Indeed, one influential recent study of Prussia suggests that conservatives hoped to preserve an authoritarian church as a surrogate for the power base they had lost in society at large. In this view, democratization could only be regarded as one of those fictions to be exploited, like the concept of the Volkskirche itself, to defend a privileged institutional position in the face of massive public indifference.[133]

Was democratization, and by extension the Volkskirche model, merely a convenient fiction? The case of Württemberg suggests otherwise. Even in Prussia, where evidence of a nationalist-conservative mentality certainly abounded, it is by no means clear that conservative churchmen simply blocked democratic alternatives as a way of shoring up a political power base.[134] Both there and in Württemberg, the protracted debates over preambles to new church constitutions suggest that a concern for confessional integrity played a major if not decisive part. Nor is it at all obvious that a more far-reaching project of ecclesiastical democratization would have redounded to the political benefit of the republic. Not only did a majority of church folk continue to ignore opportunities for participation in church affairs, but those who did participate—who in ecclesiastical terms were therefore the most "democratically" minded—tended as a group to share antirepublican convictions.

Developments in Württemberg suggest on the whole that, Voelter's caveats notwithstanding, churchmen did make an effort to explore possibilities for democratization. While the November Revolution obviously provided the immediate stimulus

[133] Jacke, *Kirche zwischen Monarchie und Republik*, pp. 151–93, 246–303; cf. Nowak, *Kirche und Republik*, pp. 11–16, 76–81, 331–39.

[134] See, e.g., Borg, *Old-Prussian Church*, pp. 97–116 and passim; Jacke, *Kirche zwischen Monarchie und Republik*, pp. 286–298, offers a more political interpretation.

for church reform, thereby inevitably investing the issue with political significance, it seems evident that the idea of ecclesiastical democracy as such was not particularly controversial for Württemberg churchmen. Certainly it did not present itself merely as the cause of a single party or church faction. In any event, the controlling frame of reference for church reform was not ideological but ecclesiastical. Whatever its specific strengths or weaknesses, the postwar church order did not reflect a disguised referendum on the republic so much as an attempt to tap latent elements of the Volkskirche model. A case might be made that the strong populist strain in Württemberg's social and religious traditions encouraged churchmen there to be more receptive than many of their fellows elsewhere to democratic possibilities in church life. The adoption of universal suffrage in 1919, however pragmatic in conception, provides one indication of this. If the church constitution of 1924 produced little in the way of genuine innovation, its also erected few obstacles to the evolution of a kind of ecclesiastical republicanism. The immediate goal, however, was to harness traditional piety and the perceived virtues of the consistorial system to whatever new spirit of lay activism the era of revolution might call forth and to do so in ways that respected pastoral considerations of mutuality and theologically disciplined tolerance. Where the church could encourage diversity and private initiative it made some effort to do so, but not at the cost of dismantling confessional standards or disrupting time-honored expressions of the communion of the saints. Hence the ambiguity of formal democratization, which promised the laity a more direct voice in setting church policy but kept them at arm's length where personnel decisions were concerned.

If democratic initiatives yielded few tangible results, either in Württemberg or elsewhere, the reason was not so much that change was resisted from above as that it remained unsupported from below. For all their emotional investment in patriarchalist practices, Württemberg churchmen were also tempted to hope that, with the church freed from state control, a new lay consciousness could be nurtured and the boundaries of the active

Protestant community expanded. Maintaining commitment is of course a problem confronting virtually every religious community; it was by no means unique to German churches or to the Weimar era. Yet to Weimar churchmen the challenge of mass mobilizaton seemed particularly pressing, inasmuch as such support provided part of the basis on which they could lay claim to a normative public role. Even in Württemberg's comparatively receptive religious climate, however, and despite gestures towards parliamentarism, despite the Volksbund, and despite evangelistic appeals, hopes for renewal proved largely hollow. It was perhaps appropriate in this regard that Jakob Schoell failed to win election as the first postwar church president; he was, after all, the chief rallying symbol in Württemberg for the optimistic liberal inclusivism that was one of the clearest casualties of the early republican era. This liberal project foundered from the beginning on both the passivity of the masses and, it might be argued, the fervor of the few. The most consistently mobilized lay community after 1918 was certainly the pietists, whose orthodox theology and devotion militated against accommodation with, and acceptance by, more marginal segments of the church. Liberals, for their part, failed to offer compelling evidence that a more latitudinarian posture than the one provided in the constitutional compromise could have produced better results. As conservatives correctly pointed out, a weakening of confessional discipline would be as likely to encourage greater indifference as to enhance what Schoell had called the "sense of belonging." In practice, therefore, exclusivity and inclusivity alike promised to subvert as much as promote the Volkskirche renewal project. This paradox revealed much about the inherent limits of church reform.

Once allowance has been made for the unique aspects of a church's situation, such as the problems attendant upon maintaining voluntary adherence to a received dogmatic position, it might be argued that the problem of ecclesiastical democracy represented a special case of the more general problem of group formation and consensus-building in Weimar Germany. The inability of churchmen to forge a vital consensus across the spectrum of classes and ideologies represented in Protestant ranks suggests parallels with political parties as well as with other social and economic interest groups. Both in Württemberg and across Germany, the church claimed to embrace some two-thirds of the entire population. A clear majority of these putative followers, however, maintained only the most tenuous identification with church organizations, cultic practices, or a confessionally prescribed way of life. If the fall of the monarchy failed to effect more than a formal separation of church and state, internal reconstruction failed to effect more than a formal integration of church and society. Churchmen's problematic place in the public order resulted from the consequent discrepancy between institutional status and social base, between the church as protected Anstalt and as vulnerable Verein. The basic problem was not new in 1918, although the revolution served to accentuate it. That churchmen failed to solve it conclusively, either in Württemberg or elsewhere, cannot be attributed simply to an anachronistic clerical ideology. If the church remained for all practical purposes a stronghold of hierarchalism, it was so less by design than out of embarrassment, an embarrassment reflecting the absence of any effective alternative.

FOUR

Clergy and the Classroom

𝕴F CHURCHMEN could not appeal unreservedly to either the authority of a benevolent state or the volition of a committed mass membership, how could they hope to effectuate the Volkskirche ideal of an all-embracing moral community? The constitutional and ecclesiastical settlements of the immediate postwar period failed to provide churchmen with any new formula in terms of which to define their place and purpose. As a result, they found themselves forced to rely more heavily than before on what might be termed an auxiliary legitimation of Volkskirche claims: on activities, that is to say, that both asserted and invoked the church's duty, as one of the historic carriers of German culture, to nurture in society the marks of a Christian public order. The centerpiece of these endeavors was public education. As a microcosm of society, the school system—particularly the *Volksschule*, the public elementary school attended by an overwhelming majority of children—constituted a crucible of Volkskirche tradition. In their efforts to promote a religiously grounded and distinctively confessional structure of education, churchmen encountered a test not only of their public influence but also of the basic viability of Volkskirche values.

From the Reformation until well into the nineteenth century, relations between church and school in Württemberg, as in most Protestant regions, had been as intimate as they were self-evident. Universal education, established in embryo after the Thirty Years' War, presupposed a reciprocity of interests between and among church, state, and society. On the one hand the school served the immediate cause of the church. It not only supplemented preaching as a means of propagating doctrine but also served as an academic winnowing ground where churchmen could recruit promising candidates for university training and a career in the clergy. On the other hand schooling fulfilled a broader social purpose, encouraging the development of a citizenry with a modicum of both literacy and piety, disciplined to fear God and to respect temporal authority. Hence religion became doubly identified with education. Not only did catechetical instruction form a capstone of the curriculum, but confessional values, tempered by the precepts of the state, undergirded and infused all learning.

Whether this confessional education ever achieved its own highest purposes is questionable at best.[1] Institutional ramifications, however, were profound and long lasting. In most cases the school bench led directly to the church pew; church officials exercised rights of review in the training and appointment of teachers and often directly monitored their classroom activity. Religious instruction, provided sometimes by schoolmasters, sometimes by pastors, and sometimes by both in tandem, dominated the Württemberg curriculum. As late as 1900, teachers remained socially and occupationally subordinate to members of the clergy, who outranked them in academic status and prestige of office. It was not uncommon for a teaching position to entail not only classroom duties but also a variety of services to the parish. Schoolmasters were typically expected to serve as church organists. Often, too, their terms of employment included such menial tasks as cleaning, heating, and maintaining the church building. With a few regional exceptions, public education throughout Germany at the time of the Great War remained organized along confessional lines. Separate schools for Catholics, Protestants, and Jews were the rule in most states, including Württemberg, while religion remained almost universally a regular and usually compulsory subject of instruction. In Württemberg itself, formal religious instruction commanded three to four hours of class time weekly in the first four grades, with as much as five hours weekly thereafter. Until 1904 such instruction was

[1] Cf. Gerald Strauss, *Luther's House of Learning* (Baltimore, 1978), especially pp. 247–308.

compulsory for all pupils, including those whose parents did not belong to a church.[2]

While external forms of instruction were slow to change, the social synthesis on which schooling had originally been based became significantly attenuated in the course of the nineteenth century. Under the influence of broadly Enlightenment notions of education and public administration, most states, including Württemberg, established ministries of education separate from the church hierarchy. The result was that churchmen, while by no means excluded from school affairs, gradually came to play a more circumscribed role than before. Meanwhile, schoolmasters themselves—underpaid and often embittered by the humiliation of enforced submission to clerical dictates—were slowly beginning to assert an independent professional identity of their own. Well before the end of the century, the confessional school was under attack by both political and educational progressives. While not necessarily disputing a place in the schools for religion as such, critics argued for the elimination of many explicit confessional elements in favor of a greater emphasis on moral and ethical themes. Above all they demanded an end to ecclesiastical controls. For these critics, the school of choice was an interconfessional school (*Simultanschule*), in which confessional separation would be observed only in religion classes themselves, other instruction being given to all pupils in common.

[2] On the development of schools in Württemberg, see Eugen Schmid, *Geschichte des württembergischen evangelischen Volksschulwesens von 1806 bis 1910* (Stuttgart, 1933); Werner Katein, "Das Verhältnis von Staat, Kirche, und Volksschule im Königreich Württemberg," *ZfWLG* 15 (1956): 53–117; Wurster, *Kirchliches Leben*, pp. 165ff.; Leube, *Tübinger Stift*; and Douglas Skopp, "Auf der untersten Sprosse: Der Volksschullehrer als 'Semi-Professional' im Deutschland des 19. Jahrhunderts," *Geschichte und Gesellschaft* 6 (1980): 383–402. Useful general surveys include Ernst C. Helmreich, *Religious Education in German Schools: An Historical Approach* (Cambridge, Mass., 1959); Peter C. Bloth, *Religion in den Schulen Preussens: Der Gegenstand des evangelischen Religionsunterrichts von der Reaktionszeit bis zum Nationalsozialismus* (Heidelberg, 1968); Folkert Meyer, *Schule der Untertanen: Lehrer und Politik in Preussen, 1848–1900* (Hamburg, 1976); and Richard H. Samuel and R. Hinton Thomas, *Education and Society in Modern Germany* (London, 1949).

Social Democrats, having declared religion a private affair, went still farther, calling in the Mannheim Principles of 1906 for abolition of all religious instruction and reconstitution of the schools on a purely secular basis.[3]

At war's end these alternatives to the confessional school had yet to make significant inroads, although the Simultanschule could be found in several parts of central Germany and was the norm in Baden, Württemberg's immediate neighbor. The ideological challenge, however, was considerable, and the upheaval of 1918 gave it new momentum. The model of confessional schools that most churchmen continued wholeheartedly to defend in effect posited religion as a public affair, merging citizenship and confession while vesting in the church an implied mandate to guard the integrity of both. In contrast, the Simultanschule derived from a more pluralistic social construct that subordinated religion, at least in its explicitly confessional aspects, to the values of civil and political society in general and to the individual conscience in particular. If the interconfessional school remained an exception in practice, the conception of education that underlay it had made major strides during the generation before 1918. In the process, the time-honored clerical image of education had begun to erode at many points. A Württemberg law of 1905, for example, severed the automatic connection between teaching posts and petty parish duties. A further school reform act in 1909 partly eliminated one of teachers' chief grievances by ending clerical supervision of local schools except for religious instruction itself.[4]

Even before the war, therefore, much of the old ecclesiastical superstructure of Württemberg education had already been dismantled, though the formal confessional framework remained.

[3] On reformist programs, see Karl-Heinz Günther et al., *Geschichte der Erziehung*, 7th ed. (Berlin, 1966), pp. 442–47, 553–85; Marius Cauvin, *Le Renouveau pédagogique en Allemagne de 1890 à 1933* (Paris, 1970), pp. 227–72; and Rainer Bölling, *Volksschullehrer und Politik: Der Deutsche Lehrerverein, 1918–1933* (Göttingen, 1978), pp. 32–103.

[4] *Regierungsblatt* (1909), p. 161; on the background to this law, see the studies of Schmid and Katein cited in note 2, above.

The November Revolution did little to alter the direction of this process. To be sure, ARTICLE 144 of the Weimar constitution explicitly placed schools under state control, thereby depriving the church of any further supervisory role, even in the area of religious instruction. Moreover, while ARTICLE 149 recognized religion as a regular part of the curriculum in all but purely secular schools, it freed teachers from any compulsion to teach religion classes; pupils, too, could opt out with parental approval. Yet these measures could be accepted, even in Württemberg, as a logical outgrowth of the previous decade's school reforms. Nor did the letter of constitutional law place confessional schools as such in any immediate jeopardy. Although ARTICLE 146 appeared at some points to envision the Simultanschule as the future norm for elementary education, it also enshrined the principle of parents' choice, and Catholic church leaders as well as many Protestants were more than ready to exploit this as a rationale for confessional education. In any case, ARTICLE 174 specified that existing arrangements should remain in force until the question of school types could be resolved by binding federal legislation. Prospects for such legislation were hardly encouraging, as the murky constitutional language itself suggested. Three times—in 1921, 1925, and 1927—draft school bills were introduced into the Reichstag, and each time they foundered on irreconcilable differences in school policy between the republic's two major mass parties, the Catholic Center and the SPD.[5]

If the legislative stalemate in Berlin meant that school policy remained for the most part a province of the separate states, the provisions of ARTICLE 174, like those of the preceding article concerning state subsidies, left churchmen in the advantageous po-

[5] See Günther Grünthal, *Reichsschulgesetz und Zentrumspartei in der Weimarer Republik* (Düsseldorf, 1968); Christoph Führ, *Zur Schulpolitik der Weimarer Republik: Die Zusammenarbeit von Reich und Ländern im Reichsschulausschuss (1919–1923) und im Ausschuss für das Unterrichtswesen (1924–1933); Darstellung und Quellen* (Weinheim and Berlin, 1970); Bölling, *Volksschullehrer und Politik*; Borg, *Old-Prussian Church*, pp. 85–96, 123–67; and Frank J. Gordon, "The German Evangelical Churches and the Struggle for the Schools in the Weimar Republic," *Church History* 49 (1980): 47–61.

sition of defending local traditions to officials more concerned with legality than innovation. Debate over school policy in Württemberg moved within relatively narrow confines. Where disagreements arose, they almost invariably involved administrative details rather than broad structural issues. Within the familiar framework of confessional schools and formal religious instruction, however, churchmen continued to face new challenges to cultural hegemony. Forms and practices once compulsory were now becoming voluntary. The normative influence of religion in schools depended increasingly on the interest and cooperation of schoolmasters and school officials. More than that, it often came to depend on pastors' own capacity to make confessional values a vital part of their pupils' mental world. The fate of the church's educational project depended not simply on constitutional structures, important though these may have been, but also on churchmen's experience in the concrete world of classroom routine, their immediate relations with schoolmasters, parents, and children. Both inside and outside the classroom, institutional specialization and the secularization of public as well as private values militated against traditions churchmen hoped to preserve. To what extent, and by what means, could the church hold society to a uniform moral and spiritual code? This question underlay the church's educational project. Responses provided not simply a token of the church's institutional power but also an index of its social legitimacy.

The Decline of Compulsion

In school policy as in other aspects of church-state relations, the constitutional settlement of 1919 encouraged the native tendency of Württemberg's republican leaders to see themselves not as innovators but as trustees of tradition. The changes that occurred in school regulations after 1918 came about either in response to constitutional mandate or as attempts to compromise the conflicting demands of church officials, the teaching corps, political parties, and the general public. As a result they served chiefly to confirm and refine the pattern of previous educational reforms. School legislation of the 1920s continued to recognize confessional interests but also affirmed the primacy of civic values in the educational system. It thereby advanced the gradual process of differentiation by which, through law and popular custom, successive sectors of life were being defined out of the church's immediate sphere of influence. The school, once a virtual department of the church, was now defined conclusively as an agency of state, one in which churchmen might still play a role but which they could not expect to control. While religious instruction by no means disappeared from the classroom, it could no longer claim its old curricular pride of place.

The framework for postwar educational policy in Württemberg was established in the so-called Little School Act (Kleines Schulgesetz) approved by the Landtag in the spring of 1920. As its name implied, the law was conceived as a transitional expedient. Although preliminary drafts began circulating several months before the school paragraphs of the Weimar constitution assumed final form, the Württemberg Education Ministry did not attempt to think beyond the familiar system of confessional schools. The only structural change envisioned in the draft was an expansion of the Volksschule curriculum from seven years to eight (a change eventually mandated throughout Germany by ARTICLE 145 of the Weimar constitution).

Given the strength of the Württemberg DDP, which, appealing to the example of neighboring Baden, stood solidly for the introduction of the Simultanschule, church officials fully expected a more determined assault on the existing structure. In February 1919, a month before the first confidential draft appeared, the Consistory informed church leaders in Hannover that while the Württemberg regime seemed unlikely to tamper with religious instruction as such, prospects nevertheless appeared dim for retention of the confessional school.[6] This pessimistic assessment, of course, took little account of the powerful forces that in retrospect could be seen to have militated against innovation in

---

[6] Evangelisches Konsistorium, Hannover, to WEK, Feb. 26, 1919, and draft reply (Schoell), n.d., both in LKA A26/779.

Württemberg. Both before and after promulgation of the Weimar constitution, the responsible state officials saw no cause to think in anything but provisional terms; like most of the other parties concerned, they could assume that basic questions of school type would be answered on the national level. Lacking the revolutionary fervor of their Prussian or Thuringian counterparts, Württemberg officials had no compelling reason to venture beyond those practical tasks dictated by the moment. Once the constitution was in force, they were duty-bound to uphold existing arrangements. Moreover, the Catholic Center, which was as pivotal a coalition partner in Stuttgart as in Berlin, always made it clear that retention of confessional schools was an important part of its price for participation in the regime. Throughout Germany, but especially in regions where Catholics constituted a minority of the population, as in Württemberg, it was a matter of principle for the church's hierarchy that Catholic rights could only be adequately protected by means of confessionally separate schools. Nor was the constituency in favor of interconfessional education as united or determined in Württemberg as the initial constellation of political forces might have implied. While both the DDP and the SPD officially supported lay teachers' demands for the "liberation of the school from all ecclesiastical tutelage," key Democratic leaders such as Johannes Hieber, a former pastor, were by no means eager to force the issue. With Education Minister Berthold Heymann reconciled to a caretaker role and heavily dependent on subordinates for policy decisions, the likelihood of independent initiatives was in fact minimal.[7]

Nor should one discount the impression created by the broad-based Protestant mobilization of early 1919, however diffuse may have been its actual political results. Church leaders across the country discovered in the school issue their most effective tool for creating a receptive mass following. Couched in terms of

---

[7] See, e.g., Bälz to WEK ("Vertraulich!"), Mar. 28, 1919, LKA A26/779. The slogan is quoted in Günther et al., *Erziehung*, p. 529; cf. Bölling, *Volksschullehrer und Politik*, pp. 77–91, 105–8.

demands for parents' rights to a voice in educational policy-making, the plea to retain a confessional presence in the schools aroused widespread support among the laity, even those not otherwise given to active involvement in church life. During the spring of 1919, as noted in an earlier chapter, churchmen in northern and central Germany mounted a massive petition drive in favor of retaining religious instruction. Subsequent grassroots agitation culminated in early 1922 with the establishment of a self-styled National League of Parents (Reichselternbund) under the aegis of the Evangelical Press Association, and this organization thereafter provided an often effective vehicle for lobbying activity. In Württemberg too, pastors and lay church leaders were quick to exploit the opportunities afforded by the school issue to score propaganda points. While the Consistory did not officially sanction the petition drive of 1919, the nascent Volksbund and the local press arm of the church sounded the same rallying cries being used elsewhere. Opponents of confessional schools, they charged, were working to undermine the nation's moral fiber. Religious instruction helped to provide a foundation for both social attitudes and personal morality and hence was essential to the "spiritual and intellectual health" of both school and society. Without a formal place in the curriculum, "all the educative influence of religion will be lost on the overwhelming part of the urban population": so declared one Protestant tract in underscoring the connection between education and the Volkskirche ideal. Without religious instruction, "our people will become heathen; public morality will suffer great harm." Nor should those who held otherwise be taken seriously: "The blind man who talks about color cannot fool . . . anyone."[8]

In Württemberg as elsewhere, to be sure, a small minority of liberal pastors, such as Stuttgart's Albert Esenwein, spoke in fa-

[8] Schoell to Kirchenregierung Cassel, Feb. 7, 1925, OKR/AR Gen. 206c/I. The following are collected in LKA D1/24,3: "Wozu Religionsunterricht in der Schule?" *Ev. Volksbund für Württemberg* 1, no. 2 (1919); Bernard Hell, "Die christliche Schulgemeinde," typescript; and *Kirche und Schule*, pamphlet ("Nicht für die Presse"). On the Protestant campaign in Prussia, see Borg, *Old-Prussian Church*, pp. 84–86, 130–42.

vor of the Simultanschule as best suited to the confessional diversity of modern society. For an overwhelming majority, however, such a conclusion remained unthinkable. Speaking against Esenwein at a conference of churchmen, teachers, and political leaders convened by the Education Ministry in May 1919, Jakob Schoell joined Catholic leaders in strongly defending confessional schools. Church and school, he argued, must work in collaboration rather than in isolation. Moreover, so long as religion retained its proper place as an integral part of the curriculum, "no church can allow itself to be excluded from participation" in school supervision.[9]

Schoell served as the Consistory's chief liaison with the DEKA on educational issues, and he was here sounding themes that, with local variations, could be heard throughout Germany and at the National Assembly. Yet as Schoell was well aware, political and administrative currents were running strongly against his demand for continued clerical supervision. If the draft school law was a model of customary bureaucratic prudence, it nevertheless adumbrated the final emancipation of the schools from clerical control. It eliminated an important symbolic vestige of the old order by freeing teachers from the obligation to serve as parish organists; in the future such services must be freely contracted. All lay instruction, including that in religion, would now fall under the supervision of an administrative council (Oberschulrat) for Protestant schools within the Education Ministry. While the church would be represented on the Oberschulrat, its influence on local schools was certain to diminish. As the Weimar constitution would later dictate, religion was to remain a regular but not compulsory subject in the curriculum. Schoolmasters could voluntarily teach religion classes, but they would no longer be required to do so, while parents and legal guardians retained the right to have their children exempted from the religion requirement. Should a teacher decline to provide instruc-

[9] SM, May 28, 1919. A similar conference held in Berlin in 1920 followed much the same pattern: Bloth, *Religion in den Schulen Preussens*, pp. 191–94; Führ, *Schulpolitik*, pp. 45ff.; Günther et al., *Erziehung*, pp. 581–85.

tion, classes would become the responsibility of pastors or others designated by church officials. On another matter of acute concern to churchmen, the draft laid the groundwork for a reduction in the number of hours allotted to religious instruction in the various school grades.

As in the concurrent negotiations over financial subsidies, officials of the Education Ministry built their case for these changes on the established logic of prewar reform. In a confidential letter of transmittal to the Consistory on March 28, 1919, the ministry took the position that the draft merely incorporated refinements of existing policy, most of which would have become necessary even without the stimulus of the revolution. Compulsion and clerical control, it was argued, did not enhance the stature of religious instruction. More often they simply created antagonism among teachers, for whom clerical control represented a painful slight to professional self-esteem. Hence the new regulations, though drafted with an eye to likely constitutional directives, should also be seen as "thoroughly in harmony" with the long-term interests not only of the schools but of the church as well.[10]

The prospect of losing rights of supervision created a special dilemma for church leaders. Unlike their Catholic counterparts, whose conception of religion as fundamentally a church affair made them willing if need be to entrust religious instruction solely to the clergy, the Consistory held firmly to a time-honored principle of the German *Kulturstaat*, namely that because religion ideally served both civic and spiritual ends, the interests of culture dictated that religious instruction be a joint responsibility of church and school, hence of both pastors and teachers. For this reason church officials hesitated to dispense with lay religious instruction, a position reinforced by recognition of the logistical problems that would arise if the full burden of instruction were to fall on church personnel.[11] In October 1919, Stuttgart Dekan Theodor Traub tested the waters on this point

[10] Bälz to WEK, Mar. 28, 1919, LKA A26/779.
[11] See Schoell speech in LKV, *Verhandlungen* (1922), pp. 1914–16.

CLERGY AND THE CLASSROOM

with a motion in the church assembly calling for an end to all lay instruction in the event clerical supervision should be curtailed. Jakob Schoell, among others, objected that this course would only serve to isolate religion from the rest of the school curriculum and would consequently diminish rather than enhance the church's influence as cultural preceptor. Evangelical interests, another assembly delegate argued, demanded "understanding and reconciliation between church and state." Traub's motion went down to a decisive defeat.[12]

But with direct clerical supervision eliminated, particularly at the local level, how could the church be assured that religious instruction would, as the Weimar constitution specified, conform to established confessional tenets? While the Consistory saw little advantage in opposing most of the new regulations, it balked on the issue of supervision.[13] For nearly a year, Consistory and Education Ministry worked to find a mutually acceptable formula within the emerging constitutional framework. Prospects for success brightened somewhat after late 1919, when the SPD withdrew from the government coalition and the education portfolio passed to the new Württemberg Staatspräsident, Johannes Hieber. As a former pastor and educator, Hieber brought to the position considerably more empathy for churchmen's concerns than did his largely passive predecessor Berthold Heymann.[14] At the same time, the powerful influence that teachers exerted in the councils of his party, whose Landtag delegation included the chairman of the Württembergischer Lehrerverein (Württemberg Teachers' Association), Johann Löchner, precluded any major concessions to the Consistory's demands. Nor did the recently promulgated constitution leave much room for maneu-

---

[12] LKV, *Verhandlungen* (1919), pp. 196, 185–222, 227–94, 302–67; "Zur Erinnerung an D. Theodor Traub," typescript, Traub Personalakten, OKR/AR Pers. See also Traub, *Kirchliche Aufsicht über Religionsunterricht* (Ludwigsburg, 1922).

[13] Thus WEK to KM, May 13, 23, 1919, LKA A26/779. The Consistory initially argued that abolition of clerical supervision was too substantial a change to be introduced via ostensibly interim legislation.

[14] See Hieber to WEK, Dec. 15, 1919, LKA A26/779.

ver. The best that church officials could hope for was a benevolent approach to implementation. As passed by the Landtag in May 1920, the school law simply followed the language of the Weimar constitution, placing all instruction under state administration and stipulating that religious instruction must be conducted "in accordance with the principles of the religious group concerned." Jakob Schoell, who served as the church's official representative on the Oberschulrat, received private assurances from Hieber that, despite the official exclusion of churchmen from local school supervision, church interests would by no means be ignored. One practical possibility, implemented in 1921, involved granting the church informal veto power over the appointment of school officials concerned with supervising religious instruction.[15]

Given the great diversity in size and types of schools involved, from one-room village schools to large urban comprehensive schools, the law of 1920 necessarily dealt in generalities, with specific applications deferred to implementing regulations. Drafting of these regulations involved two additional years of intensive and often tediously complex negotiations. Throughout 1921 and early 1922, officials of church and school conferred regularly on such matters as the establishment of new syllabi for religion classes, the division of labor between lay teachers and pastors, scheduling principles, and the like. The sticking point in most discussions involved the place and extent of religious instruction in the curriculum. Pedagogical progressives had long protested that religion classes took up a disproportionate share of school time, time better devoted to other subjects. The Oberschulrat accordingly came under strong pressure to reduce the number of hours formally allotted to religion—as much as five

[15] Christoph to Wurm, June 27, 1919, LKA D1/13,1; "Zusammendfassende Darstellung der Schritte, die das Ev. Konsistorium gegenüber dem von der Regierung vorgelegten Entwurf eines kleinen Schulgesetzes getan hat," Schoell, memorandum, Feb. 23, 1920, LKA A26/779. "Der Vertreter des Ev. Konsistoriums bei der Min.abteilung für die höheren Schulen," typescript, Apr. 14, 1920, LKA D1/25. Schoell, notes, May 8, 1920, LKA A26/779; Landtag, *Verhandlungen* (1920), Beilageband II, pp. 1203–5.

hours weekly in the upper grades—to an average of two hours a week, even less in the lowest grades. Although on administrative grounds the Consistory was willing to entertain the possibility of adjustments, it strenuously objected to such wholesale reductions. In the course of one heated session, Schoell argued that any teacher capable of covering the established syllabus in less than the allotted time "only shows that he has not understood his task as a teacher of religion."[16] Faced with the conflicting demands of teachers and churchmen, the Oberschulrat predictably chose a middle way, establishing three hours as a weekly norm in upper grades, with four hours permissible under exceptional circumstances. The Consistory had little choice but to accede. Later it grudgingly accepted a norm of between two and three hours weekly in the four lowest grades.[17]

These regulations probably represented the most that churchmen could reasonably have expected to achieve. At the same time, however, they created a public relations problem of sorts. Led by the continuing flood of hyperbolic rhetoric about "parents' rights" to assume that the future of Protestant schools still hung in the balance, the church's most loyal lay supporters saw in the extended semisecret negotiations between Consistory and Oberschulrat an unholy alliance of bureaucrats at the expense of parental desires. While Consistory members were hardly averse to using lay discontent as a bargaining counter,[18] they also felt

[16] Zeller to Mosthaf, Jan. 3, 1922; Zeller to Gauger, Jan. 3, 1922; WEK to KM, Jan. 4, 1922; and Besprechungsprotokoll, Feb. 10, 1922; all in LKA A26/781. See also Zeller to Hieber, Apr. 15, 1922, LKA D1/25, and EVB, *Mitteilungen* 21 (Jan. 1922): 360ff. The Consistory estimated that under favorable conditions—i.e., when classes were small and homogeneous—a single teacher could cover the same amount of material in three hours that would have required four or five hours if split up between schoolmaster and pastor.

[17] KM to WEK, July 9, 1921; WEK to KM, July 11, 1921; Meyding to WEK, July 18, 1921; WEK to Koehler, Aug. 3, 1921; and WEK to KM, Aug. 18, 1921; all in LKA A26/780. WEK to KM, Mar. 21, 1922; WEK, Sitzungsprotokoll (Schoell), Mar. 24, 1922; and Bälz to WEK, Mar. 27, 1922; all in LKA A26/781. See also *SAfW*, Aug. 12, 1921, Apr. 15, 1922.

[18] Cf. WEK to KM, Jan. 4, 1922, LKA A26/781; Zeller to Hieber, Apr. 15, 1922, LKA D1/25.

vulnerable to charges from within Protestant ranks that, as Schoell formulated it in a speech before the church assembly in 1922, church leaders had "not taken seriously enough their obligation to represent the church's interests in the area of religious instruction."[19] Proposals to restrict clerical influence in schools met with hostility in many parts of the core church community. The *Stuttgarter Evangelisches Sonntagsblatt*, one of the most influential of church papers, denounced the draft school law, and by implication the constitution, as a "fundamental overthrow" of elementary education, a veritable blueprint for abandoning the traditional Christian basis of public schooling.[20] Rumors about subsequent implementation proposals triggered equally negative responses. An appeal from the Volksbund in the summer of 1921 warned the Consistory that closed-door negotiations, however desirable from the leadership's standpoint, were producing uneasiness among the laity. Arguing that the "Evangelical populace will not understand if everything is decided by official agreement alone," the Volksbund demanded that any agreement between church and school authorities be submitted to full debate and possible veto in the church assembly.[21] A coalition of pietists put the issue more bluntly. Christian Kohler, editor of the strongly pietist *Christenbote*, protested to the Consistory that "the more it is asserted that our church is not a Pfarrkirche, the more shocking it is when, in the case of such a fundamental reorganization as that being undertaken in religious instruction, church members are expected to accept a fait accompli, with no prior opportunity to make their position known."[22] Pietists in Schorndorf filed a formal petition with the church assembly asking that the parents of each school district be given the right to settle questions of scheduling and supervision for themselves.[23]

Despite assurances from the Consistory that questions about

[19] LKV, *Verhandlungen* (1922), p. 1910.
[20] *SES* 54 (1920): 61, 67.
[21] EVB to WEK, June 25, 1921, LKA A26/780.
[22] Kohler to WEK, July 4, 1921, LKA A26/780.
[23] LKV, *Verhandlungen* (1921), pp. 1498–99.

school negotiations would indeed receive a full airing in the church assembly,[24] lay restiveness did not abate. It was further fueled, no doubt, by the draft national school bill placed before the Reichstag in the spring of 1921. The left-liberal tone of this draft, which in its original form refused to recognize confessional schools as a regular school type, touched off a new wave of church-inspired agitation across the country. The revived national school debate probably accounts for some of the feverish rhetoric dispensed in public statements that otherwise appears out of all proportion to the matters at issue in Württemberg. But if one purpose of mobilization was to rush Swabian Protestants into the lines to defend the once-more threatened confessional school in Berlin, the local contest over curriculum and supervision also came in for pointed attention. Taking their lead from the massive national petition drive of 1919, the major pietist groups in Württemberg joined forces with the Volksbund over the winter of 1921–22 to launch a drive aimed not at the National Assembly—already the target of a concerted Catholic petition campaign—but at the Württemberg Landtag, demanding both restoration of the deleted hours of instruction and reinstatement of some form of church supervision. Vigorous propaganda and careful organization produced some 583,000 signatures within a month, a figure representing nearly three-quarters of all adult Protestants in Württemberg. Signatures came not only from obvious strongholds of piety in small towns and the countryside but also from urban working-class districts. As the national drive had done two years earlier, the Württemberg effort provided a striking indication of the extent to which the school issue tapped a residual vein of traditionalism even among those groups on the most distant margins of the church community. It seems unlikely that all those who signed petitions shared the passions of the drive's organizers or even understood the precise positions being advanced. Still, a substantial majority of Württembergers clearly continued to regard religion in some form as a proper re-

[24] WEK to Kohler, Aug. 3, 1921, and WEK to KM, Aug. 18, 1921, both in LKA A26/780. See also *SAfW*, Aug. 12, 1921.

sponsibility of the schools; many may simply have been registering opposition to any drastic change in the accustomed order
of things.[25]

As a show of strength, the petition drive was a dramatic success. As a lobbying tactic, however, it produced minimal results.
One reason has already been suggested: the issues addressed
were fairly limited and the contending parties' freedom of maneuver correspondingly restricted. While a narrow construction
of the Weimar constitution might have permitted the state to
designate churchmen as agents for supervising religious instruction, this was hardly a feasible political option for the Hieber
government. Beyond this, implementation policies were primarily a responsibility not of the legislature but of career officials,
who were more likely to think in terms of state interests than
mass demands.

There is some evidence that Württemberg church leaders
themselves regarded their supporters' propaganda offensive
with ambivalence. To the extent that it fostered the Protestant
cause in Berlin, of course, they welcomed it. Through the DEKA
and Evangelical Press Association, the Württemberg church
joined the fray over national school legislation, if sometimes at
a discreet distance. At the same time, however, members of the
Consistory could be tempted to interpret grass-roots unrest as a
signal of distrust over the activities of all officialdom, both secular and ecclesiastical. Addressing the church assembly in 1922
shortly after the Hieber government promulgated its implementation regulations, Jakob Schoell sought to justify the Consistory's course of action since 1920, and in the process he also provided an implicit defense of his counterparts in the Education
Ministry. The Consistory, Schoell declared, did not question
school officials' basic appreciation of the importance of religious
instruction. Moreover, considering the diversity of viewpoints
with which it had to contend, the Education Ministry had loyally

[25] EVB, *Mitteilungen* 20 (Dec. 1921), 22 (Apr. 1922); [Theodor] Traub, *Jahresbericht 1921* (Stuttgart, 1922), p. 9. On national developments during this period, see Borg, *Old-Prussian Church*, pp. 135–42.

accorded every consideration to the church's proposals. Acknowledging the sometimes emotion-laden character of the issues involved, Schoell insisted that church leaders had "made every effort to approach the questions that have arisen with a calm objectivity and not to let this considered objectivity be diverted by [polemics], whatever their source." Schoell continued:

> We gave up what we were convinced was either simply outdated or impossible to retain under the changed circumstances. On the other hand we honestly strove . . . to insist upon what we consider indispensable for religious schooling and training. This calm, objective stance the Consistory will continue to maintain in the future.[26]

Although school affairs continued to generate a certain amount of friction in following years, the interest of the masses soon ebbed in the face of accomplished fact, and Württemberg was largely spared the school strikes and protracted community wrangles that plagued parts of Prussia and the north. Only once during the latter half of the decade did school policy again give promise of becoming a divisive public issue. Again the impetus came from outside Württemberg. In 1927 the DNVP minister of the interior in Berlin, Walter von Keudell, introduced into the Reichstag yet another draft school law, this one strongly favorable to conservative Protestant interests. Since the Keudell bill would have permitted existing confessional school systems to function virtually without restriction, the Württemberg church leadership, in concert with other Protestant leaders, gave it more or less enthusiastic support. Like its predecessors, however, the Keudell bill fell victim to coalition politics. Hence, the framework for Württemberg educational policy throughout the Weimar period remained as established in the ostensibly temporary agreements of 1920–22.[27]

[26] LKV, *Verhandlungen* (1922), p. 1919.

[27] DEKA Schulausschuss, Sitzungsprotokoll, July 29, 1927, and Merz to Kapler, Sept. 17, 1927, both in OKR/AR Gen. 206c/I. Jakob Schoell, "Um das Reichsschulgesetz," *SM*, Beilage, Nov. 19–20, 1927. An attempt to draft new comprehensive regulations in Württemberg in 1928–29 likewise fell victim to person-

School legislation of the early 1920s pointed up once again the ambivalence of the Volkskirche position. On the one hand, the survival of the confessional school as a normative type in Württemberg seemed to bolster churchmen's vision of a social order still based explicitly on confessional religious principles. And while this happy outcome may have been due in the first instance to Catholic intransigence and political clout, especially in Berlin, churchmen could point to the outpouring of support in the 1922 petition drive as plausible evidence for their claim that the Volkskirche in Württemberg truly rested on a bedrock of broad popular support. Yet this support, as the level of active church life indicated, remained fairly diffuse. Beneath the friendly assurances of government officials and the widespread public assent to the church's position on religious instruction, churchmen were losing ground in the struggle to define educational goals. The reduction in hours of instruction, the end of compulsion, and the elimination of clerical supervision all presaged a loosening of ties between church and school.

Churchmen would continue to have a role in schools as religion teachers; indeed, as we shall see, this role expanded considerably after 1920. Moreover, they would continue to have a voice both on the Oberschulrat in the Education Ministry and on local school councils (*Ortsschulräte*). Still, they could no longer claim to be the principal arbiters for education. In this respect, school policy, despite bows to church interests, faithfully reflected the postulates of a neutral state. To the extent that the church constituted a significant force in the community, it could count on a sympathetic hearing. But there were also countervailing demands to be considered—notably, in this case, those of the teachers' associations. The Consistory's freedom of action was therefore limited both by constitutional structures and by administrative punctilio. Jakob Schoell's speech to the church assembly showed an awareness of these new constraints; it remained to be seen what they might mean in practice.

---

ality and political-party clashes; cf. Besson, *Württemberg und die deutsche Staatskrise*, pp. 48–50. See also Borg, *Old-Prussian Church*, pp. 146–67.

SCHOOLMASTERS AND RELIGIOUS INSTRUCTION

On the surface, certainly, school policy continued to affirm traditional notions about the utility of religious instruction as a source of both personal spirituality and public virtue, of initiation into the life of the church and of preparation for responsible citizenship. If the petition drive of early 1922 was any indication, this was a model to which most of the population gave at least passive assent. To serve its intended purposes, however, religious instruction required the cooperation of those teachers, pupils, and parents, and while church leaders could appeal for such cooperation, they could hardly expect to compel it.

With clerical supervision abolished, personal attitudes of teachers took on special significance. Under ARTICLE 149 of the Weimar constitution, the confessional stance of the individual teacher became a private affair; just as children of dissidents were under no obligation to attend religion classes, so too a teacher was no longer obligated to provide such instruction. Since dissidents almost invariably constituted too small a minority to justify separate schools, and since most such dissidents in Württemberg were lapsed Protestants living in largely Protestant areas, children of dissidents almost always remained in Protestant schools. The same was likely to prove true of the teaching corps. Nor was it automatically certain that those teachers who continued to provide religious instruction would do so, as the constitution required, in conformity with church principles. Direct observation was impossible, and although the Catholic hierarchy in Württemberg had long enjoyed legal authority to evaluate prospective lay teachers of religion, the same right had not been extended to Protestants, the former church-state symbiosis in effect rendering such a provision unnecessary. The veto power over supervisory appointments vouchsafed in 1921 was a welcome tool, but it still left the church one step removed from classroom performance.

Under the circumstances, it was perhaps not unreasonable for church officials to worry about a potential dilution of the schools' confessional character. With religious instruction vol-

untary, and with no explicit provision for a confessional emphasis in other subjects,[28] there seemed little to assure retention of
the religious tenets that by the church's argument provided an
integral basis for education. How then could the church advance
its interests in the classroom without reviving the specter of
overweening clericalism? Churchmen could hardly view religious instruction as passive bystanders. On the other hand, most
forms of self-assertion risked antagonizing teachers, who ideally
would provide the linkages between religion and the rest of
classroom learning. For religious instruction to be effective, in
short, the church needed teachers' voluntary cooperation, and
many of them, as a matter of professional honor, both resented
past ecclesiastical intrusions and took a jaundiced view of
churchmen's present intentions.

In religion as in other subjects, teachers were required to follow a prescribed syllabus, thereby providing churchmen with a
measure of prior control. Although issued through the Oberschulrat, syllabi for religion classes remained a responsibility of
the church. Nor were all teachers hostile to a genuinely confessional form of religious instruction. Pietism claimed many adherents among Württemberg schoolmasters, as it did among
other lower middle-class occupations. Some seven hundred
teachers, perhaps one-eighth of the total teaching force, belonged to the pietist-dominated Evangelischer Lehrerverein
(Evangelical Teachers' Association), a group whose entire national membership numbered fewer than four thousand. The
Württemberg branch of the association generally supported the
church leadership's position in postwar controversies. Like other
educators, to be sure, pietist teachers welcomed the end of direct
clerical supervision. As they saw it, the "power-lust of many
clergymen" had in the past only served to weaken the church's
moral authority.[29] Beyond this, however, the association provided a solid phalanx of support for confessional education. The

[28] Cf. speech of Johannes Hieber, Landtag, *Verhandlungen* (1928), p. 4000.
[29] *Der Lehrer-Bote* (Apr. 1919), pp. 29–30; cf. Bölling, *Volksschullehrer und Politik*, pp. 39–40.

association's annual convention in 1919 passed a resolution attacking proposals for the Simultanschule as a "brutal assault" on families' rights to religiously grounded schooling.[30] In conjunction with the Volksbund, the Evangelical Teachers' Association played a vigorous part in the petition campaign of 1922, which it applauded as a genuine expression of popular sentiment.[31] For members of this group, cooperation with the church seemed both desirable and largely self-evident. Teachers should be involved in religious instruction both for pedagogical reasons— "in normal circumstances [the classroom teacher] can exert the most influence on the children"—and also because "in this way [the teacher] himself can best be won and kept for the service of the church."[32]

Such sentiments, however, were far from universal. "The majority of teachers in our Protestant schools are, unfortunately, hostile to the church," Consistory president Hermann von Zeller insisted early in 1919.[33] To the extent Zeller was correct, this probably had less to do with religion as such than with a conviction that the church as an institution represented a major impediment to intellectual freedom and pedagogical progress. Many also argued that to maintain confessionally segregated schools militated against a truly liberal society and polity. This was the position taken by the largest of Württemberg's teacher groups, the Württembergischer Lehrerverein, a regional affiliate of the most influential national pressure group of educators. Strongly identified since 1848 with populist-democratic currents in Württemberg politics, the Lehrerverein generally supported the fledgling republic in hopes that it would bring an end to clerical influence in schools. As an unsympathetic observer remarked early in 1919, religious instruction constituted a particular "thorn in the eye" for Lehrerverein activists, to whom the confessional school stood as a symbol of outworn ideas and craven subordination to the church. At a minimum the association

<hr />

[30] *SM*, Dec. 12, 1918; *Der Lehrer-Bote* (Nov. 1919), pp. 85–86.
[31] "Zur Schulfrage," typescript, n.d. (copy), LKA D1/24,3.
[32] Thus K. Kühnle to Wurm, Nov. 25, 1929, LKA D1/3,1.
[33] Zeller to Vibel, Feb. 12, 1919, LKA A26/322.

demanded freedom of conscience; religion should be a matter of individual choice, not legislated compulsion. If religious instruction was to remain a regular part of the teacher's task, he must be free to approach it from his own perspective, not as an automaton transmitting rote materials set by churchmen according to a rigidly prescribed syllabus. A heavy majority of these teachers favored establishment of the Simultanschule, while among younger teachers the idea of purely secular schools as demanded in the Social Democratic Mannheim Principles of 1906 aroused considerable interest.[34]

It is hardly surprising, therefore, that new Württemberg school regulations and the constitutional stalemate they reflected should have left many teachers dissatisfied, not to say bitter, convinced that the upper echelons of church and state bureaucracy were once again ignoring legitimate pedagogical concerns. Responding to the administrative agreement of 1921, which gave the Consistory veto power over supervisory appointments involving religion, the Lehrerverein declared bluntly that regardless of the limits the new regulations appeared to place on the clergy's influence, past experience showed that the church would find ways to "exploit them to the utmost."[35] In 1924, with hopes for national school legislation fading, the association's journal featured an article that related the present debate over religious instruction to the long struggle of teachers seventy years earlier to win authorization for a secular reader to supplement the Bible and catechism in elementary grades. Where school policy was involved, the article argued, progress came only after bitter struggle with "the most diverse advocates of reaction or stagnation." Nowhere was this more true than in the teaching of religion; then as now, the church was a paragon of "short-sightedness," its influence fatally weakened by a "naive"

---

[34] *Der Lehrer-Bote* (Feb. 1919), p. 16; K. Ulshöfer, "Die Schule und der Ev. Volksbund," *Württembergische Lehrerzeitung* 80 (1920): 100–101. Other representative pieces in the same volume include "Zur Reform des Religionsunterrichts," pp. 189–91, 197–99, and "In Uebereinstimmung mit der Grundsätzen der Kirche?" pp. 314–15.

[35] Printed in *SNT*, Apr. 7, 1921.

equation of "religious" and "conservative."[36] In 1927, when a diocesan synod in Crailsheim passed a resolution applauding the Keudell bill's proposed recognition of confessional schools, one-third of the district's teachers protested to the Oberkirchenrat, arguing that such resolutions violated the spirit of the Weimar constitution, which by their reading could only be taken to envision the Simultanschule as the future national norm.[37]

The critical reserve with which a substantial number of teachers regarded the existing system, including the place and purpose of religious instruction, suggested a difficult period of adjustment once new school regulations took effect. Beginning in May 1922, religion officially ceased to be a compulsory part of lay teachers' duties, and during preceding months churchmen girded themselves to deal with an expected onslaught of resignations. The Dekan in Schwenningen, for example, informed the Consistory in March that fully half the teachers in area schools had given preliminary notice of their intention to drop religion classes. From Heilbronn came a similarly somber forecast. In Langenburg, east of Heilbronn, the Dekan reported that most teachers proposed to boycott religion classes "not as a matter of principle but purely as a tactical action against the church." In response, the Consistory encouraged local church officials to make good use of the new regulations. Where teachers were uncooperative, it was suggested, parishes might revoke their contracts as church organists, depriving them of a modest source of supplementary income.[38]

In the end, a variety of factors combined to forestall the worst of the expected crisis. Of those teachers who initially threatened

[36] *Der Beobachter*, June 21, 1924; *Württembergische Lehrerzeitung* 84 (1924): 284–85. Cf. Schmid, *Volksschulwesen*; Katein, "Kirche, Staat, und Volksschule."

[37] Kirchenbezirkstagung Crailsheim, Nov. 21, 1927, Protokoll; "Vertrauliche Beschwerde evangelischer Volksschullehrer aus Anlass des letzten Kirchenbezirkstagung des Ev. Bezirks Crailsheim," Dec. 10, 1927; Dörrfuss to OKR, Jan. 12, 1928; and Röcker to OKR, July 3, 1928; all in OKR/AR Gen. 206c/III.

[38] DKA Schwenningen to WEK, Mar. 13, 1922, and DKA Heilbronn to WEK, Mar. 2, 1922, both in LKA A26/781. DKA Langenburg to WEK, Apr. 3, 1922, LKA A26/788.

to withdraw, only a fraction actually did so after the regulations of 1922 took effect. Some who announced an intention to boycott religion probably did so as a form of protest against the excessive zeal of Protestant activists during the Volksbund petition drive earlier in the year. Where refusals did occur, they were typically the actions of individuals rather than of organized groups. Moreover, some who opted out of religion classes subsequently agreed to resume instruction. In Backnang, for example, a number of teachers who retracted in this manner indicated privately that they had gone along with plans for a mass boycott under pressure from colleagues to maintain a united front. The schoolmaster in one village near Crailsheim, while inclined on principle to give up religion classes, consented to retain responsibility for the primary grades both as a token of recognition for the generally good relations between church and school in the village and out of regard for the difficulties that might have arisen for the local pastor, who by law and tradition would otherwise have been forced to provide all religious instruction himself. In the end, open noncooperation appears to have been the exception. Church leadership maintained no systematic data on teachers' actions, since the number of those who abandoned religious instruction never became large enough to pose an administrative problem. The same was true where pupils were concerned; only a very small percentage of parents or guardians formally removed their children from religion classes.[39]

Even those teachers who did sever their ties with religion remained under the indirect influence of church authorities to the

[39] DKA Backnang to WEK, Mar. 30, 1922; PfA Waldershub bei Crailsheim to WEK, July 21, 1922; and other reports in LKA A26/788. The 1920 school law, following a pattern of previous legislation going back at least to 1836, specified that religious instruction was to be the responsibility of "representatives [*Diener*] of the church" and by teachers "qualified and willing" to do so. While this language left room for church authorities to assign teachers other than pastors to religion classes, this was an unlikely option except in larger towns and cities. For analysis, see Joseph Haller, "Die Beteiligung der Geistlichen am Religionsunterricht in den Volksschulen Württembergs" (holograph copy), LKA/SS P 3/7.

extent that a representative of the Consistory sat as one of the designated members of the Oberschulrat for Protestant schools within the Education Ministry. Cases with which the Oberschulrat dealt showed that where the church's authority ran counter to an individual teacher's private opinions or freedom of action, the Oberschulrat, mindful of its constitutional mandate to uphold the existing confessional system, invariably upheld the church's position. An important test case occurred in Heilbronn shortly before the 1922 regulations took effect. In March the district of Heilbronn filed a complaint with the Consistory charging that two local teachers—neither of whom, surprisingly, had asked to be relieved of religion classes after May—had taken public stands in support of anticlerical positions. Among other things, they had signed a local freethinkers' newspaper appeal urging parents to renounce church membership and to withdraw their children from religion classes. Such activity violated no established code of teachers' conduct and hence could not by itself constitute grounds for disciplinary proceedings. The district nevertheless requested that the Consistory bring the matter to the attention of school authorities. Some months later, in July, the Education Ministry issued a policy statement declaring that to hold a position as teacher in a confessional school precluded public agitation against church membership or religious instruction. Establishment of this principle placed teachers on notice that future actions of the sort reported in Heilbronn could result in formal sanctions.[40] A test of the ruling came four years later in Schwenningen, a site of frequent clashes between churchmen and their critics. In the Schwenningen case a teacher published an article in the local Social Democratic paper urging working-class families not to allow their children to attend religion classes or take preconfirmation instruction. After church officials complained, the Oberschulrat issued an administrative reprimand. All teachers, it declared, regardless of personal political or religious convictions, bore a positive obligation to show

[40] Eytel to WEK, Mar. 23, 1922, LKA A26/409; KM, Erlass Nr. 10223, July 18, 1922 (copy), LKA A26/788.

consideration for students' religious sensitivities. The teacher in question avoided further consequences by admitting error and agreeing to refrain in the future from political agitation—in effect, by agreeing to a voluntary limitation on his constitutional rights of expression.[41]

If cases of this sort seemed to confirm teachers' complaints about continued subjugation to an ecclesiastical yoke, they also testified to an essential ambiguity in the notion of the confessional school itself. On one hand, the argument for religious instruction and separate confessional schools implied that a particular religious perspective, identified with the doctrines and practices of a particular church, was properly fundamental to the educational process. On the other hand, in token of the growing complexity of society, this religious component had come to be defined as voluntary. To the extent that the old confessional argument prevailed, the result could only be some form of compulsion at the expense of individual volition, a set of limits on free expression of the sort defined in the disciplinary cases just mentioned. To the extent that a voluntary emphasis prevailed, however, the religious perspective could hardly be considered determinative.

Like the Volkskirche itself, the confessional school depended in practice upon an active public consensus, the positive expectations of a nominally Protestant community. Where these expectations were strong and generally shared, the confessional character of the school presented no problems. This was the case, for example, in the village of Altheim, near Ulm, where a teacher was involuntarily relieved of his religion classes in early 1921 after members of the community protested that his presentation no longer reflected a "Christian standpoint."[42] Where a strong community consensus did not exist, compulsion by itself was in-

[41] Eitel to OKR, Jan. 28, 1926; Hinderer to OKR, Feb. 2, 1926; OKR to Oberschulrat, Feb. 10, 1926; and Oberschulrat to Bezirksschulrat Rottweil, Mar. 1, 1926 (copy); all in OKR/AR Gen. 206c/I.

[42] Altheim, Kirchengemeinderatssitzung, Dec. 16, 1920, Protokoll (copy); Haller, memorandum, Dec. 28, 1920; and WEK to DKA Ulm, Jan. 15, 1921; all in LKA A26/781.

sufficient to resolve attendant difficulties. We have already noted that since dissenters invariably comprised a small minority of the population in any given area, the provision of separate schools—that is, "confessional" schools without religious instruction—was out of the question on practical grounds. The result, in turn, was a de facto mixture of confessions in schools officially designated as Protestant or Catholic. Since such schools had to afford minorities the same considerations enjoyed by the majority, administrative problems inevitably cropped up, with the cumulative effect that religious instruction often lost ground in the curriculum despite its officially favored status.

In areas where substantial opposition to religious instruction existed, school officials generally attempted to arrange schedules in such a way that teachers at odds with the church had the least possible contact with pupils of active churchgoers, especially those approaching confirmation age. Where numbers permitted, conversely, pupils exempted from religious instruction by their parents were assigned to teachers who were themselves no longer involved in religious instruction.[43] Especially in the cities, where anticlerical strength was greatest, churchmen, parents, teachers, and school officials sometimes became embroiled in arguments over the boundaries of accommodation to diverse perspectives. In the factory-studded Stuttgart suburb of Botnang, for example, Erhard Schneckenberger, a schoolmaster heavily involved in left-wing youth activities, requested permission in 1923 to establish a course in nonreligious philosophy for students no longer attending religion classes. Once again the Oberschulrat intervened with a ruling favorable to the church's position. It pronounced the course inappropriate to the curriculum of a Protestant school and denied Schneckenberger his request to offer it as part of his normal teaching duties. While the course could be offered informally, outside of regular school hours, school facilities could only be used with the approval of the town fathers. Moreover, Schneckenberger would face disciplinary ac-

[43] OKR to Oberschulrat, Mar. 25, 1926; Eitel to OKR, Apr. 28, 1926; and Schoell, memorandum, Dec. 20, 1926; all in OKR/AR Gen. 206c/I.

tion if he sought to recruit prospective participants among pupils enrolled in regular religion classes.[44]

By means of such rulings, state school officials, urged on by the church leadership, sought to insulate the classroom from anticlerical sentiment and from controversies over the status of religion. Much of the latent tension to which we have alluded found its outlet not within the educational bureaucracy as such but rather in local school councils, the boards representing administrators, teachers, and the general public that ordinarily saw to the implementation of policies impinging most directly on the routines of pastors, pupils, and schoolmasters. The politicization of local school administration can be seen in the growing ambivalence with which many in the clergy regarded involvement in what had once been a natural extension of the pastor's office. Although the school law of 1909 had relieved them of direct school supervision, pastors continued to share with school superintendents the chairmanship of local school councils. The school law of 1920 altered this requirement as well, making pastors' participation on school councils optional. Symptomatically, the change met with considerable cautious approval in the Pfarrverein; in discussions of school administration in 1919 and again in early 1920, pastors in about equal numbers supported and opposed continued clerical presence on school councils. Those in the latter camp saw involvement as a double source of difficulty. Not only might the pastor become mired in ideological disputes that he lacked any authority to resolve, being himself one of the contending parties, but his very presence as a member of the school council would provide grist for the mills of those convinced that the church intended to continue meddling in education wherever possible. Although for tactical reasons the Pfarrverein later adopted a resolution approving continued participation, the vote did not reflect the triumphalism it implied.[45]

[44] Hieber to WEK, Dec. 3, 12, 1923, LKA A26/781. See also typescript report on Schneckenberger, Aug. 18, 1919, LKA D4/14x.

[45] EPW, Vertrauensmännerversammlung, Apr. 30, 1919, Apr. 27, 1920, Protokollbuch II, D/EPW 22; cf. *KAfW* 28 (1919): 132–33. On the structure of school councils, see Katein, "Staat, Kirche, und Volksschule," pp. 112–13.

It was a measure of the problems pastors foresaw in the new era that at the same time many of them were seeking to extricate themselves from local school administration, a growing number of dissidents appeared eager to take their places. Just as the confessional designation of a school did not preclude employment of teachers no longer committed to the church, so too did the school councils become magnets for dissident parents, particularly in cities and towns where the left wielded political influence. Under the school law of 1909, dissidents could be appointed to local school councils only in exceptional cases and then only with explicit dispensation from the Oberschulrat. By the mid-1920s, requests for such dispensations were becoming so commonplace that the Education Ministry for a time considered revising the provisions of 1909.[46] Church officials or sympathetic local politicians might protest, but efforts to keep school councils free of dissident influence had little effect. In 1926, for example, the town council in Zuffenhausen, another of Stuttgart's industrial suburbs, filled a vacancy on the local school council with one of its own members, a Social Democrat who had left the church three years earlier—this despite the fact that another town councillor, a Social Democrat in good standing with the church, had expressed a willingness to serve. At the request of the Zuffenhausen parish council, the Oberkirchenrat petitioned the Education Ministry to nullify the appointment, but to no avail. Three years later the same council filled another vacancy with one Gottlob Mayer, who notwithstanding his pious name was head of the local freethinkers' group. Again the church raised protests, and the local Volksbund chapter prepared to make a public issue of the matter. After lengthy negotiations the Ministry of Education voided Mayer's appointment on the grounds that no exceptional circumstances existed to warrant it. In contrast to its policies regarding teachers, however, the ministry declined to make a general ruling on the issue.[47]

[46] Schoell, memoranda, May 30, Dec. 20, 1926, OKR/AR Gen. 206.

[47] Lauxmann to OKR, Feb. 5, 1929, with copy of Kirchengemeinderat Zuffenhausen, Sitzungsprotokoll, Feb. 2, 1926; Schoell to KM, Feb. 10, 1926; Schoell, memoranda, Mar. 25, Apr. 23, May 30, Dec. 30, 1926; Lauxmann to OKR, Feb.

Similar controversy erupted over a proposal to appoint Erhard Schneckenberger, the Botnang teacher, to the school council for greater Stuttgart. Arguing that the confessional system discriminated against dissidents since they had no choice but to attend the Protestant school, supporters claimed that without one of their own in the school administration such students lacked the representation they deserved. One member of the city council, a lapsed Catholic, asserted to general merriment that personal ideology bore little relevance to the mundane work of local school administration: noodle soup was noodle soup regardless of religious confession. Conservatives on the council responded angrily. One claimed that the rationale being advanced was self-contradictory; if school councils dealt only with technical matters, then representation for dissident children was a moot consideration. In any event, the church's defenders objected, dissidents were already grossly overrepresented in Stuttgart; of twelve current members of the local school council, three had no formal religious affiliation, although a mere 3 percent of the city's Protestant school population had withdrawn from religion classes. The conclusion could only be that opponents of the confessional school system were working to undermine it from within—a charge that provoked countercharges that a backstairs intrigue of rightists was at work to deprive Social Democrats of their legal rights to appointment and representation. When the clamor subsided, the results were unchanged; Schneckenberger kept his appointment.[48]

Not all difficulties with local oversight involved ideological conflicts or political tactics. More common, in fact, were the age-old petty tensions resulting from clashes of personality, narrow bureaucratic horizons, or overzealous defense of minor prerogatives of office. Such local quarrels only rarely reached the higher offices of church or state, since they seldom involved major principles. Where grievances accumulated, however, the ef-

2, 1929; OKR to KM, Feb. 5, 1929; Schoell, memorandum, n.d.; and Bazille to Ev. Oberschulrat, Apr. 20, 1929 (copy); all in OKR/AR Gen. 206.

[48] *Amtsblatt der Stadt Stuttgart* 29 (Mar. 7, 1929).

fect on the classroom could be considerable, providing one measure of churchmen's status in the theoretical and administrative crosscurrents of the educational enterprise.

A suggestive though hardly typical example of how such friction could develop can be found in the Black Forest district of Freudenstadt. With a population dispersed among numerous small villages and isolated farmsteads, the district presented churchmen and school officials alike with a complex of knotty administrative problems arising out of both personnel limitations and the often poor facilities for transport and communication. Difficulties almost inevitably arose over the scheduling of religion classes for pastors, who might have to provide instruction in more than one location, often considerable distances apart. Unfortunately for all concerned, both the district superintendent and the Freudenstadt Dekan—himself a district school inspector before 1909—were strong-willed personalities, ill-disposed to compromise and highly sensitive of their respective claims to authority and responsibility. The uncertainties of school regulation between 1920 and 1922 produced a steady stream of jurisdictional disputes, personal feuds, and administrative squabbles that kept local church-school relations in a turmoil well beyond middecade. If the Dekan, Joseph Haller, taxed the superintendent for drawing up schedules without first consulting the pastors involved, his rival was no less quick to fault Haller for real or imagined interference in internal matters of school administration. Efforts by the Consistory and by state school officials to calm the waters had limited effect. In 1923 the superintendent, Strehle by name, was persuaded to withdraw a complaint of slander lodged against Haller the previous year, but difficulties soon commenced anew. In 1925 one finds Haller complaining to the Oberkirchenrat that his defense of church interests against the "brutal, arbitrary, and rude conduct of the local school council" was receiving insufficient support from his superiors. Church leaders could do little but suggest to Haller that his grievances might have been exaggerated and urge him to seek more harmonious working relations with school officials. As Jakob Schoell noted at one stage of the affair, quarrels in

Freudenstadt generally seemed so petty that the local adversaries had lost most of their credibility with higher officials. This did not, however, prevent area pastors and teachers from being forced to take sides in a power struggle from which no one derived any benefit.[49]

Many districts, to be sure, gave little or no evidence of open friction between pastors and schoolmasters. Confidential visitation reports at the end of the decade tended to strike a more optimistic note in this regard than did those from the troubled transitional period before 1922. In Reutlingen, earlier the scene of strong and persistent tensions, Jakob Schoell found relations between church and school in 1929 "not just merely correct, but genuinely cordial." A report submitted the following year emphasized the "laudable and effective cooperation" prevailing in Cannstatt, where bitter confrontations had likewise taken place in the past. Conditions in most districts probably fell somewhere between a state of permanent crisis and an idyll of perfect amity. Perhaps typical of this broad middle ground was the district of Calw, an area of significant pietist strength located, appropriately enough, midway between Freudenstadt and Stuttgart. An early postwar report on conditions in Calw noted that cordial personal relationships were the rule in local schools but added that the "unchurchly attitudes" of individual schoolmasters constituted a worrisome hindrance to effective religious instruction.[50]

That little of substance could be done in such situations suggests the tenuous character of the church's educational project. For reasons of both utility and principle, churchmen were unwilling to divorce religious instruction from the larger curricu-

[49] "Dekanatsamt gegen Bezirksschulamt," May 8, 1922 (statement with appended documents); Haller to WEK, Feb. 23, Mar. 7, Apr. 11, 13, 18, 1922, LKA A26/788. WEK to DKA Freudenstadt, June 19, 1923, DA Freudenstadt 38; Haller to OKR, July 14, 1925, OKR/AR Gen. 304a/I. Schoell, notes on Haller to OKR, May 16, 1925, and OKR to Haller, July 14, 1925, both in OKR/AR Gen. 203a/I.

[50] Visitation reports collected in OKR/AR Gen. 203d: Reutlingen, Visitationsbericht, Nov. 1, 1929; Cannstatt, Visitationsbericht, Jan. 10, 1930; and Calw, Visitationsbericht, Oct. 30, 1929.

lum. To the extent that separate confessional schools provided a necessary guarantee to this end, the Württemberg church, like other territorial churches, reaped continuing benefits from the Reichstag's inability to produce a definitive school law. Yet genuinely confessional schools assumed a confessional homogeneity that in many areas simply did not exist. Beyond the confessional diversity resulting from increased population mobility, the drift towards religious indifference made for diversity of a more troubling sort within the historic Protestant community itself. Under these circumstances, maintenance of anything more than a formal synthesis of confession and education depended upon active support from the teaching fraternity. Whereas churchmen had once been able to compel such support, they now depended increasingly on voluntary cooperation, and such cooperation often came only at a price. Through their professional organizations, teachers made it plain that they would not consent to serve as mere auxiliaries in an ecclesiastical project. At a minimum they demanded equality and autonomy in matters of pedagogy; where these were denied, they were certain to become antagonistic. While an obliging Oberschulrat generally held to the letter of the law in curbing outright opposition, this residual compulsion was hardly calculated to assure positive sympathy for the church's objectives. Where sympathy was lacking, however, religion threatened to become simply a variable in the educational formula rather than its defining constant.

Pastors as Pedagogues

If the church's administrative role in education continued to decline after 1918, the physical presence of churchmen in the classroom was, ironically enough, expanding substantially. In a private study drafted a decade later, Joseph Haller underscored the "remarkable fact" that "a school law signed by the Social Democratic Staatspräsident Blos . . . [and implemented] under the Democratic Staatspräsident Hieber led to a considerable expansion of pastors' religious instruction in the schools."[51] As already noted, clerical involvement in itself was not new; indeed, historically it had been more extensive in Württemberg than in many parts of Germany.[52] A school law of 1836 went so far as to declare religious instruction the responsibility in the first instance of local pastors, with "appropriate participation" by schoolmasters. In practice, as subsequent regulations made clear, "appropriate participation" meant that lay teachers continued to provide the overwhelming share of classroom instruction. Under the regulations of 1920–22, however, the old formula began to take on new significance. The Oberkirchenrat's calculations at middecade showed that, even with the continuing involvement of most lay teachers, fully one-third of all religious instruction in the Württemberg elementary schools was now being provided by parish pastors; in postelementary schools the proportion was still higher. Although local variations were legion, many pastors faced a doubling of teaching duties compared with the prewar period.[53]

Administrative factors accounted for most of this increase. One immediate source of pressure was the expansion of compulsory schooling from seven years to eight. A related factor was the gradual implementation of a so-called "single-track" approach to instruction in place of the former "dual-track" system under which pastors and schoolmasters had shared teaching duties within particular grades, the former providing doctrinal instruction while the latter dealt with church history and monitored memory work. The new system assigned either pastor or teacher exclusive responsibility for instruction in a given grade. Typically, pastors were now expected to take over the upper Volksschule grades, where doctrinal emphasis was strongest and where an important aim of instruction was the preparation of pupils for confirmation and full membership in the church. Since under this scheme the added eighth year generally became the

[51] Haller, "Beteiligung der Geistlichen am Religionsunterricht."

[52] Cf. Helmreich, *Religious Education*, p. 79.

[53] Schoell to Kirchenregierung Cassel, July 2, 1925, OKR/AR Gen. 206c/I; Haller, "Beteiligung der Geistlichen am Religionsunterricht."

pastor's responsibility, and since the single-track principle dictated that he provide all instruction, not just that devoted to doctrine, the result was usually an increase in both the amount of material churchmen were expected to impart and, despite overall curtailment of religion in the curriculum, the number of hours they were expected to spend in the classroom. Here too local variations were possible, particularly in the cities and larger towns, where more complex arrangements were possible and often necessary. In Stuttgart, for example, over half the religion classes in the upper three grades were taught not by pastors but by teachers or other lay persons commissioned for that purpose by church authorities.[54] The single-track principle, however, became the standard against which deviations were measured.

The Weimar decade thus witnessed a further evolution in relations between clergy and the schools; the pastor as administrative authority gave way to the pastor as part-time pedagogue. One result was that churchmen came to bear a greater personal responsibility for the success of the church's educational project. Some church leaders greeted this as a positive development. Through force of personal example and contact with pupils, the argument went, pastors could counter the fragmentation of education into autonomous subject areas and could promote an effective integration of religion and learning. Writing on church life in Württemberg just before the November Revolution, Paul Wurster had praised religious instruction as potentially "one of the finest and most fruitful of all pastoral tasks."[55] The new order provided ample opportunity to test this dictum.

Although evidence is somewhat sketchy, churchmen seem in general to have regarded their added responsibilities with greater earnestness than enthusiasm. If they accepted religious instruction as a pastoral task, many found it a burdensome one, the fruitfulness of which remained more pious hope than proven fact. Both pragmatic and pedagogical considerations informed this sense of ambivalence. Increased classroom time obviously

[54] Traub, *Jahresbericht 1922; Jahresbericht 1923*.
[55] Wurster, *Kirchliches Leben*, p. 169.

meant a more crowded personal schedule. Pedagogically, too, disadvantages became readily apparent. Faced with the growing professionalization of the teaching corps, many churchmen frankly acknowledged their lack of training in the latest classroom methods. This was not without a certain irony, given the supervisory authority that churchmen had so recently exercised in the schools, but it represented a far from negligible handicap at a time when advocates of religious instruction were constantly forced to assert its rightful place in the curriculum, not to mention the mind of the average schoolchild. For many pastors, products as they were of a fairly sheltered classical education, the social and psychological dynamics of preadolescent schoolchildren often presented a daunting challenge. In farming and working-class areas, class differences only reinforced the distance in temperament between pastor and pupil.

One indication of pastors' pedagogical self-consciousness was an increase in the number of church-sponsored seminars and *practica* dealing with methods of religious education. Beginning in the fall of 1922, the Consistory instituted regular colloquiums on pedagogy in both Tübingen and Heilbronn. Initial sessions attracted over five hundred participants, most of them pastors or church officials. Concern over the quality of instruction played a major part in the establishment of such seminars, which parish clergy were encouraged to supplement with local study groups on content and methods in religious instruction.[56] In this spirit, Albert Esenwein, one of the few pastors openly critical of the confessional school system in concept, initiated a working group of educators and fellow churchmen in Stuttgart devoted to the exchange of insights, experiences, and practical suggestions for improving classroom skills. While some schoolmasters also took part in Consistory-sponsored conferences, Esenwein's long identification with the DDP and his past support of the Lehrer-

---

[56] "Tagung zur Einführung in die Methodik des RUs," Schoell, memorandum, Oct. 25, 1921, LKA A26/780; cf. *Amtsblatt* 22 (1925): 48–49. Schoell, memorandum on visitation reports, Feb. 3, 1925, OKR/AR Gen. 203d; OKR, Erlass, Dec. 16, 1925, copy in DA Waiblingen, LKA C4/4.

verein program made the Stuttgart dialogues a magnet for teachers' participation.[57]

Clerical ambivalence regarding the classroom was widely recognized if never officially condoned. During the school negotiations of 1921, the *Schwäbische Tagwacht*, defending a SPD proposal that all religious instruction be handed over to churchmen, commented that it was "surely not religion that would be endangered if the pastor . . . took over all religious instruction; perhaps it would be the very leisurely life that so many village divines lead."[58] To be sure, this stock image of the idle parson hardly corresponded to contemporary reality. "We do not have an eight-hour day and do not want to have one," wrote Zuffenhausen pastor Theodor Kappus in 1924. Even so, Kappus argued, most churchmen routinely wrestled with schedules that were already too crowded to permit added attention to the classroom.[59] Parish reports and personnel documents, many of which contain painstakingly detailed accountings of pastors' official duties, suggest that leisure was indeed a rare commodity for most churchmen. Religious instruction often required from four to eight hours a week during the school year, not counting time for preparation, and classroom obligations were only a small part of the conscientious pastor's routine. Besides preparing sermons, visiting the sick, leading parish societies, and conducting special classes and services as required, pastors faced pressure from their superiors to maintain a scholarly life commensurate with their status and education. Moreover, it was far from uncommon, especially in the countryside, for a single pastor to serve several towns or hamlets consolidated into a single parish. For such pastors, new responsibilities might entail added travel—often on foot, sometimes by bicycle—between various stations of duty, an investment in time and energy inadequately reflected in bare recitals of official functions. The example of Friedrich Lörcher, who in the early 1920s appealed to the Consistory for exemption

[57] Fritz Herrigel, "Eine Arbeitsgemeinschaft," *KAfW* 31 (1922): 127.

[58] *ST*, Apr. 26, 1921.

[59] Theodor Kappus, "Die Arbeitszeit der Pfarrer," *KAfW* 33 (1924): 163–64.

from further religious instruction, may stand for many. Lörcher was pastor in Oberboihingen, a town of about fifteen hundred souls in the Neckar valley between Stuttgart and Tübingen. In addition, however, the parish included more than seven hundred Protestants in Reudern, nearly three miles away over the hills by a poor road. For Lörcher and for hundreds like him, many normal pastoral duties were doubled from the outset.[60]

In the cities, teaching assignments often competed for attention with a host of possible civic, academic, and administrative commitments. The result, to judge from fragmentary figures from Stuttgart, was a distribution of teaching duties that varied directly with a pastor's rank. As of 1922, religious instruction for the forty pastors in Stuttgart's eighteen parishes averaged four hours weekly. For the most senior pastors, however, the average was only two hours, and several had no formal instructional responsibilities whatsoever. Assistant pastors, by comparison, were assigned, on average, between four and five hours weekly; those with the rank of third pastor taught an average of seven hours per week, while for the two younger clergy designated as fourth pastors, the weekly average was closer to eight hours. Eleven vicars assisted in Stuttgart parishes as part of their training for future permanent service; their teaching assignments averaged a full ten hours weekly. Fully one-third of all religion classes offered by Stuttgart clergy, in fact, were the responsibility of these youngest and least experienced churchmen, many of whom served in a position for only a matter of months before being reassigned elsewhere. More senior churchmen, in contrast, tended to spend less time on education and more on parish administration and various kinds of public service.[61]

---

[60] Lörcher to WEK, n.d. [ca. 1922], LKA A26/781. Over 400 Württemberg parishes included more than one town or hamlet in the 1920s; cf. *Magisterbuch* (1932), pp. 10–63, and parish descriptions in Kühnle, *Die ev. Kirchenstellen in Württemberg.*

[61] Compiled from figures in LKA A26/781. Some pastors also offered religion classes by private contract at gymnasia and trade schools; these commitments, though not included in the compilations, would not materially alter the basic comparisons.

The tension between teaching and public service can be seen in the case of Gotthilf Schenkel, a junior colleague of Theodor Kappus in Zuffenhausen, like Kappus an activist on the left-liberal wing of the church and later a noted leader of the Württemberg Religious Socialist movement. In 1923 Schenkel prevailed upon the Consistory to reduce his teaching load by half, to two hours weekly, to permit him more time for participation in a national land resettlement program (Heimstättenausschuss) to which he had become strongly committed. The Consistory first reassigned Schenkel's classes to the pastor of a neighboring parish. Within a short time, however, this surrogate—a young pastor who, like Schenkel, was in his first permanent position—likewise petitioned for relief on grounds of overwork. Eventually church officials resolved the problem by appointing a new vicar solely to handle teaching duties in Stuttgart's northern suburbs.[62] Elsewhere, in similar situations, retired clergy were sometimes pressed into the breach.[63]

The creation of special teaching positions was a solution attractive to many pastors as well as to some in the church leadership, although it was an option only in the cities and therefore did nothing to ease the plight of rural pastors. As early as 1922, Stuttgart Dekan Theodor Traub drafted a proposal calling upon the Consistory to train a cadre of lay catechists for deployment in the schools. The Pfarrverein endorsed this initiative, demanding that the Education Ministry subsidize the creation of specialized positions in religious instruction under the church's jurisdiction.[64] "Why should the church have to stand in for something that is the state's affair?" asked Theodor Kappus at a meeting of Pfarrverein leaders in 1925, when it had become clear

[62] Schenkel to DKA Cannstatt, May 21, 1923, and Schenkel to WEK, May 21, 1923, both in LKA A26/789. Hozwarth to WEK, Jan. 21, 1924; Schenkel to WEK, n.d.; and Schoell, memorandum, Mar. 7, 1924; all in OKR/AR Gen. 203/I.

[63] Cf. Herzog to WEK, Aug. 27, 1923, and Merz to Herzog, n.d., both in LKA A26/799.

[64] Traub to WEK, Feb. 20, 1922, LKA A26/781; EPW, Vertrauensmännerversammlung, Apr. 16, 1922, Protokollbuch II, LKA D/EPW 22; cf. *KAfW* 31 (1922): 71.

that financial constraints doomed any prospect for an early solution. Although Theodor Traub warned that soon pastors
would "simply not be able to manage any more" without assistance, relief was slow in coming.[65]

Beyond the sheer burden of time there loomed the often bleak
experience of the classroom itself. Since the November Revolution, the anticlerical minority had become more vocal and self-
assured, and in urban areas they often worked to ensure that religious instruction would be anything but the most fruitful of a
pastor's tasks. As noted earlier, while parents had the right to exempt their children from religion classes, few exercised this option. In Stuttgart, for example, the number of children withdrawn from classes peaked in 1923 at 492, well under 3 percent
of the Protestant school population.[66] Some religious dissidents,
churchmen suspected, purposely kept their children enrolled as
a way to monitor pastors' activities, and they were quick to make
known their disapproval of statements or actions deemed objectionable. In Zuffenhausen, where organized freethinking groups
were particularly active, occasionally distributing anticlerical literature at school gates, Gotthilf Schenkel complained that a
steady undercurrent of agitation made the pastor's task a constant struggle to preserve some semblance of "religious and
moral authority." In 1923 a local SPD official filed a formal complaint against Schenkel, charging him with using religion classes
to malign freethinkers and their beliefs. School authorities dismissed the charge as frivolous, but not before Schenkel had been
forced to undergo the irritating and time-consuming formality
of an administrative hearing and a written brief defending his
views and actions. Such experiences clearly did nothing to restrain Schenkel's inclination to seek relief from teaching duties
and satisfaction in other commitments.[67]

[65] EPW, Vertrauensmännerversammlung, Apr. 14, 1925, Protokollbuch II,
LKA D/EPW 22.

[66] H. Mosapp to Oberschulrat, July 8, 1921, copy with Schoell notes, LKA
A26/781; Traub, *Jahresbericht 1923*.

[67] Schenkel to DKA Ludwigsburg, July 9, 1923; Reeder to KM, June 20, 1923
(copy); and Hieber to Reeder, Nov. 30, 1923 (copy); all in LKA A26/789.

Even where open harassment was not their normal lot, pastors had to contend with passive resistance and the indifference of both children and parents. A parish report from Bietigheim in 1924 sounded a fairly common lament: "There are many children who receive no religious influence from the home. [Some in fact] are regularly incited against the church and the pastor, and . . . in any case show little desire to exert an effort to assimilate religious materials."[68] Where such attitudes were widespread, the pastor's task could degenerate into a rear-guard action to maintain order. "Discipline is a continual, incessant struggle against pupils' inclination to disrupt," a Reutlingen pastor complained in 1924. "After all, the pastor is not there to let himself be laughed to scorn by impudent schoolboys."[69] Theophil Wurm, then Dekan in Reutlingen, echoed these complaints, suggesting that the Oberkirchenrat work to free pastors from all classroom obligations or, failing that, to seek some form of recourse such as an ordinance from school authorities invoking more rigid standards of discipline.[70] Neither alternative proved feasible, however; pastors were cast back upon their own wits and advised to cope as best they could.[71] Nor were wits enough in the most extreme cases. Vicars assigned to teach in Botnang came to regard themselves as sacrificial lambs, left to the mercy of students described by a church-appointed investigator as "thoroughly rotten." "Instruction under such circumstances accomplishes no good," this observer advised, suggesting that the church's best efforts to the contrary were likely to prove self-defeating.[72]

If problems were widespread in the elementary schools, they

[68] Bietigheim, Pfarrbericht 1924, OKR/AR OA/PfB.

[69] Finckh, memorandum, Nov. 15, 1924, with Wurm to OKR, Dec. 15, 1924, OKR/AR Gen. 203d.

[70] Wurm to OKR, Dec. 13, 1924, OKR/AR Gen. 203d.

[71] Schoell to Wurm, Dec. 13, 1924, OKR/AR Gen. 203d. Since grades in religion carried little weight and religion was not part of school-leaving examinations, pastor-teachers had few external sanctions to impose on balky pupils; cf. Helmreich, *Religious Education*, p. 91.

[72] Wilhelm Rehm, memorandum, Mar. 16, 1926; Traub to OKR, Mar. 20, 1926; and Müller to Holzinger, Mar. 26, 1926; all in OKR/AR Gen. 203d/II.

were often worse in the higher schools, particularly the trade or "continuation" school (*Fortbildungsschule*). Unlike humanistic gymnasiums, where the academic atmosphere was at least passively conducive to the teaching of religion, the trade schools seemed hopelessly barren fields to most pastors who tended them, despite the fact that those enrolled had normally attended confirmation classes and now held full membership in the church. The purpose of the trade schools was to provide instruction beyond the Volksschule level, primarily for youths entering trades or apprenticeship programs. By law, students were expected to attend classes for at least two years or until they reached the constitutional school-leaving age of eighteen. Since classes were normally held in the evening, at the end of a full workday, conditions were scarcely ripe for effective learning. Students were often listless and indifferent, if not openly resentful of the demands on their time. Unlike elementary schools, the Fortbildungsschule was not confessionally organized. After 1922, religion classes continued only where pastors agreed to continue teaching them; of ninety-one such schools in Württemberg, only thirty had some sort of arrangement with pastors in 1923.[73]

Even before 1922, pastors saw service in the trade schools as a form of temporal purgatory to be avoided if humanly possible. "The working-class population attaches no importance to [religion]," a 1920 report from Göppingen asserted, "and working-class youths constitute a consistently recalcitrant and unruly element in the trade schools."[74] That same year the Consistory temporarily suspended instruction in Botnang on the grounds that the church was "not disposed to abandon loyal clergy . . . to the rudeness of unruly youngsters"—a position that, as noted above, it was not able to extend to local elementary schools.[75] Nor were unruly youngsters the only source of frustration. No

[73] Kirn to Oberschulrat, Jan. 15, 1923 (copy), LKA A26/781; cf. Wurster, *Kirchliches Leben*, pp. 170–71.

[74] Kirn to DKA Göppingen, Dec. 2, 1920, LKA A26/781.

[75] WEK to Oberschulrat, June 9, 1920, LKA A26/787. Amthor to WEK, Oct. 27, 1920, and WEK to DKA Waiblingen, Oct. 29, 1920, both in LKA A26/781.

prophet could have felt less honored in his own country than the pastor in one small town near the northern escarpment of the Swabian Jura. During a religion class in late 1921, by his account, he was assaulted by a mob of trade school students protesting detentions he had imposed in response to alleged earlier rowdiness. Although the school custodian witnessed the disturbances, he made no move to intervene—on orders, the pastor later claimed, from the regular schoolmaster. To add insult to injury, when the pastor appeared before the district school council to lodge a complaint, several members deliberately left the meeting, depriving the council of a quorum and rendering action impossible.[76]

If this poor pastor's plight is hardly typical, it provides a vivid illustration of churchmen's changing status in school and society. For the Volksbund's August Springer, growing up in the waning years of the old century, pastors had stood at the top of the local deference scale.

> If the teachers were lords, then the clergy were their overlords. This we could tell by the servile respect shown to them . . . , the way speech became more formal when one of them entered the room. Hence pastors' religious instruction was also more impressive than that of schoolmasters. It did God's authority good that such great and highly regarded gentlemen praised him.[77]

By the 1920s conditions seemingly had changed; rarely was authority of office by itself a guarantee of classroom influence. Effective religious instruction required persuasion, tact, imagination, and even charisma, qualities with which not all pastors were richly endowed. In the context of the times it is hard to see, for example, how pupils could have warmed to the methods of someone who lamented, as did one village pastor in 1928, that children and young people in his flock showed the regrettable absence of that "wholesome training school of the old German mil-

---

[76] PfA Frickenhausen, report of Jan. 3, 1922, LKA A26/788.
[77] Springer, *Der Andere, der bist Du*, p. 16.

itary."[78] Lay teachers in Botnang claimed to experience few of the discipline problems that plagued vicars in religion classes. Any unruliness, they implied, must be the result of inept classroom methods. A report to the district school council in 1920 blamed disturbances on vicars' inability to stimulate pupils' interest and on their frequent resort to a regimen of corporal punishment that, like the proverbial rain, fell upon just and unjust alike.[79] A similar clash in perceptions could be seen in Marbach, where, according to a report of 1923, lack of order in religion classes had become a public scandal. One of the local pastors pointed out that problems became almost inevitable when one was forced, as he was, to deal simultaneously with three different classes—a total of seventy pupils—in a room with insufficient seating. The local school council, however, placed blame chiefly on the instructor, "whether it be that he is simply not capable of maintaining order or that his teaching is too unstimulating or unsuited to pupils' level of understanding." The council requested assignment of someone else to the task, arguing that constant turmoil during religious instruction did little for the "moral and intellectual service of education."[80]

This is not to say that all pastors, or perhaps even most, regarded religious instruction as futile toil in a wasteland of indifference and indiscipline. Indeed, many visitation reports from the period emphasized the diligence and skill of pastors and the interest and good deportment of pupils. "Instruction is animated and well suited; the children are stimulated": this was a fairly frequent refrain in reports from a systematic series of visitations undertaken by church officials in late 1923.[81] A Dekan's report from Backnang in the same year found that "the quiet power of religious instruction over the children" was "apparent time and again."[82] For every perduring source of trouble such as Botnang there was doubtless an oasis of peace like Ried, a hamlet in the

[78] Sielmingen, Pfarrbericht 1928, OKR/AR OA/PfB.

[79] Gehring to Ev. Bezirksschulamt, July 9, 1920 (copy), LKA A26/787.

[80] Herzog to WEK, July 19, 1923, and Vollmer to WEK, Aug. 8, 1923, both in LKA A26/798.

[81] Künzelsau, Visitationsbericht, Nov. 21, 1923, LKA A26/792.

[82] Backnang, Visitationsbericht, Nov. 17, 1923, LKA A26/792.

south Württemberg district of Biberach. Ried formed part of a consolidated parish whose pastor, as part of his established circuit, visited one afternoon a week to give religion classes in the small local school. After the regulations of 1922 went into effect, a rearrangement of teaching assignments gave classes in Ried to another pastor. When this change was announced, a good lady of the town wrote the Consistory begging that the old system be reinstated in view of the local pastor's "good influence . . . on our children."[83]

Viewed as a whole, however, the state of religious instruction after 1918 inspired little triumphalism. Jakob Schoell cautioned both that official visitations probably encouraged an overly optimistic assessment of pastors' efforts and that while general impressions might seem favorable, it would be easy to draw an "overly cheerful picture" of prevailing conditions.[84] Rudolf Daur, a designated youth pastor in Reutlingen during the early 1920s, argued pessimistically that the tendency towards greater specialization of educational functions inevitably made the pastor a "foreign body" in the classroom; despite the best intentions, his efforts could therefore not be expected to bear much fruit.[85] Visitation reports from the end of the decade described classroom obligations as "in many ways the pastor's cross," the most difficult of all his tasks.[86] Reflecting on the state of religious life in the Göppingen district, Dekan Otto Stahl confessed to colleagues in 1929 that the longer he reflected, the less able he felt to give any answer to the question of how best to instruct local youth. The range of problems associated with religious instruction left him, he said, in a position of "embarrassed helplessness." He added: "For this very reason I tell myself: Here lies our great—not to say greatest—task today, a task that we must confront in dead earnest."[87]

[83] M. Enk to WEK, Oct. 5, 1922, LKA A26/789.
[84] Schoell, memorandum, n.d. [1923], LKA A26/792.
[85] Daur, memorandum, Nov. 2, 1924, OKR/AR Gen. 203d.
[86] Thus Besigheim, Visitationsbericht, Nov. 5, 1929, and Böblingen, Visitationsbericht, Dec. 12, 1929, both in OKR/AR Gen. 206c.
[87] "Bericht des Dekans über das sittliche und religiöse Leben des Bezirkes," ad-

Part of the difficulty lay in the inherently vague definition of that task, something with which educators and churchmen alike had grappled in Germany for decades.[88] In theory, religious instruction served to nurture the moral individual as both pious Christian and virtuous citizen. By the end of his school years, a child of normal diligence and intelligence could be expected to have acquired a modest stock of memorized hymns and Bible verses, some familiarity with the classic stories of the Bible, a general knowledge of Protestant doctrine, and an introduction to local cultic practice. In the process, instruction was to be oriented more toward instinct than intellect. Syllabi for religion classes emphasized that teaching should not stress mere formal knowledge of theological formulas, ritual, and phraseology. Rather, it should concentrate on establishing and nurturing a basic moral perspective on life. "More than other forms of instruction, religious instruction must be *educative* instruction," a Consistorial directive of 1923 insisted. "Mere rote memorization of material is insufficient to train the will and disposition."[89] A syllabus for 1925 reiterated the call to consider minds and hearts alike, enjoining teachers to focus attention on the "spiritually and morally valuable" aspects of course content rather than on historical, literary, or polemical details.[90]

Shaping "will and disposition" was difficult if not impossible to measure, however, and whatever syllabi might say about character and motivation, they tended to retain memory work as the central discipline of instruction. Recitation being far simpler to test than private attitudes, school inspectors routinely used accomplishment of required memory work as a standard for evaluating instruction. Where a teacher neglected or deemphasized memorization, for whatever reason, superiors generally signaled their disapproval. In Schwenningen, for example,

dress to Kirchenbezirkstagung, Göppingen, Dec. 12, 1929 (holograph copy), DA Göppingen 142.

[88] Cf. Helmreich, *Religious Education*, pp. 85–100.

[89] WEK to Dekanatsämter, Dec. 18, 1923 (copy), LKA D1/25.

[90] *Amtsblatt* 22 (1925): 37, 211–14; *Lehrpläne für die Volks- und Mittelschulen in Württemberg, Gesamtausgabe* (Stuttgart, 1928).

where religious instruction was taxing under the best of conditions, one young vicar attempted to win his charges' confidence through a heavy diet of art and music, fields in which he happened to be gifted. Visitation reports commended his ability to maintain an admirable level of interest and attention, but they complained equally that his methods did not appear to produce enough "solid [factual] knowledge."[91] Despite interest in new pedagogical techniques, those who set and controlled policies for religious instruction found it hard to abandon older habits. Critics found all too little evidence of creative changes in method. "Instead of doing more than ever to create religious and moral values," a Stuttgart educators' conference warned in 1923, "religious instruction in the future will degenerate even further into 'didactical materialism,' " an idle exercise leaving minds dulled and hearts cold.[92]

The problem of method mirrored, once again, basic structural problems with religious instruction. In the schools, as in society at large, the church's institutional status outweighed its actual influence. While taking formal account of the Volkskirche ideal, Württemberg school regulations of the Weimar period tended in practice to expose the hollowness of actual clerical power. On paper, confessional schools remained the norm; religious instruction remained a regular part of the curriculum, its content determined and at least indirectly controlled by church authorities. Inside the classroom, however, religion functioned only sporadically as the defining core of education and, by extension, as the foundation of a Christian society. Time formerly devoted to religion was reassigned to other subjects, where by common consent confessional emphases played little or no part. Lay teachers and pastors alike, if for different reasons, came to regard religious instruction with ambivalence. For children and their parents, meanwhile, including many who willingly signed petitions demanding that confessional instruction be retained, religion

[91] Schwenningen, Visitationsbericht, 1922/23, LKA A26/793. See also Mosapp to Traub, Apr. 20, 1924, and Mosapp to Oberschulrat, Mar. 13, 1925, both in OKR/AR Gen. 203/I.
[92] Schäffler to WEK, Mar. 7, 1923, LKA A26/781.

classes constituted a matter of comparative if not total indifference.

Under these circumstances, the "embarrassed helplessness" of Dekan Stahl and his fellows was less a confession of personal failings, however justified, than an admission of the apparently intractable nature of things. Religious instruction seemed to have become an increasingly encapsulated element in the schools, one of many competing wares in the marketplace of education as of life. In this sense the classroom exposed a basic weakness of the Volkskirche ideal. If the argument for confessional education rested ultimately on a vision of society as a homogeneous community, classroom reality reflected instead a world in which churchmen were incapable of imposing either social or confessional cohesion.

FIVE

The Social Volkskirche

𝕿HE CONCERN for auxiliary legitimation reflected in churchmen's approach to the schools also found expression in their growing eagerness to assume an active social role. It was an article of faith that the Volkskirche must be a "social" church, a church of the deed as well as of the Word. This social project had both preceptorial and diaconal dimensions: churchmen sought to uphold the marks of a Christian moral order, both public and private, while also providing the proverbial cup of cold water to society's unfortunates. Diaconal imperatives were, of course, as old as the church itself. Whether carried on by lay volunteers or by commissioned pastors and deaconesses, church-related charity work had become a hallmark of Swabian religious life, particularly in its pietist manifestations, even before the "social question" became a nineteenth-century commonplace. The rise of industry and the growth of cities gave further scope to these charitable energies. They found characteristic expression in, for example, the private philanthropy of industrialists like the idiosyncratic Gustav Werner in Reutlingen or, later, Robert Bosch in Stuttgart, and in the tory social conscience that permeated the clergy of both theological camps at the turn of the century.

The November Revolution provided a renewed stimulus to such social activism, but in the process it also exposed the problematic nature of churchmen's historic social conceptions. Their reigning model of society had changed surprisingly little since the sixteenth century. It assumed that the church's task involved both the monitoring of personal conduct and the alleviation of individual distress, but always within the context of a basically fixed and stable societal order. Churchmen in Württemberg as elsewhere had been slow to comprehend or to respond to the broad social transformations of the nineteenth century. With a few notable exceptions, they attributed the ills of a changing society to personal shortcomings or to the abandonment of pious traditions rather than to structural dislocations or to economic development. As long as they could regard the state, in the person of the Christian prince, as an embodiment and guarantor of Protestant values, they could to some extent ignore pressures to articulate an independent critical perspective of their own. Until the Great War, social action remained largely patriarchal and prophylactic, designed to blunt socialist appeals and win the masses for the existing order. With the collapse of the monarchy, however, this historic function of the social Volkskirche disappeared, and the resulting problem of orientation was magnified by what most churchmen perceived to be the instability and moral neutrality of the Weimar system. One immediate challenge of the republican era therefore was to develop an autonomous Protestant social posture. This in turn raised problems of defining the role and purpose of a self-appointed social Volkskirche in a world of cultural, religious, and political pluralism.

In ways reminiscent of its education project, the church's social agenda after 1918 looked towards two related but potentially contradictory ends. On one level, social action was deemed vital if churchmen were to inculcate the vision of a Protestant moral order in a society no longer disciplined by the authority of a Christian sovereign. On another level, a vigorous social presence offered new opportunities for legitimating the Volkskirche ideal, with public pronouncements and acts of charity combining to promote reconciliation not so much between the masses and the established order as between the masses and the church itself. But if churchmen proposed to speak authoritatively from the high ground of a universally valid moral vision, they ran the risk that, in taking positions on controversial public issues, they might well alienate some part of the diverse constituency that the Volkskirche purported to embrace. How could the church open its doors to a heterogeneous society while at the same time attempting to impose a uniform conception of social order? This tension between social control and social legitimation permeated churchmen's attempts to address the social question; nor could matters be resolved simply by invoking the idea of Protestant freedom of conscience.

Thanks in part to its strong diaconal traditions and to the latitude for action afforded by a benign state government, the Württemberg church played a prominent part in efforts to grapple with these problems. After first looking briefly at the contributions of Württemberg churchmen to the formation of a general Protestant social consensus after 1918, we will attempt to trace manifestations of social commitment both in the crusade for a public moral order and in grass-roots efforts to ameliorate conditions of postwar life. As in other areas of ecclesiastical endeavor, social action in Württemberg suggests both the possibilities and the limitations of the Volkskirche project during the Weimar era.

Mandates for Activism

Broadly speaking, the church's social ideology compounded institutional traditions and an impulse to save modern society from itself. In social policy as in education, churchmen appealed to a past era of cultural consensus when the church had stood as moral arbiter and font of charity under the beneficent authority of the Christian prince. What churchmen saw in the republic, however, was not moral community but moral anarchy, not authority and common purpose but self-seeking individualism and the disintegration of public virtue. In this secular and pluralistic world, the church stood to function as little more than a guardian of private opinion. If Protestant principles were to exert continuing influence, they must be proclaimed in the marketplace of opinion and vindicated by positive action and example. In a working paper drafted for the DEKA in 1920, the Württemberg Consistory argued that since a secular state could not be depended upon to serve as an "advocate of Christian order and custom," the church must undertake to do so on its own. A Christian public consensus must be nurtured "not for the sake of church domination but for the spiritual and moral health of the nation. Where sound Christian tradition is still present it must be asserted; what has been destroyed must be built up again in new forms."[1] Eugen Reiff, leader of Group I in the church assembly, sounded the same theme in an article published at mid-decade. "Formerly," he wrote, "our church . . . was heavily dependent on the Protestant state and its cultural goals. Should the new state pull back from these goals, then the church becomes all the more indispensable to public life."[2]

This was a common theme among Protestant leaders, repeated like a litany throughout the Weimar era: the church must take upon itself the tasks of the bygone Christian state, working to preserve a moral lingua franca in the cultural Babel of secular modern society.[3] In this campaign of self-assertion, social ideology played a prominent part. Significantly, one of the first expressions of united German Protestantism after 1918 was the manifesto *Soziale Botschaft* (Social Message) adopted in 1924 at the first national congress of the newly organized Evangelical Church Federation.[4] For the first time since J. H. Wichern's Inner Mission manifesto of 1848, church leaders attempted to set forth a concise but comprehensive statement of social perspective. In a sense the *Soziale Botschaft* represented a kind of belated German Protestant *Rerum novarum*, a vigorous if tentative attempt to establish connections between unchanging religious precepts and the rapidly changing world of automation and urbanization.

Although broad in scope and ambitious in intent, the *Soziale Botschaft* made few if any pioneering contributions to a theology of social concern. Much of it recapitulated the familiar em-

[1] WEK to DEKA, June 8, 1920, and DEKA Sitzungsprotokoll, Eisenach, June 23–24, 1920, both in LKA A26/323.

[2] E. Reiff, "Wir vom Volksbund und die neuverfasste Kirche," *Evangelischer Volksbund für Württemberg* 7 (Jan. 1925).

[3] Borg, *Old-Prussian Church*, pp. 168–212; cf. Scholder, *Die Kirchen und das Dritte Reich*, 1:3–45, and Nowak, " 'Entartete Gegenwart.' "

[4] *Verhandlungen des ersten deutschen evangelischen Kirchentages 1924* (Berlin-Steglitz, 1924), esp. pp. 215–19.

phases of prewar Evangelical-Social thought.[5] Volkskirche impulses manifested themselves throughout in the assumption that social problems were not simply a matter of economic forces and material power but at heart involved moral considerations both personal and communal. Although the manifesto duly acknowledged the importance of class divisions and the impact of modern technology, it faulted both as forces that contributed to depersonalization. Between the competing materialisms of profit-oriented capitalism and class-conscious socialism it sought to interpose a religiously grounded model of social relations rooted in the affirmation of brotherhood, of individual worth, and of the ethical quality of human labor. It called for a vaguely defined culture of mutuality in which employers and employees would somehow unite in working toward a common good—a mediating vision uncannily like that propagated in *Metropolis*, Fritz Lang's popular fantasy film of the same period, which portrayed a reconciliation between "head" and "hands" (owners and workers) through the "heart" of a shared humanity. The manifesto pledged churchmen to balance their customary criticism of the labor movement's "class hatred" with a more probing critique of business insensitivity. It also declared support for wage and hour legislation (though without specific reference to current controversies over the eight-hour workday), for tighter regulation of female and child labor, and for greater labor influence in industrial management.[6]

The *Soziale Botschaft* received considerable publicity within the church and in much of the bourgeois press. It made little impression, however, on those to whom it was most specifically addressed. The labor movement ignored it almost completely. Some employers took passing note, paying polite respects to the "weight" and "value" of the church's positions, but for the most part they dismissed it as an intrusion into areas beyond the

[5] Cf. Fritz Einecke, "Die Stellung der evangelischen Arbeitervereine zur sozialen Frage" (Ph.D. diss., Cologne University, 1950), pp. 4–7, 87–161.
[6] *Die Soziale Botschaft der Evangelischen Kirche* (Berlin, 1924); Fischer, "Geschichte des Kirchenkampfes," 1:71–72; Nowak, *Kirche und Republik*, pp. 126–34; Borg, *Old-Prussian Church*, pp. 202–5.

church's competence.[7] The significance of the manifesto probably lay less in what it said or how it was received than in the fact
that it ratified the Protestant establishment's commitment to a
more active social outlook. Henceforth social concerns were not
to be simply the province of individuals or groups within the ecclesiastical ambit but rather a central feature of the Volkskirche
project. Jakob Schoell, for one, was convinced that the manifesto
enhanced the church's respectability as a social force; it provided
both a rallying point for social analysis and a point of departure
for concrete action.[8]

Through Schoell, chairman of the standing Social Committee
of the DEKA, the Württemberg church was intimately identified
with the *Soziale Botschaft* and its major emphases. Rudiments
of the manifesto can be found articulated as early as 1922 in a
lecture Schoell delivered at a seminar in Tübingen. Several
months before the national church congress in 1924, the Württemberg church assembly unanimously adopted a social proclamation of its own. Though considerably briefer than the subsequent national manifesto, it nevertheless adumbrated the
latter's central themes.[9]

Adoption of these proclamations coincided with an upsurge of
church-sponsored social involvement. Beyond the wide-ranging
private and semi-private Protestant charity work, the associations of the Evangelical-Social movement, and the social department of the Volksbund—about which more will be said presently—the Oberkirchenrat took steps to give social issues
greater prominence in the training and official duties of the
clergy. In 1925, on a joint motion of Theophil Wurm and Hans
Voelter, the church assembly established a "social information
service" (*Sozialer Aufklärungsdienst*) in each district to be ad-

---

[7] Jakob Schoell, "Die Aufnahme der Sozialen Botschaft der evangelischen
Kirche," *EGBfS* 21 (1925): 9–10; R. Dudey, "Zur 'Sozialen Botschaft' der evan-
gelischen Kirche," *Deutsche Handels-Wacht* 21 (1924): 353–54, copy in OKR/
AR Gen. 151a/I.

[8] Schoell, "Aufnahme der Sozialen Botschaft," p. 10.

[9] See Schoell, "Die volkspädagogische Bedeutung des evangelischen Christen-
tums," *MfPT* 18 (1922): 228; LKV, *Verhandlungen* (1924), pp. 2201–4.

ministered by interested pastors for the purpose of providing parish clergy with resource materials on social questions, arranging public lectures for church members, and in general promoting a greater awareness of the church's social concern.[10] After 1926, lectures on social problems formed a regular part of the curriculum for all would-be clergy.[11] In the latter year the Oberkirchenrat also agreed to provide partial support for an extended working tour of the United States by August Springer, then managing director of the Volksbund. Living and working in New York, Chicago, and Detroit, Springer hoped to observe and experience at first hand American business and labor practices, especially those associated with Henry Ford, a figure of almost endless fascination among Protestant social activists of the period.[12] The Oberkirchenrat annually dispatched several young theologians to Berlin for week-long social courses at the Evangelical-Social institute in Spandau. Seminars included a mixture of theoretical and practical topics—lectures on theological issues and open discussions of current problems. A Stuttgart vicar who attended in 1926 was struck by the contrast between the tension-riddled tenement world of Berlin and the more temperate social climate to which he was accustomed in Württemberg. While theoretical discussions were helpful, he reported, he found it harder to assess the practical benefits of participation.[13] During the second half of the Weimar decade, similar conferences brought together church social workers from around the country

[10] 1. LKT, *Verhandlungen* (1925), pp. 63–66, 68.

[11] Merz, memorandum, Jan. 10, 1927, OKR/AR Gen. 151a/I.

[12] Pfisterer to Keller, June 19, 1926; Springer to Keller, July 27, 1926; Merz to DEKA, July 26, 1926; and Mosthaf to OKR, Nov. 30, 1926; all in OKR/AR Gen. 117. See also Springer, *Der Andere, der bist Du*, pp. 307–25; EVB, *Mitteilungen* 44 (May 1927): 228; Karl Kreeb, "Die soziale und ethische Grundsätzen Henry Fords," *KAfW* 37 (1928): 58–60; and Karl Frank, "Ist Henry Fords System in der Praxis so menschenfreundlich wie in seinem Buch 'Mein Leben und Werk'?" *KAfW* 37 (1928): 124–26. Springer returned from his ten-month visit with no clear judgments; in his memoirs he later confessed to finding American life more puzzling at the end of his stay than at the beginning.

[13] Julius Eichler to OKR, n.d., reporting on 3. Sozialer Kurs, Spandau, Jan. 19–26, 1926, OKR/AR Gen. 151a/I.

for discussions of common problems, and social activists within the Württemberg church established annual conferences of their own in Ludwigsburg beginning in 1927.[14]

During the Weimar period, in short, the Württemberg church worked to enhance its social presence among the public, to increase social awareness among the clergy, and to act as a leavening influence among Protestants beyond its own borders. The latter efforts revealed a characteristic difference in emphasis and approach between south German churchmen and their fellows in the north. Whereas Prussian officials placed considerable stress on the importance of specially designated "social pastorates" within the ecclesiastical structure, the Württemberg leadership preferred to integrate social functions with normal parish duties. This reluctance to specialize may have reflected the comparative strength of religious traditions in the south. Rather than compartmentalizing social action, Württemberg's leadership could afford the luxury of hoping that pastoral example, reinforced perhaps by the para-ecclesiastical efforts of the Volksbund, would galvanize the energies of the Protestant community and in so doing underscore the church's claims to public influence.

Granting the case for social activism, what form should such activism assume? Most churchmen agreed, even when their concerns impelled them into the social or economic debates of the day, that they had different obligations than government officials, political party functionaries, or even those involved in private charitable endeavors. The church's primary task, Schoell suggested in 1927, must always be to emphasize the moral dimension of social issues. Churchmen's most effective function was a pedagogical one: the use of preaching and teaching to inform consciences and arouse individuals to action. When and if churchmen did launch into practical tasks of lobbying, mediating, or providing welfare, they should take care to serve prima-

---

[14] Schoell himself presided at the third national conference in Erfurt in 1928; Protokoll in OKR/AR Gen. 151a/II; cf. *Das evangelische Deutschland* 6 (1929): 77. On the Ludwigsburg conferences: Protokoll, Konferenz kirchlich-sozialer Facharbeiter, Karlshöhe-Ludwigsburg, Sept. 21–22, 1927 (copy), OKR/AR Gen. 151a/I.

rily as a "model and example" to others, not to present themselves as advocates for specific economic interests.[15]

Moral purposes, in short, should take precedence over material interests. The idea of the social Volkskirche assumed the possibility and desirability of an overarching public moral order. Moral principles provided the basis for the church's social witness, moral criteria were invoked to determine the scope and character of specific actions, and restoration of an explicitly Christian moral order was the ultimate goal. The new social moralism differed from that of earlier generations largely in that it operated with fewer illusions about economic life and the church's capacity to effect immediate change. On this point the upheavals of 1918 encouraged a convergence of outlook within the Württemberg church. Naumannite democrat Hans Voelter sounded the common theme in an address to Stuttgart members of the Evangelical-Social Congress in the spring of 1919. While church and state must be constitutionally separated, Voelter declared, they must remain "intrinsically" bound together. A "social state" needed a "social church"; a healthy culture was only possible where the church helped to lay its moral and spiritual foundations. These foundations were, however, more personal than structural; they included such tenets as the worth of the individual, the moral solidarity of mankind, and the need for mutual assistance. Hermann von Zeller, arguing from rather different political presuppositions, agreed that the "health . . . of public life depends not so much upon its institutions as upon the men who are active in it," thereby rooting social reform once more in the individual conscience.[16]

By emphasizing moral values, churchmen in both theological camps not only reconciled religion and social criticism but also

[15] Protokoll, Konferenz kirchlich-sozialer Facharbeiter, Sept. 21–22, 1927, OKR/AR Gen. 151a/I.

[16] Hans Voelter, "Die neue Kirche und der soziale Staat," speech, Evangelisch-Sozialer Kongress, Stuttgart, Apr. 14, 1919, copy in LKA D12/1; cf. Zeller, *Württembergische evangelische Landeskirche*, p. 23. On the tension between individual and social-structural perspectives in German Protestant thought, see Ward, *Theology, Sociology, and Politics*, pp. 44–122, 217–43.

proposed a standard for determining areas of legitimate church involvement within the political arena. In a wartime sermon on religion and politics, the future Stuttgart *Stiftsprediger* Gustav Gross had asserted that from a religious standpoint it was all the same whether government pursued an agrarian or an industrial policy. "But it is not at all a matter of indifference," Gross had continued, "whether or not we have curfews and closing laws."[17] While strictly political issues were none of the church's affair, the Consistory proclaimed in 1923, churchmen had "a right and duty to speak" whenever the "inner life" of the nation was at stake.[18] To be sure, this official formulation left the exact nature of political neutrality vague at best; from here it was only a short step to arguing, as did Jakob Schoell in 1924, that moral and material considerations were often inextricably linked, that ethics and economics could not be regarded as mutually exclusive spheres.[19] "The more rationalized society becomes, the more necessary social policy becomes," wrote an unidentified Württemberg churchman in 1927. "And who is better able and qualified to set the tone for [such policy] than the church, the Christian public?"[20] Social morality was to be the goal and at the same time the point of departure for a Protestant social witness; the church should have no qualms about acting as a pressure group for the cause of good order.

As in the case of education, churchmen saw social action as mutually advantageous to church and society. A primary objective, Theodor Traub argued, should be to awaken or restore positive relations with the many industrial workers who remained nominally within the ecclesiastical fold. This equation of social action with ecclesiastical renewal appeared rather less farfetched in Württemberg than elsewhere in Germany. An influential faction within the Württemberg SPD openly stressed the

---

[17] Gustav Gross, "Religion und Politik, Gottesdienst und Bürgerpflicht," sermon, Leonhardtskirche, Stuttgart, Nov. 7, 1915, (copy), LKA/SS.

[18] *Amtsblatt* 20 (1923): 325.

[19] Schoell, "Unternehmertum, Arbeiterschaft, und evangelische Kirche," *EGBfS* 20 (1924): 30.

[20] "Gefahren der Sozialpolitik?" *EGBfS* 23 (1927): 125.

ethical dimensions of Marxian ideology over its materialistic, "scientific" aspects. Responding to a Volksbund questionnaire in 1924, the party leadership declared Social Democrats to be in "very substantial agreement" with the social and moral perspective put forth in the *Soziale Botschaft*. Socialist goals derived from the Christian ethics of the Sermon on the Mount, and "the shocking contradiction between these teachings and reality is felt by no one more keenly than the Social Democratic party."[21]

The irony in this response was unmistakable. Two years earlier, the Social Democratic paper in Heilbronn had remarked, apropos of another Volksbund questionnaire, that "the most diligent churchgoers often turn out to be the greediest."[22] For their part, churchmen could have had few illusions about the immediate prospects for a new social gospel. Unlike 1848, when another revolution had triggered heightened interest in the social question, the church no longer stood securely on the side of the existing order. Nor could it afford simply to ring changes on the old theme of the honest laborer, diligent at work, devout at prayer, and deferential towards his betters. As in 1848, however, social activism represented in the first instance a holding action against the advance of secularity. The way to the Volkskirche ran through a restored moral community; the way to a moral community ran through the individual conscience.

The Crusade for a Moral Community

Obstacles to reviving such a moral community seemed both numerous and formidable. Surveying the first half of the Weimar decade, liberal Stuttgart pastor and future prelate Max Mayer-List, an Evangelical-Social activist who had served as one of the Württemberg delegates to the national church congress in 1924, expressed deep concern over the difficulties for church work posed by "heightened economic tensions [and a] hardening of

---

[21] Quoted in summary memorandum on Volksbund questionnaire, Nov. 11, 1924; OKR/AR Gen. 117.

[22] *Das Neckar-Echo*, Sept. 18, 1922.

political antagonisms such that nearly insurmountable barriers arise between individual fellow citizens." Concluded Mayer-List: "The heavy blows of the past years have driven hundreds of thousands to ever greater recklessness, ever greater godlessness. No effective ways have yet been found to reach them. Large circles of the educated and the working classes pose difficult questions for the church if it hopes to remain a Volkskirche."[23]

How could these "heavy blows" be counteracted? The most congenial tool available to churchmen was exhortation. Sermons and pulpit declarations provided one time-honored medium by which pastors and church officials communicated to loyal parishioners. For those outside this core group the religious press assumed an ever more important role. Parish bulletins, *Sonntagsblätter*, and a variety of other devotional publications reached a substantial part of the Protestant population, providing access to many whose identification with the church did not extend to regular attendance at services.[24] In few areas of Germany was Protestant press activity stronger and more deeply rooted than in Württemberg. The pietist *Christenbote*, a weekly published in Stuttgart since 1831, was the oldest continuous venture of its kind in Germany. During the 1920s Württemberg churchmen edited or published at least three dozen major church periodicals, from specialized theological journals to mass-circulation weeklies, with a combined press run in 1928 of nearly a million copies. While many of these circulated nationwide, readership within Württemberg itself was considerable. Even at the height of 1923 inflation, the largest church weeklies, the *Stuttgarter Evangelisches Sonntagsblatt* and the several local editions of the *Evangelisches Gemeindeblatt*, counted over 84,000 subscribers; in normal times the total exceeded 220,000.[25] Allowing for du-

[23] Max Mayer-List, "Neujahr 1927," *KAfW* 36 (1927): 1.

[24] On the religious press, see especially Bühler, *Presse und Protestantismus*; see also Gerhard E. Stoll, *Die evangelische Zeitschriftenpresse im Jahre 1933* (Witten, 1963).

[25] Hilzinger to OKR, July 13, 1928, OKR/AR Gen. 124/I; also notes on circu-

plications in subscription, it seems reasonable to assume that some form of church publication reached at least every third Protestant household. These were not official church organs, to be sure, but clergymen collaborated in their production, and their columns were almost invariably open to contributions from church leaders. Few observers in or out of church service underestimated the importance of the religious press in shaping public opinion. As Theophil Wurm put it in a speech of 1929: "The [religious press] guides, strengthens and mobilizes those church members directly involved in the life of the parish, and it reaches far beyond these circles to a substantial share of those who consider themselves, in whatever sense, members of the church at large."[26]

Church officials also sought to increase their visibility in the secular media, an arena where, except for papers in the conservative orbit, relations had often been strained. The church's principal liaison agency was the Evangelical Press Association (Evangelischer Presseverband), a loose confederation of Protestant information services established in Berlin a few years before World War I. Its director since 1918, August Hinderer, was a native of Württemberg, a Tübingen Stiftler, and a contemporary of, among others, Hermann Hesse and Hans Voelter. Under Hinderer's direction, the church's press arm cultivated editors and publishers "not so much to achieve an explicitly Christian outlook in the press as to encourage the progressive ethicization of periodicals' contents."[27] In the Württemberg branch of the association, which was absorbed into the Volksbund after 1919, Hinderer's successors provided a wide array of news and informational services to area newspapers, whose contents in turn it

---

lation figures in LKA D1/26,2. The Württemberg church numbered between 600,000 and 700,000 confirmed adult members.

[26] Theophil Wurm, "Die Bedeutung unserer religiösen Volkspresse im Haushalt des kirchlichen Lebens," *MfPT* 25 (1929): 27; cf. Ino Arndt, "Die Judenfrage im Licht der evangelischen Sonntagsblätter" (Ph.D. diss., Tübingen University, 1960), pp. 5–7.

[27] Quoted in *RGG*, 3d ed. (Tübingen, 1961), 5:549; on Hinderer, see Walter Schwarz, *August Hinderer: Leben und Werk* (Stuttgart, 1951).

carefully monitored. The bourgeois press generally paid sympathetic heed to church concerns, while even Social Democratic papers occasionally publicized church events or accepted contributions from pastors.[28] Nor did church leaders ignore the potential of other, newer media. By 1925 the Volksbund had reached an agreement with the South German Radio to broadcast devotional programs and commentaries on at least a biweekly basis. Stuttgart pastors strongly supported this radio work and in fact pressed for more frequent broadcasts of worship services, not least because surveys suggested that 75 percent or more of the burgeoning radio audience consisted of workers.[29] At a minimum such public media gave broader currency to the church's message than churchmen could achieve from the pulpit or through other traditional lines of parish communication. Beyond this the impact is harder to assess. The pastor in Markgröningen, near Ludwigsburg, may or may not have been typical in remarking that, if nothing else, his regular newspaper commentaries had "stiffened the backbone of the local police."[30]

The turbulent Weimar years gave churchmen abundant occasions for calling fellow citizens to a moral accounting. Official proclamations ordered the frequent crises of the period into a kind of perpetual morality play, each new disaster serving to symbolize another facet of the basic spiritual crisis that churchmen saw enveloping the modern world. Preoccupation with spiritual misery and moral degeneration was most acute, understandably enough, during the early years of the republic. After four years of war and the subsequent hammer blows of revolution and counterrevolution, shortages and inflation, all the old verities seemed abandoned. Integrity and compassion seemed overwhelmed by simple unbridled greed; deprivation and exploitation seemed to feed upon one another and were fed in turn

[28] E.g., Esslingen, Pfarrbericht 1925, OKR/AR OA/PfB. Cf. Dörge to Schnauffer, June 14, 1926, LKA D/EPVW 34; R. Denzel to Merz, Jan. 8, 1924, OKR/AR Gen. 124/I.
[29] EGBfS 21 (1925): 36–37, 24 (1928): 77; Theodor Traub, Jahresbericht 1926 (Stuttgart, 1927), p. 40.
[30] Markgröningen, Pfarrbericht 1926, OKR/AR OA/PfB.

by the rough victors' justice that the struggling republic had brought down upon itself in the humiliation of Versailles.

Yet these very circumstances also cried out for a reaffirmation of those common values—law and order, for example, or the need for patriotic solidarity in the face of diplomatic adversity—that would remind Germans that they remained bound together in a national community. As articulated in the church's terms, such values provided one source of hope that a true moral commonwealth, a la the Christian state of old, might eventually be restored. The Rhineland crisis of 1919–20 provided an early occasion both for jeremiads and for the invocation of this implied national consensus. Providing temporary haven for refugees from the area, Württembergers heard their full share of tales about the outrages allegedly being committed by colonial French occupation troops. The church gave place to none in expressing the nation's indignation over this "black horror on the Rhine." Both privately and officially, church leaders lent their authority to diplomatic campaigns against French policy. On May 21, 1920, the very day it approved the new church constitution, the Württemberg church assembly passed a formal resolution of protest against the use of black occupation troops. On the initiative of Consistory president Hermann von Zeller, the DEKA adopted a similar resolution the following month. Meanwhile, the Consistory attempted to use ecumenical channels in Switzerland to win a sympathetic hearing among French Protestants; disappointing results did nothing to allay wounded national pride.[31]

By themselves, however, attacks on victors' justice and the evil fruits of war did nothing to restore a stable moral order. Having defined the central crisis as moral and personal, churchmen rejected purely economic or political remedies. Indeed, as

[31] LKV, *Verhandlungen* (1920), pp. 1154–55. DEKA, Sitzungsprotokoll, Eisenach, June 23, 1920, and A. W. Schreiber (Kommission für Freundschaftsarbeit der Kirchen, Geneva) to WEK, Aug. 20, 1920, both in LKA A26/323. Cf. Keith J. Nelson, "The 'Black Horror on the Rhine': Race as a Factor in Post-World War I Diplomacy," *Journal of Modern History* 42 (1970): 606–27, and Borg, *Old-Prussian Church*, pp. 224–25.

the influential *Evangelisches Kirchenblatt für Württemberg* insisted, "a nation lives not by politics and economic measures but by the convictions that shape . . . ethical conduct." "Help and healing," the Consistory affirmed in 1919, "must come from within."[32] Hence material crises typically served to buttress homilies on the "inner life," even when church proclamations had a specific practical purpose. In a 1920 harvest message, for example, the Consistory linked the fruits of the land with the "fruits of righteousness without which our work and produce remain unblessed"—a characteristically moralistic way of admonishing Protestant farmers to cooperate with officials in holding down commodity prices.[33]

This appeal was only one of many issued in the early years of the republic. During the left-liberal ascendency of 1919–20, when state authorities were struggling to counter an epidemic of food shortages and black-marketeering, churchmen played an important part in establishing communications between Stuttgart and the rural hinterland. "If these gentlemen will speak to farmers from the pulpit, that will have an effect," Education Minister Berthold Heymann was advised in 1919.[34] Church officials were only too willing to oblige when a Social Democrat appeared to acknowledge their importance as moral preceptors. Long pastoral letters urging cooperation with the authorities were read in every church, and Protestants who did not attend services found inserts bearing the same message in parish papers. Loyalty to the community, not greed for private gain, was the duty of every church member: "If every group were to say 'I won't produce anything if things don't go exactly according to my wishes,' . . . then goodnight, German folk and Fatherland!"[35]

[32] *EKBfW* 80 (1919): 91, quoting the *Bayrischer Volksfreund*; "Ansprache der Oberkirchenbehörde und der Landeskirchenversammlung an die evangelischen Kirchengenossen," Oct. 31, 1919, in *Amtsblatt* 19 (1919–20): 101–3.

[33] "An die evangelischen Bevölkerung," Oct. 6, 1920, in *Amtsblatt* 19 (1920): 306.

[34] N. N. to Heymann, Sept. 9, 1919 (copy); Heymann to WEK, Sept. 11, 1919; and Jakob Schoell, memorandum, n.d.; all in LKA A26/1097.

[35] *Evangelisches Gemeindeblatt für Wiernsheim*, Oct. 1919; Schall (Ernäh-

In the face of inflation, unemployment, and the multiple dislocations of the postwar era, the church had no specific structural remedies to propose. To the economically afflicted, the social manifesto of 1924 could only counsel that "the more willingly we . . . take upon ourselves the unavoidable sacrifices, the better it will be for us and for the whole of society."[36] Self-discipline and personal integrity, it seemed, promised the only sure defense, yet these virtues seemed in woefully short supply. The instinctive contrast between past order and present decay infuses a remark made by one Protestant prison chaplain in a pamphlet describing his work. A hundred years earlier, he declared, the "three 'Sch's'" which instilled the most fear had been *Schultheiss, Schulmeister*, and *Schütz* (mayor, schoolmaster, and constable); now, however, the reigning trinity had become *Schnaps, Schundliteratur*, and *Schauspiel* (liquor, trashy literature, and theater).[37] Addressing a district pastors' conference in Heilbronn, Hermann Eytel complained in 1926 that too many people seemed blinded by "the dazzling charms of the word *freedom*, which is taken to mean the manifold negation of every conscious restraint. Hence 'freedom' also serves to protect those enemies of the nation: alcohol, pornography, trashy literature, open lewdness." Mass society, Eytel declared, "is devouring the soul."[38] If churchmen lacked the power and ideological vision to confront structural problems, they saw a clear mandate to take on those "enemies of the nation" that threatened moral health, family integrity, and public order.

In attacking "smut and lewdness," as in attacking French occupation methods, churchmen could be confident of voicing something like a public consensus. Unfettered expression was a watchword of few outside Weimar's cultural avant-garde. On

rungsministerium) to KM, Oct. 6, 1920 (copy); Bälz to WEK, Oct. 11, 1920; and "Erlass an Dekanatsämter," Oct. 13, 1920; all in LKA A26/1097. See also *SES* 54 (1920): 340, and note 33, above.

[36] LKV, *Verhandlungen* (1924), p. 2201.

[37] A. Bertsch, *Auf Irrwegen, Bilder aus dem Zuchthaus* (Stuttgart, 1928), p. 18, copy in LKA/SS.

[38] Hermann Eytel, speech to Heilbronn Bezirkskirchentag, Oct. 4, 1926, and *Neckar-Zeitung*, Oct. 6, 1926, copies of both in LKA D1/13,2.

the contrary, there was widespread agreement that moral laxity constituted one of the sorrier by-products of the war, that—as Berthold Heymann once put it in the Württemberg assembly— the public's "moral powers of resistance" had been severely weakened.[39] Right-wing youth groups and left-wing party functionaries alike mounted protests against, for example, the exploitation of sex in the films that crowded German screens after the postwar relaxation of censorship.[40] With the newly organized Volksbund in the vanguard, a coalition of Württemberg groups demanding the reimposition of film controls organized a statewide Committee for Cinema Reform (Landesausschuss für Kinoreform) in December 1919. Under its aegis a massive rally took place in Stuttgart on December 10. The roster of speakers dramatized the ecumenical scope of the movement, representing as it did every local party from the Bürgerpartei to the USPD. Speaking for the latter party was Klara Zetkin—surely one of the rare occasions that this doughty socialist and feminist would agree to play a supporting role in a production largely scripted by conservative churchmen. As a result of these and similar protests throughout the nation, the Reichstag speedily approved a new cinema law in May 1920 requiring predistribution review of releases coupled with age categories for theater attendance. A subsequent law, passed in 1926, extended age controls to cover printed materials as well. Both laws created networks of regional review boards to regulate the sale and distribution of materials deemed objectionable to minors.[41]

[39] Landtag, *Verhandlungen* (1920), p. 1779. Cf. Albrecht Mendelssohn-Bartholdy, *The War and German Society: The Testament of a Liberal* (New Haven, Conn., 1937), pp. 280–95, and Ernst Troeltsch's fears about a "spirit of nihilism" unleashed by the war (Fritz Ringer, *The Decline of the German Mandarins: The German Academic Community, 1890–1933* (Cambridge, Mass., 1969), pp. 345–46).

[40] See Siegfried Kracauer, *From Caligari to Hitler: A Psychological History of the German Film* (Princeton, 1947), pp. 44–47. In the early 1920s Württemberg boasted 89 public cinemas in 57 different communities, with a seating capacity of about 23,500 (*SHW 1928*, p. 284).

[41] EVB to WEK, Dec. 6, 1919, OKR/AR Gen. 117; *Reichs-Gesetzblatt* (1920), pp. 953–58, (1926), 1:505–6; EVB, *Mitteilungen* 16 (June 1921): 288–89. Re-

Passage of the 1926 law fulfilled a principal demand of another church-related pressure group, the State Committee to Combat Moral Danger (Landesausschuss zur Bekämpfung sittlicher Not). An offshoot of the original cinema reform committee, it was established under Volksbund auspices in 1921 to serve as a cultural watchdog and to provide churchmen with a convenient vehicle for moral vigilance and public advocacy.[42] In keeping with its rather bombastic name, the committee coordinated responses to any manifestation of the modernist spirit critical of religious practices or sensibilities. One frequent target was the Stuttgart *Kunstgebäude*, a significant regional forum for the artistic avant-garde. In 1924, for example, an orchestrated "women's protest" vainly sought to close down a major exhibit of new works by such expressionist masters as Otto Dix and Emil Nolde. The "brutality and raw sensuality" of the paintings were alleged to be an "offense to all sensibility and a general scandal"; even worse, the gallery was preying on the vulnerability of youth by offering students admission at a reduced price.[43]

While in this instance the committee received no satisfaction, other ventures met with greater success. In 1928 the committee brought heavy pressure to bear on the Education Ministry, the ultimate administrator of the state theater in Stuttgart, forcing major preperformance alterations in the sets and presentation of *Jonny spielt auf*, Ernst Krenek's popular jazz opera then in production at the Württemberg State Opera. Similar pressure may have contributed to an earlier decision not to include the premiere of Paul Hindemith's *Sancta Susanna* in a Stuttgart program of the composer's work.[44] In 1921 the Consistory had itself

gional review boards, each composed of a chairman and eight appointed experts, were established in Munich, Berlin, and Leipzig. The Munich board included Stuttgart youth pastor Gottlob Wüterich; cf. *Evangelischer Jugenddienst*, no. 2 (1927).

[42] The Oberkirchenrat as a matter of policy declined to give official sanction to the programs of private groups; cf. Adolf Schaal, memorandum, Feb. 17, 1927, and Engelhardt to OKR, Sept. 8, 1925, both in OKR/AR Gen. 148b/I.

[43] "Frauenprotest gegen die 'Neue Deutsche Kunst,'" *KAfW* 33 (1924): 111.

[44] Pfisterer to OKR, Jan. 19, 1928, and Landesausschuss zur Bekämpfung sitt-

intervened with the Education Ministry against one of the state theater's productions. The work in question was a comedy by Hermann Essig, a Württemberg native and minor expressionist playwright, recently deceased. In *Pastor Rindfleisch (Der Kuhhandel)*, Essig satirized a rural pastor more interested in the perquisites of office than in his spiritual obligations; to church officials this constituted a shameless attack on the "largest and strongest organization within the state." After a single performance the play was removed from the schedule, one newspaper critic remarking acidly that the theater's management should have remembered that the incumbent minister of education, Johannes Hieber, had once been a pastor himself.[45]

Among the most vigorously prosecuted battles in the campaign for moral reform was that against alcohol. Württemberg, with its strong pietist subculture, provided fertile ground for the German temperance movement, aroused to new militancy by economic distress at home and the model of America's noble experiment with Prohibition abroad. With over two hundred members, Württemberg boasted the largest regional chapter of the League of Abstaining Pastors (Bund enthaltsamer Pfarrer), a national organization established in 1903; proportionally, membership in Württemberg was double the national average.[46] At this group's urging, the Württemberg church assembly was moved to pass a resolution in 1922 commending the practice of abstinence, in the process ignoring the vigorous objections of one delegate, a brewery operator who pleaded for a distinction between distilled spirits and his "totally harmless" beer. "Alcohol is alcohol, whether in beer or in brandy," Paul Wurster rejoined; a majority of the assembly concurred.[47]

Debate on this measure appears to have been jovial; published proceedings note outbreaks of laughter and amusement during

licher Not to KM, Jan. 18, 25, 1928, both in OKR/AR Gen. 123a. On the Hindemith premieres, see Geoffrey Skelton, *Paul Hindemith* (London, 1975), pp. 62–63.

[45] Bernouli to Schenkel, n.d.; Schenkel to WEK, June 11, 1921; and press clippings and memorandum of Jakob Schoell, all in LKA A26/346.

[46] *KAfW* 38 (1929): 67; cf. *RGG*, 2d ed. (Tübingen, 1927), 1:217–18.

[47] LKV, *Verhandlungen* (1922), pp. 2019–23.

the above-mentioned exchanges. The brewer's predicament, however, illustrated a problem inherent in churchmen's efforts to promote uniformity of social comportment. In Württemberg as elsewhere, alcohol was not only a debatable pleasure but also for many a source of livelihood. By supporting abstinence, churchmen went against some parishioners' economic well-being. Along much of the upper Neckar and its tributaries, wine was the lifeblood of rural commerce, and though vintners as a class scarcely enjoyed renown as paragons of piety, they constituted a significant presence in many rural Protestant parishes, a group to be condemned only at a heavy cost in goodwill and community spirit.[48] Despite vocal arguments for abstinence, therefore, churchmen never advocated legislated prohibition with anything like the enthusiasm, for example, of their campaign for censorship laws.[49]

This is not to say that churchmen neglected opportunities to decry alcohol abuse or to encourage moderation. In larger cities, local Volksbund chapters joined with temperance groups to establish alcohol-free coffeehouses as an alternative to the beer garden and *Weinstube*.[50] At harvesttime in 1922, the Volksbund appealed to farmers to refrain from the time-honored custom of reserving part of their fruit crops for use in home distilling. At the same it called for increased propaganda on the dangers of intoxication and for tighter controls on the sale and distribution of spirits.[51] Encouraged by the Reichstag's approval in 1923 of a law increasing regulation of the alcohol trade, the Volksbund petitioned the Württemberg Interior Ministry as well as delegates to the Reichstag for early action on new legislation authorizing the exercise of local option in liquor licensing. When, by middecade, these appeals had failed to yield results, church forces joined

[48] For representative comments on rural religious attitudes and practices, see Reutlingen, Pfarrbericht 1920, LKA A29/3766; Marbach, Pfarrbericht 1922, LKA A29/2741; and Tübingen, Pfarrbericht 1923, LKA A29/4657.

[49] Discussion in EPW, Hauptversammlung, Stuttgart, Apr. 23, 1930, Protokoll, LKA D/EPW 22/II.

[50] See, e.g., Heilbronn, Pfarrbericht 1921, LKA A29/1909.

[51] EVB, *Mitteilungen* 23 (June 1922): 418.

with other disappointed temperance supporters to launch a nationwide Antialcohol Week as a way of dramatizing public support for their cause. In at least twenty-five towns and cities, Volksbund chapters sponsored rallies, signed petitions, or took out notices in local papers. The Pfarrverein pledged its support, and the Oberkirchenrat drafted a pastoral letter to be read from all pulpits, although some activists complained that church leaders in general showed insufficient commitment to the cause. Efforts on behalf of local option legislation culminated in the spring of 1926 with a national petition drive modeled on the highly successful campaign for confessional schools six years earlier. In Württemberg, the Volksbund pressed the signature drive as ''part of the great struggle we must wage to liberate our national life from the growth of corrupting hedonism and to cleanse our political life from the domination of financial interests.'' The success of canvassers in Württemberg is difficult to determine; throughout the country, however, the drive amassed more than two million signatures.[52]

Despite this burst of energy, the desired legislation failed to materialize, and in following years the fervor for reform appears to have cooled somewhat. A major reason may well have been the fact that the natural political allies of church temperance groups—the heavily Protestant parties of the right—also represented business interests opposed to increased regulation of commerce. In the Reichstag, ironically, the most consistent support for local option came from the left, an uncongenial source of allies for most of the burgher pietists, clergy, and academic mandarins who made up the core of the organized temperance movement. The controversial effects of Prohibition in the United States likewise cost significant support, especially among

[52] EPW, Hauptversammlung, Stuttgart, Apr. 15, 1925, Protokoll, LKA D/EPW 22/II; EVB, *Mitteilungen* 29 (Oct. 1923): 504, 36 (June 1925): 14, 40 (Mar. 1926): 110; cf. ''An unsere Ortsgruppen,'' Mar. 11, 1926 (copy), LKA D1/26,2. ''Die Bekanntmachung des Ev. Oberkirchenrats über die alkoholgegnerische Werbewoche,'' *KAfW* 34 (1925): 101; ''Unterschreibet bei der Unterschriftensammlung für das Gemeindebestimmungsrecht!'' *EGBfS* 22 (1926): 80. Reichstag, *Verhandlungen* 384 (1925): 684–705; *Reichs-Gesetzblatt* (1923), 1:147–51.

those not committed to total abstinence. Furthermore, the comparative prosperity of Weimar's Indian summer years made it difficult to exploit the familiar image of strong drink as a villain competing with bread and milk for the wage earner's last pfennig. In any event, abstaining churchmen could hardly avoid the melancholy conclusion that alcohol consumption probably responded more to the business cycle than to their exhortations.

Despite ritual references to the evil effects of war and revolution, neither moral abuses nor the rhetoric with which the church sought to combat them were unique to the Weimar years. Indeed, postwar church pronouncements were often all but indistinguishable in tone or substance from similar laments about the pursuit of pleasure from a century before.[53] If the *Soziale Botschaft* manifested a certain idealism in its attempt to address the economic changes of the industrial age, the moral crusades of the same period betrayed a basic frustration with cultural manifestations of this modernization process, particularly the ethos of individualism, long the stuff of conservative jeremiads. Lacking a positive theory of modern culture, churchmen often fell back upon traditional moral categories to deal with such complex problems as the relationship between public and private spheres of life or, more specifically, the nature of leisure and its relationship to the mind-numbing routines of urban factory life. As a result, one finds a strong current of cultural pessimism running through church social pronouncements. Even if they did not consciously conjure with images of some vanished Christian order, many if not most churchmen found it hard not to regard every new social phenomenon as inherently

[53] Scharfe, Schenda, and Schwedt, *Volksfrömmigkeit*, p. 70, shows a 19th-century illustration contrasting the narrow road of faith with the broad way leading—via theater, gambling, carousing and the like—to destruction. Suggestive comparative essays include J. Michael Phayer, *Religion und das Gewöhnliche Volk in Bayern in der Zeit von 1750–1850* (Munich, 1970); Edward Shorter, "Towards a History of *La Vie Intime*: The Evidence of Cultural Criticism in Nineteenth-Century Bavaria," in Michael R. Marrus, ed., *The Emergence of Leisure* (New York, 1974), pp. 38–68; and James S. Roberts, *Drink, Temperance, and the Working Class in Nineteenth-Century Germany* (Winchester, Mass., 1984).

malignant, a further threat to the health of the soul and hence of society at large.

Thus, for example, the Volksbund in 1920 urged the masses to seek "fewer pleasures, more joy," condemning the growing popularity of sporting clubs and public amusements as a "poison" being ingested by a "mortally wounded people." The pursuit of private pleasures undermined the individual and collective discipline essential to rebuild a shattered moral and political community. "A house of mourning in which there is dancing and carousing," the Volksbund warned, "will become a madhouse."[54] Given the limitations on their own moral suasion, churchmen were not about to abandon recourse to police powers where such sanctions promised to restrain the tide of self-gratification. Just as they favored controls on cinemas and beer gardens, so they urged state and local authorities to maintain vigilant supervision of public amusements and sporting events, a position justified encyclopedically on "moral, pedagogical, hygienic, social, and political grounds."[55]

The specter of "dancing and carousing" led a variety of church groups to issue grave warnings against carnivals and folk festivals which after a wartime hiatus were being revived in many areas, often on a lavish and heavily commercialized scale. In Stuttgart, church officials regularly decried excesses at the annual Volksfest, the historic state agricultural fair in neighboring Cannstatt. Youth leaders sought to counter the temptations of sideshows and beer tents by scheduling group excursions out of the city for the duration of the fair. To protect the unfortunates left behind, church officials urged city police to maintain strict enforcement of curfews and drinking ordinances. The Volksbund similarly attempted to limit merrymaking at the Shrovetide carnivals common in Catholic areas. Claiming that such events were an "insult to all serious, sensible people," fostering an "already regrettably strong tendency to moral frivolity," the

[54] "Weniger Vergnügen, mehr Freude," Ev. Volksbund für Württemberg 2, no. 1 (1920).
[55] Thus Diözesansynode Plieningen, Jan. 25, 1922, Protokoll, LKA A26/539.

Volksbund regularly petitioned the Württemberg Interior Ministry to limit the scale of celebrations. Local chapters in towns where carnivals were scheduled set about monitoring the economic and social costs of the festivities as measured by incidents of public drunkenness, bodily injury, and disturbance of the peace. Responding in part to the drumbeat of church pressure, the Interior Ministry issued a temporary ban on Lenten festivals late in 1925.[56]

Since such prohibitions did not apply to private celebrations, frivolity continued unabated in dance halls, inns, and other accommodating establishments. By 1927 pastors in Württemberg's normally sober capital were complaining that carnival celebrations had reached unprecedented proportions. Youth workers in Stuttgart patrolled the streets during carnival season in a truck emblazoned with posters denouncing the merchandising of self-indulgence. A night's take in the Stuttgart pleasure palaces, one banner proclaimed, would pay the rent on a hundred apartments or provide food for a thousand orphans for an entire year.[57] On the eve of the 1928 celebrations, youth groups distributed leaflets to every Stuttgart household urging parents to keep their offspring indoors and away from temptation. Similar concerted protests helped beat back a campaign in 1929 to liberalize police provisions and push back closing times in the city's pubs.[58]

Carnivals were only one of many leisure pursuits constantly competing with church activities for the time and interest of parishioners. Amusements, particularly sports activities, appealed to all ages and classes, but to none more than the young. By comparison, churchmen's invitations to explore the "quiet, deep-seated seriousness of the Christian world of ideas" and to cultivate the "calm, quiet contemplation of the individual" held

[56] *EGBfS* 20 (1924): 141, 143; EVB, *Mitteilungen* 6 (Jan. 1920): 99, 13 (Jan. 1921): 222, 39 (Jan. 1926): 69ff.

[57] *SES* 61 (1927): 111.

[58] *Evangelischer Jugenddienst* no. 2 (1928); "Zwei Monate Fastnachtsrummel—der Vergnügungsindustrie zulieb?" *SES* 62 (1928): 459, 508.

little allure.[59] The trend towards a shorter workweek as a result of Weimar's labor-management social contract only magnified the problem of leisure. For the church, one immediate concern lay in the challenge to traditional Sunday observance mounted by leisure organizations and activities. To be sure, legislation had long been on the books defining the Sabbath as a day of rest and prohibiting anything that was not consonant with the religious character of the day. The Weimar constitution, in ARTICLE 139, appeared to provide much the same guarantee. Yet enforcement was becoming indifferent at best; pastors found themselves increasingly hard pressed to compete for an audience with the local football club or shooting society, especially when the latter were able to sponsor cheap weekend excursions or recreational activities in comfortable proximity to an inn or clubhouse taproom. A diocesan synod in Böblingen complained that during the summer of 1921 "festive events" scheduled by sport and social clubs had interfered with attendance at services on nearly every Sunday. In 1926 on the day of the annual Solitude auto race near Stuttgart, the pastor in nearby Eltingen reported, male attendance at services was a mere 20 percent of normal, while of the 120 children normally expected at the weekly youth service only 15 appeared. In Spraitbach, near Schwäbisch Gmünd, the mere announcement of a motorcycle race in 1929 sufficed to decimate church attendance, even though adverse weather caused a last-minute cancellation of the actual event.[60]

Swelling interest in recreation and leisure activities placed heavy pressure on available facilities both public and private. Sports clubs attracted a steady flow of new recruits; the membership rosters of many groups in the late 1920s were nearly double those of 1918 or the prewar years. In all, athletic organizations boasted perhaps 375,000 members in Württemberg as of 1928, roughly one-third of whom were below age twenty. There were more than 1,350 individual groups devoted to track or

[59] *Neckar-Zeitung*, Oct. 6, 1926, copy in LKA D1/13,2.

[60] Leonhardtskirche, Stuttgart, Pfarrbericht 1923, LKA A29/4380,2; Diözesansynode Böblingen, statement, Sept. 28, 1921 (copy), LKA A26/535. Sprösser to OKR, May 17, 1926; Benzing to Schrenk, Apr. 21, 1929; and Schrenk to OKR, Apr. 23, 1929; all in OKR/AR Gen. 263.

gymnastics. Hiking and mountaineering groups claimed more than 100,000 members in over 900 local groups, while 250 amateur football clubs counted a membership of more than 40,000, and another 33,000 were enrolled in cycling clubs.[61] Given the sheer range of possibilities that resulted, it is hardly surprising that the strictest Sunday laws would often be honored only in the breach.

Even where the letter of the law was observed, the church often reaped little or no benefit. Heilbronn Dekan Hermann Eytel reported in 1921 that while local gymnastics clubs suspended practices during Sunday services, they scheduled them instead for immediately before and after the appointed hour, leaving no time for participants to put in an appearance at church. Local police normally turned a blind eye to violations of Sunday laws; intervention came only in the case of genuine public disturbances—"a position that we can tolerate, after all," Eytel observed with ironic resignation, "in view of the unchurched character of the great mass of people."[62] Complaints about lax enforcement were common. When the Stuttgart town council requested the Interior Ministry in 1921 to consider modifying Sabbath ordinances, the Consistory issued a counterplea for more consistent administration of the existing rules. While the church had no wish to denigrate the value of sports, Consistory president Zeller declared, the current passion for physical culture threatened "serious danger to the cultivation of spiritual and moral-religious values."[63] Under pressure from church groups, some village councils lined up behind the Consistory's protest. The "increasing unruliness of the youth," argued local officials in Oberschwandorf, echoing the laments of conservatives and churchmen everywhere, made it inadvisable to deprive authorities of any weapon in their already meager arsenal of disciplinary sanctions.[64]

[61] *SHW 1928*, pp. 282–84.

[62] Heilbronn, Pfarrbericht 1921, LKA A29/1909.

[63] Meyding to WEK, July 28, 1921; Bälz to WEK, Nov. 16, 1921; and Zeller to KM, Dec. 6, 1921; all in LKA A26/539.

[64] Oberschwandorf, Gemeinderatssitzung, Jan. 25, 1922, Protokollbuch II, p. 208 (copy), LKA A26/509. See also Römer to WEK, May 23, 1922, LKA A26/539;

Athletes' claims on the Sabbath presented something of a dilemma for churchmen, because they generally arose out of a moral stance little different in essentials from the church's own cultural credo. As in France after the debacle of 1870–71, the shock of military defeat in 1918 reenergized German advocates of physical culture and at the same time reinforced ethical emphases within the sports movement. A pioneer in this regard was Carl Diem, who as general secretary of the government-supported National Committee on Physical Training was the acknowledged doyen of German athletics and by most reckonings the heir to Pierre de Coubertin as prophet of the Olympic ideal. Diem wrote in 1920 that physical culture must become a means of restoring personal and social discipline, of combating decadence and strengthening moral character. "We must become strong from within," Diem declared in a phrase that might have been lifted whole from a pastoral letter.[65] Some pastors in fact were prepared to endorse Diem's basic vision. Rudolf Leyers, youth leader and pastor in the Stuttgart suburb of Feuerbach, echoed Diem in praising sport as a "school for character," one that taught "courage, diligence, endurance, patience, pure joy, self-discipline, abstinence, subordination, and cooperation"—in short, all those hallmarks of the moral personality to which churchmen so often appealed. Sport, Leyers insisted, was "not the fruit of decadence but a defense against it."[66]

Still the suspicion remained that for many in the sports movement athletics too quickly became an end in itself, an overriding passion that left no room for the church. Some churchmen saw athletic competition as feeding the same desires for personal gratification that they condemned in amusements and alcohol. While Diem argued from Olympus that athletic self-discipline would carry over into daily life to the benefit of both individual and society, church officials, especially those active in youth work, raised the specter of a leisure-crazed *Sportler* whose pas-

Vaihingen/Enz, Pfarrbericht 1920, LKA A29/4881; and Winnenden, Pfarrbericht 1922, LKA A29/5252.
[65] Carl Diem, "Die Zukunft des deutschen Sports," *Sport-Brevier* (1920): 9
[66] Rudolf Leyers, "Sport, 3," in *RGG*, 2d ed. (Tübingen, 1931), 5:710.

sion for competition left him "distracted and unreliable" on the job and a "terror of the family" at home. At a mass assembly held under YMCA auspices in 1927, church youth workers debated the advisability of expanding their own recreational offerings in hopes of shielding the young from exposure to a Diemian cult of competition.[67]

By this time, certainly, recourse to police powers was a largely moot option. In 1924 the Stuttgart city council had proceeded on its own initiative to "give the citizen back a part of his freedom," as one approving observer described it, by suspending enforcement of most restrictions on weekend amusements.[68] Over the next several years the Württemberg Interior Ministry followed suit; not only was enforced "Sabbath rest" restricted in effect to the formal duration of church services, but Sunday closing rules were relaxed, in keeping with earlier Reich legislation, to permit certain retail stores to conduct business on a limited number of Sundays during the year. Opposition to the latter provision united churchmen with members of the retail clerks' union and many SPD officials, but their protests were to no avail.[69] That this latest tribute to the advance of commerce came from the conservative government of Wilhelm Bazille was an irony not lost on church leaders. Heidenheim Dekan Othmar Schönhuth doubtless expressed the feelings of many colleagues when he lamented, in anticipation of the new regulations: "If the present government takes so little account of people's religious sensibilities, what can we expect . . . from a differently constituted regime?"[70]

To anyone inclined to draw up a balance, it was clear by the

[67] "Sport und Familie," *Stuttgarter Jugendvereins-Blatt* 21 (Nov. 1927): 8; "Fragen der Jugendarbeit," *KAfW* 36 (1927): 195–96.

[68] "Der Gemeinderat wird grosstädtisch," *SNT*, Dec. 12, 1924.

[69] Röcker to OKR, Apr. 25, 1925; Merz to Innenministerium, Apr. 30, 1925; Hermann Müller, memorandum, Dec. 11, 1925; and Bolz to OKR, Oct. 27, 1926; all in OKR/AR Gen. 262. *Regierungsblatt* (1928), pp. 461–66.

[70] Schönhuth to Innenministerium, with Schönhuth to OKR, Apr. 7, 1927, OKR/AR Gen. 264; Hofacker to OKR, July 14, 1925, OKR/AR Gen. 262; Plattenhardt, Pfarrbericht 1928, OKR/AR OA/PfB.

late 1920s that churchmen's crusade for a moral commonwealth had yielded mixed results. Prospects were by no means unrelievedly bleak. If Württemberg scarcely approximated the model of a truly Christian society, it had also not succumbed to complete moral collapse. If many of the church's exhortations went unheeded, there had also been limited successes. Films and publications were subject to review and regulation; controls on the liquor trade had been tightened in some details; Sunday protection, if considerably attenuated, had not been wholly abandoned. Significantly, the Oberkirchenrat declined to join other territorial churches in pressing for a comprehensive national law on Sunday regulations, thinking perhaps that the half loaf of protection afforded by current Württemberg regulations was preferable to the crumbs that might remain if a uniform national standard were imposed.[71] At the same time, however, there was ample evidence that even church circles had not remained untouched by the currents of an emerging consumer culture, and there seemed little alternative for churchmen but to explore possibilities for future accommodation.

A clear case in point, once again, was the sports movement, which had long since gained a firm foothold within the church, especially in its youth organizations. Gymnastics was the raison d'être for many local youth groups; in 1929 it was reported that organized sports now constituted the recreation of choice among would-be clergymen in church preparatory seminaries.[72] Younger pastors such as Rudolf Leyers continued to insist that tensions between religion and athletics were neither inevitable nor attributable solely to malice on the part of sports enthusiasts. What was needed, Leyers suggested, was an agreement by all parties to the principle of "Sunday morning free from sports, Saturday afternoon free for sports." Of all the German states, Württemberg provided proportionally the fewest playing fields and related public amenities. The church's policy should there-

[71] Merz to DEKA, Feb. 10, 1928, OKR/AR Gen. 262.

[72] EGBfS 25 (1929): 230–31; A. Desselberger, "Vom Leben im evangelisch-theologischen Seminar," Die Volkskirche 2 (1929): 47; cf. also SHW 1928, p. 280.

fore be to advocate the expansion of facilities, not to condemn the enthusiasm for physical culture; too often in the past, Leyers argued, suitable projects had fallen victim to a nay-saying triumvirate of "pastors, parish councils, and conservative town councillors."[73] Through the efforts of Leyers and like-minded members of the Volksbund, the Oberkirchenrat agreed in 1929 to consult with leaders of the principal Württemberg sports federations. By the end of the year these discussions resulted in an informal agreement in which sportsmen pledged to avoid scheduling events that conflicted with religious functions, while church leaders promised for their part to lobby for expanded public and state-subsidized recreation facilities.[74]

The examples cited reveal a fundamental self-contradiction in the church's social stance. On the one hand, adoption of a "social" posture arose out of what might be called missionary impulses. In every sense, social action represented an earnest of good faith to those outside the church's core community, an attempt, like the surface democratization of church polity, to win the active allegiance of nominal members. On the other hand, the crusade for a moral society harked back to an anachronistic throne-and-altar triumphalism. It invoked a uniformity of values that flew in the face of modern conditions and conjured an identity between church, state, and society that existed only as a nostalgic ideal. Could churchmen set themselves up as arbiters of conduct, appealing to a social vision that many fellow citizens did not fully share, and at the same time expect such an assertion of social commitment to legitimate their role among marginal members of the church? This implicit paradox set churchmen apart from the civil servants, army officers, and academic mandarins with whom they have often been grouped. The universities, however embattled, remained at least formally a preserve of high culture. Civil servants and army officers still controlled the

[73] *RGG*, 2d ed. (1931) 5:710; Rudolf Leyers, "Unsere Kirche und die Sportbewegung," *Die Volkskirche* 2 (1929): 22–24, 29–31.

[74] Leyers to Müller, June 4, 1929; Müller to Leyers, June 20, 1929; Leyers to Müller, Sept. 3, Dec. 1, 1929; and Müller, memorandum, Dec. 30, 1929; all in OKR/AR Gen. 262.

coercive apparatus of the state, often to the detriment of the republic itself, while new pretenders to mandarin status such as industrialists wielded the potent weapon of wealth in an openly plutocratic society. Despite its privileged constitutional status, however, the church no longer had an unambiguous claim to social influence. Its position was not that of a universally accepted cultural preceptor but of a moral pressure group whose effective influence depended upon the vagaries of mass opinion.

Württemberg churchmen felt these problems keenly, if only because the strong residual piety evident in much of the region's social life made the old role of cultural preceptor seem more viable than in the pervasive secularity of the northern cities where, as we have noted, it has been suggested that the Volkskirche ideal was little more than a "vital lie" used to justify institutional and financial privileges.[75] If secularity was less blatant in the south, however, its effects were much the same. So too, inevitably, were the practical problems facing churchmen. The weakness of the church's moral crusade did not lie first in its emphasis on individual renewal. Churchmen were no doubt well advised to concentrate on possible religious dimensions of social problems, even if exhortations to self-discipline and quiet contemplation spoke only in the vaguest terms to the causes of unemployment, the distribution of wealth, or the dangers of anti-Semitism. Difficulties arose rather from the fact that social action, even when limited to a struggle against "enemies of the soul," did not specifically legitimate churchmen's claims to moral hegemony. As Social Democratic support for alcohol controls and limited Sunday protection showed, the church's positions could presumably be arrived at from diverse ideological starting points. Nor was active church membership normative for all members of the community. Personal piety was but one institutionally circumscribed option among others in an essentially private sphere of values. What one person found in the church pew another might find on the athletic field, or around a

[75] See, in general, Jacke, *Kirche zwischen Monarchie und Republik*, pp. 305–23.

neighborhood *Stammtisch*, or in a ramble through the countryside; the clergy in Öhringen, near Heilbronn, reported plaintively in 1928 that "love of nature" often lured even members
of the parish council away from Sunday services.[76]

Such problems were hardly unique either to German churches
or to the period under discussion. What they underscored, however, was the frustration inherent in any attempt to model cultural consensus in a pluralistic society. As moral preceptors
churchmen had only limited powers of coercion; as pastors they
had only limited powers of persuasion. The effort to maintain
both roles led to ambiguities that rhetoric alone could not resolve, and as a result Protestant moral alarms often served to
confirm the very pluralism they were designed to obviate.

The Diaconal Imperative

"When we've had lunch, your preaching can begin": Mack the
Knife's sardonic refrain spoke to churchmen as well as to the
philistines of the *Threepenny Opera*.[77] The social Volkskirche
manifested itself not only in churchmen's crusade for morality
and good order but also in their assertion of the church's diaconal
obligations to give food to the hungry, shelter to the homeless,
and aid to the orphans and the helpless. While Bismarck's state
socialism of the 1880s had set in motion a trend towards government control and provision of relief services, the "applied Christianity" of the Iron Chancellor's social insurance system nevertheless left wide scope for private involvement. Cooperation
between church and state was as extensive in the welfare field as
it had once been in education. But assuming churchmen were indeed ready to offer the "same service to the . . . democratic state
as to the old conservative state,"[78] they did so less to serve the
dictates of the state than to serve interests of their own. During

[76] Öhringen, Pfarrbericht 1928, OKR/AR OA/PfB.

[77] Bertolt Brecht, *The Threepenny Opera*, English lyric by Eric Bentley (New
York, 1964), p. 66.

[78] See above, p. 63; cf. *KJ 1921*, p. 111: "What the church receives in aid from
the state, the Inner Mission reimburses with rich interest."

the Weimar era, it may be said, diaconal endeavors probably came closer to providing legitimation of the church's posture as an all-embracing community than any appeal to doctrine or morality.[79]

One effect of the November Revolution was to encourage greater consolidation and coordination of existing church relief work. The idea of a unified Protestant charity program went back at least to 1848, when J. H. Wichern, in his famous address to the Protestant church congress at Wittenberg, called upon the churches to launch an "Inner Mission" to the poor and suffering of their own towns and countryside. This counterrevolutionary appeal to embrace charity as a tool for social stability met with a strong response in Württemberg, where by 1848 hospitals, orphanages, and other charitable institutions were already well-established features of the ecclesiastical landscape. Württemberg pietism had typically combined concern for the soul with charity for the body; humanitarian endeavors in nearby Switzerland also left their mark on church practice. By 1775 a privately supported orphanage was operating in Göppingen, and a host of other facilities followed throughout the kingdom. In Stuttgart alone such facilities were numerous enough by 1830 to support establishment of a pietist-dominated Evangelical Society (Evangelische Gesellschaft) to coordinate Protestant charitable work. Expansion continued throughout the century, although formal consolidation of Inner Mission efforts in Württemberg did not occur until 1914.[80]

The scope of this work can be indicated by a few examples. Church-related hospitals, orphanages, and rest homes provided a capacity of almost fourteen thousand beds in Württemberg by the early twentieth century, approximately one-third of all such facilities in the kingdom. The amalgamation of Inner Mission work in 1914 brought together more than thirty different organizations and social programs, ranging from an Evangelical Wom-

[79] Cf. Yorick Spiegel, *Der Pfarrer im Amt: Gemeinde, Kirche, Öffentlichkeit* (Munich, 1970), esp. pp. 127–30.

[80] Shanahan, *Social Question*, 1:26–27, 32; Evangelische Gesellschaft, *Jahresbericht 1918/19* (copy), LKA A29/4371.

en's League and the major Protestant youth group, each with a
membership of 150,000 or more, to parish Sunday School associations, youth hostels, and even a Society for the Assistance of
Barmaids. In the Württemberg capital alone by 1920, Inner Mission establishments included several large hospitals, a sewing
school and other women's programs, a 13,000-member life insurance cooperative, and a full range of youth services including
several orphanages, some twenty kindergartens, a dozen day-
care centers, boarding schools of various sorts, an institute for
the blind, and numerous apprenticeship programs. These programs employed more than three thousand full-time workers
and countless part-time volunteers. Financial contributions
from the Protestant population annually exceeded the total of all
other freewill offerings collected by the church.[81]

In both its latent political orientation and its approach to social
policy, Inner Mission work was solidly conservative. The concern to relieve individual distress inevitably took precedence
over analysis of the causes of that distress. Orphanages sheltered
abandoned and delinquent children, hostels afforded urban
youth modest facilities for recreation, trained welfare workers
looked after the handicapped and undernourished: such diaconal
care constituted a keystone of the welfare edifice in heavily Protestant areas like Württemberg. Nor had the growth of state welfare a la Bismarck posed an immediate challenge to the primacy
of Inner Mission efforts. Health, accident, and old age insurance
met needs beyond the capacity of private charity to provide
while not undermining the utility of such private care where it
could be offered. The emerging system of social welfare rested
initially on a symbiosis of public and private efforts. Public subsidies supplemented private donations; laymen, churchmen, and
public officials cooperated on everything from volunteer relief
boards to the highest levels of bureaucracy.

Even so, the church's historic diaconal status was potentially

[81] Wurster, *Kirchliches Leben*, p. 295; *Die Innere Mission in Württemberg im
Jahre 1925* (Stuttgart, 1925), pp. 13–90; *Die Innere Mission in Württemberg im
Jahre 1928* (Stuttgart, 1928), pp. 40–64; Martin Remppis, "Die Innere Mission
in Stuttgart," *EGBfS* 25 (1929): 314.

precarious. The growing cartellization of economy and politics after the 1880s implicitly called into question the sufficiency of private welfare efforts. The precepts of Prussian state socialists and liberal "socialists of the academic chair," not to mention Marxian socialists of whatever stripe, pointed towards broader government influence in the area of social policy. At the same time, the gradual extrusion of the church from the fabric of public administration evident in the separation of church and school and increasingly casual enforcement of Sabbath-protection laws threatened to force church-oriented charity efforts towards the periphery of the nascent welfare state. In an age of increasing social organization, even voluntary activities depended upon a united front. This was one of the motives behind the consolidation of Inner Mission programs in 1914.

By 1918, then, the "communalization" of welfare work was already a central concern within the Inner Mission ambit. Especially in the early months of the republic, "communalization" suggested not so much the symbiotic relationship of old as the systematic implementation of a new and explicitly secular model, one in which private interests—religious ones in particular—would lose their former pride of place.[82] Throughout Germany, similar apprehensions worked to drive the hitherto semiautonomous Inner Mission program towards closer institutional ties with the ecclesiastical establishment. Efforts to achieve greater cohesion in this regard received the unanimous support of the Württemberg church assembly in 1920. Without the protective support of the church, alarmists predicted, Protestant social work might be absorbed by a confessionally indifferent state. By the same token, separation of church and state made such charity work more indispensable than ever: "The Inner Mission is a daughter of the church, but as such it must do its part to feed and sustain its mother."[83]

[82] See, e.g., *KJ 1925*, p. 147, and *KJ 1921*, p. 112. As late as 1927 youth leaders in Berlin were speaking of the "communalization" of charity programs as a "violation of conscience" ("Kommunilisierung der Wohlfahrtspflege," *Evangelischer Jugenddienst*, no. 8/9 [1927]).

[83] LKV, *Verhandlungen* (1920), p. 1368; cf. *KJ 1921*, p. 111: "At present the

The foremost concern involved child welfare and youth work. Not only did these areas represent the heaviest concentration of Inner Mission resources, but they also bore directly on the church's project to nurture a Christian society. Orphanages and youth activities took up the burden where home and school set it down. Both inside and outside the classroom, argued a Württemberg youth pastor shortly after the war, the physical, intellectual, and moral nurture of the young was a legitimate community concern, and the Protestant community must of necessity commit itself to a vision of youth work decisively colored by religious principles. "The more the church's influence in the school is restricted, the more important it becomes to neglect nothing [that might affect] preschool youth": so declared the Württemberg Consistory in commending the postwar expansion of Evangelical child-care facilities.[84]

The specific catalyst for action after 1918 was a measure, conceived before the war and revived shortly after the revolution, to coordinate all youth-related programs in Württemberg through a system of local youth bureaus (*Jugendämter*). These agencies would bring together representatives of both public and private organizations, confessional as well as nonconfessional, in hopes of achieving greater uniformity in programs involving the young. In concept, Evangelical youth workers had no objection to such a proposal. They did, however, harbor reservations about its practical implications, fearing that to establish a board where churchmen would have only a consultative voice might lead either to the dilution of Inner Mission influence in youth work or to some impairment of its "cultural basis." This in particular was the argument of Stuttgart pastor Gottlob Wüterich, who since 1904 had devoted his energies exclusively to youth work and who assumed the directorship of all Evangelical youth activities in Württemberg after the war. Wüterich argued repeatedly that without a guaranteed status of codetermination for private

church and the Inner Mission have become more dependent upon each other than ever before."

[84] Otto Schuster, "Jugendgerichtshilfe," speech to Nürtingen Jugendpflege, n.d. [ca. 1920], Protokollbuch, LKA D5/1; *Amtsblatt* 19 (1919): Beiblatt, p. 6.

charities and churches, the potential value of a comprehensive administration would be more than offset by increased bureaucratization; the impersonality of administrative routines would replace the flexibility and personal contact that the Inner Mission sought to cultivate. Hence, Wüterich advocated a precautionary consolidation of all Evangelical youth programs into a network of "secretariats" (*Jugendsekretariate*), private committees that could function as a Protestant pressure group in establishing and implementing future government social policies. Wüterich had already established such a secretariat for the Stuttgart area in 1910. It provided a clearinghouse for the exchange of information on youth activities and a forum for discussing problems that exceeded the scope of individual church youth programs.[85]

In early November 1918, only days before the end of the monarchy, Wüterich and fellow youth workers received the official state charter for a new umbrella organization, Evangelical Youth Work in Württemberg (Evangelische Jugendarbeit in Württemberg), designed to coordinate church-related youth programs and to bolster the church's capacity to make a show of strength in dealing with public agencies.[86] When, as anticipated, the provisional government moved quickly to establish a central advisory council on youth policy (Landesjugendamt), the newly chartered Protestant youth consortium automatically qualified churchmen for participation. On the more informally constituted local youth boards established at the same time, clergymen took an active part as a matter of course. In practice, despite earlier dire predictions, new youth boards served a chiefly consultative function; they seldom if ever dictated policies to their constituent organizations. Most local boards in fact convened only

[85] Gottlob Wüterich, *Evangelische Jugendarbeit in Württemberg* (Stuttgart, 1920); see also Wüterich to OKR, Dec. 5, 1927, LKA A29/4373,1.

[86] Ev. Jugendarbeit in Württemberg, e. V., Satzung, Nov. 4, 1918 (copy), LKA A29/4374,1; Wüterich to WEK, Nov. 7, 1918, LKA A29/4373,3; Evangelischer Jugendverein, Mitgliederversammlung, resolution of Nov. 4, 1918 (copy), LKA A26/380; Wüterich to WEK, Dec. 12, 1918, LKA A26/380.

once a year, usually for no other purpose than to approve formal reports on youth activities in a given area.[87]

Far from suffering under enforced "communalization," in short, the church's organized youth work flourished as never before in the republican climate. The financial exigencies of the early 1920s notwithstanding, most programs not only survived but also enjoyed a spurt of expansion. By 1926 Gottlob Wüterich was reporting to the Oberkirchenrat on a half-decade of "exemplary cooperation" between church and state, thanks to which Protestant forces had been able to consolidate "a network of endeavors . . . to be found nowhere else in Germany, at least not in the same plenitude." As proof Wüterich pointed to the more than 450 Inner Mission day-care centers in Württemberg, nearly one-fourth of all such facilities in the nation.[88] The church leadership regularly provided loans and subsidies for the maintenance and expansion of such facilities, while public funds were often available to offset the operating costs of local church programs, particularly in the area of child welfare.[89] A model of collaboration between church workers and civil authorities, known and imitated well beyond the borders of Württemberg, was Stuttgart's Wichern House, a boarding-school apprenticeship program for juvenile delinquents and wards of the court. Established before the war by the Inner Mission in conjunction with Stuttgart youth pastors, the house came under municipal supervision after 1918, when its facilities were expanded and its administration entrusted to a board drawn jointly from the local Jugendamt and Protestant youth secretariat. The board also included two Protestant pastors, five city and state officials repre-

[87] Bälz to WEK, June 14, 1919, LKA A26/380; *Regierungsblatt* (1919), p. 305; *Evangelischer Jugenddienst* no. 7 (1927), no. 12 (1927), no. 1 (1928).

[88] Jahresbericht, Evang. Reichsverband für Kinderpflege, 1925–26 (copy), OKR/AR Gen. 148b/I; Wüterich to OKR, Jan. 30, 1926, LKA A29/4374,3; cf. Trautwein, *Religiosität und Sozialstruktur*, p. 38.

[89] See, e.g., Marbach, Pfarrbericht 1922, LKA A29/2741; correspondence between Wüterich and OKR in LKA A29/4373,1; Stuttgarter Jugendverein, *Jahresbericht, 1924–25* (Stuttgart, 1925), *Jahresbericht, 1927–28* (Stuttgart, 1928); and "Erholungsfürsorge für 14- bis 18-jährige Jugendliche," *Evangelische Jugendhilfe* 2 (1926): 182–88.

senting the police and courts, and two private citizens. Wüterich shared the directorship in the early 1920s with a Social Democratic town councilman.[90]

Other aspects of the church's charity work manifested a similarly comfortable symbiosis of private and public elements. Most parish pastors continued to play a prominent part in local relief administration, even though, as in the case of the school councils, such participation ceased to be mandatory after 1918. The Consistory strongly encouraged pastors to assert their claims as providers of charity. A decree of 1923 directed that parish benevolence programs be carried out "as much as practicable in conjunction with and in close consultation with the civil work."[91] Since diligent pastors made some systematic attempt to visit the homes of parishioners, they were often more conversant with family circumstances than was any other local authority. It was not uncommon for pastors to serve as conduits for relief requests, sharing with town fathers the information gathered in the course of their regular rounds. In small towns, relief matters might be entrusted completely to the pastor.[92]

The result, at best, was something like the Volkskirche ideal, a spirit of community cooperation cutting across political and social boundaries, and sometimes the boundaries of confession as well. In Öhringen, for example, charity work created a bond of sorts between Protestants and the small local Jewish community. According to a parish report of 1928, relations between church and synagogue were "almost friendlier than those with the Catholic congregation"; members of the Jewish community adopted Protestant charities as their own, regularly visiting the vicarage with gifts for distribution.[93]

Similarly cordial working relations developed in a number of localities between churchmen and socialist officials. Reporting to

[90] Wichernhaus, Stuttgart, "Am tiefsten Punkt," Jahresbericht 1923 (Stuttgart, 1923), p. 4.

[91] Amtsblatt 22 (1923): 20.

[92] See, e.g., Bietigheim, Pfarrbericht 1928, OKR/AR OA/PfB, and Hausen ob Lontal, Pfarrbericht 1920, LKA A29/1842.

[93] Öhringen, Pfarrbericht 1928, OKR/AR OA/PfB.

the Oberkirchenrat in 1924, the Dekan for Urach noted that Social Democrats elected to the town council since 1918 had, on the whole, shown a greater interest in the church's charity work than had their bourgeois counterparts. A report from Böblingen some years later complained in effect that the lack of social conscience among conservative churchgoers was driving pastors into an alliance of necessity with the "completely unchurched" left, at least where problems of relief were concerned. Clergy in Schwenningen, where a conjunction of vocal anticlericalism and vigorous pietism kept religious tensions high throughout the period, reported that relief work and other joint business with town authorities was always "disposed of smoothly." In Ebersbach, a growing industrial town near Göppingen, relations were more than correct. The Social Democratic mayor was an active member of the parish council and, according to the pastor, "warmly disposed" towards the church. Even the Communists, one pastor near Stuttgart reported in 1928, cooperated loyally with the clergy in dealing with community problems. To be sure, it was not uncommon for pastors to encounter opposition from individual officials, but in general the left's postwar gains in local politics had little effect on the traditionally close relations between town hall and manse.[94]

Beyond relief activities normally associated with the Inner Mission and parish-pump noblesse oblige, the manifold crises of the Weimar decade created rich opportunities for initiatives. Occasions were never lacking for the church to demonstrate, in the words of one 1922 parish report, its "great value" to civic authorities as a social agency. Foremost among postwar concerns was an acute shortage of housing, the result of the concentration of laborers in war industries since 1914. Gotthilf Schenkel estimated that in 1924 a million families in Germany lacked adequate shelter. A half-decade of raging inflation, with its attend-

[94] Urach, Pfarrbericht 1924; Böblingen, Pfarrbericht 1928; Ebersbach, Pfarrbericht 1929; and Plattenhardt, Pfarrbericht 1928; all in OKR/AR OA/PfB. Schwenningen, Pfarrbericht 1921, LKA A29/4151; Tailfingen, Pfarrbericht 1920, LKA A29/4552; Kuchen, Pfarrbericht 1922, LKA A29/2422; Mittelstadt, Pfarrbericht 1923, LKA A29/2869.

ant credit crises and rampant speculation, had only exacerbated the problem.[95] In this as in most social problems, churchmen saw significant moral issues at stake. Lack of adequate shelter threatened family stability, and because it hit hardest at new arrivals from the countryside, homelessness seemed a natural correlate of social rootlessness, delinquency, and mindless political radicalism. These threats to good order drove churchmen like Schenkel into the battle for housing reform. In an effort to determine the actual extent of housing needs in Württemberg, the Volksbund undertook a detailed canvass of individual parishes, and in 1924, with a coalition of other private groups, it prevailed on the austerity-minded Württemberg government to underwrite a new lending bank for home construction. Some individual Volksbund chapters pooled members' resources in order to set up modest building cooperatives of their own.[96] Through Schenkel's efforts, the national Homesteads Committee held a major meeting in Stuttgart late in 1924, attended by leading figures in ecclesiastical and political life. Jakob Schoell, who represented church president Johannes Merz, reported after the meeting that while speakers reflected a "totally Social Democratic" viewpoint, they were at least unequivocal in both their support of private property and the sanctity of the family and their opposition to the employment of women outside the home—all positions central to the church's social philosophy.[97] In the following years, Schoell and other members of the Oberkirchenrat provided symbolic support for the group's efforts, appearing at its conferences and on occasion addressing public assemblies. The church's patronage of housing reform was sufficiently visible for the municipal housing office in Stuttgart to request Merz's personal support in a drive to secure increased state appropriations for the 1925 building season.[98]

[95] Gotthilf Schenkel, "Unsere Verantwortung gegenüber der Wohnungsnot," EVB, *Mitteilungen* 33 (Sept. 1924): 581–83.

[96] EVB, *Mitteilungen* 31 (Apr. 1924): 521; *EGBfS* 21 (1925): 195.

[97] Schenkel to OKR, Nov. 10, 1924; Jakob Schoell, memoranda, Nov. 13, 17, 1924, OKR/AR 151a/I.

[98] Wohnungsamt Stuttgart to Merz, Jan. 1925; Merz to Wohnungsamt Stutt-

The church also gave limited support to other programs aimed at easing population pressures. This was especially true in the late 1920s, when rising unemployment added further to the woes of displaced rural workers. With an upsurge in the number of Swabians seeking emigration (in 1927 the American consulate in Stuttgart reported more than sixteen thousand applications pending to the United States alone),[99] a variety of private and semipublic agencies sought to encourage internal migration, especially resettlement programs in thinly populated territories along Germany's eastern borders. With the blessing of the Oberkirchenrat, churchmen and the Volksbund sought to publicize these efforts. Silesia was particularly favored for such projects, not least because of its political significance; other efforts aimed at transplanting western Germans to locations in Mecklenburg and Pomerania.[100] The strongest impetus to participation came in 1927, when the German Settlement Bank purchased a Silesian estate of former Duke Albrecht of Württemberg. Ethnic as well as religious considerations played a role in the affair; Silesian churchmen appealed to their Württemberg counterparts for support in expanding the Protestant minority along the Polish frontier.[101] Success, however, was modest at best. Despite continued appeals from eastern church officials and the various settlement movements, scarcely two hundred volunteers a year

gart, Mar. 27, 1925; Rittich to OKR, Dec. 27, 1926; and Merz to Rittich, Jan. 4, 1927; all in OKR/AR Gen. 151a/I.

[99] Süddeutsche Siedlungsgenossenschaft (Stuttgart), circular to Württemberg clergy, July 1, 1927 (copy), OKR/AR Gen. 151c. The church provided indirect support to would-be emigrants through the Deutsches Auslandsinstitut in Stuttgart, whose director of emigration, Manfred Grisebach, was a pastor seconded to the Inner Mission. See Grisebach to WEK, Nov. 20, 1920, LKA A26/377, and Grisebach papers in National Archives Microcopy T–81, rolls 428, 600.

[100] Collection of materials in OKR/AR Gen. 151c; cf. Nowak, *Kirche und Republik*, pp. 135–36.

[101] Ev. Konsistorium, Breslau, to OKR, Feb. 24, Nov. 26, 1927, OKR/AR Gen. 151c. The confessional politics involved are evident in a resettlement official's remark that it would be "politically more expedient, whenever possible, to settle Protestant German stock along the frontier as a bulwark against the [Catholic] Poles" (Kehler to Merz ["persönlich!"], Jan. 12, 1927, OKR/AR Gen. 151c).

could be found willing to brave resettlement. Few of these came from Württemberg, where church leaders became skeptical of the merits and motives of some migration schemes and, while agreeing to publicize the ventures, declined to commit any other resources.[102] Württemberg went unrepresented at a major conference on resettlement held in Kassel under Inner Mission auspices in 1929, although the Oberkirchenrat did send one delegate to a subsequent seminar in Berlin.[103]

Even before the whiplash of the Wall Street panic struck with full force in late 1929, worsening economic conditions in Germany were straining local and national social support systems and were once again threatening Weimar's tenuous political balance. As early as the summer of 1926, levels of unemployment in the larger Württemberg cities equaled or exceeded those of the worst days of the 1923–24 crisis; times were little better for farmers.[104] The magnitude of the problems mocked any pretense that the church's charity efforts alone could have a significant meliorative impact. "How happy we would be if we could provide *work*," a Volksbund communiqué declared at the beginning of the new slump. "That would be the best help!"[105] Where possible, the church did attempt to ferret out opportunities for work,[106] but job relief was clearly a matter for public unemployment offices. Out of both necessity and conviction, the church marshaled its energies largely to ease the cultural and psychological burdens of unemployment. One unnamed pastor, writing in the Pfarrverein journal in 1926, sounded a familiar theme when he argued that it would be a mistake for churchmen to separate the moral and social dimensions of the growing crisis.

[102] "Sieben magere Jahre der Siedlungsbewegung," *EGBfS* 24 (1928): 67; Friedrich Hilzinger, memorandum, Aug. 1929, OKR/AR Gen. 151c.

[103] Heimstättenausschuss-Ev. Siedlungsstelle to OKR, May 23, 1929; Carl Bonn to OKR, Aug. 22, 1929; and Hilzinger to Rinckh, Oct. 17, 1929; all in OKR/AR Gen. 151c. "Ein Schwabendorf in Pommern," *Deutsches Volksblatt*, Nov. 7, 1929 (copy), OKR/AR Gen. 151c.

[104] Unemployment series in *SHW 1928*, p. 127.

[105] EVB, *Mitteilungen* 38 (Nov. 1925): 52.

[106] Ibid., p. 53. Zeller to OKR, June 7, 1929, and Wurm to Ev. Bund, Stuttgart, July 24, 1929, both in OKR/AR Gen. 151.

"Our means of material assistance are for the most part more than modest—all the more reason for us to exploit the great advantage of church charity: its pastoral and personal manner." Since the church could not hope to solve the problem of material want, it should work primarily to encourage a "gain in the forces of morality for times to come."[107]

In this spirit, various church groups, with the Volksbund in the vanguard, concentrated their resources on what they considered to be the cultural needs of the unemployed. The Volksbund in particular experimented with ways of serving as an honest broker between capital and labor. Beginning in the fall of 1926, the Volksbund's current chairman, Heinrich von Mosthaf, arranged a series of retreats at which small groups of workers and businessmen could meet for a day or more to discuss economic conditions in hopes of bridging the gaps between classes. The largest of these conferences, held in Stuttgart in March 1927, drew slightly more than a hundred participants, half of whom turned out to be pastors and others involved in church social programs. Even the most optimistic accounts could point to few tangible results from such discussions. Nor did they attract interest outside a narrow circle of committed Evangelical shopkeepers, factory owners, and skilled workmen; the true proletariat was all but unrepresented.[108] Much the same could be said of other retreats organized primarily for the benefit of the unemployed. Designed to promote "genuine recreation, reconciliation between the classes, inner growth, and strengthened personal self-reliance," these retreats provided stays of from several days to several weeks in country hostels, often free or at minimal expense, while offering cultural enrichment in the form of lectures, discussions, or musical events. As with most such endeavors, results were mixed. In Haigerloch, where the Volksbund expected to attract enough participants for two successive weeklong retreats in the spring of 1926, a mere twelve persons regis-

[107] "Erwerbslos," *KAfW* 35 (1926): 106; Karl Edler, "Arbeit an Arbeitslosen," *KAfW* 39 (1930): 125.

[108] *EGBfS* 23 (1927): 17–18; EVB, *Mitteilungen* 40 (Mar. 1926): 100–101, 44 (May 1927): 250–51.

tered. By contrast, evening entertainment programs in working-class districts attracted a more varied audience, including some not usually known to frequent parish activities.[109]

After 1929 these "evenings for the unemployed" were about all that remained of the project to promote culture as a means of social welfare. While other efforts continued sporadically, increasingly desperate economic conditions forced church groups to transfer most of their attention and resources to simple relief. Given the straitened state of public finances, it is hardly surprising that relief itself became an issue polarized along administrative, class, and party lines, in Stuttgart no less than in Berlin. Churchmen also felt the impact of this polarization. Göppingen Dekan Otto Stahl reported in 1931 that if churches in his area had set up few relief programs of their own, the reason was "not just because congregations in general lack sufficient means for comprehensive action but above all because an explicitly church-oriented operation would incur suspicion from the start." Church groups therefore preferred to offer assistance to "organizations established by a neutral party."[110]

Demands for such assistance came from all sides. From 1926 on, Volksbund chapters in the Stuttgart area maintained soup kitchens in several parishes to supplement municipal relief facilities. After 1929 such services became increasingly common, often underwritten jointly by voluntary contributions and grants from hard-pressed local relief agencies. During the cold months, virtually every parish organized a Winter Help campaign of some sort, with pastors and church councils supervising the distribution of foodstuffs, used clothing, and in some instances small token Christmas gifts for needy children. Ironically, economic disaster achieved what evangelization and the Volksbund had not been able to accomplish. Pastors almost everywhere threw open parish halls to those seeking a "warm, well-lighted place," thereby creating a Volkskirche in miniature,

[109] EVB, *Mitteilungen* 41 (May 1926): 141, 44 (May 1927): 241–42; *KAfW* 39 (1930): 125–29; Pfarramt Heidenheim to OKR, Feb. 9, 1931, OKR/AR Gen. 151a/III.

[110] DKA Göppingen to OKR, Feb. 20, 1931, OKR/AR Gen. 151a/III.

its members drawn together less by a shared faith than by shared misery.[111]

To be sure, such efforts could be no more than short-term palliatives. "At a time when the warehouses are overflowing, when the ruling class is carrying on in unheard-of luxury, bourgeois and Social Democratic welfare agencies have gone cadging with the princes of the church to boil up a beggar's brew for the needy": so proclaimed the Communist *Süddeutsche Arbeiterzeitung* in an editorial of 1931 that circulated among members of the Oberkirchenrat.[112] For its part, the church was impotent to do more than tend the soup kettle. Beyond taxing the church's relief capacities, the new economic crisis once again called into question the coherence of the church's social vision. Hans Voelter, tireless in promoting a liberal social perspective among churchmen, posed the issue clearly in an article published only weeks before the deluge in 1929. Was it really possible, Voelter wondered, for the church to influence social and economic conditions? He for one remained optimistic. The church was itself a part of society and therefore shared responsibility for the existence of social ills. It could neither withdraw from the public arena nor sanctify a single ideology or approach to social welfare. Its primary task must be to promote cooperation and community, to serve as "conscience-pricker" where injustices surfaced, and withal to uphold a "consciousness of spiritual unity" in the face of economic and political animosities.[113]

But what forms of involvement were effective or proper? The politicization of even simple charity, as in Göppingen, confirmed the difficulty if not impossibility of churchmen taking explicit

[111] Schairer to Kübler, Dec. 22, 1926, OKR/AR Gen. 151a/I. Ev. Pfarramt Flein to DKA Heilbronn, Feb. 10, 1931; Pfarramt Mühlacker to DKA Knittlingen, Feb. 18, 1930; and DKA Marbach to OKR, Feb. 21, 1931; all in OKR/AR Gen. 151a/III. *SM*, Jan. 8, 1927; "Wie helfen die evang. Gemeinden in den heutigen Erwerbslosennot?" press release, Ev. Presseverband, Mar. 3, 1931 (copy), OKR/AR Gen. 151a/III.

[112] "Bettelruf statt Hilfe," *Süddeutsche Arbeiterzeitung*, Sept. 16, 1931 (copy), OKR/AR Gen. 151a/III.

[113] Voelter, "Hat die Kirche die Möglichkeit, die sozialen und wirtschaftlichen Verhältnisse zu beeinflüssen?" *Die Volkskirche* 2 (1929): 68–71.

positions on social issues while at the same time claiming to stand above class or party. In a pluralistic society, to adopt a specific position on any public question usually meant favoring the cause of one group over another. The result, as Max Mayer-List acknowledged, was a dilemma from which churchmen could never fully escape. Ideally the church might fill the role prescribed by Voelter, seeking to educate and prick consciences, but "in specific cases," Mayer-List noted, "it is then taken amiss when the church casts its weight on a particular side of the balance."[114] Nor for that matter could churchmen reach agreement among themselves over the resulting implications for either theory or social practice.[115]

This sense of dilemma must be emphasized, particularly since the vigorous cultural conservatism of so many public church pronouncements seems to reinforce the conclusion that Weimar churchmen simply resorted to an authoritarian social mythology as a way of masking an actual loss of social function. The political dimension of this problem needs to be examined further. Here it is worth observing that, occasional triumphalist rhetoric aside, most influential churchmen in Württemberg appear by 1930 to have abandoned any illusions about their capacity, however "social" the church's appeals, to exert more than a marginal influence on the existing moral contours of society. Commitments to social activism, moreover, paid few immediate dividends in the form of increased lay loyalty. While from churchmen's standpoint public morality and private charity should have been mutually reinforcing, in practice this was only coincidentally the case. The church as charitable agency was not coterminous with the church as spiritual association; a person accepting charity from the Volksbund did not thereby embrace the church's vision of society or become active in the core parish

[114] Mayer-List, "Neujahr 1927," p. 1.

[115] See, e.g., Protokoll, Konferenz kirchlich-sozialer Facharbeiter, Sept. 21–22, 1927, OKR/AR Gen. 151a/I; Adolf Schaal, "Leitsätze für die 1. württ. kirchl. soz. Facharbeiter-konferenz am 21. u. 22. Sept. 1928 [sic] auf der Karlshöhe b. Ludwigsburg," OKR/AR Gen. 151b; and "Pfingstagung der Ev. Arbeiter und Arbeiterinnenvereine in Tuttlingen," KAfW 38 (1929): 95–96.

community. To be sure, the likelihood of such convergence may have been somewhat greater in Württemberg than in many parts of Germany. Despite an often congenial small-town culture, however, and despite residual institutional advantages, Württemberg churchmen had no effective way of constructing the moral community of their rhetoric. Indeed, rhetoric notwithstanding, much of the church's day-to-day social activity hinted less at the restoration of a bygone Christian society than at accommodation to a more pluralistic order in which the preaching came after the lunch, if it came at all.

SIX

Politics and
Pastoral Responsibility

𝕴N 1927 the national church congress in Königsberg adopted a widely publicized proclamation on the responsibilities of Christian citizenship. The *Patriotic Message* (*Vaterländische Kundgebung*) reasserted the church's familiar claim to stand "above parties," and from the vantage point of this self-imputed neutrality it called upon loyal Protestants to fulfill their duties as citizens, enjoining them always to "be subject to the state for the sake of God's Word." Like its predecessor, the *Soziale Botschaft* of 1924, the Königsberg statement originated in the DEKA's social committee. Its bland generalities expressed the *Vernunftrepublikaner* sentiments of Jakob Schoell and like-minded members of the committee. In this respect it was a characteristic product of Weimar's Indian summer, that brief period at middecade when the German economic nightmare seemed to be ending and the election of former field marshal Paul von Hindenburg as Reichspräsident gave the republic a father figure congenial to those nostalgic for the old order. Its benign phraseology notwithstanding, the Königsberg declaration had provoked heated intramural debate. The original draft called upon church members to be subject to the "present"—that is, republican—"state," but after considerable wrangling the document emerged with the crucial adjective deleted. As finally adopted, the *Patriotic Message* provided a ringing commendation of patriotism but failed to identify the fatherland specifically with the existing republic. While those so inclined could interpret the call for responsible citizenship as a belated endorsement of the new order, others would be equally justified in reading the repeated invocation of authority as an indictment of party democracy. The document, in short, was designed to be all things to all people.[1]

Because of this ambiguity, the Königsberg declaration has been taken as evidence both of a rapprochement between church and republic and of the church's continuing authoritarian and antirepublican bias.[2] Either view is tenable to some extent. As the document itself suggests, many churchmen remained deeply ambivalent towards the republic nearly a decade after the November Revolution. Institutional pragmatism, if nothing else, encouraged a spirit of accommodation between the church and the new state; nor was there anything in their tradition that would incline churchmen to preach civil disobedience rather than loyal citizenship. Yet the republic was incontestably a monument to national humiliation, and like most national-minded Germans, churchmen found it difficult or impossible to accord full legitimacy to a regime spawned by defeat and revolution, boasting a parliamentary system that seemed to many to preclude any possibility of stable authority by subjecting government to incessant competition between ideologies and interest groups.

Beyond this, the divided loyalties betrayed in the 1927 declaration manifested yet another dimension of the basic problem confronting a self-professed Volkskirche in a fragmented and ideologically pluralistic society. In its political form, the problem was this: how could churchmen reconcile their insistence on remaining "above parties," open to all elements of society regardless of political persuasion, with the fact that virtually every institution and aspect of public life, including the church, had become politicized to some degree since the founding of the Bismarckian-Wilhelmian Reich?[3] Until the November Revolution,

---

[1] *Vaterländische Kundgebung der Evangelischen Kirche* (Berlin, 1927); *Verhandlungen des zweiten deutschen evangelischen Kirchentages 1927* (Berlin-Steglitz, 1927).

[2] E.g., Wright, *"Above Parties,"* pp. 60–61; Nowak, " 'Entartete Gegenwart,' " p. 110; Nowak, *Kirche und Republik*, pp. 173–77.

[3] Fischer, "Protestantismus und Politik," and for an early formulation, Ernst Troeltsch, "Aufsätze zur Geistesgeschichte und Religionssoziologie: Das Neun-

the church could partially avoid this problem by retreating behind the bulwark of the monarchical Kulturstaat. Now, however, with the state itself an object of political controversy, churchmen could no longer simply preach subjection to authority as a self-evident political principle. Nor, as continuing debates over education and social policy made clear, could it simply assert "Evangelical principles" as an a priori framework for the organization of either public or private affairs.

Hence, the appeal to political neutrality posed as many problems as it promised to resolve. The general politicization of society impelled churchmen ineluctably into the public arena as advocates of Protestant values. Where controversial issues were involved, however, this very advocacy promised to alienate one or another of the various constituencies the Volkskirche hoped to unite in a common spiritual community. In this context, the *Patriotic Message* may be taken as an attempt to establish common norms for citizenship in a pluralistic, politically divided society, a society whose every division was also reflected within the church. The ambivalent tone of the document mirrored the confusion of churchmen caught between competing impulses of political involvement and pastoral responsibility.

How, if at all, could this tension be resolved? Many observers have concluded that the pursuit of neutrality, like the Volkskirche ideal itself, was at best an illusion, at worst the flimsy trapping of a consciously partisan ideological stance. According to a widely accepted view, most Protestant churchmen joined the conservative nationalist "flight into mythology," staking out a generous plot in the antimodernist and antirepublican seedbed of the Third Reich.[4] This is, however, only a partial picture. What is striking about Württemberg, at least, is not only the degree of uniformity but also, paradoxically, the degree of diversity in churchmen's responses to political circumstances. If the Novem-

---

zehnte Jahrhundert," in *Gesammelte Schriften*, vol. 4 (Tübingen, 1925): 614–49. Hans-Ulrich Wehler provides a provocative general analysis in *Das Deutsche Kaiserreich, 1871–1918* (Göttingen, 1973); see also Kouri, *Protestantismus und soziale Frage*, and Borg, *Old-Prussian Church*, pp. 1–28.

[4] See above, p. 7, note 8.

ber Revolution drove most into the conservative opposition, it stimulated a minority to explore political options, particularly on the left, that had previously been considered beyond the bounds of clerical respectability. If Weimar's political tensions led some to seek salvation in activism, it led many more to abjure political involvement in the name of a higher pastoral imperative.

In short, the conservative image the Württemberg church shared with Protestant churches everywhere in Germany should not be allowed to obscure new currents of commitment set in motion by the multiple upheavals of the Weimar era. These currents and crosscurrents help mark the Weimar years as a transitional period, a time in which churchmen, having long defined themselves primarily as servants of the state, began to conceive of themselves increasingly as servants of society, potential bridge-builders between the heterogeneous elements of a nominally Protestant population.

THE VOLKSKIRCHE AND THE PARTY STATE

There is little reason to exclude Württemberg from the purview of the oft-cited Weimar epigram that "the church is politically neutral—but it votes German-National."[5] Notable exceptions notwithstanding, the most characteristic Protestant political stance of this era was indisputably nationalist and conservative, distinctly antirevolutionary, and instinctively antirepublican. Such instincts were hardly a clerical monopoly, of course. If churchmen longed for a return to the national pride and heady statesmanship of Bismarck's day, and if they nurtured corresponding feelings of contempt for the latter-day "party state," with its scheming political hacks and craven diplomats, these were commonplaces of the German conservative classes. Yet such opinions followed consistently from central assumptions in

[5] The phrase is quoted in Dahm, *Pfarrer und Politik*, p. 104; cf. Wright, *"Above Parties,"* pp. 49ff.; Dahm, "German Protestantism and Politics, 1918–39," *Journal of Contemporary History* 3 (1968): 29–49; and Nowak, *Kirche und Republik*, pp. 85–107 and passim.

the Volkskirche tradition. When churchmen weighed the republic in the balance of their norms, they found it wanting not only on its immediate merits—humiliation abroad, instability at home—but also because it violated basic principles about the proper ordering of state and society. Implicit in Volkskirche ideology was a vision of the nation as an organic cultural whole, a moral entity modeled by the church itself in its role as both preceptor and all-embracing community. Parliamentary democracy, in contrast, bore the stigmata of a corrupting, self-seeking individualism. Instead of promoting community, it unleashed those forces of fragmentation that churchmen saw reducing the nation to a quasi-Hobbesian state of moral and social anarchy. At the same time, the neutrality of the republic in matters moral and spiritual militated firmly against the ideal of a Christian state. Unlike the monarchical system, in which the personality and power of the king offered at least some hopes for realizing a symbiosis of Christianity and German culture, the republic, it seemed, could never be anything more than a utilitarian convenience, an impersonal broker of private selfishness. Nor, for that matter, did the Weimar Republic appear to be merely passive in its neutrality. Its revolutionary origins and the ideological positions of its chief supporters made it the very antithesis of all that was genuinely Christian and German, a monument to the unholy trinity of crass individualism, godless socialism, and lurking ultramontanism. To the extent that churchmen shared such convictions, it is not surprising that they would find a natural home in Weimar's major conservative parties. The generally moralistic tenor of the church's public pronouncements, coupled with the highly visible role of pastors and prelates as decorative fixtures at military and patriotic functions, only served to reinforce this identification with the symbols and vocabulary of the nationalist right.[6]

No medium did more to feed impressions of a monolithic Protestant conservatism than the church press. As previously

[6] On Protestant conservatism, see Borg, *Old-Prussian Church*, pp. 13–20, 174–202, 246–71, and the sources cited in the previous note.

noted, parish papers and Sonntagsblätter were not, strictly speaking, official publications. A comparison of the popular religious press with the *Kirchlicher Anzeiger*, the professional journal of the Württemberg Pastors' Association, reveals striking differences both in tone and in the range of perspectives represented. The fact that many church papers bore a more or less pietistic stamp may have tended to exaggerate their more reactionary features. All the same, their wide circulation and the fact that most were written and edited by churchmen inevitably identified them with the ecclesiastical establishment. Given their mass circulation, furthermore, their role in shaping public opinion within the Evangelical community can hardly be underestimated. Columns on current politics and diplomacy were a regular feature of many church papers; these columns provided the most explicit and arguably the most influential political commentary offered by the Weimar church.

"For the tactful editor, explicit party-political leanings must automatically be ruled out. On the other hand, the cultivation of monarchical and patriotic sentiment is one of the rights and duties of the Sonntagsblatt." This prewar maxim, cited by Theophil Wurm at the 1928 Evangelical Press Congress in Cologne, followed naturally from a characteristic conservative distinction between citizenship, understood as loyalty to the powers that be, and partisan politics. Wurm, who yielded to no one in his own monarchical sentiments, admitted that the republic demanded a new principle.[7] Yet for the church press as a whole, the advent of the republic encouraged not greater flexibility but a more rigid adherence to the old verities. The Social Democratic *Schwä-*

[7] Theophil Wurm, "Die Bedeutung unserer religiösen Volkspresse," *MfPT* 25 (1928): 23–33. Wurm argued that a monarchist stance was no longer possible because it would alienate large parts of the population, but he also decried "blind devotion" to the republic on the curious grounds that the church had already suffered quite enough for its *Staatsfrömmigkeit*. Wurm sought to propose a middle ground, with the press "collaborat[ing] loyally in all areas involving the common weal and [asserting] the demands of the Christian conscience, without regard for party or class, in all areas of life, if possible in accord with the leadership of the state, but if necessary in opposition to its principles" (p. 32).

bische Tagwacht, hardly a voice of rabid anticlericalism, was not wholly unjustified when in 1924 it dismissed Germany's oldest church weekly, the venerable pietist *Christenbote,* as a mere "Nationalist propaganda sheet."[8] In tone and substance, the principal church papers in Württemberg—notably the *Stuttgarter Evangelisches Sonntagsblatt* and the several regional *Gemeindeblätter*—seldom strayed far from the broad path of antirepublican rhetoric outlined above. Even a brief perusal of their pages yields abundant evidence of a tendentious political Protestantism cloaked in imperial mythology and set implacably against the structures and values of the republic.[9]

Much of this commentary reflects the same heavy moralism we have seen pervading the church's social formulations. Indeed, most writers equated alcoholism, pornography, and similar social evils with what they saw as the near-total collapse of order and authority in Germany since the end of the monarchy. The violence of postwar society flowed from the same source; both the random mayhem of the home or the street and the calculated brutality of the political terrorist bore sorry witness to the "terrible degeneration of morals wrought upon the German people by war and upheaval."[10] Moral decadence, in short, simultaneously reflected and fed upon political fragmentation. Taking recent incidents as convenient points of departure, columnists produced a litany of cultural pessimism replete with examples of the republic's failure to measure up to traditional standards either as a Christian state or as an organic moral community.

Since these themes have been analyzed at length in a variety of studies, exhaustive documentation hardly seems necessary here; a few examples should suffice to convey the general tone of the Württemberg clergy's contributions. Like other "unpolitical Germans,"[11] Protestant writers were quick to lament the

[8] " 'Der Christen Bote'?" *ST,* Nov. 19, 1924.

[9] The concept of a "political Protestantism" is developed in Christ, *Politische Protestantismus.*

[10] *SES* 60 (1925): 67.

[11] Fritz Stern, "The Political Consequences of the Unpolitical German," in Stern, *Failure of Illiberalism,* pp. 3–25.

extent to which, in their view, the republican party state sacri-
ficed the "great spiritual idea" of the nation to idols of materialism and economic egoism. Weimar politics and culture were
routinely held to represent forces alien to the Protestant German
tradition—in particular, Catholicism, bolshevism, and world
Jewry. If the republic remained hopelessly infected with the
"childhood diseases of parliamentarism," as the *Stuttgarter
Evangelisches Sonntagsblatt* was still insisting in 1926,[12] few
readers would have missed the implication either that the most
dangerous bacilli came from Rome and Moscow or that Jews
were their most dreaded carriers. Whether attacking Jews as
traitorous internationalists or decrying them as paragons of the
decadent modern spirit, the church papers did as much as any
politician of the time to propagate anti-Semitic instincts among
a large and often politically unreflective constituency.[13] Economic misery, declared the *Christenbote* in a typical formulation, was an inevitable result of "Jewish and Jesuitical intrigues."[14] Commenting on the presidential election of 1925, the
Stuttgart *Sonntagsblatt* portrayed Weimar democracy as the de-
formed product of a liaison between socialism and political Catholicism, the one "international and papist," bent upon rolling
back the Protestant Reformation, the other "hostile to the
church and bent upon setting class against class."[15]

Like the nationalist right in general, religious writers were
fond of juxtaposing this doleful picture with carefully burnished
images of the old empire—that "splendid, united Fatherland," as
the *Sonntagsblatt* called it in 1921, in which Germans had been
a "nation of brothers . . . [whose] lot improved from year to
year." To be sure, even that halcyon world had begun to show
signs of the "lamentable party strife that has so often fearfully
ravaged the German people," and this it was, the paper insisted,
that had encouraged foreign enemies to launch their fatal attack

[12] *SES* 60 (1926): 508.
[13] Arndt, "Die Judenfrage im Licht der evangelischen Sonntagsblätter"; on
the general problem, see Richard Gutteridge, *The German Evangelical Church
and the Jews, 1879–1950* (London and New York, 1976), pp. 35–64.
[14] *Christen-Bote*, Aug. 15, 1920, p. 187.
[15] *SES* 59 (1925): 172.

in 1914.[16] Since the war, the "nation of brothers" had become hopelessly embroiled in political strife. In an issue appearing just before the 1924 Landtag elections, the *Gemeinschaftsblatt* of the Old Pietists, largest of the Württemberg pietist federations, recommended halfheartedly that readers exercise their franchise but cautioned that "even in the loyal fulfillment of patriotic duty we will want to remain . . . on guard against all party-political intrigues, knowing that the things of this world will pass away."[17] Some of the faithful took such admonitions seriously indeed. One voter in Stuttgart reportedly crossed out all the parties and candidates on his ballot and appended the notation "Isaiah 41:24"; the text in question reads: "Behold, ye are of nothing, and your work of nought: an abomination is he that chooseth you."[18]

Church papers made much of the notorious flag crisis of 1926, when disputes over a presidential decree authorizing increased use of the old imperial colors led to the collapse of the governing coalition in Berlin. "The flag is the symbol of a nation," raged the Stuttgart *Sonntagsblatt*, ". . . and what do the parties of the Reichstag make of it? An affair of politics."[19] This and a host of similar jeremiads against interest-group rule bore a striking generic resemblance to the famous statement by Italo Balbo, the Italian Fascist, about a parliamentarism that "made a merchandise of every ideal."[20] Small wonder that despite nationalist suspicions of Mussolini's foreign policy, the church press greeted Il Duce's regime warmly after 1922. The Blackshirts had strengthened Italian national pride, the *Sonntagsblatt* concluded, and had eliminated with one stroke the menace of a "red upheaval." In contrast to the German republic with its endless parliamen-

---

[16] *SES* 55 (1921): 20.

[17] "Zur Wahl," *Gemeinschaftsblatt für die verbundenen altpietistischen Gemeinschaften in Württemberg* 18 (May 1924): 25–26.

[18] Eberhard Lempp, "Erfahrungen im Wahlkampf," *EGBfS* 20 (1924): 73–74.

[19] *SES* 60 (1926): 223.

[20] Quoted in Herman Finer, *Mussolini's Italy* (London, 1935; reprint, New York, 1965), p. 139.

tary bickering, Italy was now a state ruled by action, not mere words.[21]

The verdicts on Weimar leaders, it follows, were rarely positive. On occasion an individual or coalition—even a Social Democrat like Friedrich Ebert or Württemberg Staatspräsident Wilhelm Blos—might earn grudging recognition for upholding law and order, particularly when police powers were exercised with vigor against "revolutionaries."[22] For Foreign Minister Walther Rathenau, a victim of rightist gunmen in 1922, there were qualified tributes for a willingness to sacrifice private comfort for the demands of public service and the quest for a lasting peace.[23] Typically, however, the leaders of the day figured as impotent or impious, not to mention unpatriotic. A year before Rathenau's death, when ex-Reich Finance Minister Matthias Erzberger, a native (albeit Catholic) son of Württemberg, was similarly cut down by the bullets of right-wing fanatics, the *Sonntagsblatt* expressed righteous outrage and strongly condemned Erzberger's "cowardly assassins." For the victim, however, there were only bald references to a controversial career set in obloquy of the most thinly veiled sort:

> No matter how many bitter enemies Erzberger made with his ruthless egotism, and no matter how much he scandalized his fellow Catholics, it was for his political activity that his countrymen . . . most faulted him; he was seen as the one who destroyed the Reich, the man most to blame for the loss of the war, the collapse of the monarchy, and the shameful . . . peace treaty.[24]

If acts of political violence came most frequently from the right, church journalists were quick to discern that the true threat lay elsewhere. In 1920, when the Kapp Putsch in Prussia drove the national government to take temporary refuge in Stuttgart, the *Christenbote* issued a routine condemnation of

[21] *SES* 56 (1922): 390.
[22] E.g., *Christen-Bote*, Sept. 12, 1920, p. 206, and *SES* 61 (1927): 314.
[23] *SES* 56 (1922): 220; cf. ibid., p. 52.
[24] *SES* 55 (1921): 229.

political coups "from whatever side they come, right or left" but hastened to add that the great objection to this abortive attempt from the right was that it would deflect attention from the "real danger" on the left.[25] On this score the church press followed counterrevolutionaries everywhere in identifying the left indiscriminately with Russian bolshevism. Editors uncritically detailed every lurid rumor about the "horror of immorality" said to be rampant in the new Leninist state.[26] At the height of the Ruhr crisis in 1923, the pietist *Gemeinschaftsblatt* described Germany as trapped between the "Egyptians" in the occupied Rhineland and the "Red Sea" beyond the eastern frontiers. "The *Red* Sea lies before us in more than one sense: a red flood of the blood and tears that flow where there is war, a red flood of bolshevist godlessness."[27] Against this tide few statesmen of the republic could be expected to hold their ground. Gustav Stresemann, the target of much undeserved rightist abuse for his foreign policy of "fulfillment," spoke in Stuttgart shortly before receiving the Nobel Peace Prize in 1927. Of his speech, which stressed the importance of peace both at home and abroad, the *Sonntagsblatt* remarked that "fine words" hardly measured up to the "hard facts of reality and the bitter experiences of the present time."[28] Two years later the same paper would greet the Hugenberg-Hitler agitation against the Young Plan not only as a patriotic revolt against the fetters of Versailles but equally as a "flaming protest against an impotent and incompetent system of government."[29]

The one great exception to this sorry pattern, of course, was Paul von Hindenburg, the hero of the Great War who became

[25] *Christen-Bote*, Mar. 28, 1920, pp. 73–74; Apr. 11, 1920, p. 86.

[26] Thus *EKBfW* 80 (1919): 133–34.

[27] *Gemeinschaftsblatt für die verbundenen altpietistischen Gemeinschaften in Württemberg* 17 (May 1923): 17.

[28] *SES* 61 (1927): 250.

[29] *SES* 63 (1929): 472. The article unleashed a political tempest of its own in Württemberg, where DDP and SPD papers attacked it vigorously; see *Neckar-Echo*, Nov. 26, 1929; *ST*, Nov. 26, 1929; *Der Beobachter*, Nov. 23, 1919; and clippings file in LKA D1.

the republic's second president in 1925. Protestant publicists everywhere trumpeted the old field marshal's election as both a political and a religious event of the first magnitude, the triumph of Protestant and German ideals over Catholic, socialist, and "internationalist" schemings. After 1925, Hindenburg functioned for many as a surrogate kaiser, a pious and patriotic link with the past under whose leadership conservatives could finally make a peace of sorts with the republic. It was a "divine gift of incalculable worth," wrote *Gemeindeblatt* editor Gotthold Kneile, a Stuttgart pastor, that though Hindenburg could accomplish no miracles, nevertheless the nation with all its woes at least enjoyed the guidance of one "in whom all the best and noblest from the old German monarchy is embodied."[30] For those who shared this conviction, Hindenburg functioned less as a political leader than as an antidote to politics, a symbolic alternative to the party state whose president he had become.

The same assumptions cultivated so assiduously in the church press also found a variety of institutional expressions. Officially, to be sure, churchmen enjoined each other to keep to the high ground of a conscientious neutrality. In 1918 and again in 1920, Consistory decrees warned against partisan involvement in the "clash of parties and political opinions"; the Oberkirchenrat repeated the warning informally in 1926.[31] The neutrality thus decreed did not, however, preclude continued attempts to cultivate patriotic—if not monarchical—sentiment. If anything, the call to remain above party strife implied an obligation to identify with familiar symbols of national unity in hopes of stemming the tide of democratic disorder and factionalism. In the name of patriotism the church therefore paid loyal tribute to departed royalty while leaving republican leaders and state occasions all but ignored. Memorial services and the tolling of church bells marked the death of the former kaiser's wife in April 1921, and the passing of Württemberg's own beloved former king six

[30] "Hindenburg," *EGBfS* 23 (1927): 446; see also "An die evangelischen Wähler," *EGBfS* 21 (1925): 139; *SES* 59 (1925): 172.

[31] WEK, Erlass, July 6, 1920 (copy), LKA D1/26,9; other materials (Dec. 1918, Jan. 1926) in LKA 426/151.

months later triggered an outpouring of sentiment that reached into every pulpit and belfry in the land. By contrast, the death of Weimar's first president, Friedrich Ebert, in 1925, brought polite expressions of official regret but no formal remembrances. And while the fiftieth anniversary of Bismarck's *Reichsgründung* called forth special religious observances, symbolic dates on the republican calendar passed in virtual silence.[32]

Members of the clergy and church leadership regularly conveyed tacit ecclesiastical sanction on the countless military ceremonies, unveilings of war monuments, and services of dedication with which the Weimar years abounded, occasions that almost invariably served as showpieces of nationalist mythology.[33] But while churchmen could invoke the sacred cause of the fatherland, raise thanks for the "heroic deaths" in the trenches and implore the Almighty to accept these sacrifices in token of "a new future . . . and a new freedom for our people,"[34] their actions revealed a consistently narrow construction of patriotic values. When a coalition of trade unionists in Stuttgart requested permission to use one of the city's churches for a rally against war in 1924, local church officials turned them down on the ground that the church could not lend its facilities to support any partisan political cause. Those planning the rally, most of them nominal Protestants, found such reasoning incomprehen-

[32] Zeller, notes, Dec. 3, 1920; Urach Kirchengemeinderatssitzung, Apr. 12, 1921, Protokoll; Ulm Kirchengemeinderatssitzung, n.d. [Apr. 1921], Protokoll; Merz to DEKA, Feb. 28, 1925; and Kapler to Merz, Mar. 3, 1925; copies of all in LKA A26/582,2. See also *SM*, Jan. 17, 18, 19, Apr. 17, Oct. 4, 5, 7, 9, 10, 1921.

[33] For examples, see *SM*, June 29, Nov. 24, 1919, Oct. 25, 1921, May 8, 1922, Nov. 23, 1926, July 9, Oct. 29, Nov. 26, 1928, and June 28, 1929. The church also retained close connections with the army at another level. Discussions in the Pfarrverein executive committee suggest that the Reichswehr customarily turned to the clergy for personal references on potential recruits, requesting that responses be sent privately to officers' homes rather than to official addresses (EPW, Vertrauensmännerversammlung, Apr. 6, 1926, Protokollbuch II, LKA D/EPW 22).

[34] Thus Stuttgart pastor Ernst at the dedication of the municipal war memorial, July 15, 1923 (*Ehrenbuch der Gefallenen Stuttgarts, 1914–1918* [Stuttgart, (1923)], p. viii). Ernst was a former pastor in Strassburg "forced to leave his homeland as a victim of his loyal German convictions" (*SM*, Apr. 10, 1919).

sible. How, demanded the *Schwäbische Tagwacht*, could the church hide behind a claim of neutrality "when at a memorial service in Stuttgart two clergymen proclaim the stab-in-the-back legend and yearn for the return of the [imperial] black-white-red flag? . . . If the church still had any point of contact with Christianity, it would certainly throw its doors wide open for an antiwar day. Failing to do so, it condemns itself."[35]

Church president Johannes Merz became an accidental symbol of this perceived double standard in 1926 during the controversial national referendum on a proposal to authorize uncompensated expropriation of property belonging to the former princely houses. Instigated by the Communists with lukewarm support from Social Democrats, the referendum was itself an exercise in political symbolism—an effort to humiliate the old order while exploiting the economic resentments of the workers and the numerous petit bourgeois elements disinherited by postwar inflation. Though the campaign never had serious prospects of success, it helped restore the vitriol to Weimar political discourse by playing on the strong passions of all concerned.[36] Churchmen rushed to join the vanguard of opposition, insisting that, in Merz's words, the church could have "nothing in common with a movement that violates eternal laws of right and justice."[37] The national church leadership drew up a public resolution condemning the measure. In Württemberg, where the state government had already reached a compensated settlement with the former royal household and where surviving members of the king's family obliquely pressured church leaders to take a clear stand, Merz chose the occasion of a parish assembly in Stuttgart to warn Protestants of the grave moral evils lurking in the ex-

[35] Reported in [Theodor Traub], *Jahresbericht 1924* (Stuttgart, 1925), pp. 12–13. The reference is presumably to the memorial service mentioned in the previous note.

[36] For a general analysis, see Ulrich Schüren, *Der Volksentscheid zur Fürstenenteignung 1926: Die Vermögensauseinandersetzung mit den depossedierten Landesherren als Problem der deutschen Innenpolitik unter besonderer Berücksichtigung der Verhältnisse in Preussen* (Düsseldorf, 1978).

[37] Merz to Gemmingen, May 18, 1926, LKA D1/26,9.

propriation proposal. The referendum, he argued, called for an arbitrary revocation of basic property rights, something the church could never tolerate regardless of whom it might harm or benefit.[38]

While innocuous in itself and differing little in substance from a host of public utterances on the issue across the political spectrum, Merz's statement triggered a storm of controversy that in parts of Württemberg overshadowed the referendum itself. At issue was not so much what Merz said as his warrant to speak publicly about the matter at all. The *Schwäbische Tagwacht*, whose editors probably shared Merz's basic conclusions on the merits of the case and whose tepid support for the referendum arose largely out of a fear of being tactically outflanked by the Communists, took Merz roundly to task for intruding into a purely political debate.[39] Trade unionists similarly denounced Merz as a propagandist for the princes.[40] Nor were workers Merz's only critics. Bitter responses also came from artisans and shopkeepers—normally among the church's most loyal supporters—many of whom had been ruined financially by inflation and by the Reich government's austere currency revaluation program of 1924–25. The Oberkirchenrat had in fact endorsed demands by the DEKA for greater fairness in calculating revaluation, but this was apparently not communicated effectively to those on whom the blows fell most heavily. One anonymous parishioner wrote Merz demanding to know why the church had had "so little to say on behalf of the expropriated middle classes" while now lending such "handsome support" to the princes.[41]

The scope and intensity of the criticism caught Merz by sur-

[38] Reported in *SES* 60 (1929): 244; cf. *KAfW* 35 (1926): 95; also Gemmingen to Merz, May 16, 1926, LKA D1/26,9.

[39] *ST*, May 26, 1926.

[40] Vereinigten Gewerkschaften Lauffen, statement of May 1926 (copy), OKR/AR Gen. 285a.

[41] Unsigned letter to Merz, n.d., OKR/AR Gen. 285a; cf. Fischer, "Geschichte des Kirchenkampfes," 1:95–97. Church officials did attempt to use their influence to aid persons in particular need; see Feller to Merz, July 28, 1926, Oct. 14, Nov. 17, 1927; OKR to Reichsentschädigungsamt, Oct. 21, 1927; and OKR to DEKA, Oct. 21, 1927; all in OKR/AR Gen. 285a.

prise. He would later claim somewhat lamely that he had meant his remarks to refer only to Württemberg, where a property settlement acceptable even to Social Democrats was already on the books. In no case had he intended to violate Protestant freedom of conscience by dictating to church members. In a letter to former DDP Staatspräsident Johannes Hieber, Merz pleaded with his old friend to take his part in the quarrel, insisting that he had "carefully refrained from identifying with any political party or its position and also from . . . telling fellow church members how they should vote." His remarks were not to be taken as an ex cathedra pronouncement but only as an expression of "moral feelings."[42] Elsewhere in the church the tone was less apologetic. The Volksbund and the Evangelical Press Association mounted a counteroffensive, circulating public statements by prominent Social Democrats that resembled Merz's position.[43] In a widely circulated article, former Consistory president Hermann von Zeller branded the referendum as an exercise in simple theft and urged fellow church members to "raise loud our voices against this injustice contrived by Russian bolshevism."[44]

Zeller claimed to be speaking as a private citizen. It is unlikely, however, that in so doing he saw himself as merely the spokesman for a particular interest group, hoping to advance his cause. His manifest outrage, like the bewildered innocence of Johannes Merz, betrayed rather a sense of being compelled by circumstances to point out a simple principle of good order and authority to which all church folk—indeed, all of society as properly constituted—should be expected to adhere as a matter of course.[45] By church standards this comported fully with the dic-

[42] LKV, *Verhandlungen* (1926), pp. 201–3; Merz to Hieber, May 28, 1926, LKA D1/26,9.

[43] EVB, statement, n.d. (copy), LKA D1/26,9.

[44] "Zur Fürstenenteignung," *SDZ*, June 10, 1926, reprint, *SES* 60 (1926): 263.

[45] For a general discussion of this mentality, see Dahm, *Pfarrer und Politik*, pp. 96–110, 148ff. Zeller had earlier provoked a minor journalistic and parliamentary furor by implying, shortly after his retirement as Consistory president, that only the rightist parties fully deserved Protestant voters' support. Coming as it did so soon after the Landtag had approved the favorable church-state settlement of 1924—a settlement that the Württemberg right, for tactical reasons,

tates of neutrality in that it transcended the specific interests of any party—bolshevism being by definition less a political orientation than a moral condition. To take such a stand, whether in a quasi-official capacity like Merz or as a private citizen like Zeller, represented an effort not so much to tilt the balance in a particular political contest as to confront a soulless and divisive party state with the historic ideal of the nation as collective moral personality. In this way churchmen sought to reconcile the Erastian implications of the Volkskirche outlook with the reality of a state whose moral authority they could find no clear and acceptable basis for upholding. Yet as the controversy swirling around Merz indicated only too clearly, political neutrality thus conceived was itself a form of partisan commitment. The vocabulary of nationalist conservatism provided one way—for many the only conceivable way—of accommodating Volkskirche ideology to the exigencies of the republican system. In the process, however, the church was dragged ineluctably into the very mire of party strife from which it so steadfastly claimed to hold aloof.

Politics in the Parish

If efforts to uphold the nation as moral community led unmistakably in the direction of the political right, efforts to embrace a politically diverse society within the confessional framework of the Volkskirche set up contrary currents of commitment. The church's institutional stance reflected the magisterial tradition of Christian-state theory. Churchmen's behavior, by contrast, increasingly reflected a heightened sense of pastoral responsibility, a new sensitivity to the problems of dealing honestly with the economic, ideological, and sociological complexity of the Protestant community. The result, ironically enough, was that despite the church's often monolithic public image, pastors as a

had refused to ratify—Zeller's remark outraged party leaders of the center and left. Zeller, "Staat und evangelische Kirche," *SDZ*, Dec. 2, 1924; *Württembergische Lehrerzeitung* 84 (1924): 522; Landtag, *Verhandlungen* (1925), p. 1071.

group manifested a greater diversity of political orientation after 1918 than before.

A fundamental problem arose from the lack of any authoritative consensus in terms of which to define acceptable political behavior. Until 1918, even in the comparatively progressive climate of Württemberg politics, boundaries of commitment had been all but self-evident. In the halcyon days of the empire, August Springer later noted wryly, "the conservative pastor was a truism, the National Liberal a tolerated exception, the democrat a rarity, and the Social Democrat an impossibility."[46] The Blumhardt case of 1899 testified to the self-evident character of these principles: renegade pietist Christoph Blumhardt was stripped of his pastor's robes on the assumption that Christianity and Social Democracy were mutually exclusive. Within the unspoken limits personal tastes might differ; Adolf Stoecker and Friedrich Naumann were both significant lights on Württemberg's Evangelical horizon. But defense of the established monarchical and burgher order remained the first and unchallenged principle of pastors' political commitments.

In 1918, however, the captains and the kings departed, leaving the Social Democrats, erstwhile "enemies of the state," as pillars of the new political establishment. Under the circumstances the old formulas ceased to be fully compelling. The result was a blurred vision of both the purposes and the permissible boundaries for political activity. Problems confronted even those who declined to recognize the basic legitimacy of the Weimar system, who saw a church standing "above parties" as one of the last mighty fortresses of the unpolitical German.

During the first months of the republic, as noted elsewhere, a common response was to embrace party politics as a tool of institutional self-defense. In 1918, Urach Dekan Albert Leube later recalled, many pastors "considered it nothing short of their

---

[46] August Springer, "Pfarrer und Politik," *Württemberger Zeitung*, May 9, 1932, quoted in Gerhard Schäfer, ed., *Die Evangelische Landeskirche in Württemberg und der Nationalsozialismus*, 5 vols. to date (Stuttgart, 1971–), 1:135.

duty to take a political stand."[47] Such convictions, however, proved relatively short-lived. Significantly, none of the church-men who won seats in the Württemberg assembly in 1919 still held them two years later. They either declined renomination, as in the case of the Democrats Lamparter and Esenwein, or chose to subordinate political influence to ecclesiastical preferment, as in the case of Theophil Wurm, who despite winning reelection in 1920 resigned his mandate to accept appointment to the favored position of Dekan in Reutlingen.[48] This retreat from activism occurred across a broad front. By one reasonably informed estimate, fewer than fifty of the approximately twelve hundred pastors in Württemberg took any active part in party politics between 1920 and 1930.[49]

Among those who did render unto Caesar, a clear generational pattern soon manifested itself. As might be expected, the revolution had little effect on the loyalities of churchmen already active in public life before 1914. For this group August Springer's dictum still held substantially true: the great majority belonged to one of the conservative parties on the Württemberg spectrum, either the Bürgerpartei or its larger rural counterpart, the Bauernbund, both associated after 1918 with the right-wing DNVP. A smaller group, including Jakob Schoell and Volksbund directors Hermann Ströle and Richard Lempp, preferred the more moderate conservatism of Gustav Stresemann's DVP. Lempp, a graduate of both the Tübingen Stift and Harvard Divinity School who before the revolution served briefly as court preacher in Stuttgart, was a token DVP candidate in the 1924 Landtag election. The Bürgerpartei, as its name implied, remained a classic party of burgher notables, the *alte Herren* of the academy and the bureaucracy. In theory, if not always in prac-

[47] Notes on Hermann Ströle, "Kirche und Arbeiterschaft," typescript, n.d., LKA D4/24x; cf. Voelter, "Bietigheimer Tag," p. 36.
[48] Wurm admitted in his memoirs that he played a "fairly passive role" in legislative matters (Wurm, *Erinnerungen*, p. 69).
[49] Fischer, "Geschichte des Kirchenkampfes," 1:170; this figure does not include approximately 50 pastors who joined the Nazi Pastors' Association between 1929 and 1933.

tice, it stood for traditional Protestant values, and the upper echelons of the church hierarchy were well represented in its ranks. Former Consistory president Hermann von Zeller was an active member; so too were future church president Wurm and his fellow Landtag delegate, Tübingen theologian Paul Wurster, as well as members of the Oberkirchenrat such as Gerhard Schauffler, a number of Dekans, and most of the politically active leaders of the state church assembly.

Few of these could be called young men. Wurm was already over fifty in 1918, Zeller seventy, while the designation *a.D.* (Ret.) figured prominently on the membership roster of the church assembly. A similar generational coloring characterized the liberal minority. Hans Voelter, pastor in Bietigheim and later in Heilbronn, a left-liberal stronghold since the days of Naumann, was among the younger activists to join the postwar DDP, having been born in 1877. Both of the DDP pastors in the 1919 Landtag, Albert Esenwein and Eduard Lamparter, were approaching the end of their careers. Esenwein, a contemporary of Wurm, served in the Stuttgart parish of Gaisburg throughout the Weimer decade, but the period of his greatest political activity came before the war.[50] Lamparter retired from active parish service in 1924, devoting his last years to a lonely struggle against the anti-Semitism that he saw poisoning both the church and secular politics. His essay *Evangelische Kirche und Judentum*, a critique of the anti-Semitic tradition in Lutheranism published in 1928, was one of the few significant challenges to the prevailing tenor of church pronouncements on the subject.[51]

War and revolution exerted a much more dramatic impact on the orientations of younger pastors, many of whom bore the physical and spiritual stigmata of experience in the trenches. Here too activists constituted a distinct minority. They were,

[50] Esenwein Personalakten, OKR/AR Pers. E/102. On Esenwein's work in the Naumannite cause, see also Heuss, *Erinnerungen, 1905–1933*, p. 48, and Heuss, *Friedrich Naumann*, p. 169.

[51] Lamparter Personalakten, OKR/AR Pers. See also Gutteridge, *The Evangelical Church and the Jews*, pp. 57–58, and Scholder, *Die Kirchen und das Dritte Reiche*, 1:146–47.

however, more likely than their elders to find a political home outside the boundaries of the old consensus. On the right, a small faction followed the extreme logic of nationalist conservatism into the alternative camp of a folkish-racialist political theology. On the left, another faction challenged the old lines of demarcation between socialism and the Christian gospel. Yet another group emerged from pietist quiescence in an effort to create a Protestant alternative to the Catholic Center, namely an explicitly Christian political movement on social-conservative but not necessarily antirepublican foundations. These new departures resulted in an unprecedented range and diversity of viewpoints within the clergy, forcing churchmen both individually and collectively to search for some revised guiding principle to govern the place of politics in the pastor's heirarchy of roles.

Of the new political orientations, racialism has understandably garnered the greatest attention since 1933. It was also closest in spirit to mainstream conservative Protestant nationalism, from which it was to some extent a radicalized outgrowth. The folkish-racialist outlook did not coalesce into a homogeneous movement during the Weimar era. It encompassed a variety of groups, most notably perhaps the Berlin-based League for a German Church (Bund für deutsche Kirche), not a few clerical *Einzelgänger*, and varying degrees of radicalism in theological or political commitment. Like orthodox Lutheran conservatism, racialism proceeded from an understanding of the nation, or folk, as an organic moral and ethnic community if not in fact a distinct, divinely ordained order of creation and, as such, a kind of transcendental constant in the nature of things. But if such creation-order theology was congenial to many conservative churchmen after the war, racialists insisted on carrying the implied synthesis of Christianity and German spirit to its extreme, finding spiritual meaning in the peculiar genius of the racial community itself. Salvation, in effect, was to be found as much in the restoration of a true folk community as in the Cross of Protestant orthodoxy. This did not necessarily imply acceptance of a conscious neopaganism such as that propounded by former field marshal Erich von Ludendorff. It did, however, lead typi-

278

POLITICS AND PASTORAL RESPONSIBILITY

cally to an insistence on adapting Christian tradition to the service of national values. Thus many if not most racialists proposed
stripping Protestant faith of its non-German elements, for example by giving Christ an Aryan pedigree or by dismissing the
Old Testament from the scriptural canon. From such convictions
the politics of anti-Semitism followed almost as a matter of
course.[52]

Although it won little mass support, folkish theology in its
various forms found resonance in a number of churches, especially in northern Germany, where adherents gained seats in
several church assemblies. Württemberg, however, proved comparatively unreceptive to such appeals. While many Württemberg churchmen certainly shared latent inclinations toward a
hard-core nationalism, and while the Protestant anti-Semitism
decried by Eduard Lamparter would in later years gain scholarly
credence through the work of the prominent Tübingen theologian Gerhard Kittel,[53] a number of factors militated against
widespread acceptance of racialist postulates. Perhaps most important was the persistent strength of pietism, which served as
the chief leaven of Protestant orthodoxy in the region. For all the
affinity between hypernationalism and the pietist rhetoric of crisis so typical of the church press after 1918, pietists' fervent devotion to the Bible made them largely immune to a racialist theology that appeared to play even faster and looser with the Word
than did traditional Protestant liberalism. Hence, the formation
of a self-styled folkish-social "study group" among Württemberg pastors in 1925 failed to attract significant interest. The
small cadre of active supporters put out a manifesto that was a

[52] Borg, *Old-Prussian Church*, pp. 174–202, provides the best brief summary
of the various folkish and racialist movements; see also Scholder, *Die Kirchen
und das Dritte Reich*, 1:93–109, 124–250. For theological dimensions, see esp.
Wolfgang Tilgner, *Volksnomostheologie und Schöpfungsglaube: Ein Beitrag
zur Geschichte des Kirchenkampfes* (Göttingen, 1966); also Hans Buchheim,
Glaubenskrise im dritten Reich (Stuttgart, 1953).

[53] On Kittel, see esp. Robert P. Ericksen, *Theologians under Hitler: Gerhard
Kittel, Paul Althaus and Emanuel Hirsch* (New Haven, Conn., and London,
1985), pp. 28–78.

pastiche of similar statements issued throughout the country over the previous half-decade. Attacking Versailles as a violation of "the spirit of Christian love and justice," they swore fealty to Luther in his most militant guise, proclaimed "honesty" and Christian charity as the essence of a genuine social policy, and, predictably, declared war on alleged Jewish influences as inimical to true religion and a threat to the "purity and rectitude of the German soul."[54]

The principal activists were all younger pastors from small-town parishes. They included Rudersburg pastor Friedrich Ettwein; Karl Steger, pastor in Massenbach; and Wilhelm Rehm, vicar in Botnang, near Stuttgart, who later assumed a pastorate in Simmersfeld. Ettwein, the oldest of this trinity, was born in 1886; the youngest, Rehm, was still in his teens during the November Revolution. Both Ettwein and Rehm—the latter a veteran of the Western Front—were naturally militant personalities, in heavy demand as firebrand orators at rightist and paramilitary functions.[55] For much of the decade, however, the most prominent member of the group was Steger, who served from 1924 to 1928 as a delegate of the Folkish-Social party in the Württemberg Landtag. Holder of a doctorate in history and economics from Tübingen, Steger was at once pastor, politician, and scholar, with an outlook and temperament more akin to the older Christian-Social tradition of Adolf Stoecker than to the virulent Aryanism of his confreres. Whereas both Rehm and Ettwein became early converts to Hitlerism, Steger's attitude remained ambivalent until well after the Nazi breakthrough of 1930, when

[54] Manifesto, Feb. 18, 1925 (copy), LKA D1/29,2. The folkish movement tended to be most visible on the fringes of the church community, including some youth organizations. The subsequent Nazi education minister in Württemberg, Christian Mergenthaler, was an early and active proponent of folkish ideas in the theocratic pietist community of Korntal, outside Stuttgart (Lehmann, *Pietismus*, pp. 306, 327ff.).

[55] Notes in Rehm Personalakten, OKR/AR Pers. Typical is a self-styled "German" sermon delivered at an open-air rally in Stuttgart in April 1925 praising strength, uncompromising self-discipline, and the hope that the German people would rise again (*Die Reichs-Sturmfahne* [Stuttgart], Apr. 11–14, 1925 [copy], Rehm Personalakten).

he briefly reemerged as a leader among Württemberg German-Christians. While in the Landtag he occasionally defended Hitler's cause; he took the floor in 1925, for example, to protest Stuttgart authorities' refusal to permit the Führer, then recently released from Landsberg prison, to speak at a public rally in the city. However, when the tiny Folkish-Social faction formally joined the Nazis in 1927, Steger renounced the merger and chose to serve out the last months of his legislative tenure as a guest of the Bürgerpartei.[56]

Not until after 1930, and then largely under the pressure of external events, did the folkish faction assume any real importance either in Württemberg politics or within the church. As late as 1928, in a confidential assessment supplied to the DEKA in Berlin, the Oberkirchenrat dismissed the radical right as virtually insignificant in both numbers and influence.[57] A more widely debated development at middecade was the emergence of Religious Socialism, a loose, largely Protestant alliance of pastors, theologians, and lay persons committed to the cause of reconciling the church and the Marxist working classes. If the folkish position took its point of departure from a conservative Protestant ideal of the nation, Religious Socialism arose out of the ideal of the church as an all-embracing spiritual community. It reflected a conviction that the Volkskirche would indeed remain a hollow concept unless churchmen could realize a new sense of solidarity with the working classes and that the struggle for a moral society involved not simply injunctions to individual probity and patriotism but also active engagement on behalf of political and economic justice. Whereas racialists were tempted to equate Christianity with the folk ethos, Religious Socialists were tempted to see in the socialist tradition a powerful if sometimes perverted expression of authentic Christian values.

Building on scattered nineteenth-century antecedents, Religious Socialism first emerged as an identifiable force shortly before World War I in the Reformed churches of northern Switz-

[56] Landtag, *Verhandlungen* (1925), p. 1529, (1927), pp. 4176–77.
[57] OKR to DEKA, Feb. 29, 1928, OKR/AR Gen. 151b.

erland, where its major spokesmen included the noted Zurich churchmen Hermann Kutter and Leonhard Ragaz as well as the young Karl Barth. Within Germany the November Revolution served as a powerful catalyst, spawning a variety of local groups around Berlin, in Thuringia, and especially in Baden. Most though not all of these groups had coalesced by middecade to form the League of Religious Socialists in Germany (Bund der religiösen Sozialisten Deutschlands).

Like the term *Religious Socialist* itself, the league embraced a wide range of contradictory positions. Some adherents, including the so-called "Neuwerk circle," Berlin pastors like Günther Dehn, and especially the theologians associated with Paul Tillich, emphasized a theoretical and theological dialogue with Marxism. Others, including many in Thuringia and Baden, were more concerned with socialist praxis. Some stressed political action, others concentrated their energies on ecclesiastical reform. Many were essentially bourgeois idealists; a few, notably the Thuringian Emil Fuchs and his colorful Badenese counterpart Erwin Eckert, identified increasingly with a proletarian ethos. In the end the movement foundered between the "religious" and the "socialist," between a skeptical party leadership and an even more skeptical church leadership. Its significance, most would agree, lay less in any immediate achievements than in its symbolic role as a harbinger of more consequential openings to the left in German Protestantism after 1945.[58]

In Württemberg, the same sociological factors that moderated working-class politics in general helped create a potentially fertile recruiting ground for Religious Socialists.[59] While slower to organize than their neighbors in Baden, the spiritual heirs of Blumhardt stepped forward in small but growing numbers after 1924 to claim their inheritance. The band of active Religious Socialists among the Württemberg clergy quickly outstripped the

[58] Breipohl, *Religiöser Sozialismus und bürgerliches Geschichtsbewusstsein*; Balzer, *Klassengegensätze in der Kirche*; Ernst August Suck, "Der religiöse Sozialismus in der Weimarer Republik," (Ph.D. diss., Marburg University, 1953); Bredendiek et al., *Zwischen Aufbruch und Beharrung*, pp. 90–152, 193–220.

[59] Cf. Balzer, *Klassengegensätze in der Kirche*, pp. 39–54.

folkish faction in size and influence. Württemberg furnished several prominent leaders to the national movement, notably Gotthilf Schenkel, who at decade's end assumed editorship of the *Sonntagsblatt des arbeitenden Volkes*, the principal Religious Socialist publication.[60]

As a group, Württemberg Religious Socialists reflected the diversity of commitments in the national movement, if without the extremes of personality or ideology. Once again a distinct generational pattern developed, with a heavy representation of younger pastors, most still in their thirties. Except for the odd visionary and eccentric,[61] those drawn to the cause could best be described as radicalized offspring of Württemberg's strong Evangelical-Social movement. Some, like Schenkel and Winnenden pastor Reinhold Planck, were former liberals driven leftward by the November Revolution. Planck, the group's elder statesman, born in 1866, played an active part in a short-lived association of Christian Revolutionaries in Stuttgart during the early 1920s. A document in Planck's personnel file summarizes a speech of 1921 in which he stressed the need for an ongoing "revolution of the spirit" and attacked conservative colleagues for attempts to "herd their sheep into the fold of the rightist parties."[62] For others, such as Eberhard Lempp and Paul Weitbrecht, prior political attitudes seem to have played little part. Both of these pastors came to socialism in the Blumhardt manner, striving to demonstrate good faith to their working-class parishioners by taking a stand with the major working-class party. To this core of members should be added a small circle of liberals, the most prominent of whom were Hans Voelter, the Volksbund leader August Springer, and the young Waiblingen (later Stuttgart) pastor Ernst Lachenmann, who sympathized more or less

[60] Müller to Volk (Eisenach), Mar. 14, 1932, OKR/AR Gen. 151b; Reinhold Planck Personalakten, OKR/AR Pers.

[61] See, e.g., Theodor Rohleder Personalakten, and Max Stürner Personalakten, both in OKR/AR Pers.

[62] Planck, "Kirche und Christentum in der Stunde der Entscheidung," speech at Christrevolutionäre assembly, Stuttgart, June 13, 1921, report in Planck Personalakten, OKR/AR Pers.

openly with the aims of Religious Socialism without abandoning the liberal fold.[63]

Within Württemberg Social Democracy, Religious Socialists found sympathy if not open encouragement for their often vague aims. Socialist editors generally opened the party press to their contributions, and Religious Socialist pastors occasionally appeared as speakers before local party gatherings.[64] For their part, pastors sought to make the church more attractive to workers by making parish facilities available to workers' groups, by scheduling special services led by Religious Socialist clergy, and by pressuring the Oberkirchenrat to appoint members of the group to symbolically important posts.[65] Progress on these several fronts was often halting. When Gotthilf Schenkel spoke at a SPD meeting in Aalen in 1929, one observer reported that he spoke from an intellectual plateau beyond the attainment of most in his audience. A year earlier, the SPD chairman in Rohracker had refused to take part in a scheduled party meeting be-

[63] Cf. Voelter, "Christlicher Aktivismus: Gedanken über Kirche und Politik," *KAfW* 21 (1922): 53–54, 57–59; "Von den Religiösen Sozialisten," *Württembergische Arbeiterzeitung* 34 (Jan. 15, 1926); and Springer, *Der Andere, der bist Du*, passim. In 1925, at the instance of the Oberkirchenrat, Voelter filed a warmly positive report on the Berlin Religious Socialists, to which Jakob Schoell appended a laconic note questioning whether Voelter distinguished clearly enough between his own Naumannite views and those of Religious Socialists (Voelter to OKR, Dec. 7, 1925, OKR/AR Gen. 151b).

[64] For examples, see Eberhard Lempp, "Reformation," *ST*, Nov. 1, 1926, and Lempp, "Wider den Antipazifismus," *ST*, May 21, 1927; cf. Göppingen, Pfarrbericht 1930, Persönliche Beilage, OKR/AR OA/PfB; clippings in LKA D1/13,2 and D1/28,7.

[65] E. Kunkel and R. Gauss to OKR, Dec. 4, 1929, OKR/AR Gen. 151b. Stuttgart Religious Socialists were particularly anxious to see one of their number installed in a prestigious city pastorate; Gotthilf Schenkel served in Zuffenhausen, an outlying Stuttgart suburb. Petitions for church services were, of course, in addition to regular services, which pastors in the movement led as a matter of duty. In 1928 special services or meetings were authorized in Tailfingen as well as in the Stuttgart suburbs of Rohracker and Wangen. Pfleiderer to OKR, Jan. 12, 1928; Leitz to OKR, Mar. 21, 1928; Rohracker, Kirchengemeinderatssitzung, Mar. 25, 1928, Protokollbuch II, p. 315 (copy); and Gonser to OKR, Nov. 20, 1928; all in OKR/AR Gen. 151b.

cause a Religious Socialist had been invited to speak.[66] Still, the Württemberg movement enjoyed a steady if unspectacular growth in membership, largely among white-collar intellectuals and skilled laborers. By the end of the decade Württemberg ranked with Baden and Thuringia as a leading center of Religious Socialist influence, boasting a statewide organization and local chapters in most industrial towns.

Both the folkish and Religious Socialist movements can be viewed as attempts to reconstrue existing relationships between religion and the secular order. In challenging the church's ambiguous official commitment to neutrality, they provided common testimony to the tension between traditional Volkskirche ideals and the pluralistic, conflict-ridden world in which churchmen actually lived. Each movement sought in its own way to restore a measure of identity between and among church, state, and society. Radical folkish theology did so through a near-apotheosis of the racial community, while Religious Socialism did so by invoking the latent moral energy of the proletariat. If Religious Socialists hoped to transcend class constraints in the name of a more or less Marxian version of the Kingdom of God, racialists hoped to transcend pluralism in the name of an organic national community that identified the blood of the Lamb with the blood of the Volk.

While both movements were syncretistic in the sense that they accommodated theological principles to some species of secular politics, a third new postwar movement proposed to avoid this difficulty by elevating theology itself to the status of a political program. Such at least was the intent of the Christlich-Sozialer Volksdienst (Christian-Social People's Service, or CSVD), a quasi-theocratic party whose nerve center in Württemberg was the pietist community of Korntal, near Stuttgart. Like the other movements, the CSVD was an affair of the young, most of them idealists steeped in pietist tradition and radicalized by the experience of war and defeat, which they regarded in apocalyptic

---

[66] Kübler to OKR, Nov. 21, 1928, OKR/AR Gen. 151b; clippings on Schenkel (Oct. 19, 21, 1929) in LKA D1/28,7.

fashion as signs of divine judgment on an apostate society. The party's founders became activists in spite of themselves, drawn into the struggle for votes out of frustration over what they saw as the lack of a uniquely Christian political alternative. Appalled alike by ideologues of the right and of the left and by what seemed to them the utilitarian and self-serving behavior of existing parties, the *Volksdienstler* saw themselves as veritable missionaries to politics charged with the moral regeneration of public life. What they sought, according to their initial manifesto in 1924, was "not the re-establishment of the fallen idols, the restoration of our nation's external greatness, but the restoration of its [inner] health, its moral renewal."[67] This vague formula comported to some extent with the rhetoric of mainstream Protestant conservatism, especially in its implied view of the nation as organic moral community. Unlike most conservatives, however, those in the CSVD did not pine for the return of a Bismarckian-Wilhelmian Reich—the "fallen idol" of the party statement—but sided with the minority of clerical Democrats and Religious Socialists in declaring unqualified support for the republic. Appeals to piety aside, the party's program drew heavily upon the paternalistic formulas of the old Christian-Social tradition; it was, in effect, Stoecker in sober republican dress, purged of both anti-Semitic dross and antisocialist triumphalism.[68]

Like both folkish Protestantism and Religious Socialism, the CSVD was perhaps less important for what it achieved than for what it symbolized. It represented yet another attempt, this one anchored in the tenets of pietism, to realize and at the same time to overcome the constraints of the Volkskirche tradition, to point the way towards an integration of confession and social order. Of all these initiatives, however, the CSVD made the greatest direct political impact, especially within Württemberg itself. While the

[67] *Christlich-soziale Blätter* 1 (1924): 3, quoted in Lehmann, *Pietismus*, p. 304.
[68] On the Volksdienst generally, see Günter Opitz, *Der Christlichsoziale Volksdienst* (Düsseldorf, 1969); on the Württemberg branch, see Lehmann, *Pietismus*, pp. 303ff.

other movements had their origins and chief loci of activity elsewhere in Germany, the CSVD was to a significant degree a native product, and its implicit aim of becoming a genuinely confessional counterpart to the Catholic Center was perhaps less farfetched there than in areas that lacked Württemberg's vigorous pietist subculture.

The Württemberg CSVD had its roots in a discussion group founded in 1919 by a young Korntal teacher and former soldier, Wilhelm Simpfendörfer, and by others disillusioned by the failure of the bourgeois political front to incorporate their Christian ideals without compromise. In 1924, responding to an appeal from Bielefeld theologian Samuel Jäger, they expanded to form a statewide group, one of a loose network of *Gesinnungsgemeinschaften* then being established around the country. While Simpfendörfer insisted that he and his friends were not forming a political party and indeed had no taste for politics as usual, by 1925 they had begun nominating candidates for local office, winning town council seats in Stuttgart and Ludwigsburg as well as in a number of smaller communities. The Landtag elections of 1928 brought further advances. Now formally entered in the lists as the Christlich-Sozialer Volksdienst, the party managed to capture about 4 percent of the vote in Württemberg and send three delegates to the assembly in Stuttgart. In the epochal Reichstag election of September 1930 the party reached the modest pinnacle of its success. Attracting support from Protestants disgruntled over the demagogic course of Alfred Hugenberg's DNVP, the CSVD won 2.5 percent of all votes cast nationwide and gained fourteen seats in the new Reichstag. In Württemberg the results were more impressive. The CSVD total reached 6.5 percent of the votes cast, exceeding 10 percent in more than a dozen heavily Protestant districts and reaching nearly 18 percent in the Black Forest pietist stronghold of Freudenstadt.[69]

[69] Election statistics in Joseph Griesmeier, "Die Reichswahlen im Wahlkreis Württemberg von 1919–1930," *Württembergisches Jahrbuch für Statistik und Landeskunde 1930/31* (Stuttgart, 1931), p. 110.

If the CSVD, like the Nazis, benefited from the decay of the established parties—particularly the nationalist-conservative Bürgerpartei, whose share of the Württemberg vote declined nearly 40 percent between 1924 and 1930—its appeals failed to find significant resonance within the ecclesiastical hierarchy. Eugen Reiff, leader of Group I in the church assembly, was sympathetic. So too were *Christenbote* editor Christian Kohler, well-known Tübingen theologian and exegete Adolf Schlatter, and Hermann Müller, a lay member of the Oberkirchenrat who served briefly as a CSVD delegate in the Württemberg assembly. Most churchmen, however, kept their distance from the party, whose leading figures were, like Simpfendörfer, pietist schoolmasters. The CSVD cause probably drew more support from Baptist, Methodist, and other free church clergy than from those in the Evangelical establishment.

This lukewarm reception resulted most immediately from the party's failure to win over such influential *Bürgerparteiler* as Theophil Wurm, whose endorsement Simpfendörfer and others eagerly courted. "While you may fear that the Volksdienst will bring about a questionable linkage of religion and politics," Simpfendörfer contended in a letter to Wurm in 1928, "we for our part see the most fateful mix . . . precisely in the Bürgerpartei. . . . It is common knowledge that the . . . leaders of the party are not particularly church-oriented at all, much less positively Christian."[70] The leaders in question, quick to see connections between CSVD gains and their own declining fortunes, pressured Wurm to uphold his old loyalties.[71] While admitting in a letter to Reiff that the Bürgerpartei tried his patience at times, Wurm still insisted that the CSVD represented a potentially greater evil, not only because it threatened a possibly irreparable schism in the conservative front but also, significantly, because Wurm saw its self-conscious Protestantism as contrary

[70] Reiff to Wurm, Dec. 17, 1927; Simpfendörfer to Wurm, Feb. 1, 1928; and Simpfendörfer to Wurm, Feb. 16, 1928; all in LKA D1/28,5.
[71] See, e.g., Wider to Wurm, May 2, 1928, OKR/AR Gen. 124/I. Commentary on the political calculations involved can be found in *ST*, Jan. 17, 1928, and in *Der Beobachter*, Jan. 28, 1928.

to the spirit of the all-embracing Volkskirche. Given the social and political diversity in the Protestant community, Wurm found the CSVD lacking in "prudence and maturity" when it sought to establish an exclusive "politics of faith." For the church to adopt the CSVD cause, in his view, would be to violate the Protestant emphasis on freedom of conscience. The church's message for society, Wurm argued, could not be embodied in a single political movement; nor, ultimately, could the regeneration of the nation be achieved by political means at all.[72] Other overtures met similar rebuffs. When a parish paper in the village of Mühlheim, near Sulz, carried a guarded endorsement of the CSVD before the 1928 elections, the regional church press, partly at the urging of church officials, countered with statements reasserting the church's neutrality and denying the claims of any party to church members' exclusive support.[73]

Even with the concerted assistance of church officials, the CSVD would have had little prospect of becoming a significant national force. Without such assistance, it was condemned even in Württemberg to remain a splinter movement. To the extent, however, that it absorbed much of the Protestant vote lost to the older parties of the center and right, it did pose a significant if temporary barrier to the spread of National Socialism. Württemberg Nazis managed only 9.4 percent of the vote in 1930, scarcely half their nationwide percentage and the lowest total for any electoral region in the country.[74] This was the CSVD's major achievement. Lacking experienced leadership and a mass base outside the pietist community, however, it could not long resist the pull of more powerful political currents.

The failure of the CSVD to reorient Protestant political alignments did more than attest to the national-conservative grip on leading churchmen's outlooks. It also reflected the inability to find a compelling formula for mediating the claims of confes-

[72] Wurm to Reiff, Dec. 20, 1927, and Wurm to Simpfendörfer, Feb. 2, 1928, both in LKA D1/28,5. Wurm, "Evangelische Politik?" *MfPT* 24 (1928): 160–63.
[73] *Evangelisches Gemeindeblatt für Mühlheim*, Apr. 1928 (copy), and Ev. Gesellschaft, Quell-Verlag, to Müller, May 9, 1928, both in OKR/AR Gen. 124/I.
[74] Griesmeier, "Reichswahlen im Wahlkreis Württemberg," pp. 78ff.

sional solidarity and freedom of conscience in a seemingly fragmented political order. Wurm's primary argument against the new party—that the church's internal diversity rendered a distinctively Protestant party self-contradictory—in fact reflected what for a majority of pastors and officials was becoming an inhibitant to political activism of any kind. "Here politics is off limits," declared an Evangelical Press Association pamphlet about the church. "An individual is not involved as a Social Democrat or . . . Conservative *but only as a person*."[75] The Consistory's 1920 decree on political neutrality emphasized that parishioners' "trust in the Word and its preacher" would suffer if pastors took partisan stands, especially in official or semiofficial capacities. The pastor's central duty must be to "take account of the diversity of the parish in both theological and political areas, within the unity of the faith, and, setting aside all that could divide, to strengthen and encourage unity of spirit."[76] Christian Schnaufer, head of the Pfarrverein and a supporter of the Bürgerpartei, sounded the same theme in his annual report for 1921. "The position of us pastors in public life," he wrote, "is different from that of other officials. It is important for our congregations to be made strongly aware of this, and also to be reminded of it regularly ourselves."[77] Paul Wurster made such reminders a central feature of an article on preaching written after his own retirement from political life. The newspaper, he wrote, was the appropriate vehicle for discussing current events; the sermon should present eternal concerns. "Whether [God] chooses to save our people in a monarchical or republican form, by more socialist or more conservative means, is his affair. Our task is to show parishioners what in any case is the certain path of Christian salvation, a renewal that begins from within."[78]

These declarations represent not simply a conventional conservative denigration of politics but also the expression of a ten-

[75] Evangelischer Presseverband, *Arbeiter, Religion, und Kirche* (n.p., n.d. [ca. 1919]), copy in LKA D12/5; italics in original.
[76] Konsistorialerlass, July 6, 1920, draft in LKA A26/151.
[77] Schnaufer, "Jahresbericht," *KAfW* 30 (1921): 70.
[78] Wurster, "Zeitpredigten," *MfPT* 16 (1920): 145–46, 148.

tative new criterion for political activity, one that emphasized the clergy's role as shepherds of the flock rather than as representatives of public authority. Confirmation of this consensus can be found in numerous visitation records and *Pfarrberichte*, the detailed reports on parish life that all pastors were required to file periodically with the Oberkirchenrat. Unlike statements intended for public distribution, Pfarrberichte were confidential working papers that circulated only among members of the church hierarchy. In their mixture of idiosyncrasy and cliché and in the often revealing marginalia added by Dekans and higher officials, such reports provide candid glimpses into pastors' attitudes as well as their superiors' assumptions and policies.[79]

Many parish reports testify to pastors' growing awareness of political factors in assessing their stewardship in office. Typical of many is a 1920 report from Musberg-Leinfelden, a parish comprising two small villages a short tram ride outside Stuttgart. As a result of the growth of industry in Leinfelden, two separate communities were developing within the parish, one of farmers and the other of factory workers. Describing these demographic and social changes, the local pastor remarked that by siding with the strong Bauernbund faction in area politics he could doubtless woo some religiously indifferent farmers but only at the cost of alienating himself from working-class parishioners. He therefore chose to remain "impartial" in hopes of retaining credibility with both groups.[80]

In those parishes where pastors did venture public involve-

[79] Investigation of *Pfarrberichte* for this study was necessarily selective; time constraints precluded a thorough reading of all reports from every Württemberg parish for the Weimar period. I therefore concentrated on parishes served by known political activists as well as on major urban and diocesan centers. In addition I took a more or less random sampling of other parishes reflecting the social and geographic contours of the church as a whole. As with all such documents, reports vary considerably in quality and utility. Taken as a whole, however, they provide the best available picture of pastors' attitudes and the texture of church life at the parish level.

[80] Musberg-Leinfelden, Pfarrbericht 1920, LKA A29/2998; cf. Kumpf to OKR, Feb. 20, 1928, OKR/AR Gen. 427/I.

ment, reports almost invariably include some evaluation of political behavior and its impact on a pastor's effectiveness in the
parish. Relatively homogeneous parishes presented few problems, provided that a politically vocal pastor shared the views of
his flock. Another visitation report from 1920 discusses conditions in Gaildorf, whose current Dekan, Theodor Schrenk, it de-
picts as "a sworn opponent of the democratic system . . . in its
present form." In conservative Gaildorf, where the right regularly won a solid majority and where the local gentry retained
patronage rights in the church, Schrenk's stance appeared on
balance to reinforce rather than to undermine his clerical role.
Not only did it ensure a sympathetic ear on the part of the patron, but the church council, queried privately by a visiting prelate, found nothing in the arrangement to protest. The Dekan's
political frankness, members insisted, was an asset to his pastoral
work, since it left no one in doubt of where he stood on current
issues.[81]

In Urach, as in Gaildorf, church offices were situated in a former patron's castle. There, however, the resemblance ended.
Urach Dekan Albert Leube reported that most townfolk opposed
any political role for their clergy. A predecessor's vocal conservatism, wrote Leube, "may have found favor among many (but
not all) parishioners sympathetic to the Bürgerpartei," but it left
"those of other persuasions . . . rather offended." Leube himself admitted to sharing the conservative outlook, but he ab-
stained from any attempt to "illuminate political questions from
a religious standpoint"; his junior colleague did likewise.[82]
Leube's flock at least made their opinions known more conventionally than some parishioners in Aldingen, near Tuttlingen,
where in 1919 anonymous threats, underscored by a grenade
tossed through a window of the manse, called attention to alleged "warmongering" by the village pastor. Police investiga-
tions having failed to uncover a culprit, the Consistory in Stutt-

---

[81] Gaildorf, Pfarrbericht 1920, LKA A29/1390. In 1930 Schrenk became titular
prelate and *Stiftsprediger* in Stuttgart.
[82] Urach, Pfarrbericht 1924, OKR/AR OA/PfB.

gart eventually arranged to have the pastor in question transferred to another post.[83]

Political activism also caused problems in Böblingen, where Albrecht Schäfer, an outspoken Bauernbund member, had taken up duties in 1919. Intelligent, opinionated, and self-possessed, Schäfer did not lack for admirers, but fellow churchmen regarded his partisan posturing as disruptive in a town like Böblingen, where the coexistence of a growing factory class with a strong pietist community taxed pastoral and administrative skills under the best of circumstances. A 1928 visitation report concluded that, while postwar tensions may have moderated over time, Schäfer remained "more a politician . . . than a pastor." With Communists and Social Democrats competing for the largest bloc of local voters, Schäfer's rightist stance threatened good relations between parish leaders and the town hall. Schäfer responded to criticism by threatening to resign, an intention that church officials did nothing to discourage; a marginal comment noted that "the attempt to transfer him to another church post would involve no little difficulty."[84]

Perhaps the most painful conflict between political and pastoral norms during the period occurred in Ditzingen, another of the newly industrializing towns in the greater Stuttgart area. Maximilian Kappler came to Ditzingen as pastor in 1926 after more than two decades in an outlying rural parish, and though he had long sought promotion to a larger community, his political views remained emphatically those of the countryside. Kapp-

[83] Haller to Schnaufer, Aug. 5, Oct. 23, 1919, LKA D/EPW 34; cf. *Magisterbuch* (1932), p. 104. The local Dekan speculated that the grenade attack was the work of local "profiteers" whose operations the pastor in question, Heinrich Gommel, had allegedly castigated.

[84] Notes in Böblingen, Pfarrbericht 1928, OKR/AR OA/PfB. Schäfer, who apparently had an independent income, did in fact resign his pastorate in 1930, although he by no means retired from church politics in Böblingen, where he seems to have retained a strong following among the faithful. In the 1931 church assembly elections he won an overwhelming victory as a theological independent, garnering nearly 70% of the votes cast in the district. Cf. *Magisterbuch* (1932), p. 165; 2. Landeskirchentag, *Verhandlungen* (1931), Beilage 2, "Ergebnisse der Wahlen zum Landeskirchentag vom 8. März 1931."

ler's immediate superior, the Dekan for Leonberg, predicted on Kappler's arrival in Ditzingen that his "one-sided" sympathies would "make it difficult for him as a pastor to win the confidence of the workers." A Christmas homily that appeared in the parish paper the following year seemed designed to fulfill this prediction. Its blunt attack on German socialists and what Kappler called their "dreary whimpering about a rotten world peace" attracted attention far beyond the small circle of parishioners to whom it had originally been addressed. In early 1928 it provided grist for the editorial mill of the *Schwäbische Tagwacht*, which lampooned Kappler's position as "even more miserable than the German in which it is couched." Ditzingen Social Democrats sought to force Kappler to defend his charges at a party meeting. In response Kappler announced plans for a Bauernbund rally of his own; the *Tagwacht* attack, he declared, had only strengthened his convictions about the duty to "fight openly and unequivocally" against the socialist movement in all its forms. With the affair thus threatening to escalate, the Oberkirchenrat considered it prudent to intervene. At its suggestion, Leonberg Dekan Eugen Lachenmann, a onetime classmate of Kappler's in Tübingen, met with his outspoken subordinate to urge tact in dealing with Ditzingen's working-class public. Lachenmann asked how Kappler's position as pastor could "tolerate, let alone require" crusades against a political party, particularly one to which so many parishioners belonged. Other pastors in the area formally condemned Kappler's position and disassociated themselves from his public statements. Meanwhile, town officials in Ditzingen ordered the Bauernbund rally canceled on the grounds that the hall rented for the occasion could not hold the anticipated crowd. There the matter rested for the moment. The Oberkirchenrat, which had prepared a contingency decree forbidding Kappler's appearance at his own rally, contented itself with a caution against further acts of provocation. A subsequent visitation report found little to praise in Kappler's approach, which by then had led him into the ranks of the National Socialists. In Ditzingen, the report concluded, the pastor and hence the church as an institution had become hopelessly alienated from most of the population.[85]

It is hard to imagine an antisocialist zealot arousing comparable disapproval in the prewar church. After 1918, however, as the Ditzingen case showed, not even the most fervent conservatism exempted a pastor from the obligation to consider first the politics of his constituency. Parish reports from folkish and Religious Socialist pastors show appeals to the same criterion of behavior. A good example is that of Karl Steger, whose position as Landtag delegate after 1924 gave him particular visibility. Visitation reports from Massenbach, Steger's post during most of the period, resemble those from Gaildorf cited earlier. They suggest that Steger was able to persuade church officials of his ability to meet political commitments without either neglecting pastoral duties or offending parishioners who did not share his views. Steger enjoyed the confidence of the Massenbach patron, and widespread political apathy among the local population was seen as buffering the impact of Steger's racialism on parish morale.[86] Steger's political credentials in fact appear to have enhanced his credibility in some circles. Admirers in another town, including a fellow Landtag delegate, petitioned the Oberkirchenrat in 1927 to appoint Steger to their currently vacant parish.[87]

Steger's racialist comrade Friedrich Ettwein, pastor in Rudersberg between 1922 and 1930, earned a more qualified appraisal

[85] Ditzingen, Pfarrbericht 1926, Pfarrbericht 1930, OKR/AR OA/PfB; Kappler to OKR, May 19, 1925; *Evangelisches Gemeindeblatt für Ditzingen*, Dec. 1927; *ST*, Jan. 16, Feb. 7, 13, 1928; OKR to Dekanatamt Leonberg, Feb. 8, Mar. 6, 1928; Lachenmann to OKR, Feb. 13, 14, 1928; Lachenmann to Kappler, Feb. 8, 1928 (copy); Kappler to OKR, Feb. 22, 1928; Lachenmann to Schoell, Mar. 4, 1928; all in Kappler Personalakten, OKR/AR Pers. K/32.

[86] Massenbach, Pfarrbericht 1926, OKR/AR OA/PfB; Steger Personalakten, OKR/AR Pers.

[87] Landtag, *Verhandlungen* (1927), pp. 4331, 4365, 4382–83; Unterensingen, Besetzungsakten, OKR/AR OA. While the requested appointment was in fact made, Steger declined it. Perhaps the parish in question seemed too small for his ambitions; two years later he successfully applied for transfer to a more substantial post in Friedrichshafen, the bustling harbor town on Lake Constance (Steger Personalakten, OKR/AR Pers.).

from superiors. In the margin of a 1924 report, the supervising Dekan in Welzheim stressed the political tone of Ettwein's preaching and speculated that his "energy" and "combative nature" threatened at times to become sheer "ruthlessness"—a prescient observation in view of Ettwein's subsequent role as a National Socialist hotspur.[88] Equally mixed were the evaluations of Wilhelm Rehm, who assumed his first regular pastorate at Simmersfeld in 1926. Reports of earlier service as a vicar stressed Rehm's zeal and vigor but warned that political enthusiasms could easily interfere with his potential as a pastor. "It would be a pity if all his good energies should be consumed by [political] tiffs," commented one supervising pastor in 1924. Jakob Schoell, who in his capacity as prelate for Reutlingen attended a Sunday service in Simmersfeld in the late 1920s, expressed displeasure with Rehm's sermon, which he called a "conscious political harangue." Rehm, however, found a defender in his immediate superior, Wilhelm Otto, Dekan for Nagold. Despite pietist roots, Otto was mildly sympathetic to the folkish cause, and he argued that Rehm's admitted partisanship did not constitute a hindrance to pastoral effectiveness in what would prove to be one of the first Nazi strongholds in the state. In any event, Otto insisted, Rehm did not carry his politics over into work with parishioners. "He is a capable pastor," concluded the Dekan in 1930, "and promises to become even more so."[89]

Perhaps the clearest evidence for the primacy of pastoral functions comes from those parishes served by Religious Socialists. Unlike other political views, all of which had at least some prior pedigree among churchmen and were therefore tied to vested church interests, socialism was a new departure with only negative precedents to serve it. Pfarrberichte for the Weimar period, however, show that the Blumhardt precedent no longer obtained. The prevailing albeit skeptical position was to treat Reli-

[88] Rudersberg, Pfarrbericht 1924, OKR/AR OA/PfB.

[89] Report of May 26, 1924, Rehm Personalakten, OKR/AR Pers.; notes on Simmersfeld, Pfarrbericht 1930, OKR/AR. The National Socialists won nearly 23% of the vote in the Nagold district in September 1930, the highest percentage in Württemberg.

gious Socialism as a permissible option for pastors in areas where it promised to aid in building rapport with parishioners. Speaking with the blessing of church president Merz, liberal Vaihingen Dekan Ernst Welsch told the church assembly in 1927 that Religious Socialists should expect no difficulties with the church leadership on account of their principles. Rather, they deserved the "freedom and opportunity to show to what extent they can succeed in healing the . . . painful wound in the body of the Württemberg church, the alienation of the working masses from the church."[90]

The motives invoked by Welsch can be seen at work in the case of Eberhard Lempp, who assumed his first regular pastorate at Baltmannsweiler in 1919. Described by superiors as shy and conscientious, Lempp was not by temperament a political activist. In Baltmannsweiler he confronted a socially evolving parish, many townsmen having abandoned their marginal farms for jobs in the railway yards at nearby Plochingen. It was largely in hopes of halting the deterioration of local church life that Lempp turned to the most active political movement in the town. By the time of his first formal report in 1920, Lempp already claimed to see hopeful signs. Two Social Democrats had accepted nomination to the parish council. They did so, Lempp insisted, not for political reasons but because "with the present pastor Social Democrats have no cause to stay away from church." In a community that, like many in Württemberg, combined new proletarian mores with older habits of small-town piety, Lempp's identification with working-class politics established a productive point of contact with his parishioners. The Dekan for Schorndorf, whose district included Baltmannsweiler, endorsed Lempp's own evaluation and reported seeing definite improvements in the town's religious life since the war. In a later report, written under the impact of the 1923–24 economic crisis, Lempp

[90] 1. Landeskirchentag, *Verhandlungen* (1927), p. 293. Upon invitation, the Oberkirchenrat sent official observers to the state conferences of the Religious Socialists as well as to a national congress in Mannheim in 1928; the 1930 national congress was held in Stuttgart. See notes on Eckart to OKR, July 12, 1928, OKR/AR Gen. 151b; and below, pp. 318–27.

admitted that the initial breakthroughs had yet to yield significant dividends, but he stressed again the importance of cordial ties between the church and Social Democratic officials. A Dekan's report from 1926, after Lempp had become a founding member of the Württemberg Religious Socialist group, struck a generally positive note, with special commendation for Lempp's "understanding and tact" in winning workers' confidence without alienating pietist-inclined traditionalists in the parish.[91]

Similar themes recur in the career of Paul Weitbrecht, who joined the Religious Socialist movement while serving in Tailfingen and who later became pastor in the northern Württemberg parish of Neckargartach. A heavily working-class suburb of Heilbronn, where the SPD could count on as much as 75 percent of the vote, Neckargartach was much more heavily proletarian in character than the smaller Baltmannsweiler. Like Eberhard Lempp, however, Weitbrecht used socialism primarily as a tool to gain credibility in a parish where anticlerical prejudices ran strong. By visiting local factories and by using the parish paper to support workers' economic and political demands, Weitbrecht evolved what he himself called a "parish-oriented socialism" having little to do with explicit party-political activity. Heilbronn Dekan Karl Gaub, in commenting on conditions in Neckargartach, questioned whether it was necessary for Weitbrecht to "assume the prejudices" of his parishioners "in order to help them religiously." The new prelate for Heilbronn, Theophil Wurm, was more categorical, commenting in the margin of one report that "to share false opinions with others can never help." Both, however, found much to praise in Weitbrecht's work. Gaub expressed a general view when he commended him as "the right man in the right place."[92]

Arguably the capital of Württemberg Religious Socialism at the end of the decade was Göppingen, in the foothills of the Swabian Jura southeast of Stuttgart. The center of a district that was

[91] Baltmannsweiler, Pfarrbericht 1920, LKA A29/293; Pfarrbericht 1924; and Visitationsbericht, Nov. 11, 1926; all in OKR/AR OA/PfB.

[92] Neckargartach, Pfarrbericht 1928, OKR/AR OA/PfB.

more than 60 percent industrial—statistically the second-heaviest such concentration in the state—Göppingen was both a stronghold of Social Democratic militancy and the mecca of the Blumhardt cult, Blumhardt having spent the years before and after his dismissal from church service in the nearby health resort of Bad Boll. This environment peculiarly favored Religious Socialism. By 1930, according to one report, the local Religious Socialist chapter included many SPD officials and at least three of the town's six pastors, among them Blumhardt's future biographer Eugen Jäckh. The town council, with Social Democrats casting the decisive votes, agreed in 1929 to fund a new position for religious instruction in local intermediate schools. Churchmen's earlier requests for such an appointment had encountered firm Social Democratic opposition, but "now [that] we have a religious socialism," as one party leader explained, the matter appeared in a more favorable light. Pastors also reported changed hearts among ordinary parishioners; Religious Socialist events such as special May Day services attracted many who otherwise rarely found their way into a pew. These achievements did not meet with universal acclaim, to be sure, particularly among pietists in the area. From the Religious Socialist perspective, however, Göppingen provided an attractive model for the Weimar church, one in which the Volkskirche ideal was still truly alive.[93]

Despite local successes like Göppingen, Religious Socialists faced the same problems as their pietist counterparts of the Volksdienst when they made efforts to transcend the status of a "tolerated exception" within the Weimar church. The unprejudiced neutrality promised by Johannes Merz did not preclude deep skepticism. Few except committed Religious Socialists seriously considered the proposition that socialism and Protestant Christianity might share significant common ground. An unsigned article in the Stuttgart *Evangelisches Gemeindeblatt* expressed a general sentiment when it asked rhetorically "whether

[93] Göppingen, Pfarrbericht 1930, OKR/AR OA/PfB.; Göppingen, Kirchengemeinderatssitzung, Jan. 27, 1928, Protokoll (copy), Göppingen Besetzungsakten, OKR/AR OA; Göppingen Kirchenbezirkstag, Protokoll, DA Göppingen 31.

these [Religious Socialist] circles, whose idealism deserves every recognition, are not in danger of losing touch with the church . . . without establishing any real contact with the working masses in exchange?"[94] The same report from the Oberkirchenrat to the DEKA that dismissed racialist groups as insignificant also expressed doubts about Religious Socialists' prospects of success among "religiously intolerant" socialists.[95] Theophil Wurm, a titular member of the Oberkirchenrat as prelate for Heilbronn, put the objection with his usual bluntness. "We really have enough [proletarian consciousness] in Germany," wrote Wurm. "That will not save us."[96] In lay circles attitudes were often anything but understanding. "Not everyone in church-minded circles," wrote Waiblingen Dekan Friedrich Buck, whose purview included the parish of Religious Socialist Reinhold Planck in Winnenden, "is simply prepared to tolerate having a pastor in the church as a Social Democratic huckster and greeted as 'our comrade' in the *Tagwacht*."[97]

The widespread rejection of Religious Socialist formulas should not obscure the fact that both Religious Socialists and their critics began with essentially the same assumptions. Both affirmed the imperative nature of the church's task, as Volkskirche, to serve as a bridge-builder between and among the diverse segments of a class-ridden society. Having affirmed the primacy of pastoral tasks, however, they drew different conclusions from existing conditions. A majority rejected the Religious Socialist initiative, in part out of a belief that while its supporters could never hope to succeed in penetrating the "godless" core of the workers' movement, their efforts to do so were certain to antagonize the largely conservative core of faithful parishioners. For their part, Religious Socialists acted out of a conviction, by no means limited to their own ranks, that the future of the Volks-

[94] "Evangelische Sozialisten," *EGBfS* 20 (1924): 124. See also Schoell, notes on Voelter, to OKR, Dec. 7, 1925, OKR/AR Gen. 151b; Traub, *Jahresbericht 1927* (Stuttgart, 1928), p. 40; Paul Wurster, "Die Sozialdemokratie von heute und unsere Kirche," *MfPT* 16 (1920): 88.
[95] OKR to DEKA, Feb. 29, 1928, OKR/AR Gen. 151b.
[96] Wurm, "Kirche und Arbeiterschaft," *KAfW* 36 (1927): 94.
[97] Buck to OKR, Apr. 10, 1929, OKR/AR Gen. 151b.

kirche depended precisely upon its ability to construct new avenues of understanding to its own *Randsiedler*, those marginal members of whom the largest and most important body were working class and socialist. Thus problems of political involvement echoed problems of ecclesiastical renewal: in a complex and culturally pluralistic society, where uniformity of outlook could not be assumed and where conformity of practice could not be compelled, was the Volkskirche truly viable in either theory or practice? As the above-mentioned divergence of conclusions testified, commitment to the primacy of pastoral responsibility served more as an acknowledgement of political fragmentation than as a sure means of overcoming it. To the extent that this principle condoned political activism as a way of commending pastors to parishioners, it underscored the church's own lack of inner unity. To the extent that it made such activism dependent on the circumstances of parish life and subordinated politics to prior obligations of the pastoral office, it threatened to become a formula for clerical impotence in a party state.

The Church and the Proletariat

If attempts to reconcile politics and pastoral responsibility were at heart a response to the question of how the church could strengthen its influence among parishioners both active and nominal, the cases reviewed above suggest that this question came most clearly into focus where relationships with the working classes were involved. Postwar political and economic conditions lent new urgency to the search for possible bridges between pastors and the proletariat. Through the Inner Mission and other agencies of social Protestantism, churchmen attempted to revive some of the worker-oriented impulses that had animated the early Wilhelmian Evangelical-Social movement. Such efforts were particularly common in Württemberg, where the social and political encapsulation of the working classes appeared less advanced than in many industrial areas and where the Evangelical-Social tradition itself had suffered less than elsewhere—Prussia, for example—from factional disputes or from the kaiser's famous condemnation of social-political activism in

1896. Both before and after the war, Württemberg churchmen of every outlook and station, from prelates and Dekans to vicars fresh from the security of the Tübingen Stift, undertook to promote the cause of the workers as they understood it.[98]

But if a concern to make contact with the proletariat was by no means new in Württemberg after 1918, churchmen's understanding of the task underwent considerable chastening as a consequence of war, revolution, and social upheaval. Prewar gestures towards the working classes almost invariably reflected paternalistic assumptions about the social order. The "good worker" of Protestant imagination was someone who knew both the hymn book and his proper place in life, a model of patriotism and piety content to remain a junior partner in the national enterprise. With the collapse of the old order, however, such images became a sentimental irrelevancy. If prewar churchmen had seen themselves called to win workers for the established order, those of the republican era felt compelled primarily to win them for the church itself. Nor could they bring to this task the implicit triumphalism of an earlier day. The Volksbund functionary and Evangelical-Social leader August Springer, himself a laborer by birth and training, later recalled the new awareness of complexity with which his most astute clerical contemporaries sought to grapple after 1918:

> I was forced to recognize . . . how complicated things had become. . . . It was easier . . . for a pastor to be "social" [before the war]. He could believe in, and confidently hope for, simple solutions. . . . Now all that had changed. The economic fabric had become grayer, and as the world lost its distinctive shades of color the once sharp line between right and wrong was also blurred. Man seemed more puzzling, and we knew less about him than in the springtime of the Evangelical-Social movement.[99]

[98] On the Evangelical-Social tradition in Württemberg, see Voelter, "Bietigheimer Tag," pp. 3–25; for the general context, see Kouri, *Protestantismus und soziale Frage.*

[99] Springer, *Der andere, der bist Du*, pp. 282–83.

What did this loss of certainty imply for churchmen struggling to realize the broad-based spiritual community of the Volkskirche? To Springer, the obvious conclusion was that true understanding between the church and its working class members could only come about on the latter's terms; churchmen must recognize the integrity of a worker's outlook, not simply seek to entice him out of his proletarian milieu. Speaking at the 1924 convention of the Evangelical-Social Congress in Reutlingen, Springer contended that the church should not ignore the very real barriers of antagonism separating most workers from the "pious class." This meant, among other things, that pastors should put aside a priori judgments and seek to understand why workers might be attracted to Marxian doctrines of economic determinism and class struggle. "The great question," Springer insisted, "is whether members of the organized Christian community can in fact remain together if they are in a state of [economic] struggle against each other. I think that they can, if each will recognize that his adversary, like himself, often finds himself in the grips of an overriding necessity and is forced to reckon with conditions which he himself did not create." Hence Springer rejected attempts to "cure the worker of socialism" as both futile and unjustified. Churchmen should harbor no illusions about social conflict; easy formulas for reconciliation were no more relevant within the church than in society at large.[100] Most of Springer's fellow travelers on the Evangelical-Social course in Württemberg shared his sober conclusions. "What can the church do to change conditions?" Hermann Ströle had asked in a speech at a 1921 Volksbund seminar in Tübingen. His frank answer was: "Perhaps nothing." Former court preacher Richard Lempp agreed, confessing that when dealing with workers he often felt as if he were "standing in front of a wall." Workers, he admitted, "belong to a cultural world totally different from our own."[101] Pastors' reports abounded with similar statements.

[100] Evangelische-Sozialer Kongress, 31. Tagung, *Verhandlungen*, p. 90; cf. Voelter, "Bietigheimer Tag," pp. 25–26, 32–33.
[101] Notes on Ströle, "Kirche und Arbeiterschaft," typescript, LKA D4/24x.

This consciousness of entering an alien world may have inhibited forays into working-class society, but it did not prevent them. The Volksbund and its local chapters sought wherever possible to declare a truce in the class war, holding between 150 and 200 seminars, lectures, and discussion meetings each year for the benefit of workers and their bourgeois neighbors. Reports on such meetings routinely claimed that a "beginning" had been made in breaching class barriers, though evidence of more substantial success was rare and usually proved premature.[102] Such projects as the Evangelical Workers' League (Evangelischer Arbeiterverein), established by Theodor Traub as early as 1888, may have been too closely identified with Wilhelmian values to bear fruit in the new political climate. Despite the best efforts of Eduard Lamparter and, after 1921, Hans Voelter, membership in the Evangelischer Arbeiterverein hovered around three thousand for most of the decade, only half the pre-war total; a women's organization, the Evangelischer Arbeiterinnenverein, added at most fifteen hundred more. The economic havoc wrought by war and inflation left both groups dependent upon subsidies from the church leadership to maintain even a skeleton operation.[103] And while thanks to the influence of Jakob Schoell, a founding father of the Württemberg Evangelical-Social movement, the Oberkirchenrat showed a new sensitivity to worker interests when making appointments to parish posts, church life remained institutionally weighted towards rural and small-town concerns.[104] For all its efforts to provide bridges between workers and the pious classes, the old Evangelical-Social cadre found its field of operation limited and few on either side of the divide eager to risk crossings with any regularity.

Bridge-building of a different sort was the aim of the so-called

[102] EVB, *Mitteilungen* 15 (Apr. 1921): 262–63, 27 (Apr. 1923): 474, 31 (Apr. 1924): 528, 35 (Apr. 1925): 623; *EGBfS* 23 (1927): 129; "Gefahren der Sozialpolitik?" *EGBfS* 23 (1927): 124–25.

[103] Voelter to OKR, Mar. 26, 1926; Schaal to Voelter, Apr. 17, 1926, Mar. 22, 1927; Krockenberger to OKR, Mar. 3, 1927; and Merz to Krockenberger, Mar. 5, 1927; all in OKR/AR Gen. 151.

[104] Voelter, "Bietigheimer Tag," pp. 29–39.

Bietigheim Days, a series of more or less annual conferences held from 1921 in the town of the same name. Established under the direction of Hans Voelter, pastor in Bietigheim from 1917 to 1923, these conferences aimed not at grass-roots contact between classes but rather at fostering dialogue at a higher level. Those invited to participate included church officials, prominent Evangelical-Social figures, and leaders of the trade unions and the SPD. Bietigheim marked one of the earliest occasions on which churchmen systematically confronted leaders of the socialist camp as equals and largely without preconditions. In Voelter's own words, the conferences represented "an attempt to put the church's political neutrality into practice by encouraging unprejudiced, sober, but at the same time sympathetic and warmly personal exchanges between church and socialism, [to provide] a neutral ground on which the various groups in public life, which had been slipping progressively towards almost insuperable antagonism, could come together for objective discussions." By limiting the dialogue to a relatively small circle of participants, architects of the experiment hoped to promote greater frankness and an "honest effort to achieve an open exchange of views, however conflicting."[105]

The first Bietigheim Day took place April 21–22, 1921; a second followed in June 1921 and a third in January 1922, and thereafter they continued annually for the rest of the decade. The first conferences established a format for following meetings. After an opening religious service, participants retired to the intimate confines of the Bietigheim parish hall to hear several addresses, usually from representatives of both the church and the socialist movement, on a general topic chosen as the conference's organizing theme. At the first Bietigheim Day, discussion dealt with the spiritual outlooks of workers and peasants. Later topics included the youth movement, the place of women

[105] Voelter, "Der 'Bietigheimer Tag,' " *Württembergische Arbeiterzeitung* 30 (Apr. 2, 1922); quoted also in Voelter, "Bietigheimer Tag," p. 44. Cf. August Springer: "This forum proved a success. The tone was conciliatory—as it could well be, since only churchmen with social insight and only socialists with a respect for the Christian faith met together" (*Der andere, der bist Du*, p. 282).

in economic life, and socialist ideology. The main speeches served, in turn, as a stimulus to the principal conference activity, an open discussion between the speakers and members of the audience. Evangelical-Socials like Jakob Schoell, August Springer, and DDP Staatspräsident Johannes Hieber made up one of the most faithful contingents, while Religious Socialists played a growing role as years went by. Among regular Social Democrats, in addition to a fair number of lesser functionaries, moderate leaders such as state party chief Wilhelm Keil, an old ally of Christoph Blumhardt, proved sympathetic. Former education minister Berthold Heymann shared the rostrum with Jakob Schoell at the second conference, while Anna Blos, wife of Württemberg's first president, spoke at the following session.

By middecade the Bietigheim Days were shedding some of their provincial flavor, drawing conferees from Baden and the Rhineland as well as from Berlin. Former Reich interior minister Wilhelm Sollmann, probably the most religiously inclined among national Social Democratic figures, took part in 1927 and again in 1929. Ironically, the very popularity of the conferences cost them some of their original intimacy, since swelling attendance forced Voelter to move proceedings from the parish hall to a much larger athletic facility. At the end of the decade, however, with the onset of economic catastrophe and the sudden emergence of National Socialism as a burning issue, the Bietigheim experiment lost its original momentum. The twelfth conference, in May 1931, proved the last of the republican era. A thirteenth did not take place until seventeen years later, in 1948, when two old veterans of Weimar's political wars, Theophil Wurm and Wilhelm Keil, reopened the dialogue under vastly altered circumstances.[106]

If the Bietigheim Days attracted little popular attention, that was not their intent.[107] They probably deserve to be seen as one

[106] An extended summary of the meetings is given in Voelter, "Bietigheimer Tag," pp. 43–90; documentation also in press clippings and notes, LKA D12/2.

[107] Cf. Voelter: "This meeting was a young, tender, and modest little plant. It was oriented not towards the wider masses but towards leading circles on both sides" (Voelter, "Bietigheimer Tag," p. 44).

of the seeds that flowered in Bad Godesberg in 1959, when Social Democrats invoked "Christian ethics, humanism, and classic philosophy" as the foundation stones of the party. While hardly typical of party leaders in the Weimar era, Wilhelm Sollmann nevertheless expressed more than an isolated opinion when he told assembled churchmen in 1929 that "much may divide us, but when I speak before an assembly of people who I sense are striving to express Christian convictions, I have a feeling of being in the presence of kindred spirits."[108] When the party press commented on the proceedings, it usually did so in politely favorable terms such as those used by the Heilbronn *Neckar-Echo*, which emphasized the "earnest and mutually recognized social concern" in evidence at the 1927 discussion of socialist ideology.[109] Gotthilf Schenkel summarized the view of most Religious Socialists when he praised Voelter for daring to "forge a course whose importance and rightness becomes clearer from year to year."[110]

The Bietigheim strategy contradicted an assumption shared by many churchmen that while good church folk could certainly attempt to persuade or convert socialists, true dialogue between the church and the party was both a contradiction in terms and dangerous from an apologetical standpoint. In agreeing to speak in 1921, Jakob Schoell remarked ruefully that he anticipated a flood of letters from outraged colleagues castigating him as a prelate and prominent church leader for the impropriety of sharing a platform with a socialist.[111] In 1929, when interest and participation were at a peak, an unnamed critic charged in the *Kirchlicher Anzeiger* that the conferences had become "more an advertisement for the socialist party line . . . than a convention to clarify major problems."[112]

Even among the active participants there were some who harbored doubts about the Bietigheim spirit. One of the speakers in

---

[108] Quoted in *SM*, Apr. 30, 1929.
[109] *Das Neckar-Echo*, Mar. 16, 1927.
[110] Schenkel to Voelter, n.d. [1929], LKA D12/2.
[111] Schoell to Voelter, June 2, 1921, LKA D12/2.
[112] "Kritisches zum Bietigheimer Tag," *KAfW* 38 (1929): 91.

1922, Mathilde Maisch, a Stuttgart lay woman deeply involved in the Volksbund and a variety of Evangelical-Social organizations, later wrote Voelter that "the socialist front knows exactly what it wants and *adheres* to it; *our* side, on the other hand, is a priori too intent upon understanding, upon the *desire* to understand at all costs, rather than upon keeping the truth from being obscured!" Elly Heuss-Knapp, the wife of Theodor Heuss and a conference speaker in 1928, confessed to a "guilty conscience" that Evangelical participants did not take a stronger stand in defense of the church, "which . . . in spite of everything is still a green meadow compared to the gray of socialism."[113]

The Bietigheim Days never fully overcame such reservations, nor did they bridge all the differences between participants. At the same time, however, the very objection that Evangelical positions may have been too feebly defended suggests the extent to which the experiment succeeded in its purpose of providing a neutral ground for dialogue. In this respect the Bietigheim discussions were fully consonant with the new pastoral outlook of the Weimar years; it could be argued that they represented its most vigorous expression. The impulse at Bietigheim, as in parish work, was to make contact with Social Democrats not as a way of winning workers to the state but as a first step in reconciling them to the church. Rather than preaching submission, Bietigheim sought to promote understanding. If this goal was a modest one, it nevertheless required a significant change in the church's political self-definition. Wilhelm Menn, a Düsseldorf pastor who was the Rhineland church's official "social pastor" and who spoke at Bietigheim along with Wilhelm Sollmann in 1927, stressed the significance of this shift. "One must dare to go beyond the [bounds of established church interests]," he wrote to Voelter, "and conditions are such that you in Württemberg can much more easily dare to do this than we."[114]

Perhaps Menn expected more from his colleagues along the

---

[113] Maisch to Voelter, Mar. 12, 1928, and Heuss-Knapp to Voelter, Mar. 19, 1928, both in LKA D12/2.

[114] Menn to Voelter, Mar. 28, 1927, LKA D12/2; cf. *EGBfS* 23 (1927): 129.

Neckar than they were able to provide. He was correct, however, in suggesting that behind the facade of institutional conservatism that the Württemberg church shared with the rest of mainstream German Protestantism, new stirrings of social engagement could be detected as pastors sought to rethink their understanding of the church's position in a pluralistic society. The very diversity of political responses after 1918 gives evidence of a struggle to discover and apply new norms for pastoral activity. On the one hand, confrontation with a neutral party state born out of revolution encouraged commitment to a hypertrophied version of traditional national-conservative Protestant values. On the other hand, emancipation of the Volkskirche from the restrictive security of the old monarchical order encouraged new clerical openings to the left. The politicized atmosphere of the republican era provided a spur to clerical activism, but it also encouraged quiescence in the name of a higher pastoral responsibility. The historic defensive alliance between Protestant orthodoxy and political conservatism found powerful expression during the Weimar period in the attitudes and pronouncements of many churchmen. Yet developments in Württemberg indicate that it would be misleading to portray the church simply as a bulwark of antimodernism. If the Volkskirche tradition set pastors against a system that appeared to deny or at least ignore their claims as the moral preceptors of society, it also brought a growing conviction that the church's integrity and vitality ultimately depended not upon favored legal status or a sympathetic state but upon its capacity to claim the masses and to mold them into a strong confessional community. If, as Wilhelm Menn was willing to argue, conditions in Württemberg encouraged creativity in this search for new openings to society, the modest achievements of the Weimar decade attest to the strong inhibitants with which even the best of clerical intentions still had to contend.

SEVEN

Toward National Renewal

THE LAST YEARS of the decade were a time of comparative equilibrium in Württemberg church life. No new controversy emerged to strain relations between theological factions. No issue became weighty enough to set pastors against either each other or their superiors. Relations with government officials were invariably correct, if not cordial. The work of the Volksbund and other church agencies suggested that churchmen were gradually coming to accept, if hardly to affirm, their ambiguous position between a state to which they retained no organic connection and a social order from which they sometimes felt threatened with extrusion.

But if an equilibrium of sorts developed, it remained in many ways a fragile one. Even in Württemberg's congenial cultural climate, the church confronted continuing tensions between institutional advantage and social marginality, between its pretensions as a moral nestor and its seemingly negligible significance in everyday life. The democratic gestures in church order since 1918 had done little to expand or revitalize the church's mass base. In the classroom, pastors could no longer count automatically on their old authority as *Respektspersonen*, while repeated admonitions to moral discipline and self-denial seemed to find little resonance among ordinary people preoccupied with both recurrent economic woes and the temptations of a burgeoning culture of leisure. To some extent churchmen gave evidence of accepting that in a pluralistic world, where an all-embracing spiritual community could be neither created by fiat nor maintained by compulsion, the Volkskirche ideal dictated a strategy of slow and patient pastoral action aimed at nurturing a "living parish" within the framework of a religiously heterogeneous so-

310

ciety. At the same time, however, the church's old role as pillar
of public order and authority continued to exert a strong if not
intensified residual attraction. The result was a contrast between, for example, the antimodern moralism of many official
pronouncements and the largely nonideological character of social service programs or between the antiliberal tenor of much
ecclesiastical symbolism and the concurrent pastoral emphasis
on accommodation and bridge-building. On the one hand were
censorship campaigns and the clerical nationalism of the church
press, on the other the Bietigheim conferences and the Volksbund's parish work.

It was against the background of these conflicting impulses
that the church confronted the multiple crises that eventually
gave rise to the Hitler dictatorship. Considerable scholarly energy has been expended on the subject of churchmen's attitudes
towards National Socialism, particularly the extent to which
Protestantism may have provided a sociological and ideological
catalyst for the Nazi rise to power. The themes are familiar
enough and probably do not require detailed rehearsal at this
point. Certainly there is abundant evidence that the nationalism
and social conservatism congenial to so many in the church made
them at least passively sympathetic to party appeals. Exploiting
the rhetoric of Protestant antirepublicanism, the Hitler movement claimed to offer the most effective vehicle for deliverance
from a moribund Weimar democracy equated with political impotence, social atomization, and moral relativism while also providing a powerful antidote to the dread disease of bolshevism. In
their desire to witness the restoration of the nation as a true
moral community, many churchmen were only too ready to
place a favorable construction on Nazi calls for national renewal.[1]

[1] See, e.g., Thalmann, *Protestantisme et nationalisme*; Nowak, " 'Entartete
Gegenwart' "; Nowak, *Kirche und Republik*, pp. 131–39 and passim; Richard V.
Pierard, "Why Did German Protestants Welcome Hitler?" *Fides et Historia* 10,
no. 2 (1978): 8–29; Hans Tiefel, "The German Lutheran Church and the Rise of
National Socialism," *Church History* 41 (1972): 326–37; Jonathan Wright, "The
German Protestant Church and the Nazi Party in the Period of the Seizure of

At the same time, however, the Nazi campaign against Weimar itself served to challenge churchmen's understanding of their place and purpose in society. The frequent dissonance between party rhetoric and party practice had troubling implications for Volkskirche ideology, with its dual emphasis on the state as exemplar of the national ethos and on the church as spiritual community encompassing and transcending societal divisions. Churchmen found themselves confronted with an incipient paradox: while Nazi promises of national renewal raised hopes of escape from the gray limbo of Weimar pluralism, the party's radical racism and the ruthlessness of its political tactics seemed designed to increase the very confusion and polarization from which the church hoped to provide a refuge. To the extent that loyal parishioners became caught up in the clash of political passions thus engendered, the existing equilibrium in church life threatened to disintegrate. In effect, therefore, Nazism could be seen as itself a radical manifestation of the pluralism against which the church sought to contend. How Württemberg churchmen responded to this dilemma is the central concern of what follows. While their reactions may not have been representative in every particular of German Protestantism as a whole, they did exemplify basic patterns of commitment established during the course of the republic, the full contours of which would not become evident until after the rubble of Hitler's Reich had been cleared away.

CHALLENGES TO THE VOLKSKIRCHE SYNTHESIS

In May 1929, at the age of seventy-two, church president Johannes Merz died after a brief illness. To succeed him the church assembly elected Theophil Wurm, who had joined the Oberkirchenrat in 1927 as prelate for Heilbronn. Once again the choice of a president occasioned controversy both inside and outside the church. Wurm's former association with the Bürgerpartei and

---

Power, 1932–3," in Derek Baker, ed., *Renaissance and Renewal in Christian History* (Oxford, 1977), pp. 393–418; and, more broadly, Tilgner, *Volksnomostheologie und Schöpfungsglaube.*

the fact that he had been the advance choice of Group I led some to dismiss him as a pawn of political and theological reaction. The *Schwäbische Tagwacht* labeled the election a "fateful step to the right" that belied the church's pretensions to be a true Volkskirche.[2] Many liberals in Group II expressed unhappiness that their own spokesman, Jakob Schoell, would once again be denied an honor for which his prominence in the church leadership should have recommended him. Despite vigorous campaigning on his behalf, Schoell's candidacy foundered, as it had in 1924, on the theological scruples of the pietist rank and file. After two inconclusive ballots, which failed to give him even a simple majority let alone the two-thirds required for election, Schoell withdrew as the choice of Group II in favor of Stuttgart pastor Max Mayer-List, a veteran Evangelical-Social activist and long-time editor of the Pfarrverein journal. This face-saving maneuver accomplished, enough of Schoell's followers broke ranks to assure Wurm of election.[3]

Wurm would later recall the first years of his presidency as a time when ecclesiastical conditions were "still relatively uncomplicated." To some extent this represented a tribute to Wurm's own skill as a church politician. Although long identified with Württemberg's pietist subculture, Wurm was no hidebound partisan where theological matters were concerned. In later years he would describe himself as intellectually beholden to liberal scholarship but emotionally rooted in the biblicistic tradition of pietist orthodoxy. Theological and tactical considerations alike encouraged Wurm to present himself as a bridge-builder between factions. When a seat on the Oberkirchenrat fell vacant a few months after his election, Wurm arranged to have the post offered to his recent challenger, Mayer-List. Jakob Schoell remained highly visible as Wurm's official deputy and principal spokesman on social and theological questions. By the end of 1929, Wurm had won over skeptics in the liberal camp without

[2] "Die Machtprobe der Konservativen in Württemberg," *ST*, June 15, 1929. Religious Socialists declared their confidence in Wurm's leadership; see statement of Lempp, Weitbrecht, and Stürner, *KAfW* 38 (1929): 114.

[3] Wurm, *Erinnerungen*, pp. 78–79.

unduly straining the loyalties of conservatives, and he could reasonably claim to personify the vital center of a church whose interests he stoutly defended, committed to a policy of evenhanded moderation and open to the best impulses from every quarter of the Protestant community.[4]

Among these impulses, however, were new theological and political commitments that revived earlier debates on the nature and purpose of the church and that, together with the looming crisis in Weimar polity, marked Wurm's election as a turning point in postwar church life. The most powerful theological current was that set in motion by the so-called dialectical theology associated with Karl Barth and his circle. Developed in Switzerland during the latter stages of World War I and counting the Blumhardt tradition in Württemberg among its contributing sources, the theology, first developed in Barth's epochal commentary on Romans (1919), exerted a pervasive and almost instantaneous influence on German churchmen. By the late 1920s, if not before, Barthianism could reasonably be called the party of theological movement in German church life. Particularly among younger theologians—those most deeply affected by the collapse of optimistic liberalism as a result of the war—Barth's ideas won widespread adherence, although older colleagues were attracted as well; Wurm, for example, found many of Barth's formulations "extraordinarily sympathetic."[5] Barth weighed and found wanting the prevailing liberal Protestant conception of man as moral personality and human society as immanent manifestation of the Kingdom of God. Against both liberal ethicism and an unreflective Volkskirche conservatism he counterposed an older Augustinian and Lutheran-Calvinist orthodoxy, emphasizing the radical antithesis between righteous God and sinful man and rejecting any equation of divine revelation with corrupted nature, of true biblical piety with smug bourgeois "religion."[6]

[4] Ibid., pp. 33, 82–84.

[5] Ibid., p. 85.

[6] Scholder, *Die Kirchen und das Dritte Reich*, 1:46–64, provides a good brief summary of Barth's impact.

In purely theological terms, Barth's impact on Württemberg churchmen was scarcely revolutionary. The prevailing theological atmosphere, among churchmen at large as well as within the Tübingen theological faculty, was unquestionably congenial to many of the chief emphases of neoorthodoxy. Homiletics professor Karl Fezer, for example, perhaps the fastest-rising star among Tübingen theologians after 1930, was a convinced Barthian (and was trusted enough by conservatives to ensure his election to the church assembly in 1931 as a member of Group I).[7] What Barth's thought brought was not so much a theological challenge as a potentially unsettling critique of the Württemberg church's sturdily institutional version of the Volkskirche project. On the question of the church, as indeed on many other questions, Barthians by no means formed a united front. Most, however, shared a conviction that to equate the church with an institutional structure or to define its role primarily as that of social conscience-pricker and spiritual omnium-gatherum was to ignore or distort the radical emphasis of the Christian gospel.

This sense of tension between institutional and confessional imperatives, between a visible church structure and an invisible "church of faith," found its strongest expression in what later became the Church-Theological Society (Kirchlich-Theologische Sozietät), a study group of young Württemberg pastors around Hermann Diem and Paul Schempp, including the sometime Religious Socialist Ernst Bizer, organized during the early 1930s. "We are discovering," the group declared in an early statement, "that a basic deficiency [of the existing church system] is that we no longer know how to tell ourselves and our age

---

[7] On Fezer, see Leonore Siegele-Wenschkewitz, "Karl Fezer und die Deutsche Christen," in Eberhard Jüngel, ed., *Tübinger Theologie im 20. Jahrhundert*, Zeitschrift für Theologie und Kirche, Beiheft 4 (Tübingen, 1978), pp. 35–37. For years the moderate conservatism of Tübingen theologians such as Adolf Schlatter had attracted students seeking alternatives to the liberal Protestantism dominant in many northern universities. Thanks to this heavy influx of "outsiders," Tübingen regularly boasted the largest enrollment of any German theological faculty.

315

in binding terms what the gospel is."[8] If leaders of the Volksdienst, the natural heirs of pietist quiescence, were looking outward to the transformation of politics and society, some Barthians were turning inward in search of a more uncompromising
commitment to gospel and confession. The result was an often
deeply critical attitude towards the existing church and its leadership, a reserve not uncolored by feelings of generational distance from the "old men" who dominated the Oberkirchenrat.
It is not surprising that the most radical of these critics, notably
Diem and Schempp, were suspected of harboring free church
tendencies. For them the Volkskirche idea no longer functioned
as a self-evident starting point for thinking about the church's
task or its place in society; the Volkskirche as actually constituted seemed at best problematic, at worst a positive hindrance
to the unfolding of faith.

This sense of the church as problematic was not confined to
the small Diem circle. As social and economic tensions mounted
after 1929, the perceived gap between pastors and parishioners
again became a subject of debate among the clergy at large. Soar-
ing unemployment made some pastors acutely sensitive to their
image as comfortably paid bureaucrats immune from the material cares of the layman. As one of them complained in the worst
days of the depression: "We take too little nourishment from
the Word; we concern ourselves far too much with finances."[9]
Writing in *Das Evangelische Deutschland*, Jakob Schoell called
upon colleagues to face the "bitter fact" that economic troubles
required all public institutions, not least of all the churches, to
set an example of thrift and self-denial.[10] When he presented his

---

[8] Quoted in Theodor Dipper, *Die Evangelische Bekenntnisgemeinschaft in
Württemberg, 1933–1945* (Göttingen, 1969), p. 17. On the society's attitudes
toward the church and its leadership, see also Ernst Bizer, *Ein Kampf um die
Kirche: Der "Fall Schempp" nach den Akten erzählt* (Tübingen, 1965), pp. 1–
13; cf. Schäfer, ed., *Landeskirche und Nationalsozialismus*, 5:xii–xiii.

[9] Grüner to Buck, May 4, 1932, LKA C4/4; cf. Oscar Planck, "Wege der Volkskirche zum Volk," *Die Volkskirche* 1 (July 15, 1928): 2–3.

[10] Jakob Schoell, "Bittere Tatsachen," *Das Evangelische Deutschland* 6
(1929): 77–79.

first budget to the church assembly, Theophil Wurm struck an uncharacteristically defensive note. "The church today is [often] viewed as a problem," he acknowledged, but he denied that it was "swimming in money" at a time of extreme public and private austerity.[11]

A vocal minority of pastors, most of them young, argued for more than simply a rhetoric of self-denial. During Weimar's economic Indian summer, as we have seen, the Württemberg clergy had allied with other civil servants to lobby for improvements in salaries and pension benefits. Now, some insisted, pastors must confess to the "sin of income," break their ties with civil service interest groups, and accept reduced salaries as a token of identification with hard-pressed parishioners.[12] The generational character of this agenda is suggested by a remark of Pfarrverein chairman Schnaufer, born in 1874, who suggested during a meeting of the association's officers in 1930 that "the young people should first wait and learn more" before taking or proposing action.[13] Ernst Lachenmann, a Stuttgart pastor born in 1897, spoke for many of these "young people" in a letter to Schnaufer the following year. Calling for the Pfarrverein's withdrawal from the National Association of Higher Civil Servants, Lachenmann declared, "It weighs painfully on me that on the one hand we preach a willingness to sacrifice and a sense of community and on the other hand strengthen by our affiliation an 'interest-group crowd' whose [response to economic retrenchment] has been nothing less than ominous and has had a corresponding effect [on the public]." Lachenmann later transmitted to the Oberkirchenrat a postcard from an anonymous parishioner that appeared to underscore his contention:

> i [sic] don't know you, but you strike me as a well-paid and well-fed man that can speak or write well, but what have you accomplished? . . . The clergy ought to set a good ex-

[11] 1. LKT, *Verhandlungen* (1930), pp. 631–44.

[12] "Gehaltsünde," *Christlicher Volksdienst* 7, no. 35 (Aug. 9, 1931).

[13] EPW, Vertrauensmännerversammlung, Apr. 22, 1930, Protokoll, LKA D/EPW 22/II.

ample for a change and not wait until salaries are reduced officially[.] . . . are you a pastor just to earn money or for salvation's sake!![14]

Minor in itself, the issue of salaries nevertheless provided a symptom of more deep-seated problems. For most of the Weimar period, we have suggested, church leaders had sought to subordinate political action to the higher criterion of pastoral duty. After 1929 the always tenuous consensus on this point began to disintegrate. Under the compound pressures of theological critique and societal crisis, the pastoral role itself threatened to become politicized. Most pastors no doubt still agreed with Hans Voelter when he reiterated the familiar argument that the church could not deny its internal diversity by sanctifying a single social or political perspective. Yet a growing minority was also beginning to insist that the classic Volkskirche notion of neutrality in the name of a "consciousness of spiritual unity" was in fact an illusion and that the church could only maintain integrity in the face of the growing crisis if churchmen were willing to take a clear political stand.[15]

Such attitudes were evident among many supporters of the Volksdienst. They were strongest and most explicit, however, among the Religious Socialists, whose influence and activism reached a peak in the period between 1929 and 1931. The controversies surrounding this movement deserve to be reviewed in some detail. While subsequently overshadowed by the issues of the Church Struggle—Wurm's memoirs, for example, are strangely silent on the subject—internal battles over Religious Socialism during this period largely determined the framework within which the Württemberg church would eventually grapple with the Hitler movement and its promise of a national moral and patriotic renewal.

Although hardly a mass organization, the Württemberg Re-

[14] Lachenmann to Schnaufer, Nov. 6, 1931, LKA D/EPW 31; "Viele Arme" to Lachenmann, n.d. [1932], LKA D/26,8.

[15] "Hat die Kirche die Möglichkeit, die sozialen und wirtschaftlichen Verhältnisse zu beeinflüssen?" *Die Volkskirche* 2 (Sept. 15, 1929): 68–71.

ligious Socialist group had by 1929 expanded considerably from its modest beginnings. Total membership can only be roughly estimated, but it was at least several hundred and may well have been considerably higher; local chapters flourished in virtually all urban centers.[16] While lay persons made up most of the rank and file, clergy continued to exercise a dominant leadership influence. In addition to founding members such as Gotthilf Schenkel, Eberhard Lempp, Paul Weitbrecht, and Reinhold Planck, a new postwar generation of vicars and theology students helped to swell the rolls. The most notable of the new recruits was probably Ernst Bizer, later professor of church history in Bonn, who was assigned as a vicar to the Religious Socialist stronghold of Göppingen in 1930. Activist pastors maintained a level of visibility that belied their numbers. Schenkel, chairman of the Württemberg organization, spoke at nearly forty public gatherings during 1929 alone. Where local chapters were strong, as in Göppingen or Heilbronn and around Stuttgart, liturgical celebrations of May Day briefly became an annual tradition. Bad Boll, the shrine of the Blumhardts, hosted yearly conferences of Religious Socialists and fellow travelers, culminating in a week-long Easter retreat in 1932 that attracted participants from throughout Germany and from neighboring Switzerland.[17]

While Religious Socialists pursued their program as a token of the church's friendly intentions towards the working classes, many of their undertakings, and the May Day services in particular, had the all but literal effect of red flags waved in the faces of active church members. This was especially true in the worsening economic and political climate of the last Weimar years. If conservatives had been inclined from the beginning to regard Religious Socialists as witting or unwitting tools of secular party interests, they found abundant justification for such suspicions

[16] Membership estimates for Germany in 1930 range from 2,000 to as high as 30,000; the Religious Socialist *Sonntagsblatt des arbeitenden Volkes* reached a circulation of 17,000 in 1931. See Balzer, *Klassengegensätze in der Kirche*, p. 54.

[17] Göppingen, Pfarrbericht 1930, OKR/AR OA/PfB; *ST*, May 21, 1930; *KAfW* 39 (1930): 76, 40 (1931): 84–85, 157–58, 41 (1932): 86; and undated materials in OKR/AR Gen. 151b.

in the increasingly outspoken radicalism of a few of the movement's most prominent national figures. Of these activists on the left, none had a more telling impact on Württemberg than Erwin Eckert, the moving spirit behind a large and active Religious Socialist group in neighboring Baden. Nominally a parish pastor, first in Meersburg on Lake Constance and later in Mannheim, Eckert in fact functioned as a circuit rider for his own flamboyant brand of socialism, a gospel couched in rhetoric more familiar to the factory floor than the chancel. Thanks to his frequent forays across the border as pastor and public agitator, Eckert probably enjoyed wider recognition in Württemberg than did any local pastor active in the movement. Eckert's personality and opinions allowed little room for neutrality. One sometime Religious Socialist found him "bull-headed," "dogmatic," and "incapable of listening to reason."[18] Paul Pfleiderer, a pastor in Tailfingen, expressed the view of many Württemberg churchmen when he suggested that Eckert's Religious Socialism "triply underscored the 'socialist' and put 'religious' in double quotes."[19] Whether it was a product of radical idealism or simple demagogic instincts, Eckert's insistence on the centrality of class struggle led to a progressive estrangement not only from church authorities in his native Baden, where he came under official censure in 1929, but also from moderate Social Democrats. By 1931, convinced by the deepening depression that the final crisis of capitalism was at hand, he was applying for membership in the German Communist party, an act that led to his outright dismissal from church service. Shortly thereafter he was once again in Württemberg, speaking to a crowd of nearly ten thousand in Stuttgart, where he drew acid contrasts between "the godless KPD, which accepted me as a pastor the way I am, supported me, and sought to understand me," and a church "that cannot support me as a Communist because it is Christian and longsuffering."[20]

[18] Dehn, *Alte Zeit, vorige Jahre*, p. 223; Balzer, *Klassengegensätze in der Kirche*, paints a much more sympathetic portrait.

[19] Pfleiderer to OKR, Mar. 22, 1928, OKR/AR Gen. 151b.

[20] OKR Mannheim, judgment of censure, June 21, 1929, copy in OKR/AR Gen.

Shortly before censure proceedings against Eckert began in Baden in 1929, Theophil Wurm had expressed the opinion that the Württemberg clergy, Religious Socialists included, would doubtless be "more repelled than attracted" by what to Wurm was Eckert's "sheer, unrestrained demagoguery."[21] In this he was completely correct. Both theoretically and in practice, Württemberg members of the movement held to a different definition of the Religious Socialist task. The tension was already visible at the Mannheim congress of Religious Socialists in 1928. Württemberg delegates, represented by Eberhard Lempp and Leonbronn pastor Paul Stürner, argued for an essentially theological understanding of socialism and its possibilities, taking traditional Protestant doctrine as the starting point for a "religious" socialism and affirming a conception of the church compatible with Volkskirche ideals. For Eckert, in contrast, the primary aim was not church renewal but furtherance of the proletarian cause. The church, he declared in another of his frequent Stuttgart speeches, was "by no means a community of saints but rather an instrument of power within the political struggle." That struggle, and not social harmony, must be the lodestar of the Religious Socialist cause. If Württemberg colleagues like Lempp turned to Religious Socialism as a means of animating the old Volkskirche ideal, Eckert proposed simply to abolish it. Proletarian solidarity, not spiritual unity, was to be paramount.[22]

The rift grew deeper among the more than two hundred delegates who attended the fifth national congress of the movement, held in Stuttgart during the summer of 1930. For the host Württemberg group, the Stuttgart congress represented an opportunity to enhance their image among church leaders and per-

---

151b. "Bericht über die Eckert-Versammlung am Samstag, 10. Oktober 1931 in der Stadthalle in Stuttgart," typescript, OKR/AR Gen. 151b. On Eckert, see also Balzer, *Klassengegensätze in der Kirche*, and Breipohl, *Religiöser Sozialismus*.

[21] Wurm to OKR, Jan. 22, 1929; OKR/AR Gen. 151b.

[22] Report on Mannheim congress in OKR/AR Gen. 151b; "Was wollen die religiösen Sozialisten?" typescript report (Hilzinger) to OKR, Apr. 17, 1930, OKR/AR Gen. 151b.

haps to win new supporters from among friendly but hitherto uncommitted clergy, particularly on the social-liberal front. Eckert, for his part, had no patience with such strategies. Already estranged from his nominal superiors in Baden, he used his prerogative as chairman to prevent any concessions to the local ecclesiastical establishment, pointedly ignoring the presence of Oberkirchenrat member Adolf Schaal as an unofficial representative of the Württemberg church leadership and controlling the agenda to limit the visibility of spokesmen for conciliation. The natural result was a hardening of fronts both within the movement itself and between Religious Socialism and the clerical majority. Stuttgart's Ernst Lachenmann was probably referring to himself when he wrote that the proceedings as a whole left a negative impression on outside observers, "even those who had reckoned with the possibility of being induced, under the impact of the congress, to join." For Lachenmann, at least, the heavily political tone encouraged by Eckert, coupled with what Lachenmann perceived to be a shallowness of theology—hardly a commendable feature among conservative Württemberg Protestants—militated against further support. However urgent the need for new responses to current dilemmas, Lachenmann concluded, "this one will not do!"[23]

There can be no doubt that Erwin Eckert's posturing reinforced prior dispositions to dismiss Religious Socialism as a tool of party politics and as a program to politicize church life. Theophil Wurm expressed this consensus in an address to the church assembly in 1930. His objection to the Eckert line revealed not only the perdurance of conservative instincts but also a sense of the need to establish a new foundation for church life independent of the old monarchical synthesis. "Have we given up the equation 'Christian equals conservative,'" he asked, "only to arrive at the equation 'Christian equals socialist'? Have we freed ourselves from the formula 'for throne and altar' . . . only to

[23] Adolf Schaal, note on Rais to Wurm, Oct. 17, 1932, OKR/AR Gen. 151b; Ernst Lachenmann, "Ein Nachwort zum V. Kongress der 'Religiösen Sozialisten,'" *KAfW* 39 (1930): 153–54; cf. *KAfW* 40 (1931): 44–45, 60–61.

take up the formula 'for party and pulpit'?"[24] Despite grave reservations, however, neither Wurm nor other high church officials proposed to declare Religious Socialism off limits to pastors. Indeed, at about the same time that he made his statement to the assembly, Wurm also met privately with Religious Socialist clergy and reaffirmed the movement's right to a place within the Protestant community. While they had few expectations of success, church leaders remained reluctant to reject out of hand any potential bridge-building effort within the Protestant ambit, however marginal its status.[25]

The resulting policy was perhaps best expressed by Pfarrverein chairman Schnaufer, who declared during a meeting of the association's officers in 1930 that "if we have people who want to get closer to the worker, well and good. But [Religious Socialist] pastors should not transgress against their [conservative] congregations and make fools out of themselves."[26] It was a policy that satisfied virtually no one. The political and theological right protested against any toleration of Religious Socialist ideas among the clergy. As early as the spring of 1929, shortly before Wurm became church president, a press campaign in Waiblingen demanded that church officials take action against Religious Socialist pastor Reinhold Planck, who had recently addressed a local meeting, for allowing a pamphlet by Eckert to be circulated and thus "permitting the church which pays him and to whose service he is pledged" to be "reviled" by Eckert's attacks.[27] The following year, rightists in Heilbronn unleashed a similar broadside against Planck's younger colleague Paul Weitbrecht. According to a published statement, copies of which circulated among

[24] 1. LKT, *Verhandlungen* (1930), p. 636.

[25] Gotthilf Schenkel, "Landestagung, Verband der religiösen Sozialisten, Stuttgart," *ST*, May 21, 1930.

[26] EPW, Vertrauensmännerversammlung, Apr. 22, 1930, Protokoll, LKA D/EPW 22/II; cf. *KAfW* 39 (1930): 60–61, 98–99.

[27] *Remstalbote* (Waiblingen), Apr. 2, 3, 4, 5, 6, 1929; *ST*, Apr. 6, 1929; Planck to Buck, Apr. 5, 1929; Planck to OKR, Apr. 6, 1929; Buck to OKR, Apr. 10, 1929; and OKR to Buck, Apr. 16, 1929; all in OKR/AR Gen. 151b. Planck insisted that the pamphlet in question had been distributed against his will and without his assistance; the Oberkirchenrat took no action in the matter.

members of the Oberkirchenrat, "a pastor can no more belong to the Social Democratic party . . . than someone can be a tavern owner and at the same time head of the temperance society." Weitbrecht, the statement continued, was a "model of what a pastor should do to alienate Christians from the church."[28]

Religious Socialists complained in turn of the apathy and administrative obstacles with which they saw themselves having to contend. The use of church facilities provided a frequent source of controversy. In a few strongholds of the movement, notably Göppingen, churches and parish halls were readily available, special services such as those on May Day encountered little opposition, and other activities found support or at least benevolent neturality in many quarters. More often, however, parish councils and pastors outside the movement turned a deaf ear to requests for assistance. This was true even in the Stuttgart area, where Religious Socialists constituted a significant and often vocal minority.[29]

The stance of the Oberkirchenrat was similarly ambiguous. Responding to an appeal from the Stuttgart Religious Socialist chapter, the Oberkirchenrat appointed a young member of the group, Karl Honecker, as vicar to the veteran liberal Albert Esenwein in the working-class Stuttgart district of Gaisburg. Elsewhere, however, even though a parish council specifically requested that a vacancy be filled by a young Religious Socialist, the Oberkirchenrat chose not to act. Yet another young Religious Socialist vicar, Gerhard Kraft, welcomed an appointment to Ebersbach, an industrial satellite of Göppingen, only to find himself transferred almost immediately to a farming village. In a private letter to Wurm, Kraft protested that his transfer would destroy any ties between workers and the church that he might have established in Ebersbach and that a rural post would render

[28] "Kann ein Christ Sozialdemokrat sein?" *Heilbronner Beobachter*, Mar. 22, 1930, copy in LKA D1/49,1.

[29] Paul Weitbrecht, report on Pforzheim conference, Apr. 23–26, 1930, in *KAfW* 39 (1930): 75–76; Wurm to Kühlewein (Karlsruhe), Nov. 22, 1930, OKR/AR Gen. 151b.

him "utterly useless for the special tasks that we Religious Socialists have."[30]

Religious Socialist activism reached a peak in 1931, when the
Württemberg group mounted a challenge to the entrenched theological groups in the March church assembly elections. The
model was once again Baden, where a bloc of eight Religious Socialists had occupied seats in the church assembly since 1926.
Württemberg Religious Socialists presented candidates in
thirty-two of the forty-nine electoral districts, and their efforts
made the election the most actively contested in many areas
since 1919. If the basic social mix of their slate, dominated by
pastors and schoolmasters, was not unlike that of the traditional
groups, the Religious Socialists nevertheless made clear efforts
to broaden the occupational boundaries of participation. Candidates included several skilled and unskilled laborers, including
railwaymen, shop foremen, and mechanics, as well as six white-
collar workers and four artisans.[31]

If Religious Socialists hoped to mobilize working-class parishioners for their cause, the election results proved a grave disappointment. Despite often hectic campaigning and the encouragement of the Social Democratic press, the masses refused to be
moved. In terms of total votes cast, the 1931 election actually
represented a marginal decline in participation from 1925. This
could be partially explained by the fact that in nearly one-fourth
of the electoral districts only a single candidate presented himself, usually because of informal prior agreements between the
two main theological groups. In such cases, according to the revised church election laws, no balloting need take place. Where
seats were contested, the level of participation seems to have
been almost identical to that in 1925. Of some 297,000 votes

[30] Bund der Religiösen Sozialisten, Ortsgruppe Stuttgart to OKR, Dec. 4, 1929,
and Müller to Volk (Eisenach), Mar. 14, 1932, both in OKR/AR Gen. 151b. Kraft
to Wurm, Dec. 12, 1929, LKA D1/28,2.

[31] "Ergebnisse der Wahlen zum Landeskirchentag vom 8. März 1931," 2. LKT,
Verhandlungen (1931), Beilageband, pp. 11–16. Gotthilf Schenkel was the most
tireless of the Religious Socialist candidates, presenting himself for election in no
fewer than six districts.

cast, Religious Socialist candidates were able to claim 37,000, or about 12 percent of the total. In no district, however, did they achieve a majority or even a plurality. Their best results came in the traditional Evangelical-Social stronghold of Heilbronn, where they captured a full third of the votes, and in Ludwigsburg, where they won nearly one vote in four. In other areas with active Religious Socialist chapters, notably Stuttgart, Göppingen, and Reutlingen, the results ranged around 15 percent, scarcely better than the statewide average.[32]

Perhaps predictably, the principal beneficiaries of the Religious Socialist challenge were probably candidates representing Group I. Given the apparent lack of increased participation in working-class districts, it seems likely that Religious Socialists drew most of their support from voters who would otherwise have supported a candidate of Group II. In some districts, moreover, the mere presence of a Religious Socialist candidate probably served to bring out conservatives who might otherwise have neglected to vote at all. This may have happened in Göppingen, for example, where a candidate of Group I narrowly gained a seat formerly claimed by Group II; in the Göppingen district, the combined votes for the liberal and Religious Socialist candidates far outstripped the total for Group I.[33] A similar result obtained in Reutlingen, while in Urach and in the Stuttgart suburbs the combination of Group II and Religious Socialist votes would have sufficed to deny the conservative group seats they had narrowly won in 1925.

In most cases, to be sure, Religious Socialist candidacies amounted to no more than a token gesture. If breakthroughs occurred, they came not in the church assembly elections but in the concurrent elections for members of parish councils. In these elections, unlike those for the assembly, Religious Socialists did not always have to mount a separate slate of candidates, nor was the requirement of a plurality as significant an obstacle. By ne-

[32] Ibid.

[33] Ibid.; the result was: Gruppe I 4,022, Gruppe II 3,979, Rel. Soz. 1,476. See also the analysis by Göppingen Dekan Otto Stahl, Göppingen Kirchenbezirkstag, Nov. 30, 1931, Protokoll, DA Göppingen 142.

gotiating for places on a common list of nominees, like the *Volksdienstler* before them, Religious Socialists succeeded in gaining representation on parish councils in most of their strongholds, particularly around Heilbronn, Stuttgart, Reutlingen, and of course Göppingen. Since no compilations by group exist, the number of seats won in this manner can only be estimated, though the total certainly remained quite modest. An occupational tabulation of parish council members in the Göppingen area, for example, listed eighty-six farmers and thirty-two artisans, most of them probably from the pietist hinterlands, with thirty-three listed as "worker," or about 15 percent of the total. It seems fair to assume that many—though hardly all—of those in the latter category were either active Religious Socialists or at least sympathetic to the cause.[34]

The major casualty of intrachurch developments after 1929 was the liberal Volkskirche outlook. Under pressure from Religious Socialism on one side and Barthian neoorthodoxy on the other, liberals emerged from the 1931 elections a distinct and declining minority. Of fifty-eight elected delegates to the new assembly, thirty-seven adhered informally to the conservative Group I, while Group II dropped from its previous twenty-four members to sixteen. Only five of the latter were pastors—a symptom, perhaps, of at least a modest theological migration toward neoorthodoxy among Württemberg clergy. In this context it may also be worth noting that the number of self-described independents in the assembly increased to five, all of them present or former churchmen.[35]

The new assembly convened under a cloud of criticism. Reporting on the election, the *Schwäbische Tagwacht* charged that the assembly merely confirmed the reality of a "purely bourgeois and consciously antisocialist church, which may *put up with* socialist members as taxpayers and churchgoers but not as

---

[34] Göppingen Kirchenbezirkstag, Nov. 30, 1931, Protokoll, DA Göppingen 142. Another 64 persons, about 30% of the total sample, were not classified; these presumably included teachers, professionals, and civil servants.

[35] Among these was former Böblingen pastor Albrecht Schäfer, who had stood unsuccessfully as a candidate for Group I in 1925.

participants in its governance and administration."[36] Social Democrats were not alone, however, in arguing that for a group supported by one voting parishoner in eight to go unrepresented in high church councils was unjust. Heilbronn pastor Ernst Drück, one of the five nonaligned members elected in March, introduced a resolution calling upon the assembly to award one of the discretionary seats provided for in church election laws to a Religious Socialist. Drück's proposal triggered a flurry of private bargaining, the leaders of the two established groups having already agreed on a joint list of nominees for these seats. By a vote of thirty-five to twenty-three the assembly turned down the motion, rejecting any explicit gesture to the left. Having been blocked from immediate participation, the Religious Socialists next formally petitioned the assembly for yet another revision in election procedures to provide for some form of proportional representation. Support for this proposal came from representatives of the districts where Religious Socialism was strongest, including Göppingen, Heilbronn, and Öhringen; a number of local Volksbund chapters also supported the measure. Since the church had become accustomed to two theological groupings, Göppingen Dekan Otto Stahl suggested, there was no reason why it could not learn to accommodate a third.[37]

What is noteworthy about this argument is its frank acknowledgment of the church as a pluralistic community. While the reigning Volkskirche ideal also recognized diversity, its adherents sought to ignore or to transcend social complexities in the name of a higher spiritual unity. The Religious Socialist petition, finding fault with a system "allegedly based solely on personality but behind which in actuality strong group antagonisms lurk," underscored the intrinsic weakness of the old synthesis.[38]

[36] "Kritik an diesen Kirchenwahlen," *ST*, Mar. 12, 1931; italics in original.

[37] 2. LKT, *Verhandlungen* (1931), pp. 11–12, (1932), p. 130. Bund der religiösen Sozialisten Württembergs to LKT, Apr. 29, 1931, copy in OKR/AR Gen. 151b; "Übersichtsbericht des Dekans," Göppingen Bezirkskirchentag, Nov. 30, 1931, DA Göppingen 142.

[38] Bund der religiösen Sozialisten Württembergs to LKT, Apr. 29, 1931, OKR/AR Gen. 151b.

Not only was the ideal of unity far removed from contemporary reality, but the church had so far demonstrated little success in mobilizing a wider constituency through the agency of what Theophil Wurm in 1930 called "a [pastoral] office that, standing above economic conflicts and mundane questions, proclaims the great basic truths of the gospel as they relate to the present and its needs."[39] On this score, as election statistics indicated, Religious Socialism showed little greater promise. For the moment, in any event, the arguments over representation remained unresolved. By the middle of 1931, the political sea change created by the Nazi success of the previous September, when the party vaulted out of insignificance to capture 108 seats in the Reichstag, was beginning to reflect itself in the atmosphere of Württemberg church life. During the next six months the Hitler movement all but totally eclipsed Religious Socialism as the focus of debates over the nature and future of the Volkskirche.

Unlike Religious Socialism, which despite the Eckert faction had grown up largely independent of the regular SPD, National Socialism owed its growing prominence in church affairs almost exclusively to the party's own efforts. Nazi mobilizers in Württemberg cultivated a stridently Protestant image, hoping no doubt to exploit confessional differences in an area where, despite Catholics' minority status in the population, the Catholic Center functioned as the de facto government party. Party rhetoric, with its incessant calls for national renewal and its infinitely malleable appeals to a "positive Christianity," was finely calculated to strike a responsive chord among church folk, including church officials tempted to seek parallels with the *annus mirabilis* of 1914, when a wave of patriotic fervor had sent the masses crowding back into church pews. To Lutheran conservatives the Nazi party offered promises of a reinvigorated Christian-German ethos purged of alien Roman and ecumenical influences. To pietists it offered ringing endorsements of traditional morality and a healthy family life. Its anti-Semitic catch phrases parroted the customary fare of the parish press; so too did most of its so-

[39] 1. LKT, *Verhandlungen* (1930), p. 632.

cial positions. To all factions it promised a healthy nationalism infused with the best influences of religion, a movement for renewal whose positive Christianity avoided the pitfalls of a sectarian "politics of faith" in the manner of the Volksdienst no less than the uneasy fusion of spirituality and materialism in the Religious Socialist mode.

Despite intense propaganda efforts, the number of recruits among the Württemberg clergy remained negligible; one estimate puts the figure at no more than fifty in the early days of the Third Reich.[40] Nor did these clerical brownshirts share a common theological orientation or conception of political priorities. The divisions that had existed in the extreme national-conservative camp throughout the Weimar period persisted into the 1930s. A few pastors, notably pioneer folkish radicals like Wilhelm Rehm and Friedrich Ettwein, grounded their commitment in a genuinely racist position; ultimately they were prepared to regard the Volk as a source of divine revelation that transfigured if it did not totally supercede traditional Christian doctrine. Most sympathizers, however, probably leaned more toward a folkish-Christian synthesis of the sort advanced by such nationally known theologians as Emanuel Hirsch or Paul Althaus and characterized by a conviction of the inherent affinity between Christian values and the German folk ethos as well as by an insistence that great events of recent history—for example, the defeat of 1918 and its consequences—represented specific manifestations of divine judgment and redemption in the life of the nation as corporate moral personality.

Both of these general orientations found organizational expression in Württemberg, with the boundaries between groups overlapping to some extent and frequently shifting as a result of personal or principial conflicts. On what might be called the ecumenical wing could be found those who inclined toward the more moderate version of folkish theology, many of whom regarded National Socialism, at least in theory, as only one among a number of possible means to a broader restorationist

[40] Fischer, "Geschichte des Kirchenkampfes," 1:170.

end. This in essence was the position taken by the self-styled Christian-German Movement, Southern Branch, established in Stuttgart in September 1931 by Otto Lohss, a former missionary to China now serving as an evangelist under the auspices of the pietist-dominated Basel Mission. Like their northern counterparts, led by Mecklenburg bishop Heinrich Rendtorff, Lohss and his followers envisioned their organization as a kind of ecclesiastical Harzburg Front, a common vehicle for all those seeking national and religious renewal along folkish lines. Anti-Catholic and stridently anti-Communist, Lohss's organization described itself, somewhat awkwardly, as "nonpartisan in the sense of a political coresponsibility for the entire patriotic freedom movement." Its avowed aim was to realize the folkish implications of the Volkskirche ideal. To this end, in good antimodernist fashion, it called for the "organic reconstruction of a popular and constitutional state in which the devastating and inflammatory class struggle is superseded through recognition of a sacred, God-given community of blood and birth."[41]

While Lohss sought to distinguish his new political evangelism from the more traditional variety sponsored by the Basel Mission, he never strayed far from the pietist subculture that provided him with his natural constituency. Symptomatically, he regarded the Volksdienst as his major source of competition. There was some sense in this, since both groups drew political conclusions to some extent from what they regarded as the judgment of God on the German nation manifested in defeat and postwar difficulties. In place of the vague republicanism of the Volksdienst, however, Lohss offered a correspondingly vague pastiche of antirepublican moralisms adapted for the most part from the conventional rhetoric of the Protestant conservative front. If he appeared to accept racialist formulations as a means to the end of a renewed Christian *Volksgemeinschaft*, he did so more in the sense of an older hypernationalist rhetoric than in

---

[41] Rundschreiben, Nov. 1931 (copy), LKA D1/29,2; "Leitsätze, 'Christlich-Deutsche Bewegung' " (copy), with Lohss to Wurm, Dec. 10, 1931, LKA D1/29,2. These and many of the documents subsequently cited can be found in Schäfer, ed., *Landeskirche und Nationalsozialismus*, 1:73ff.

solidarity with apostles of a purely Aryan faith. By the end of 1931, his summons to patriotic commitment had earned a following of perhaps a hundred active members, most of them apparently Protestant laymen in Württemberg.[42]

Over time, to be sure, Lohss abandoned his original pretense to ecumenicity. Convinced like many on the right that Hitler offered the only alternative to a Communist revolution, he moved steadily towards exclusive identification with National Socialism. Ironically enough, he thereby put himself at odds with the Rendtorff group in the north, which was simultaneously struggling to break free of a narrowly Nazi course. Still, the Christian-German group continued to emphasize its Christian orientation, and single-minded commitment to the Nazi cause was not a prerequisite for membership. More sectarian racialist impulses found expression in the Württemberg League of National Socialist Pastors (NS-Pfarrerbund), a creation of Wilhelm Rehm and Friedrich Ettwein. Unlike Lohss's group, the NS-Pfarrerbund preached a gospel of national revolution exclusively through the party of Hitler. Moreover, Rehm and Ettwein went beyond Lohss in their willingness to recast the church's message in purely Aryan terms. If the latter argued for a natural affinity between national and religious renewal, the former saw the Nazi movement itself as the norm for renewal on both fronts; the church was called upon to enlist in the cause, not seek to define its values. Embracing the führer ideology with characteristically ruthless enthusiasm, the NS-Pfarrerbund presented itself not as a fraternal association or a fledgling mass movement but as a disciplined cadre committed to the internal conquest of ecclesiastical structures. Within the group, Rehm and Ettwein brooked little challenge to their leadership. In dealings with other churchmen, moreover, they displayed a growing disregard for the conventional patterns of ecclesiastical deference that linked pastors, prelates, and Dekans. This faint aura of insubordination, together with the NS-Pfarrerbund's uncompromising

[42] Lohss to Wurm, Dec. 10, 1931, LKA D1/29,2; cf. Lehmann, *Pietismus*, pp. 317–19.

aims, may help explain why Rehm and Ettwein attracted only a small number of willing followers. As late as October 1932 a membership conclave in Stuttgart drew a mere fifteen persons.[43]

By the time of the *Machtergreifung*, to be sure, the number of sympathizers had grown considerably. A list presumably drawn up in early 1933 includes contact persons in forty-two of forty-nine Württemberg districts. The collective profile of these *Vertrauensmänner* conforms to the familiar image of National Socialism as preeminently a youth movement. Of the forty-two churchmen listed, thirty-six were under fifty years of age; nineteen, or nearly half, were in their thirties, seven having been born since 1900. The Front Generation was well represented: at least twenty-four had seen military service during the Great War, of whom five earned officers' commissions, four were decorated or mustered out because of wounds, and two were interned in prisoner-of-war camps. As their comparative youth and the inevitable career interruptions of the war years would lead one to expect, most held junior positions in the church hierarchy, almost invariably in small towns or the rural hinterland. All but two were simple parish pastors; the two higher churchmen, Dekans in Geislingen and Weinsberg, were both among the active-duty veterans.[44]

Rehm and Ettwein had already established themselves as activists on the right long before the Nazi ascendancy. Most of their comrades, however, boasted little previous political involvement and appear to have been drawn to the movement under the impact of depression-era crises and the growing conservative conviction that a "national revolution" provided the only sure way of forestalling a proletarian revolution and the establishment of a truly godless state along Soviet lines. Symbolic if not necessarily typical of this polarization process was the case of Immanual Schairer, pastor in Hedelfingen, part of the Neckar valley conurbation between Stuttgart and Esslingen. Born in

[43] Pressel to Wurm, Oct. 10, 1932, LKA D1/29,3.
[44] Compiled from data in *Magisterbuch* (1932) and "Vertrauensmänner des N.S.-Pfarrerbundes," undated typescript (copy), LKA D1/29,2.

1885, Schairer was among the older and better-known church-men in the group. At Tübingen, where he earned a doctorate in 1912, he had been a classmate of both Friedrich Ettwein and Religious Socialist Eberhard Lempp, and he had been active in various church organizations since 1918; he delivered one of the major addresses at the 1930 Bietigheim conference. In Hedelfingen, Schairer found himself caught both literally and figuratively in the crossfire between militants on the left and right. In response to a wave of political vandalism that included, among other things, anticlerical placards affixed to church buildings and even some random sniping directed at the parsonage, local storm troopers offered their services to protect church property. Convinced that the attacks were the work of local Communists, Schairer welcomed the protectors and eventually embraced their politics. With Wilhelm Pressel, then a popular university chaplain in Tübingen, and two younger pastors seconded to the Volksbund directorate, Friedrich Hilzinger and Kurt Hutten, Schairer played an active role in the Nazi front's frequent internecine struggles, attempting to mediate between NS-Pfarrerbund zealots and rank-and-file Christian-German supporters.[45]

Nazi activists in Württemberg made up in missionary fervor what they lacked in numbers. As noted in the previous chapter, the 1930 Reichstag elections had not brought the party the same degree of success in Württemberg achieved elsewhere, nor did coalition politics in Stuttgart suffer as yet from the paralysis that in Berlin was destroying what remained of parliamentary government. This marginal position in local politics only spurred the party to redouble its agitation in a relentless drive to secure a respectable mass base. If party strategy called for elaborate gestures in the direction of Protestant piety, Lohss and the NS-Pfarrerbund were only too eager to oblige. Like the Religious Socialists, but with greater vigor and consistency, they pressed to establish symbolic linkages between the church and their cause. A favorite device was the holding of well-publicized outdoor services for storm troopers, a device familiar to many church-

[45] Fischer, "Geschichte des Kirchenkampfes," 1:169.

men from postwar veterans' reunions, at which such services were a common occurrence. Lohss, for one, defended such political prayer meetings as a legitimate extension of the church's missionary enterprise, and given the striking similarities in technique between tent-meeting evangelism and the mass political revivalism practiced by the Nazis, it is perhaps understandable that a professional evangelist like Lohss would find a fusion of the two forms both reasonable and congenial.[46]

Besides such specifically party-oriented functions, local brownshirts also sought to take propaganda advantage of normal parish activities. Probably the most common tactic, in Württemberg as elsewhere, involved group attendance at church services in full party regalia, often after a closed-formation march from party headquarters. Coupled with escalating demands to use church facilities for all manner of ostensibly patriotic purposes, these deliberately provocative practices posed an awkward problem for church leaders. To tolerate a uniformed presence at worship was to fuel the indignation of the many loyal parishioners outside Nazi ranks. Explicit restrictions, on the other hand, would be difficult to justify in view of past considerations extended to such groups as the Religious Socialists, while a general prohibition against uniforms would affect not only Nazis but also others, such as youth groups, whose participation the clergy was only too eager to encourage.

An Oberkirchenrat directive of 1931 reflected the resulting sense of dilemma. It advised pastors that to set specific dress requirements would be "neither possible nor advisable from an Evangelical standpoint," the more so since in the present case it "would have the undesirable consequence that attendance at services would cease." On the contrary, "if . . . church order is maintained and the appearance of partiality avoided, the church can only welcome having the widest possible participation at services." The only possibility seemed to be a delicate compromise: uniformed groups should be tolerated, but closed-formation entrances must be prohibited, preferential seating avoided,

---

[46] See, e.g., Sayler and Lohss to OKR, July 7, 1932, LKA D1/29,2.

and all flags and banners barred from the sanctuary. Controversy continued, however, and while President von Hindenburg's ban on uniformed political formations in December 1931 temporarily alleviated the problem, it brought no resolution of the underlying tensions.[47]

The debate over uniforms was only one symptom of the reorientation taking place in Württemberg church politics during Theophil Wurm's first years in office. Although the familiar test of strength between orthodox and liberal factions continued, its significance was rapidly becoming overshadowed by Barthian critiques of Volkskirche theology and by the radical revisionism of the Religious Socialist and National Socialist minorities, both of which argued in different ways that the church's commitment to social renewal remained inadequate without overt political engagement. Of these challenges, that of the National Socialists was by far the more consequential, not only because the Nazi cadre within the church was so vocal and aggressive but also because Nazi appeals were in many ways so ideally suited to penetrate the vulnerable national-conservative core of the active Protestant community. Barthian objections to a bureaucratic triumphalism masquerading as theology had a profound long-term effect on church life, but for the moment they served churchmen primarily as a stimulus to introspection and self-criticism, not as the action program of a self-conscious ecclesiastical party. Religious Socialism, for its part, remained too marginal a movement to alter the church's central agenda; despite good intentions and isolated achievements, it was a victim of the very ecclesiastical class structure it condemned. The National Socialist challenge, especially during the years of the party's national mobilization, was at once more vague and more radical. What Nazi churchmen implicitly faulted in the existing Volkskirche synthesis was its incapacity to inspire or promote a genuine national renewal, both political and spiritual. In place of the Wei-

---

[47] OKR, Erlass, Oct. 14, 1930, in *Amtsblatt* 24 (1930): 295; Erlass "Über das Verhalten gegenüber politischen Bestrebungen," Jan. 27, 1931, in *Amtsblatt* 25 (1931): Beiblatt 2; Erlass, Oct. 10, 1931, reprinted in Schäfer, ed., *Landeskirche und Nationalsozialismus*, 1:35–36.

mar settlement, they proposed in effect to revive some spiritual equivalent to the old alliance of throne and altar, albeit with a führer in place of a king and with the integrative symbols of monarchy replaced by the evolving iconography of Hitler's promised national revolution.

That this revolution lacked any clear focus only strengthened its appeal. It encouraged churchmen, like a host of other Germans, to become victims of their own wishful thinking, to read into the movement the content of their own most cherished hopes for a future fatherland. The party's repeated invocation of a "positive Christianity" as its moral and spiritual basis was shrewdly calculated to facilitate such a process. Not only did the term "positive" carry the spurious ring of orthodoxy—it was in fact the designation of choice for conservative confessional factions in many of the territorial churches—but the rhetoric of moral renewal invited recollections of 1914 and the hope that patriotic fervor, arising out of a restored sense of national purpose and folk cohesion, might once again prove the means for arousing a mass piety that the church in its own right seemed unable to summon forth. At the same time, however, the brutality of Nazi methods and the movement's ruthless intolerance not only heightened the already bitter polarization of public life but also threatened the church's claim to stand "above parties" and above specific party dogmas—all the more so when the dogma in question placed race and folk above gospel and church. If National Socialism promised churchmen salvation from the frustrations of pluralism, it did so on terms that many if not most were unprepared to pay. Even when it appeared to speak the cultural language of the Volkskirche, Hitler's national revolution posed a clear challenge to Volkskirche ideals, and it did so at a time when churchmen themselves were perhaps less confident of those ideals than at any time since the November Revolution.

Between Activism and Neutrality

A year after the 1930 Reichstag election, Nazi *alte Kämpfer* still remained confined to a narrow beachhead in Protestant Württemberg. But if their numerical strength among churchmen scarcely exceeded that of the Religious Socialists, the deepening national crisis catapulted their ideology to the center of ecclesiastical debate. By late 1931, seminars and retreats sponsored by the Pfarrverein or Volksbund that earlier would have been devoted to discussions of education or social issues now dealt almost invariably with some aspect of National Socialism.[48] Other issues in church life came to be subsumed by the question of churchmen's stance towards the Nazi crusade. The advance guard in the NS-Pfarrerbund pressed to define alternatives as starkly as possible: either a "national revolution" or a bolshevik revolution, either the triumph of "positive Christianity" or the triumph of Soviet godlessness. In the autumn of 1931, writing in the Pfarrverein journal, the *Kirchlicher Anzeiger*, Gingen pastor Rudolf Brügel, a comparative moderate within the Nazi clerical cadre, predicted the imminent eclipse of "old party constellations" in a new era of uncompromising, elemental mass movements. Wrote Brügel: "Who knows how long it will be before we *must* decide for one movement or another!"[49]

Despite such challenges, the church leadership and the greater part of the clergy remained reluctant to take any unequivocal stand. However disinclined to mourn Weimar's moribund parliamentarism, however eager to see an end to the country's desperate economic and political woes, few churchmen gave evidence of anticipating the total destruction of the existing system or of abandoning the official doctrine that the church, by its very nature, must claim and defend the high ground of political neutrality. Neutrality need not, however, imply indifference or total detachment from the arena of conflict. A Volksbund resolution of 1931 construed neutrality in practice as implying that "the church recognizes and fosters the good that animates a movement while warding off and denouncing the bad. Any absolutization of . . . a system, or a race, or a people or a state, must be

---

[48] See reports in *KAfW* 41 (1932): 41–43, 47, 58, 122–23, 131–32, 166; EVB, Informationskurs, Stuttgart, Sept. 20–22, 1932, agenda, OKR/AR Gen. 117.

[49] "Nochmals 'Pfarrer und Parteien,' Ein offenes Wort," *KAfW* 40 (1931): 138.

opposed."[50] As in the prior case of Religious Socialism, the effort
to define a consistent position towards National Socialist demands arose out of a basic sense of ambivalence. The ideal of a
church open to all encouraged accommodation with the Hitler
movement despite its unsavory features. Theophil Wurm was
fond of arguing, not without a certain degree of special pleading,
that the church should not "repeat its mistake towards socialism" by holding aloof from or condemning a movement to
which growing numbers of parishioners belonged.[51] Against
this, however, stood the often vulgar spectacle of Nazi behavior
and the ominous possibility of an uncontrolled politicization of
church life. An unnamed pastor objected in mid-1931 that

> if there are religious Socialists, there can equally well be re-
> ligious National Socialists, and the more that pastors them-
> selves descend into the arena of political struggle the more
> this is likely to become the case. But in such a case ecclesi-
> astical and religious viewpoints would no longer be deter-
> minative [in church affairs]; rather, partisan political con-
> siderations would be decisive. And that would mean the end
> of our church.[52]

As this statement implies, the key issue, both symbolically
and practically, involved the political role of the clergy. Far more
than the other parties in which pastors remained active, National
Socialism was exclusivist, with no tolerance for competitors and
hence no patience with the church's claim to an autonomous position of neutrality. To Hitler's followers, neutrality could only
be interpreted as an expression of hostility. As Nazi pastors grew

[50] "Bericht über den Vertretertag 1931 in Stuttgart," Apr. 23, 1931, OKR/AR
Gen. 117; internal evidence suggests that the report was submitted by Friedrich
Hilzinger, himself a recent convert to Nazi ranks. On the general position, see
also Scholder, *Kirchen und das Dritte Reich*, 1:183, and Wright, "*Above Parties*," pp. 99–109.

[51] "Kirchliche Stellungnahme zu den gegenwärtigen politischen Verhältnissen und Bestrebungen," memorandum for DEKA (Berlin), Nov. 24, 1932, LKA
D1/42; cf. Schäfer, ed., *Landeskirche und Nationalsozialismus*, 1:127–29.

[52] H. St. [*sic*], "Pfarrer und Parteien," *KAfW* 40 (1931): 114.

more prominent, they inevitably imposed their Manichaean outlook on the continuing debate over the church's proper role, demanding ever more forcefully that fellow pastors join their ranks and accusing those who held back of insufficient enthusiasm for the national cause. Their stridency in turn provoked a backlash of protest among non-Nazis, who still constituted a clear majority of parishioners virtually everywhere in Württemberg. By 1932, far from offering a refuge from the fray, the church stood in danger of succumbing to the same polarization that was causing blood to flow in German streets. The incessant and increasingly violent political contests of 1932 saw the church leadership caught between the common desire of Protestant officials everywhere to assist in bringing about national renewal, or at least to avoid being left impotent on the sidelines, and an equally strong pastoral desire to keep political passions from becoming a crippling impediment to the nurture of "living parishes."

Official policy, we have already noted, sought to strike a balance between these conflicting impulses. Individuals and groups were to be encouraged to participate in church functions, even if the wearing of uniforms served to flaunt political convictions. At the same time, pastors were expected to exercise care that church facilities not be exploited for purely political purposes through special assemblies, displays of party banners, or any concession to a particular party that "might give offense to those of other political convictions."[53] While Oberkirchenrat directives discreetly avoided mention of any specific party, no one was under any illusion after 1931 about where the central problems lay. Beyond invoking official neutrality, however, churchmen did not share a common perspective on the Nazi challenge. A substantial number, especially among those identified with the Evangelical-Social tradition, regarded Hitlerism as a mortal threat to the integrity of Protestant institutions and values. In a circular to fellow pastors, Religious Socialists Eberhard Lempp

[53] Erlass, Nov. 10, 1931, in Schäfer, ed., *Landeskirche und Nationalsozialismus*, 1:35–36.

and Paul Weitbrecht warned against a "so-called positive Christianity" in which "Christian moral principles are only tolerated to the extent that they 'do not contradict German racial consciousness' [and in which] force and terror are glorified."[54] Paul Bausch, cofounder of the Württemberg Volksdienst, decried the "fantastic and visionary messianism" of a movement that served only to "sow the seeds of hate and discord . . . a thousandfold" in church and society alike.[55] If Religious Socialists and Volksdienstler had obvious reasons for speaking out, their views found widespread agreement among Volksbund leaders as well as in the Oberkirchenrat. Before the spring presidential elections of 1932, when Hitler launched his unsuccessful frontal assault against Paul von Hindenburg at the polls, both Jakob Schoell and former court preacher Konrad Hoffmann, since 1927 prelate in Ulm, joined Vernunftrepublikaner throughout Germany in signing public election appeals supporting the old field marshal.[56]

On this point they parted company with Württemberg's church president, who lent the considerable force of his office and personality to a more benevolent view of the Hitler movement. While Theophil Wurm held aloof from the Nazi party as such, he did not hesitate to send signals that party members could interpret favorably. A variety of considerations dictated Wurm's choice of tactics. One was unquestionably the basic missionary impulse implied in the Volkskirche ideal. In particular, the Nazis' carefully burnished image as a movement of youth encouraged hopes that a policy of benevolent neutrality might open new avenues of understanding between the church and the younger generation. Wurm clearly had Hitler's party in mind when he insisted to the Württemberg clergy at the end of 1931 that "groups which have hitherto been somewhat removed from

[54] "An unsere württembergische Amtsbrüder," Dec. 1932 (copy), LKA D1/28,6.
[55] "Was ist Wahrheit?" leaflet [Spring 1932] (copy), LKA D1/28,5.
[56] Reports on Volksbund gatherings in Stuttgart, Apr. 17–18 and Sept. 14, 1932, in LKA D1/59,1 and OKR/AR Gen. 117; "Ein evangelischer Pfarrer" to Hoffmann, n.d. [1932], in LKA D1/29,2; cf. Schäfer, ed., Landeskirche und Nationalsozialismus, 1:51–52.

church life should not be repulsed if they seek contact with the church and show a desire to place themselves under the guidance and uplifting power of the gospel."[57]

As for his own sympathies, Wurm doubtless saw much that was attractive in the professed aims of National Socialism. Like others in the national conservative camp, he found it easy to project his own ideals onto the movement and to take at face value the claim that an elemental mass movement could effect a moral transformation of society. Wurm's shrewd political instincts also warned him against losing touch with what might prove to be the eventual winning side. The church did not carry out its task "by the grace of political and economic potentates," he said in the spring of 1932, but to be truly vital and effective it must "apply its full energies in exploiting the open doors presented to it."[58] Even before the 1930 elections he had identified Hitler as the "coming man" in national affairs. By 1932, despite great admiration for Hindenburg, he too had become convinced that a Hitler regime, for all its possible drawbacks, was the only viable alternative to an impending dictatorship of the left. Wurm apparently entertained expectations that in practice National Socialism would bring some sort of postparliamentary order not unlike the authoritarian "Christian state" envisioned by Franz von Papen and his cronies, a state in which churchmen might reclaim a recognized corporative voice in public affairs, perhaps as members of some new chamber of notables. In a brief prepared for the DEKA in the fall of 1932, Wurm paid obeisance to the Volkskirche ideal of neutrality—"the spiritual cohesion of church members [forms] one of the preconditions for the civil cohesion of compatriots"—but he placed equal emphasis on the church's obligation as "a guardian of national culture, an advocate of justice and equity, a voice of admonition against morally dubious public measures" to take the lead in marking out the way to a new national order.[59]

[57] "An die Geistlichen der evang. Landeskirche in Württemberg," Dec. 16, 1931, Amtsblatt 25 (1931): 11.
[58] Ev. Pressedienst release, May 1932, copy, with Wurm notations, in LKA D1/29,2.
[59] Wurm to Frasch, May 7, 1933, LKA D1/42; Voelter, "Bietigheimer Tag," p.

Though he harbored few illusions about Hitler's character or the party's political methods, Wurm, like many of his kind, clearly hoped that National Socialism could be tamed of its worst excesses. He believed, moreover, that to encourage this process would ultimately serve the church's own interests: once the "healthy" elements in the movement prevailed, the party could assume its proper role as a carrier of moral and political renewal in concert with the church and other national institutions. In an effort to foster his own version of an ecclesiastical Harzburg Front, Wurm actively sought out and encouraged moderate churchmen sympathetic to the Nazi cause. Chief among these confidants were Karl Fezer, since 1930 director of the Tübingen Stift, and Tübingen chaplain Wilhelm Pressel. Born in 1895, Pressel was a veteran of the trenches and enjoyed considerable esteem among the university's Nazi student leaders. Pressel's membership in the party, by his own testimony, was "not without considerable mental reservation." He had joined in part for the usual patriotic reasons but even more out of a sense of what he termed an "obligation *pro iuventute*," a conviction that "the intelligentsia and we Christians have left this movement too long to its own devices."[60] The affinities with Wurm's own position are clear. Throughout 1932 Pressel served Wurm as a key liaison with the constantly shifting factions in the Nazi camp.

Wurm's policy, in sum, represented a logical extension of basic Volkskirche ideology. Wurm hoped to lend positive moral support to a self-proclaimed movement for national renewal without sacrificing either the church's institutional autonomy or its internal tranquillity. These goals, however, could not be achieved simultaneously, since Hitler's followers, including the hard core of Nazi pastors, aimed precisely at politicizing the church and subordinating it to party dictates. The disintegration of parliamentary government in both Württemberg and the Reich during 1932, which raised the stakes of political agitation

---

75; "Kirchliche Stellungnahme zu den gegenwärtigen politischen Verhältnissen und Bestrebungen," Nov. 24, 1932, LKA D1/42; draft letter to parishioner (Bad Cannstatt), Mar. 1932, LKA D1/26,9. Cf. Wright, *"Above Parties,"* pp. 108–9.

[60] Pressel to (unidentified) Volksdienst supporter, n.d. [May 1932] (copy), LKA D1/28,5.

and made campaigning a perpetual activity, forced Wurm and the Oberkirchenrat to unite behind a new strategy. Over the course of the year, events moved them to curtail and eventually to interdict public political activity by clergy, thereby opting for internal peace at the risk of a rupture with the forces of national revolution.

The shift in interpreting church neutrality began in the spring of 1932, when a double round of presidential balloting as well as state legislative elections sent voters in Württemberg to the polls three times within a six-week span in March and April. This period of frenetic activity left passions at an unprecedented fever pitch and threw state government, hitherto only indirectly affected by the larger political crisis, into a paralysis from which it never fully emerged. Württemberg Nazis, who had previously boasted only a single Landtag delegate, now scored a belated breakthrough, gaining twenty-three of the eighty seats to emerge as the largest single faction. When negotiations over a new coalition collapsed, Württemberg was left with a minority caretaker government under former Catholic Center minister Eugen Bolz. The result was a virtually free field for the sort of parliamentary irresponsibility and public demagoguery at which National Socialists excelled.[61]

These developments had direct consequences for churchmen. In their drive to destabilize governing coalitions anchored in the Catholic Center—Brüning in Berlin, Bolz in Stuttgart—National Socialists ruthlessly exploited every possible Protestant connection, including a highly visible role for Nazi clergy as political agitators. Throughout the early months of 1932, the NS-Pfarrerbund in Württemberg maintained a steady barrage of propaganda against the alleged "red-black dictatorship" holding sway in the state and national capitals. Its most prominent firebrands, Wilhelm Rehm and Friedrich Ettwein, ignored few opportunities to leap into the fray. During the period of intense spring campaigning, Ettwein in particular became an all but full-time circuit rider for the cause, delivering harangues on such

---

[61] Besson, *Württemberg und die deutsche Staatskrise*, pp. 253–73.

themes as "Why Must Every True Christian Vote NSDAP?"
Seemingly impervious both to private admonitions from superiors, who formally forbade further speeches on the aforemen-
tioned theme, and to the protests of outraged parishioners, at
least one of whom threatened to bring him to court on a charge
of slander, Ettwein presented himself as an Erwin Eckert of the
right, fusing pastoral identity and political involvement to a degree seldom if ever previously encountered in Württemberg.[62]

NS-Pfarrerbund tactics provoked a strong response from
many quarters of the church. The church assembly, which convened for its spring session in Stuttgart one day after the April
legislative elections, roundly condemned what several speakers
denounced as the abuse of pulpit and clerical office by political
activists. Liberal lay delegate Prince Hohenlohe-Langenburg
suggested that, under existing conditions, pastors should consider accepting the status of "political castrati" for the sake of internal harmony; his fellow members strongly agreed.[63] Although the assembly itself took no formal action, the
Oberkirchenrat was at work behind the scenes on a new statement of policy that would effectively rein in Nazi activists without resorting to an outright ban on political activity. Wurm and
others remained reluctant to take the latter step, perhaps because
it smacked of an unconstitutional restraint on pastors' civil
rights. When Paul von Hindenburg dissolved the Reichstag on
June 4, raising the prospect of yet another bitter election struggle, the Oberkirchenrat was ready with a new decree. Directed
specifically to the clergy, it combined an appeal to conscience
with an official directive setting up more stringent criteria for
political behavior. The basic theme remained the same: pastors
must scrupulously avoid "anything which is incompatible with
the church's stance of impartiality." That Nazi activists were the

[62] "An die Evang. Christen Württembergs," leaflet, Apr. 1932 (copy), LKA
D1/29,2. OKR to DKA Cannstatt, Apr. 15, 1932; Kübler to Holzinger, May 21,
1932; and Holzinger to OKR, May 26, 1932; all in Ettwein Personalakten, OKR/
AR Pers.; cf. Schäfer, ed., Landeskirche und Nationalsozialismus, 1:55–56.

[63] 2. LKT, Verhandlungen (1932), esp. pp. 48–49. For National Socialist criticisms, see Schäfer, ed., Landeskirche und Nationalsozialismus, 1:133–42.

primary targets is implicit in one sentence, which makes specific reference to "young pastors" and suggests that the "many-sided task of the modern-day pastorate" should provide "so much to do that for this reason alone party-political activity should rule itself out." Most importantly, the decree reaffirmed the church's long-standing policy that active political involvement was only permissible when carried on during an authorized leave of absence. Since such leaves could only be granted by the Oberkirchenrat, the leadership could, if it wished, exercise an effective administrative veto over clergy action. [64]

If the new policy failed to accomplish its intended purposes in full, it at least served to buffer the church against the excesses of the previous spring. Although Nazi pastors continued their vigorous propaganda efforts, particularly among fellow clergymen, the level of public appearances, and hence of parish controversy, remained well below that of March and April. Most affected by the decree, ironically, were the Religious Socialists. Despite complaints that the prevailing rightist tone of Protestant rhetoric would soon destroy what little confidence they had managed to build up among workers, they withdrew from all direct party work and loyally heeded the injunction to silence. Thereafter they ceased to be a significant part of the church-political mosaic. [65]

Before the summer was over, however, the turmoil of national politics was again undermining the church's arrangements. The recision of Hindenburg's uniform ban in mid-June raised political violence to a new pitch. Casualty lists from private mayhem and pitched street clashes between left and right lengthened al-

[64] "Über die parteipolitische Betätigung der Geistlichen," June 9, 1932, in *Amtsblatt* 25 (1932): Beiblatt, pp. 14–16. Copies of earlier working drafts can be found in LKA D1/29,5; cf. Schäfer, ed., *Landeskirche und Nationalsozialismus*, 1:148–51. The requirement for leaves of absence had been in effect for over 20 years; Theophil Wurm applied for such a leave in 1919, as did Richard Lempp in 1924.

[65] "An die Herren evang. Geistlichen Württembergs," July 31, Sept. 27, 1932, copies in LKA D1/29,3; Bund der religiösen Sozialisten Württembergs, Rundschreiben, Dec. 1932 (copy), LKA D1/28,6; Mosthaf to OKR, OKR/AR Gen. 117; Rehm to OKR, Nov. 26, 1932, Rehm Personalakten, OKR/AR Pers.

most daily, and churchmen's pleas for peace were all but drowned out, confirming once more the weakness of the church's position as moral preceptor. The incontrovertible propensity for violence displayed by Hitler's forces could be condemned as incompatible with an ordered society, but it thereby increased the pressure on those who, like Wurm, persisted in holding that National Socialism represented a basically healthy impulse with which the church could and should in some way identify.

The turning point for Wurm came in the notorious Potempa incident of early August. On August 9, the same day Franz von Papen's cabinet of barons resorted to an emergency decree extending the death penalty to acts of political killing, a band of storm troopers in the Silesian town of Potempa invaded the home of a Polish Communist and trampled him to death before his mother's eyes. Arrested and tried almost immediately before a special tribunal in Beuthen, five of the Nazi thugs received death sentences under the new decree. Sensational as was the crime itself, the response of Adolf Hitler was even more sensational. In a widely quoted telegram and subsequent newspaper manifesto, Hitler proclaimed his solidarity with the assassins and pledged to win their freedom while declaring it the party's duty to "fight against a regime under which [such a sentence] was possible." For many burghers, churchmen included, previously willing to give Nazis the benefit of the doubt, Hitler's minatory rhetoric and apparent glorification of murder came as the rudest of shocks. Seeing his civic strategy crumbling away, Theophil Wurm poured out his frustrations in a private letter to Wilhelm Pressel. From Wurm's standpoint, Hitler's failure to condemn violence had dangerously sullied his party's cause. "The triumph of a freedom movement on a Christian and national basis, for which I yearn as intensely as any member of the younger generation, has seemingly been endangered, if not rendered impossible, by Hitler's conduct regarding recent events." Wurm pleaded with Pressel and like-minded party members, especially from among the clergy, to take an open stand against the party's course. Wrote Wurm: "The National Socialist clergy

347

are, I am convinced, called to such a [step], which may perhaps be considered politically inopportune at the moment and [which] may bring . . . disciplinary measures from the Brown House, but which is sure to have a good effect."[66]

Predictably enough, this naive resort to moral suasion proved abortive. Pressel, who was no less appalled than Wurm by the mailed-fist tactics of the party leadership and who had become further disillusioned by rumors of secret coalition negotiations between party officials and the despised Catholic Center, did indeed attempt to mobilize an intraparty opposition. To Wilhelm Rehm he expressed shock and revulsion at Hitler's position. In the name of some thirty party members in the Volksbund, he formulated a declaration to Württemberg storm troopers and their local *Gauleiter*, Wilhelm Murr, appealing on the basis of the party's self-proclaimed positive Christianity for an official denunciation of political violence.[67] The only effect was to heighten tension between the Pressel circle and hard-core Nazi clergy. Rehm, Ettwein, and their comrades left no doubt that for them the dictates of the Führer superseded all other moral considerations. Their reaction to Potempa provides graphic evidence of the extent to which a politicized theology fusing religious and national impulses could tolerate a total relativization of ethical standards, justifying even murder in the name of patriotism. The Hitler telegram, Immanuel Schairer tried to convince Pressel, and perhaps himself, was "an elemental outcry of blood for blood: inarticulate, unclear, primitive, unstatesmanlike, undiplomatic—but genuine!"[68] Rehm went still further. In one of his regular "Sunday meditations" for a local party paper, Rehm condoned the Potempa action as an act of justified patriotic self-

[66] Wurm to Pressel, Aug. 26, 1932, LKA D1/29,3; on the general church response to Potempa, see Scholder, *Die Kirchen und das Dritte Reich*, 1:227–29.

[67] Pressel to Rehm, Aug. 27, 1932, quoted in Schäfer, ed., *Landeskirche und Nationalsozialismus*, 1:157; Pressel to NSDAP, Gauleitung Württemberg [Sept. 1932] (copy), LKA D1/29,2. The "thirty colleagues" referred to were presumably part of a larger group who participated in a Volksbund-sponsored seminar on folkish theology at Tübingen; EVB to OKR, Oct. 22, 1932, OKR/AR Gen. 117.

[68] Schairer to Pressel, Sept. 2, 1932, LKA D1/29,2.

defense. The convicted men's only crime, he argued, was "to love folk and Fatherland above all." In private correspondence with Pressel he stressed the duty to close ranks behind the leader, adding a thinly veiled warning that "those who don't trust us can get out; we'll find new ones to take their place."[69] Party officials took the same line. In October Pressel was summoned to a hearing before Gauleiter Murr in Tübingen and accused of insubordination; only the intercession of student leaders prevented his summary dismissal from the party.[70]

The Potempa affair and its aftershocks resulted in a certain clarification of fronts within the church. Specifically, it created a demarcation of the previously fluid boundary between those who saw national renewal as a cause that transcended the power interests of the Nazi party alone—a group including Fezer, the Pressel circle, and many in Lohss's Christian-German movement—and those, notably in the NS-Pfarrerbund, who saw national revolution as the party's exclusive preserve. At the same time, it marked off those who held the Hitler movement accountable to extrinsic moral or theological standards from those who saw the movement as generating its own intrinsic standards. For the church leadership, struggling to prevent complete disintegration of the Volkskirche ideal, it exposed the hollowness of Wurm's positive neutrality as a strategy for social influence. With public life so heavily politicized, to assume the mantle of

[69] Rehm to Pressel, Sept. 7, 1932, LKA D1/29,2; Rehm, "Saet euch Gerechtigkeit und erntet Liebe," NS-Kurier, Aug. 27, 1932, excerpted in Schäfer, ed., Landeskirche und Nationalsozialismus, 1:156–57. This astonishing piece takes as its ostensible text a verse from Hos. 10: "Sow to yourselves in righteousness . . . for it is time to seek the Lord, till he come and rain righteousness upon you." Significantly, Rehm omits mention of the next verse, which continues: "Ye have plowed wickedness . . . because thou didst trust in thy way, in the multitude of thy mighty men."

[70] Baetzner to Pressel, Sept. 2, 1932, and G. Berger [Standartenführer-SA, Untergruppe Württemberg] to Pressel, Sept. 3, 1932, both in LKA D1/29,2. On subsequent measures, see Pressel, aide-memoire, May 8, 1935, "Bericht zum Potempa-Fall und den sich daraus ergebenden bzw. folgenden Massnahmen der Partei, der NSDAP, 1932," in Schäfer, ed., Landeskirche und Nationalsozialismus, 1:171–72.

moral preceptor meant to be ignored: this the fate of countless church proclamations showed. Conversely, cultivation of openings to the contending political forces only increased centrifugal pressures on an already divided church community.

In the case of National Socialism, the latter policy risked total subordination of autonomous Protestant principles to the pragmatic interests of a movement impelled not by some generalized positive Christianity but, as Hitler's recent maneuvers made only too clear, by the naked lust for power. A semiofficial statement from the Volksbund's press service, referring to Rehm's published defense of the Potempa killers, protested the "perversion and paralysis of ethical consciousness" by self-serving political calculations. The only response the Volksbund could mount, however, was to observe that "for the serious Christian . . . participation in political affairs will doubtless always bring difficult inner struggles, decisions, and encumbrances, and no one can set himself up as an infallible judge of others." Political violence should "weigh as a distressing burden on the Christian conscience" and could only be dealt with using the "weapons of the Spirit."[71]

The tone of resignation in these lines is as revealing as any explicit message they conveyed. Aside from a token role as moral preceptors condemning the scourge of political violence, the only realistic alternative remaining to church leaders seemed to be a passive neutrality, the renunciation of active public leadership for the sake of pastoral service to parishioners. This inclination to passivity gained momentum after September 12, when, with the Potempa controversy still smoldering, the machinations of both Papen and Hitler led to dissolution of the newly convened Reichstag and hence the prospect of yet another full-scale election campaign, the fifth for Württembergers in nine months. Within the Volksbund, where sentiment for a self-imposed political truce had been growing since the spring elections, the response was almost immediate. By midmonth the executive com-

[71] "Politische Gewalttaten und christliches Gewissen," in Schäfer, ed., *Landeskirche und Nationalsozialismus*, 1:158–60.

mittee had discussed the new situation and had drafted a formal petition to the Oberkirchenrat asking that the church stiffen its injunctions to neutrality. The document appealed to the old ideal of the church as "a community, a place where political striving must come to a halt and the passions of partisanship be overcome." From this familiar starting point the logic of passivity proceeded almost inexorably.

> The more that serious-minded groups among our people turn away disillusioned in their hopes for political salvation, alienated by fruitless and venomous party wrangling, the more important it is for the church to be mobilized to welcome them in. It must awaken the understanding that only a community centered on the gospel can bridge political and economic antagonisms and provide the nation [*Volksgemeinschaft*] with an ultimate anchor and the innermost energies for renewal. We are convinced that the unswerving fulfillment of this task, which is nothing less than pastoral service to our sick age, will secure a new place for the church in public life.

The document continued with a request that church officials go beyond past appeals to establish a strict ban on political activity, including the kind of disguised polemics perfected by Rehm in his newspaper meditations.[72]

Deliberations within the Oberkirchenrat led to a similar conclusion. On September 29, church leaders took the unprecedented step of expressly forbidding pastors from engaging in any sort of public political activity for the duration of the impending campaign. Except for Wurm's November memorandum to the DEKA, this Muzzle Ordinance, as it came to be known, constituted the Württemberg church's last programmatic statement before Hitler's accession to power. It underscored the preoccupation with pastoral office evident in the church's posture throughout the Weimar era. Referring to the "excessive passion

[72] Mosthaf to OKR, Sept. 19, 1932, in Schäfer, ed., *Landeskirche und Nationalsozialismus*, 1:173–77. As usual, no specific names are mentioned.

and bitterness" of the current political scene, it asserted that church officials had been receiving complaints from laymen that the "political initiatives of particular pastors" were "giving offense, undermining the confidence of parishioners in the equitable performance of the pastor's offical duties, and taking away time and energy from . . . service to the parish." This, the Oberkirchenrat warned, constituted a serious threat to the "repute and pastoral efficacy of the clerical office." The Oberkirchenrat therefore declared itself

> bound to urge emphatically upon all clergy, regardless of their political orientation, that for the sake of their office they refrain from any political agitation during the coming Reichstag campaign, and especially that they refrain from appearing at rallies as representatives of a party; that they lend their names to no election appeals or proclamations, regardless of party; that they refrain from making propaganda for any party in the press.[73]

Responses to the new policy, originally designed to apply only during the impending election campaign, indicated the prevailing constellation of positions in church circles. Although little specific evidence is available, there can be no doubt that an overwhelming majority of pastors and active lay persons either submitted to the dictates of the Oberkirchenrat out of a sense of duty or positively welcomed the new policy as an overdue reprieve from political tension. Included in this majority were not a few party members; Pressel wrote Wurm in early October that the decree "rescued [many] from conflicts and pangs of conscience."[74] In the case of Rehm, Ettwein, and the dozen or so colleagues that formed the activist core of the NS-Pfarrerbund, reaction was very different. At a stormy session in Stuttgart on October 5, which saw Pressel and one other member, Karl Hettler from Unterboihingen, resign in protest, the NS-Pfarrerbund

---

[73] Erlass, Sept. 29, 1932, in Schäfer, ed., Landeskirche und Nationalsozialismus, 1:177–78.
[74] Pressel to Wurm, Oct. 6, 1932, LKA D1/29,3.

determined to attempt a stand against the new policy. In written appeals and personal audiences, they complained to church leaders that the September 29 decree was both high-handed, in that none of them had been consulted in advance, and discriminatory, in that its effects fell principally on their own group, leaving them branded as "second-class pastors."[75]

The Nazi press provided covering fire for the NS-Pfarrerbund, attacking the Oberkirchenrat's action as a "stab in the back of the National Socialist German freedom movement" and as a "capitulation to those who are corrupting our people and to those philistines who want nothing but to be left in peace." A special dose of vitriol was reserved for Volksbund leaders, whose petition of September 19 the party apparently saw as the main cause for the shift in policy.[76] Württemberg party officials, loathe to abandon one of their most effective means of agitation, privately sought to persuade the Oberkirchenrat, and especially Wurm, whose friendly public expressions in the past had not been forgotten, to relax the newly announced restrictions. In a conference with Wurm on October 17, the party's Landtag chief, Christian Mergenthaler, requested a written statement from the Oberkirchenrat indicating how strictly church leaders proposed to interpret their injunction and whether violation of the decree would bring official disciplinary sanctions—an indication that Nazi pastors and party strategists were looking for some way to circumvent the ban without paying too high a price.[77]

Despite pressures and protests, the Oberkirchenrat held firm, although it did concede pastors the right to continue providing advice and serving in other supporting roles out of the public

[75] Thus Rehm to Wurm, Oct. 9, 1932, Rehm Personalakten, OKR/AR Pers. See also Ettwein to Wurm, Oct. 6, 1932, and Schairer to Wurm, Oct. 27, 1932, both in LKA D1/29,3, and Besprechungsprotokoll (Müller), Oct. 6, 1932, OKR/AR Gen. 317a.

[76] *NS-Kurier*, Oct. 8, 12, 1932, in Schäfer, ed., *Landeskirche und Nationalsozialismus*, 1:189–95. The Volksbund responded with a vigorous circular of its own, "Parteipolitik und Evang. Volksbund" (copy), LKA D1/29,2.

[77] Gauleitung Württemberg to Wurm, Oct. 14, 1932; Wurm to Murr, Oct. 14, 1932; Besprechungsprotokoll, Oct. 17, 1932; and OKR to Gauleitung Württemberg, Oct. 18, 1932; all in LKA D1/29,3.

eye. In the case of unsigned press articles, for example, church officials would "not make it their task . . . to search out the author."[78] On the ban's explicit provisions, however, there could be no compromise. In a letter to Mergenthaler, Wurm explicitly rejected any contention that "only within the NSDAP is a [true national] standpoint possible and in fact present," and he declared himself in total agreement with the full Oberkirchenrat "in recognizing the objective ecclesiastical necessity" for the decree of September 19.[79] To those pastors who voiced objections, the Oberkirchenrat, after considerable deliberation, drafted a letter over Wurm's signature that expressed "full understanding" of activists' frustrations but reiterated the injunction to restraint as a sacrifice that all pastors were being called upon to make for the higher cause of the church and its "faithfulness in executing its commission to advance the gospel entrusted to it."[80] In the end clerical discipline prevailed. Even Wilhelm Rehm, despite obvious chafing, reportedly declared it to be a matter of honor to heed the Oberkirchenrat's directives, and the election passed without major incident.[81]

In a review of conditions published at the beginning of 1933, the new editor of the Pfarrverein's *Kirchlicher Anzeiger*, Richard Fritz, wrote that "the church would not be so courted by the most varied political tendencies if it were not more of a force in the life of our people than is often thought."[82] This was in many respects a typical piece of ambivalent Volkskirche rhetoric, combining as it did wistful insistence on the church's continuing public significance and implied alarm at the threats to internal unity represented by the social and political struggles of the day. Even the most optimistic rhetoric, however, could not gainsay the fundamental passivity of the church's postwar stance. The

---

[78] Besprechungsprotokoll, Oct. 6, 1932, OKR/AR Gen. 317a.

[79] Wurm to Mergenthaler, Oct. 19, 1932, LKA D1/29,3.

[80] Copy in OKR/AR Gen. 317a. The files contain no fewer than five different drafts of this letter prepared over a three-day period; cf. undated letter in LKA D1/29,3.

[81] DKA Nagold to OKR, Nov. 28, 1932, Rehm Personalakten, OKR/AR Pers.

[82] *KAfW* 42 (1933): 1.

Weimar years had furnished ample support for the conclusion that in a pluralistic society the church courted political influence only at the cost of pastoral integrity. Conversely, cultivation of a diverse mass constituency in the name of pastoral responsibility all but assumed a retreat from politics. In the near-total politicization of the early 1930s, the great majority of Württemberg churchmen saw little alternative but to embrace the pastoral option. If the improvised revolution of 1918 had impelled them to mobilize across a broad political front in defense of their institutional status, the impending counterrevolution saw them moving in virtually the opposite direction, towards an internal demobilization motivated by concern to preserve a fragmenting social base.

CONCLUSION

ⓄN JANUARY 30, 1933, weeks of back-room maneuvering ended with the appointment of Adolf Hitler as chancellor in a coalition cabinet of the right. For this study to conclude without consideration of the *Machtergreifung* and its consequences may appear somewhat arbitrary, especially in view of the enthusiasm with which most churchmen moved to embrace the new order. Indeed, the sense of resignation and passivity previously so prevalent in church circles gave way, almost literally overnight, to a new hope that the day of national and spiritual renewal might finally be at hand. For conservatives such as Theophil Wurm, Hitler's appointment signified less the breakthrough of National Socialism than a long-delayed consolidation of the national front. As early as February 2, Wurm was writing to Bishop Heinrich Rendtorff of Mecklenburg that "the agreement between Hindenburg, Hitler, and Hugenberg has created a new situation. So long as the groups represented by these names and personalities stood opposed to each other, there was great inner tension within the Protestant electorate. Their union [now] provides a clear solution for at least 80% of committed Protestants."[1] The new chancellor's early public gestures did nothing to dispel this sense of anticipation. When Hitler solemnly affirmed the regime's intention to reanimate the Christian basis of German life, as he did in a Stuttgart speech on February 16, churchmen felt entitled to celebrate the imminent fulfillment of their cultural ambitions.[2]

Nor did signs of an emerging terror system cloud confidence in Hitler as a loyal drummer for the cause of a restored moral commonwealth. With the Nazis in the role of a court party, the

[1] Wurm to Rendtorff, Feb. 2, 1933, LKA D1/36,2.

[2] Helmreich, *German Churches under Hitler*, p. 129; in an ironic portent of tensions to come, a radio broadcast of the speech fell victim to censorship of sorts when saboteurs cut the power supply in midtransmission.

Potempa precedent lost its power to disconcert. Untoward incidents could be dismissed, Wurm would later write, as "minor blunders attributable to the fact that a social stratum with cruder manners had come to power, which for that reason alone constrained [churchmen] not to hold themselves aloof."[3] The Oberkirchenrat officially reiterated warnings against becoming embroiled in party strife, but in effect it quietly removed the muzzle from partisans of the new order. Prominent critics of Nazi intentions such as Jakob Schoell and Volksbund functionary August Springer were eased into retirement. In July the church assembly moved to revoke the title of church president and confer on Wurm the designation *Landesbischof*. Despite Wurm's own insistence that this action represented a confirmation of the essentially spiritual rather than administrative authority of his office, National Socialists applauded the change as a first application of the führer principle to church life.[4]

Although in Württemberg and elsewhere the Nazi Machtergreifung thus inaugurated a fleeting era of good feelings between church and state during which churchmen showed every willingness to accommodate themselves to the dictates of the national revolution, the apparent rapprochement should not unduly color interpretations of the entire preceding Weimar era. Churchmen may have greeted the Third Reich with varying degrees of hope and confidence, but few played any direct role in bringing it about. Without the machinations of such self-appointed power brokers as Franz von Papen and Alfred Hugenberg, there is no reason why the Muzzle Ordinance of 1932 might not have remained almost indefinitely a defining feature of Württemberg church life. Moreover, the new patriotic rhetoric by no means negated the pastoral emphasis reflected in that ordinance, and pastoral concerns continued to exercise a tempering influence even when hopes were brightest for cooperation between church and state and for a restoration of the church's

---

[3] Wurm, *Erinnerungen*, p. 87.
[4] Springer, *Der andere, der bist Du*, pp. 339–42; Wurm, *Erinnerungen*, p. 86; Schäfer, ed., *Landeskirche und Nationalsozialismus*, 1:262–64, 269–74, 491–94, 507–15, 566–71.

CONCLUSION

moral power in society. When he accepted the bishop's cross, Wurm saw himself in effect reasserting the church's claim to an autonomous moral and pastoral mandate. If the church was called to serve the new order, he wrote in the spring of 1933, it was "not [as] an armed combat soldier but [as] a compassionate medical corpsman" concerned to bind up the wounds of all, regardless of party or ideology. Restoration of national unity, by whatever means, was a worthy goal. But unless and until such unity manifested itself, one of the church's chief obligations must continue to be "the cultivation of a spirit of fraternity that avoids anything that might give offense to another within the community of Christ."[5] Nowhere did Wurm state more succinctly the essence of the pastoral orientation.

This new self-consciousness about the pastoral task, as the foregoing study has attempted to show, represented one of the church's chief legacies from the Weimar period. It arose in good measure out of efforts to confront the challenges of pluralism in postwar German society. Like the Volkskirche ideology that informed them, churchmen's responses to pluralism were ambiguous, vacillating as they did between authoritarian and voluntaristic conceptions of the church. Beyond the conflicting tendencies common to all religious associations—those reflected, for example, in Ernst Troeltsch's classic distinction between church and sect, between inclusivity and exclusivity—the sense of pastoral task manifested by clergy in the German territorial churches historically embraced impulses toward both state and society, impulses that potentially stood in tension with one another. Ideally the church was to mediate between state and society. In their official capacities, churchmen would help reinforce public order and social cohesion in the course of preaching the gospel and nurturing the spiritual commitments of their parishioners. Theologically the church might understand itself as a body of believers united around the Word, the creeds, and the

5 "Kirche, Volkstum, und Staat," *EGBfS* 29 (1933): 117; see also *KAfW* 42 (1933): 65–66, and draft in LKA D1/42, as well as Wurm's open letter to Württemberg clergy, Mar. 26, 1933, in *Amtsblatt* 26 (1933), Beiblatt.

sacraments. But in its institutional manifestation as Volks-kirche, the church also constituted a model of the public order as moral commonwealth—an image and token of the Christian-German synthesis in which the nation was to find its ultimate identity. Hence if pastoral concerns had always oriented church-men toward society by means of the "cure of souls" and attempts to evangelize the indifferent, they also implied service to the state as advocates of right behavior and obedience to the established order.

This dual orientation need not produce serious tension in churchmen's roles so long as clergy could be confident of operating within the framework of a general cultural consensus—so long, that is, as the images and symbols of religious orthodoxy were also to a significant extent those of civic virtue. In the German Evangelical tradition, this ideal of congruence found its classic expression in the idea of the Christian state. But if churchmen were capable of exerting considerable power as moral and cultural preceptors so long as they could articulate a general consensus, they could not by themselves create or maintain such a consensus. Hence the Volkskirche could neither resist nor ignore the complex of social, political, economic, and cultural forces tending towards what Richard Sennett has called the "fall of public man."[6] To the extent that it functioned as an agency of public order, the church became marked by the growing politicization of that order. To the extent that it remained a community of voluntary assent, it became exposed to the effects of a growing privatization of belief. As a would-be mediator between state and society, it both manifested and fought to retard the trend toward a distancing of public and private spheres of conduct and commitment. The theological diversity and practical indifference characteristic of much Protestant church life mirrored the complexity of society at large in which churchmen found it increasingly difficult to assume or assert a position of cultural hegemony.

[6] Richard Sennett, *The Fall of Public Man* (New York, 1977); cf. Habermas, *Strukturwandel der Öffentlichkeit*.

CONCLUSION

Problems of pluralism did not therefore originate with the November Revolution. A generation and more before 1918, churchmen already faced the whole range of tensions inherent in their dual role as cultural preceptors and shepherds of a voluntary communion of belief. Such tensions would undoubtedly have continued to exercise a major influence on the church even without postwar upheavals. The immediate significance of the Weimar system was that abolition of the monarchy eliminated the historic integrative symbol of the Volkskirche project. It was this rather than any specific provision of disestablishment that decisively informed churchmen's efforts at adjustment to the new order.

In their effort to recover a vital center of the Volkskirche tradition, churchmen predictably moved to address postwar pluralism along two separate and potentially contradictory avenues, one rooted in the orientation toward society and private commitments, the other in the orientation toward the state and the idea of a public moral order. The former avenue led to various projects aimed at revitalizing the church community. In the case of Württemberg, these found positive expression in, for example, the quasi-democratic spirit of the new church constitution, in the Volksbund, and in the practical manifestations of the "social" church. Negatively, they informed churchmen's ambivalent attitude toward the political sphere, which included both party involvement in the name of rapprochement with parishioners and, more typically, a commitment to at least formal neutrality in hopes of avoiding parish polarization. The public dimension of Volkskirche ideology found expression in the sometimes overweening moralism of many public pronouncements, in churchmen's claims to codetermination in the area of public education, and especially in the utopian antirepublicanism of the national-conservative ethos with its appeals for a revival of moral community.

That such impulses should have reasserted themselves powerfully during the latter months of the republic is hardly surprising, especially against the background of churchmen's repeated disappointments over attempted openings toward society

360

after 1918. The national revolution presented itself as a new vital center that would again accommodate both dimensions of Volkskirche ambition. Not only did the revolution promise to restore genuine national community, but the resulting upsurge of healthy patriotic spirit might perhaps do what lay organizations and social programs seemed incapable of doing: stimulate mass participation in church activities and new enthusiasm for church teachings. Compelling precedent seemed ready at hand in the August Days of 1914, already fixed firmly in Protestant mythology as a time of both societal and ecclesiastical Volksgemeinschaft when the nation seemed united and church pews were packed with parishioners. Having failed in their own efforts to reintegrate church, state, and society, churchmen were tempted to look for some latter-day equivalent of Luther's princes whose drive to rebuild national pride would also create the preconditions necessary for a restored Christian commonwealth. To the extent that such thinking prevailed in Württemberg and elsewhere, some degree of enthusiasm for the new order of 1933 was a logical outgrowth of basic Volkskirche ideology. But it was also in some senses a confession of clerical impotence. Although the Weimar years had been a time of unprecedented activism on the societal front, churchmen's efforts had apparently done little to reverse their long-term slide towards marginality as a shaping force in national culture.

In this respect, as in others, what Waldemar Besson observed about local politics also holds true for church life: developments in Württemberg tended to follow national patterns, albeit with local variations. If conditions anywhere in Germany might have fostered a republican conception of the Volkskirche project, it ought to have been in Württemberg. Yet Württemberg churchmen did not constitute a force for republican consolidation after 1918; they proved little more inclined than any other German Protestants to come to terms with the new order.

This conclusion, while perhaps obvious, is hardly trivial. The case of Württemberg argues strongly against the position that antirepublicanism in the Weimar church can be explained as a mirror image of republican anticlericalism, a largely defensive reaction against genuine political and ideological threats. Perhaps nowhere in Germany, and certainly not in any of the major states, did a stronger potential exist in 1918 for cordial relations between church and state. At no time were the Württemberg church's established interests ever in jeopardy, even from a revolutionary Einzelgänger of the Prussian or Saxon ilk. It is even possible, as we have noted elsewhere, that pastors' strictly institutional status might have improved marginally as a result of the November Revolution. Collectively they had won an unprecedented freedom of action without having been forced to pay any prohibitive penalty in either financial support or institutional prerogatives. Despite this, however, rapprochement with republican institutions and adoption of republican ideals failed to materialize. Taken in sum, the public rhetoric and private commitments of Württemberg churchmen differed little from those of other German Protestant leaders. Rooted both emotionally and ideologically in a tradition of monarchical authority, most churchmen were ultimately incapable of seeing in the republic a legitimate successor to the Second Empire. For them, as for others of their class and kind, Weimar would always bear the ugly birthmarks of defeat and revolution, national humiliation and social upheaval. Political estrangement aside, moreover, churchmen still found it difficult to accept or affirm the republican order; as the constitutional embodiment of unfettered pluralism, it appeared to militate against their efforts to advance church interests as they usually conceived of that task.

It is ironic that the very absence of a radical disestablishment after 1918 spared these same churchmen from the need to seriously reevaluate their role. That a root-and-branch separation of church and state would have been vastly traumatic goes without saying. Yet a shock of such magnitude to the Volkskirche tradition would certainly have forced churchmen to reappraise, in ways that few otherwise felt compelled to do, the central emphases of that tradition and their implications for the pastoral role. What if clerical doomsayers' worst fears had been realized in 1918, and revolutionary leaders had in fact managed to reduce the territorial church to a simple "free church," a purely voluntary association? A plausible case might be made that such a church would not only have survived but might ultimately have prospered in a modest way. This would seem especially true for Württemberg, with its strong tradition of pietist lay activism and respect for things ecclesiastical. In actuality, of course, circumstances demanded no such radical rethinking of church order. Efforts to democratize procedures or to mobilize the populace therefore took place within the framework of inherited structures and assumptions. This may have been one reason why such efforts remained superficial in their impact, producing little long-term change either in church life or in churchmen's notions of their place and role.

In sum, if Volkskirche rhetoric proved more than flexible enough to surmount the immediate postwar crisis, it also discouraged church leaders and their supporters from identifying or seeking to confront more deep-seated problems of identity and purpose. Such problems, in practice, were instead typically deflected into critiques of the republican system, which condemned itself in the eyes of many churchmen for its refusal or inability to foster a Christian-German national synthesis. In the process, of course, churchmen implicitly dismissed any possibility that a sustaining public philosophy might be developed for the republic and that such a public philosophy might in time mitigate, if not totally overcome, the instability and lack of unity for which they were so quick to fault the Weimar order.

This having been said, it is necessary to emphasize once again the significance of the emerging new pastoral orientation. While the republic did not force churchmen into a radical redefinition of institutional purpose and in fact encouraged them instead to pursue the chimera of a Christian-German Volksgemeinschaft, it nevertheless served to raise in new ways the question of their proper role in a pluralistic society. The resulting shift in orientation, towards a conception of mission rooted more explicitly in the analysis of existing social conditions, constitutes one of the chief distinguishing accents of the Württemberg experience. Incomplete and half-hearted though it may have been, it pointed away from the Volkskirche synthesis of earlier times and toward a more nuanced, less prepossessing conception of ecclesiastical purpose. If after 1918 as before churchmen found it natural to issue preachments to society, they also sought increasingly to explore new modes of pastoral service. If they appealed for the return of a Christian state, they also labored to nurture "living parishes" in a substantially secular society. If they continued instinctively to defend the high ground of institutional privilege, they also became more willing to descend into the lowlands of mass society, where values were likely to follow the ways of the marketplace and where strength lay primarily in numbers.

Although this affirmation of pastoral tasks sometimes became drowned out by national-conservative rhetoric during the first heady days of the Third Reich, the ensuing Church Struggle restored it to the forefront of churchmen's debates over their basic mission and identity. The exclusivity of Nazi claims to power proved utterly incompatible with the vision of a national moral consensus nurtured by church leaders such as Theophil Wurm. For his part, Wurm could not long reconcile his insistence on the institutional and pastoral autonomy of the church with demands that the church tailor its teachings to the doctrines of the party and its practice to the whims of local party chieftains. Disillusionment grew rapidly. By the fall of 1933, when the NS-Pfarrerbund and other hard-core supporters of the regime made a bid to consolidate a more or less dictatorial position within the Württemberg church, Wurm was prepared to throw down a gauntlet of his own, appealing personally for the loyalty of rank-and-file clergy. The result was a dramatic vindication of Wurm's position. Membership in German-Christian groups and the NS-Pfarrerbund shrank almost as rapidly as it had once expanded. Some members, such as Wilhelm Pressel, were summarily dismissed. Many resigned outright, including Karl Fezer, now rector-elect of Tübingen University, who as personal confidant of the Württemberg bishop and designated representative of the German theological faculties had worked vainly since spring, in concert with several Tübingen colleagues, to moderate the policies of national German-Christian leaders such as Joachim Hossenfelder and would-be Reich bishop Ludwig Müller. Less than

a year after the Nazi seizure of power, the overwhelming majority of Württemberg churchmen had abandoned any unalloyed
optimism over the prospects for national renewal, returning to
an emphasis on inner-church renewal and the primacy of pastoral tasks.[7]

Thanks to the personal tenacity of its bishop and the support
he commanded among parish clergy, the Württemberg church
remained "intact" throughout the Nazi era, stubbornly fending
off every attempt at *Gleichschaltung* from within or without. In
spirit it formed part of the so-called Confessing Church, those
within German Protestantism who made common cause around
the gospel and historic confessions in opposition to Nazi doctrines and attempts to dictate the nature of church life and witness. Bishop Wurm himself would eventually earn the cachet of
a minor resistance hero for repeated protests against the Third
Reich's policies sounded in sermons, decrees, and a series of remarkably candid letters to party luminaries ranging from the
Württemberg Gauleiter to Heinrich Himmler and the Führer
himself.[8]

Resistance remained confined, to be sure, within fairly well
defined institutional and ideological limits. Radical proponents
of a pastoral church such as Hermann Diem and Paul Schempp
often reproached Wurm for concerning himself unduly with the
fate of ecclesiastical structures rather than with the integrity of
the church's gospel and confession.[9] In any event, Wurm was too
much a German patriot, too much an old-school Lutheran conservative, to abandon the Volkskirche values of a lifetime. His
opposition to Hitler bore witness less to a change in political consciousness than to simple disillusionment over Nazi behavior,
particularly over the regime's refusal to grant the church the
role it claimed in shaping a new national order. "The tragic thing

[7] Wurm, *Erinnerungen*, p. 91; Schäfer, ed., *Landeskirche und Nationalsozialismus*, 1:293–347, 566–71; Siegele-Wenschkewitz, "Karl Fezer."

[8] Wurm's role as a leader of the Confessing Church is documented exhaus-
tively in Gerhard Schäfer, ed., *Landesbischof D. Wurm und der nationalsozialistische Staat, 1940–1945* (Stuttgart, 1968).

[9] See Bizer, *Ein Kampf um die Kirche*.

was and is," Wurm would write to one of his pastors near the end of World War II, "that a movement for political renewal, which we welcomed and with which we fully sympathized—in part because we expected it to exercise beneficial influence in a moral respect—proved to be so closely tied up with a folkish counter-religion [*Freidenkertum*]."[10] Despite extensive contacts in resistance circles, Wurm refused on principle to countenance active measures against the Führer; this, in his mind, remained tantamount to treason. Wurm's own resistance, and by extension that of the church he represented, took the form not of political action but of pastoral appeals, calls for the same moral renewal he had hoped the regime itself would set in motion. Constrained by Romans 13 and its injunction to obey the powers that be, Wurm never challenged the legitimacy of the Third Reich, only what he considered its aberrant practices. That the two were inseparable posed a problem that Wurm and many of his contemporaries never found an adequate formula to resolve.[11]

As his own comments implied, one of the most powerful factors commending National Socialism to churchmen of Wurm's mentality was its carefully orchestrated claim to share their repugnance over the Weimar system as a cultural model. The sad irony, of course, was that Nazi counterpluralism resulted in a system far more baneful and ultimately far more inimical to the Volkskirche project than that which it superseded. It might well be argued that National Socialism could itself be understood, mutatis mutandis, as a radically secularized version of Volkskirche ideology. In his penultimate speech at the 1934 Nuremberg party congress, Hitler declared: "[Our] goal must be that all upstanding Germans become National Socialists. Only the best National Socialists will be fellow members of the party."[12]

[10] Wurm to "Stadtpfarrer X," Feb. 11, 1944, in Schäfer, ed., *Wurm und der nationalsozialistische Staat*, pp. 354–55.

[11] On the context of Wurm's position, see David J. Diephouse, "The Triumph of Hitler's Will," in Joseph Held, ed., *The Cult of Power: Dictators in the Twentieth Century* (Boulder, Colo., and New York, 1983), pp. 51–76.

[12] *Der Kongress zu Nürnberg vom 5. bis 10. September 1934* (Munich, 1934), p. 211.

What is this but a translation into totalitarian political terms of the Volkskirche model, with its broad nominal membership ("all upstanding Germans") and its living core of committed activists?

That the Württemberg church generally held fast to its principles despite the unremitting pressures of a police state testified not only to the force of Theophil Wurm's personality but also to the peculiar strengths of local church life: the consciousness of occupational cohesion that bonded members of the clergy; the perdurance of pietism as an alternative matrix of faith and practice within the Volkskirche; and, more broadly, the persistence of small-town cultural traditions, a conservative populist sense of community that fostered respect for clerical authority (if not always for clerical actions) and that, as we have noted frequently, encouraged Württemberg churchmen to regard the Volkskirche project as inherently realizable. The Church Struggle represented something of a last stand for these forces of tradition. Far from restoring a symbiotic relationship between church and state, the Nazi seizure of power brought with it a formidable new obstacle to churchmen bent upon a role as heralds of public authority. The republican state had in practice maintained a more or less benevolent neutrality with respect to the church and its claims to cultural hegemony. Hitler's state, by contrast, denied and sought to suppress such claims. To be sure, the institutional settlement of 1918 was little affected by the resulting church-state struggles. Yet the gap between churchmen and the state widened considerably; persecution or its threat drove the church back upon its base in society, back to a search for vitality and moral authority rooted not in public privilege but in the loyalty and initiative of ordinary church members.

This continuing preoccupation with parish-building can be seen, for example, in the reorganization of the Württemberg Volksbund after the initial power struggle of 1933. Despite close ties with the church hierarchy, the Volksbund had been founded as an autonomous organization and functioned independently of formal ecclesiastical structures. In December 1933—partly, no doubt, because its status as a mass organization rendered it vulnerable to dissolution or Gleichschaltung—the Volksbund transferred its functions to a new agency, the Evangelischer Gemeindedienst (Evangelical Parish Service), under the direct supervision of the Oberkirchenrat. The very name of the successor organization betrayed a concern for pastoral effectiveness at the grass-roots level.[13]

During the Weimar years, pastors' confrontations with pluralism had the effect of impeding the stabilization of a new public order in Germany. Since the collapse of the Hitler millenium, conditions have changed significantly. In the east, the formula "church within socialism" testifies to a hard-won new Protestant identity in a political climate scarcely more hospitable to Volkskirche ambitions than that of the Third Reich. For those in the west, the struggle to become a "church within capitalism" has generally redounded to the benefit of a democratic consolidation. In the process, however, western churchmen, including those in Württemberg, have had to abandon or substantially alter their former lines of defense against pluralism. Many aspects of church life and government have persisted, to be sure, despite the establishment of two German states, attendant shifts in population and confessional balance, and the general dislocations of the postwar era. Yet if territorial churches like that in Württemberg retain inherited structures and legal standing, and if church life as conventionally understood remains in many cases a shrinking preserve of petit bourgeois piety,[14] the idea of the Volkskirche has assumed a distinctly more pluralistic character. Wholesale rapprochement between chastened churchmen and a pragmatic Social Democracy since the Adenauer era has done much to offset the old equation of Protestantism with national conservatism. Where once the blessing of arms was an all but self-evident ecclesiastical function, the postwar church has more typically presented itself as a patron of peace movements. The "Evangelical academies" established in many areas after the war

[13] Schäfer, ed., *Landeskirche und Nationalsozialismus*, 1:499–576.
[14] On this point see, e.g., the critical sociological profile in Bormann and Bormann-Heischkeit, *Theorie und Praxis kirchlicher Organisation*, pp. 61–90.

express the church's attempt to provide a forum for dialogue between and among all segments of society, while in the massive biennial Church Congresses (Kirchentage) the churches have created a national rallying point for young people and social activists of every shade, including many not customarily associated with ecclesiastical endeavors.[15]

Meeting in Stuttgart in October 1945, Theophil Wurm joined with fellow bishops and territorial church leaders to declare that clergy and laity shared "in a community of suffering but also in a solidarity of guilt"; they reproached themselves for "not having borne witness more courageously, prayed more diligently, believed more joyously, and loved more ardently."[16] The character of the postwar church and its programs inevitably reflects this moral legacy of the Church Struggle. More often than not, however, one can discover prototypes for latter-day church ventures in the pastoral initiatives of the first republican era. In this respect the Württemberg church furnishes interesting examples of continuity. The reorientation toward Social Democracy, for example, can be seen adumbrated in the Bietigheim conferences of the 1920s. The first of the postwar Evangelical academies was established in Bad Boll, where pietism and socialism had first embraced a half-century earlier in the person of the younger Christoph Blumhardt. The goals of lay involvement and ecclesiastical Sammlung that animated the Württemberg Volksbund can be found, albeit conceived on a very different scale, in the postwar national Kirchentage. It is appropriate, in this regard, that the guiding spirit of the 1983 Hannover Kirchentag, with its

[15] For a sampling of opinions on the postwar church, see Helmreich, *German Churches under Hitler*, pp. 413–41; Frederic Spotts, *The Churches and Politics in Germany* (Middletown, Conn., 1973); and Fischer, *Evangelische Kirche und Demokratie nach 1945*. See also Wolfgang Lück, *Das Ende der Nachkriegszeit: Eine Untersuchung zur Funktion des Begiffs Säkularisation in der "Kirchentheorie" Westdeutschlands, 1945–1965* (Bonn and Frankfurt, 1976), and Martin Greschat, "Kirche und Öffentlichkeit in der deutschen Nachkriegszeit (1945–1949)," in Armin Boyens, Martin Greschat, Rudolf von Thadden, and Paolo Pombeni, *Kirchen in der Nachkriegszeit* (Göttingen, 1979), pp. 100–124.

[16] *KJ 1945–48*, pp. 26–27; cf. Spotts, *Churches and Politics*, pp. 93–95, and Helmreich, *German Churches under Hitler*, pp. 420–21.

strongly pacifist and antiestablishment tone, should have been the maverick Social Democrat and active lay churchman Erhard Eppler, a native of Ulm and child of the Weimar era whose earliest ideological impulses were those of the Naumannite pastors and schoolmasters among whom he spent his boyhood.[17]

It is a long way from the jeans and peace scarves of Hannover to the high collars and imperial banners of the Weimar years. Then as now, however, churchmen faced the challenge of reconciling stubborn contradictions between the church as ecclesiastical agency and as voluntary association. Then as now they struggled to forge a coherent role in a society whose complexity mocked easy appeals to spiritual unity. Whatever its specific strengths and weaknesses, the latter-day Volkskirche project owes much to the flawed vision of Weimar churchmen, those backward-looking pioneers whose faith in a natural harmony of interest linking church, state, and society was so painfully shaken in 1918.

[17] "Natürlicher Rückgang," *Der Spiegel,* May 30, 1983, pp. 50–53. Erhard Eppler, with Freimut Duve, *Das Schwerste ist Glaubwürdigkeit: Gespräche über ein Politikerleben* (Reinbek bei Hamburg, 1978), esp. pp. 11–21, 35–37, 53–65, and pp. 38–49 on Eppler's relationship to the Evangelical-Social tradition; cf. Eppler, *Liberale und soziale Demokratie: zum politischen Erbe Friedrich Naumanns* (Villingen/Schwarzwald, 1961).

SOURCES

$\mathcal{T}$HIS STUDY relies heavily on manuscript church records, including correspondence and working documents of the Württemberg church leadership, personnel information, and periodic reports of parish clergy. The Landeskirchliches Archiv (LKA), Stuttgart, contains materials through 1924. I consulted holdings under the following classifications: A26 (Generalia), A27 (Personalia), A29 (Ortsakten), and A100 (Synodus). Material since 1924 is to be found, for the most part, in the archive (Altregistratur) of the Evangelischer Oberkirchenrat, Stuttgart, classifications Generalia, Personalia, Ortsakten, and Pfarrberichte. A complete list of folios consulted would require several pages; footnotes provide specific citations. Research in the thousands of local parish reports and visitation records was necessarily selective, and though I was able to peruse a reasonably generous sampling, I undoubtedly overlooked much of interest. In addition to the central archives, some local records are also available. I reviewed holdings from the following districts: Calw, Cannstatt, Freudenstadt, Gaildorf, Göppingen, Heilbronn, Ludwigsburg, Reutlingen, Urach, and Waiblingen (the latter incorporated into the LKA as Bestand C4).

Papers of several Weimar-era churchmen can also be found in the LKA. By far the most significant of these collections is the Theophil Wurm Nachlass (LKA D1). While the bulk of the documentation comes from the Nazi era, there is also considerable material from the 1920s. A narrative companion to the Wurm papers is Richard Fischer, "Die Geschichte des Kirchenkampfes in Württemberg (1933–1945)," an unpublished manuscript in nineteen bulky binders housed in the LKA; the first section includes coverage of the Weimar years. Much less extensive but still useful is the Sammlung H. Voelter (LKA D12), which includes material on church politics and Evangelical-Social activities. Other holdings of at least some use include the Knapp Archiv (LKA D2), the Nachlass Liesching (LKA D3), the Nachlass Dr. Martin Plieninger (LKA D4), the Nachlass Schuster (LKA D5), and the Nachlass Kolb (LKA D14). Manfred Grisebach, a pastor seconded to the Deutsches Ausland-Institut in Stuttgart during the 1920s, left a small collection of papers in the institute's files; I consulted these on microfilm (National Archives Microcopy No. T–81, rolls 428, 600). Papers of other leading churchmen, notably Jakob Schoell, are either no longer extant or could not be located. There is a small Hermann von Zeller Nachlass in the Zeller family papers, but it contains little from the Weimar era. The LKA also houses a collection of minute books and other records of the Württemberg Pfarrverein covering most of the 1920s (LKA D/EPW). Unfortunately, nothing comparable is available for other organizations such as the Volksbund. The same is true for the Württemberg Kultusministerium, many of whose files were destroyed during World War II. In many cases, of course, copies of important documents can be found in church archives.

Both the reference library of the Oberkirchenrat and the Württembergische Landesbibliothek, Stuttgart, contain extensive holdings of published primary sources. These include the proceedings of the Württemberg Landtag and the successive church assemblies, *Amtsblätter* for both church and state as well as for the city of Stuttgart, and more or less complete runs of leading regional newspapers and church periodicals. Of the newspapers, the richest source of material was the *Schwäbischer Merkur*, the paper of choice among moderate middle-class Protestants. I was also able to sample holdings of the semiofficial *Staatsanzeiger für Württemberg*; the *Schwäbische Tagwacht*, organ of the Württemberg SPD; the left-liberal *Stuttgarter Neues Tagblatt*; and the conservative Stuttgart *Süddeutsche Zeitung*. In many cases, relevant articles from these and other papers could be found as clippings filed in church archives. Among the church papers, the *Kirchlicher Anzeiger für Württemberg*, monthly journal of the Pfarrverein, was particularly useful. So too, though to a lesser extent, were the periodic *Mitteilungen* of the Volksbund, as well as runs of the major church weeklies, including the *Stuttgarter Evangelisches Sonntags-blatt*, the *Evangelisches Gemeindeblatt für Stuttgart*, the *Evangelisches Kirchenblatt für Württemberg*, and the *Christenbote*. A further repository of printed source material in the LKA, the "Sammelstelle für evangelisches Schrifttum," houses a variety of leaflets, brochures, fugitive numbers of periodicals, and other ephemera, the most useful of which included the annual reports of various church-related agencies, especially those associated with the Inner Mission.

Other primary sources, including memoirs and contemporary monographs, are listed in the footnotes. Mention might be made, however, of several specialized reference works that proved indispensable. Paul Wurster, *Das kirchliche Leben der ev. Landeskirche in Württemberg* (Tübingen, 1919), provides an insider's portrait of the church and its traditions at the beginning of the Weimar period. For detailed information on individual parishes, Friedrich Kühnle, *Die ev. Kirchenstellen in Württemberg* (4th ed., Esslingen, 1931), was helpful, while the several editions of the *Magisterbuch* (Stuttgart, 1920, 1925, 1928, 1932) performed a similar function for the clergy and other former Tübingen Stiftler. More detailed biographical data on churchmen could often be found in the manuscript compilation by Christian Sigel, "Das evangelische Württemberg: Seine Kirchenstellen und Geistlichen von der Reformation an bis auf die Gegenwart," a labor of love begun in 1910 and substantially complete through the Weimar period; copies of this work (typescript, 14 volumes in 22) are housed in the Württembergische Landesbibliothek and the LKA. For composite statistical information, Joseph Haller, *Das evangelische Pfarrhaus in Württemberg* (Berlin, 1937), was of some use; so too were the 1924 and 1928 editions of the *Statistisches Handbuch für Württemberg*.

Scholarly literature dealing with the general topic of this study is extensive, and it continues to accumulate steadily. A full listing of all works consulted would require an unwarranted amount of space; the list that follows is selective and perhaps a bit arbitrary. The most relevant secondary sources have been cited in the notes, and all works to which reference is thus made have been included in the index under the name of the author. Taken together, the books by Borg, Helmreich, Jacke, Nowak, Scholder, and Wright listed below provide a definitive bibliography for Germany as a whole, with particular emphasis on Prussia. For Württemberg, in addition to works cited, good starting points are the occasional compilations published in the *Zeitschrift für württembergische Landesgeschichte* and the *Zeitschrift für württembergische Kirchengeschichte*.

Arndt, Ino. "Die Judenfrage im Licht der evangelischen Sonntagsblätter von 1918–1933." Ph.D. diss., Tübingen University, 1960.

Balzer, Friedrich-Martin. *Klassengegensätze in der Kirche: Erwin Eckert und der Bund der Religiösen Sozialisten.* Cologne, 1973.

Benz, Wolfgang. *Süddeutschland in der Weimarer Republik: Ein Beitrag zur deutschen Innenpolitik, 1918–1923.* Berlin, 1970.

Besson, Waldemar. *Württemberg und die deutsche Staatskrise, 1928–1933.* Stuttgart, 1959.

Bizer, Ernst. *Ein Kampf um die Kirche: Der "Fall Schempp" nach den Akten erzählt.* Tübingen, 1965.

Blackbourn, David. *Class, Religion, and Local Politics in Wilhelmine Germany: The Centre Party in Württemberg before 1914.* New Haven, Conn., 1980.

Boos-Nunning, Ursula, and Egon Golomb. *Religiöses Verhalten im Wandel: Untersuchungen in einer Industriegesellschaft.* Essen, 1974.

Borg, Daniel R. *The Old-Prussian Church and the Weimar Republic: A Study in Political Adjustment, 1917–1927.* Hannover and London, 1984.

Bormann, Günther, and Sigrid Bormann-Heischkeid. *Theorie und Praxis kirchlicher Organisation: Ein Beitrag zum Problem der Rückständigkeit sozialer Gruppen.* Opladen, 1971.

Bredendiek, Walter. *Zwischen Revolution und Restauration: Zur Entwicklung im deutschen Protestantismus während der Novemberrevolution und in der Weimarer Republik.* Berlin, 1969.

Breipohl, Renate. *Religiöser Sozialismus und bürgerliches Geschichtsbewusstsein zur Zeit der Weimarer Republik.* Zurich, 1971.

Buchheim, Hans. *Glaubenskrise im dritten Reich.* Stuttgart, 1953.

Bühler, Karl Werner. *Presse und Protestantismus in der Weimarer Republik: Kräfte und Krisen evangelischer Publizistik.* Witten, 1970.

Cazelles, Henri. *Église et état en Allemagne de Weimar aux premières années du IIIe Reich.* Paris, 1936.

Christ, Herbert. *Der politische Protestantismus in der Weimarer Republik: Eine Studie über die politische Meinungsbildung durch die evangelischen Kirchen in Spiegel der Literatur und der Presse.* Ph.D. diss., Bonn University, 1967.

Conway, John. *The Nazi Persecution of the Churches, 1933–45.* London, 1968.

Dahm, Karl-Wilhelm. *Pfarrer und Politik: Soziale Position und politische Mentalität des deutschen evangelischen Pfarrerstandes zwischen 1918 und 1933.* Cologne and Opladen, 1965.

Eckstein, Harry. *A Theory of Stable Democracy.* Center of International Studies Research Monograph no. 10. Princeton, 1961.

Eyck, Erich. *A History of the Weimar Republic.* Trans. Harlan L. Hanson and Robert G. L. Waite. Cambridge, Mass., 1962. Reprint, New York, 1970.

Fischer, Fritz. "Der deutsche Protestantismus und die Politik im 19. Jahrhundert." *Historische Zeitschrift* 171 (1951): 473–518.

Fischer, Hans Gerhard. *Evangelische Kirche und Demokratie nach 1945.* Lübeck, 1970.

Freytag, Justus, and Kenji Ozaki. *Nominal Christianity: Studies of Church and People in Hamburg.* Trans. Marjorie Sandle. London, 1970.

Greschat, Martin, ed. *Der deutsche Protestantismus im Revolutionsjahr 1918/19.* Witten, 1974.

Groh, John E. *Nineteenth-Century German Protestantism: The Church as Social Model.* Washington, D.C., 1982.

Gutteridge, Richard. *The German Evangelical Church and the Jews, 1879–1950.* London and New York, 1976.

Habermas, Jürgen. *Strukturwandel der Öffentlichkeit: Untersuchungen zu einer Kategorie der bürgerlichen Gesellschaft.* Neuwied, 1962.

Hasselhorn, Martin. *Der altwürttembergische Pfarrstand im 18. Jahrhundert.* Stuttgart, 1958.

Hermelink, Heinrich. *Geschichte der evangelischen Kirche in Württemberg von der Reformation bis zur Gegenwart.* Stuttgart and Tübingen, 1949.

Helmreich, Ernst C. *The German Churches under Hitler: Background, Struggle, and Epilogue.* Detroit, Mich., 1979.

———. *Religious Education in German Schools: An Historical Approach.* Cambridge, Mass., 1959.

Hunt, James C. *The People's Party in Württemberg and Southern Germany, 1890–1914.* Stuttgart, 1975.

Jacke, Jochen. *Kirche zwischen Monarchie und Republik: Der preussische Protestantismus nach dem Zusammenbruch von 1918.* Hamburg, 1976.

Köster, Reinhard. *Die Kirchentreuen: Erfahrungen und Ergebnisse einer soziologischen Untersuchung in einer grosstädtischen evangelischen Gemeinde.* Stuttgart, 1959.

Kouri, E. I. *Der deutsche Protestantismus und die soziale Frage, 1870–1919: Zur Sozialpolitik im Bildungsbürgertum.* Berlin and New York, 1984.

Kupisch, Karl. *Das Jahrhundert des Sozialismus und die Kirche.* Berlin, 1958.

———. *Zwischen Idealismus und Massendemokratie: Eine Geschichte der evangelischen Kirche in Deutschland von 1815–1945.* Berlin, 1955.

Lehmann, Hartmut. *Pietismus und weltliche Ordnung in Württemberg vom 17. bis zum 20. Jahrhundert.* Stuttgart, 1969.

Lersner, Dieter von. *Die Evangelischen Jugendverbände Würt-*

tembergs und die Hitler-Jugend 1933/1934. Göttingen, 1958.

Leube, Martin. *Das Tübinger Stift, 1770–1950.* Stuttgart, 1954.

Martin, David. *The Religious and the Secular: Studies in Secularization.* New York, 1969.

Matthes, Joachim. *Kirche und Gesellschaft.* Reinbek bei Hamburg, 1969.

Mehnert, Gottfried. *Evangelische Kirche und Politik, 1917–1919: Die politischen Strömungen im deutschen Protestantismus von der Julikrise 1917 bis zum Herbst 1919.* Düsseldorf, 1959.

Meier, Kurt. *Volkskirche, 1918–1945: Ekklesiologie und Zeitgeschichte.* Munich, 1982.

Motschmann, Claus. *Evangelische Kirche und preussischer Staat in den Anfängen der Weimarer Republik: Möglichkeiten und Grenzen ihrer Zusammenarbeit.* Hamburg and Lübeck, 1969.

Nowak, Kurt. *Evangelische Kirche und Weimarer Republik: Zum politischen Weg des deutschen Protestantismus zwischen 1918 und 1932.* Göttingen, 1981.

Opitz, Günter. *Der Christlich-Soziale Volksdienst: Versuch einer protestantischen Partei in der Weimarer Republik.* Düsseldorf, 1969.

Pressel, Wilhelm. *Die Kriegspredigt 1914–1918 in der evangelischen Kirche Deutschlands.* Göttingen, 1967.

Rendtorff, Trutz. *Die soziale Struktur der Kirchengemeinde.* Hamburg, 1958.

Rosenberg, Arthur. *A History of the German Republic.* London, 1936.

Schäfer, Gerhard, ed. *Die Evangelische Landeskirche in Württemberg und der Nationalsozialismus.* Vol. 1, *Um das politische Engagement der Kirche, 1932–1933.* Stuttgart, 1971.

———. *Kleine württembergische Kirchengeschichte.* Stuttgart, 1965.

———, ed. *Landesbischof D. Wurm und der nationalsozialis-*

tische Staat, 1940–1945: Eine Dokumentation. Stuttgart, 1968.

Schmid, Eugen. *Geschichte des württembergischen evangelischen Volksschulwesens von 1806 bis 1910.* Stuttgart, 1933.

Scholder, Klaus. *Die Kirchen und das Dritte Reich.* Vol. 1, *Vorgeschichte und Zeit der Illusionen, 1918–1934.* Frankfurt am Main, 1977.

Shanahan, William O. *German Protestants Face the Social Question.* Vol. 1, *The Conservative Phase, 1815–1871.* Notre Dame, Ind., 1954.

Simon, Klaus. *Die württembergischen Demokraten: Ihre Stellung und Arbeit im Parteien- und Verfassungssystem in Württemberg und im Deutschen Reich, 1890–1920.* Stuttgart, 1969.

Spiegel, Yorick. *Der Pfarrer in Amt: Gemeinde, Kirche, Öffentlichkeit.* Munich, 1970.

Spotts, Frederic. *The Churches and Politics in Germany.* Middletown, Conn., 1973.

Stoll, Gerhard E. *Die evangelische Zeitschriftenpresse im Jahre 1933.* Witten, 1963.

Thalmann, Rita. *Protestantisme et nationalisme en Allemagne (de 1900 à 1945).* Paris, 1976.

Tilgner, Wolfgang. *Volksnomostheologie und Schöpfungsglaube: Ein Beitrag zur Geschichte des Kirchenkampfes.* Göttingen, 1966.

Trautwein, Joachim. *Religiosität und Sozialstruktur: Untersucht anhand der Entwicklung des württembergischen Pietismus.* Stuttgart, 1972.

Weller, Karl. *Die Staatsumwälzung in Württemberg, 1918–1920.* Stuttgart, 1930.

———, and Arnold Weller. *Württembergische Geschichte im südwestdeutschen Raum.* 7th ed. Stuttgart and Aalen, 1972.

Ward, William R. *Theology, Sociology, and Politics: The German Protestant Social Conscience, 1890–1933.* Bern, 1979.

Wright, J. R. C. *"Above Parties"*: *The Political Attitudes of the German Protestant Church Leadership, 1918–1933.* London, 1974. Expanded German version: *"Über den Parteien." Die politische Haltung der evangelischen Kirchenführer, 1918–1933.* Göttingen, 1977.

INDEX

Aalen, 112, 284
Abraham, David, 9n
academies, Evangelical, 368–69
advisory council, pastors' (Pfarrer-
    beirat), 81, 98
Albrecht of Württemberg, Duke, 251
Aldingen, 292–93
Althaus, Paul, 330
Altheim, 186
amusements, church views on, 232–
    35
anticlericalism. *See* freethinkers
antimodernism, 265–66, 309, 329,
    331, 360
antirepublicanism, 6–7, 264–71, 361–
    62
anti-Semitism, 240, 265, 277, 279–
    80, 286, 329
Apelt, Willibalt, 75n
Association for a Free Volkskirche
    (Freie volkskirchliche Vereini-
    gung), 47, 63
Association of Higher Civil Servants
    (Verband höher geprüfter Beam-
    ten), 80, 317

Backnang, 184, 204
Baden, 27, 163, 306; church life in,
    51, 61, 85; Religious Socialism in,
    282, 285, 320, 322
Balbo, Italo, 266
Balingen, 149
Baltmannsweiler, 297–98
Baptists, 23, 26n, 288
Barth, Karl, 12, 282; influence in
    Württemberg, 314–16, 327, 336
Basel Mission, 331
Bauer, Ludwig, 86

Bauernbund, 33, 34, 35, 65. *See also*
    Bürgerpartei
Bausch, Paul, 341
Bavaria, 3, 27, 51
Bazille, Wilhelm, 90, 92–93, 94, 95–
    96, 100, 237
Beisswänger, Gustav, 65, 87, 89, 96
Bengel, Johann Albrecht, 48
Berlin, 14, 136, 282
Berlin City Mission, 45
Besigheim, 139–40
Besson, Waldemar, 80, 361
Biberach, 152
Bietigheim, 115, 201
Bietigheim Days, 304–8, 311, 334,
    369
Bigler, Robert M., 6n
Birkach, 151
bishop, office of, in Württemberg,
    127, 357, 358
Bismarck, Otto von, 241, 243
Bizer, Ernst, 315, 319
Blaufelden, 111–12
Blos, Anna, 306
Blos, Wilhelm, 56n, 57, 71, 74, 193,
    267
Bloth, Peter C., 162n
Blume, Wilhelm von, 60, 61, 89
Blumhardt, Christoph, 45–46, 275,
    282, 296, 299, 306, 314, 319, 369
Böblingen, 234, 249, 293
Böhm, Friedrich, 150n
Boll, Bad, 45, 299, 319, 369
Bölling, Rainer, 163n
bolshevism, 265, 268
Bolz, Eugen, 344
Borg, Daniel R., 21n
Borscheid, Peter, 30n

381

Evangelical Church Association
(Evangelische-kirchliche Vereinigung), 48
Evangelical League, 62, 66
Evangelical-Lutheran church in
Württemberg, 10, 26, 78, 101–4;
administration of, 37–40, 42, 57,
125–26, 128; as case study, 24–25;
constitutional provisions concerning, 73–74, 133, 360; finances, 40,
58–59, 75, 78–80, 316–17; religious life in, 50–51, 105–6, 131–33,
135, 140–41; theological factions
in, 46–50; in Third Reich, 356–58,
364–68; and workers, 301–4
Evangelical Parish Service (Evangelische Gemeindedienst), 368
Evangelical People's League in Württemberg. *See* Volksbund
Evangelical Press Service, 67, 70, 74,
168, 273, 290, 350; and Volksbund,
221–22
Evangelical-Social Congress, 217, 303
Evangelical-Social movement, 46, 63–
64, 74, 213–14, 340–41; and workers, 301–4
Evangelical Society (Evangelische Gesellschaft), 49, 50, 242
Evangelical Teachers' Association
(Evangelischer Lehrerverein), 180–
81
Evangelical Women's League, 242–43
Evangelical Workers' League, 142,
304
Evangelical Young Men's League
(cvjm), 147
Evangelical Youth Work in Württem-
berg, 246
Evangelisches Gemeindeblatt (Stutt-
gart), 220, 299–300
*Evangelisches Kirchenblatt für Würt-
temberg*, 224
Eytel, Hermann, 131–32, 225, 235

farmers, 29–30
fascism, Italian, 266–67
Feldman, Gerald D., 9n
Fezer, Karl, 315, 343, 349, 364
Finance Ministry, Württemberg, 81–
82, 85, 96, 97
Finer, Herman, 266n
Fischer, Hermann, 12n
Fischer, Johannes, 66
flag crisis, 266
folkish movement, 278–81
Folkish-Social party, 280–81
Ford, Henry, 215
Fox, Charles James, 32
franchise, in church elections, 104,
107
Frasch, Karl, 153
free churches. *See* Baptists; Method-
ists
freethinkers, 76–77, 137–38, 185, 189
Freudenstadt, 191–92, 287
Friedrichshafen, 295n
Fritz, Richard, 354
Fuchs, Emil, 282
Führ, Christoph, 164n

Gaildorf, 292
Gaisburg, 277, 324
Gaub, Karl, 298
Gauger, Samuel, 114, 145
Gehring, Paul, 31n
Gemeinschaftsblatt (Old Pietist), 266,
268
General Church Order of 1559, 37
German-Christians, 281, 364. *See
also* Christian-German movement;
NS-Pfarrerbund
German Evangelical Church Commit-
tee (deka), 22–23, 94, 223, 272;
Social Committee of, 214, 258; and
Weimar assembly, 72–74
German Evangelical Church Federa-
tion, 22–23, 212

German National People's party
(DNVP). *See* Bürgerpartei
German People's party (DVP), 34, 276
German Settlement Bank, 251
Godesberg, Bad, 307
Goldschmidt, Dieter, 18n
Gommel, Heinrich, 293n
Göppingen, 33, 116, 202, 242, 254,
255, 327; Religious Socialism in,
298–99, 319, 324, 328
Gordon, Frank J., 8n, 164n
Graf, Friedrich Wilhelm, 12n
Greiner, F., 18n
Greschat, Martin, 369n
Griesmeier, Joseph, 287n
Gross, Gustav, 218
Grube, Walter, 34n
Gruner, Gustav, 155
Grünthal, Günther, 164
Günther, Karl-Heinz, 163n
gymnasium, religious instruction in,
198n

Hackler, O., 16n
Haffner (church assembly president),
119
Hahn, Michael, 49
Haigerloch, 253
Haller, Joseph, 43n, 191–92, 193–94
Hamburg, church life in, 135, 136
Hannover, Elizabeth and Heinrich, 9n
Hannover, 26; church congress in,
369–70
Harnack, Adolf von, 19, 47
Hausen, 105–6
Hedelfingen, 333, 334
Hegel, Georg Wilhelm Friedrich, 41,
44
Heidenheim, 139
Heilbronn, 27, 29, 37; church and
schools in, 183, 185; in church
elections, 107, 116, 153; church life

in, 131–32; Religious Socialism in,
319, 323–24, 326, 328
Heim, Karl, 44n
Hermelink, Heinrich, 45
Herrmann, Immanuel, 137
Herrnhut Brethren, 48–49
Hertzman, Lewis, 65n
Hesse, Hermann, 44, 136, 221
Hettler, Karl, 352
Heuss, Theodor, 20n, 28n, 31n, 46n,
56, 57
Heuss-Knapp, Elly, 308
Heymann, Berthold, 56, 60, 63–64,
167, 224, 226; and 1924 church
law, 88, 89; and Bietigheim Days,
306
Hieber, Johannes, 63, 66, 83, 92, 167,
193, 228, 273; and church finances,
81, 82, 86–87, 93–94, 96; and
schools, 171, 172; and Bietigheim
Days, 306
Hildenbrand, Karl, 75
Hilzinger, Friedrich, 334, 339n
Himmler, Heinrich, 365
Hindemith, Paul, 227
Hindenburg, Paul von, 258, 268–69,
336, 341–42, 345–46, 356
Hinderer, August, 74, 109, 221
Hinderer, Paul, 122
Hinrichs, Carl, 21n
Hippel, Wolfgang von, 30n
Hirsch, Emanuel, 330
Hitler, Adolf, 25, 68, 341, 347–48,
350, 356, 366
Hofacker, Ludwig, 48
Hoffmann, Adolf, 58
Hoffmann, Konrad, 109, 341
Hohenlohe-Langenburg, Ernst Fürst
zu, 109, 119, 129, 345
Holborn, Hajo, 19n
Homesteads Committee (Heimstät-
tenausschuss), 250
Honecker, Karl, 324

Schneider, Johannes, 17n, 18, 21, 53
Schoell, Jakob, 47, 49, 114, 158, 171,
    250, 316; in church elections, 115,
    152–53; and church polity, 105,
    108–9, 110, 154; and church presi-
    dency, 133–34, 313; political atti-
    tudes of, 258, 276, 296, 341; retire-
    ment of, 357; and school policy,
    169, 172–74, 176–78, 191–92, 205;
    social views of, 214, 216–18, 304,
    306, 307; and Volksbund, 142, 144
Schömberg, 151
Schönhuth, Othmar, 237
Schöntal, 153
school councils, 178, 188–90, 203,
    204. *See also* Oberschulrat
schools, 160–64, 360; in Landtag,
    163, 166–67, 177n–78n, 189, 194;
    in Reichstag, 164, 175, 177
Schorndorf, 174
Schorske, Carl E., 34n
Schreiber, Ernst, 105–6
Schrenk, Theodor, 292
Schubert, Daniel, 148
Schüren, Ulrich, 271n
Schwäbisch Hall, 153
Schwäbischer Merkur, 69, 116
Schwäbische Tagwacht, on church as-
    sembly, 313, 327–28; on church
    press, 263–64; on clergy politics,
    271, 272, 294; on religious instruc-
    tion, 197
Schwarz, Walter, 221n
Schwenningen, 33, 183, 185–86, 206–
    7, 249
sects, 132, 146
secularization. *See* pluralism
seminaries, preparatory, 97, 238
Sennett, Richard, 359, 359n
separation of church and state, 5, 53–
    62, 72–73, 76–77, 99–100, 362–63
Shorter, Edward, 231n
Siegele-Wenschkewitz, Leonore,
    315n

Silesia, 251, 347
Simmersfeld, 296
Simpfendörfer, Wilhelm, 287–88
Simultanschule, 162–63, 164, 182,
    183
Skelton, Geoffrey, 228n
Skopp, Douglas, 162n
Social Democrats, 5, 75, 163, 237,
    240, 275, 318, 369, 370; at Bietig-
    heim Days, 306–8; and church-
    state relations, 58, 88; and 1926
    referendum, 271–73; relations
    with church, 45–46, 67, 69–71,
    150, 153, 218–19, 297, 325, 327–
    28; and Religious Socialism, 284–
    85; in Württemberg, 33–34, 35,
    55–57, 82–83
"social information service," parish,
    214
Society for the Assistance of Bar-
    maids, 243
Sollmann, Wilhelm, 306–7, 308
*Sonntagsblatt des arbeitenden
    Volkes*, 283
South German Radio, 222
Soziale Botschaft, 212–14, 219, 231,
    258
Spandau, Evangelical-Social institute
    in, 215
sports, church views on, 232, 233–39
Spraitbach, 234
Springer, August, 31, 203, 215, 275,
    276; on Bietigheim Days, 305n,
    306; on church and workers, 283,
    302–3; retirement of, 357; and
    Volksbund, 110, 142
Stahl, Otto, 205, 208, 328
State Committee to Combat Moral
    Danger, 227
Steger, Karl, 280–81, 295
Stern, Fritz, 7, 7n
Stier-Somlo, Fritz, 76n
Stift, Tübingen, 36, 43–44, 52, 97,
    154

LIBRARY OF CONGRESS CATALOGING-IN-PUBLICATION DATA

Diephouse, David J., 1947–
Pastors and pluralism in Württemberg, 1918–1933.
Bibliography: p.
Includes index.
1. Evangelische Landeskirche in Württemberg—
History—20th century. 2. Lutheran Church—Germany
(West)—Württemberg—History—20th century. 3. Church
and state—Germany (West)—Württemberg—History—20th
century. 4. Württemberg (Germany)—Church history.
I. Title.
BX8022.W7D54 1987   284.1'4347   87–3293
ISBN 0–691–05501–7

David J. Diephouse is Professor of History at Calvin College.